Dedicated to those who seek to change themselves, in order to change the world

First published in 2016 by
Speechmark Publishing Ltd,
5 Thomas More Square, London E1W 1YW United Kingdom
www.speechmark.net

© Ian Long 2016

All rights reserved. The whole of this work, including all text and illustrations, is protected by copyright. No part of it may be copied, altered, adapted or otherwise exploited in any way without express prior permission, unless in accordance with the provisions of the Copyright Designs and Patents Act 1988 or in order to photocopy or make duplicating masters of those pages so indicated, without alteration and including copyright notices, for the express purpose of instruction and examination. No parts of this work may otherwise be loaded, stored, manipulated, reproduced, or transmitted in any form or by any means, electronic or mechanical, including photocopying and recording, or by any information storage and retrieval system, without prior written permission from the publisher, on behalf of the copyright owner.

002-6020 Printed in the United Kingdom by CMP (uk) Ltd

British Library Cataloguing in Publication Data
A catalogue record for this book is available from the British Library

ISBN: 978 1 90930 173 3

CONTENTS

How to use this book iv

About the author v

Ranges of feelings 1

Sad feelings 2

Angry feelings 3

Dispirited to obsessed feelings 4

Positive feelings 5

Rejection feelings 6

Scared feelings 7

Close feelings 8

Individual feeling words 9

Opposite pairs of feelings 323

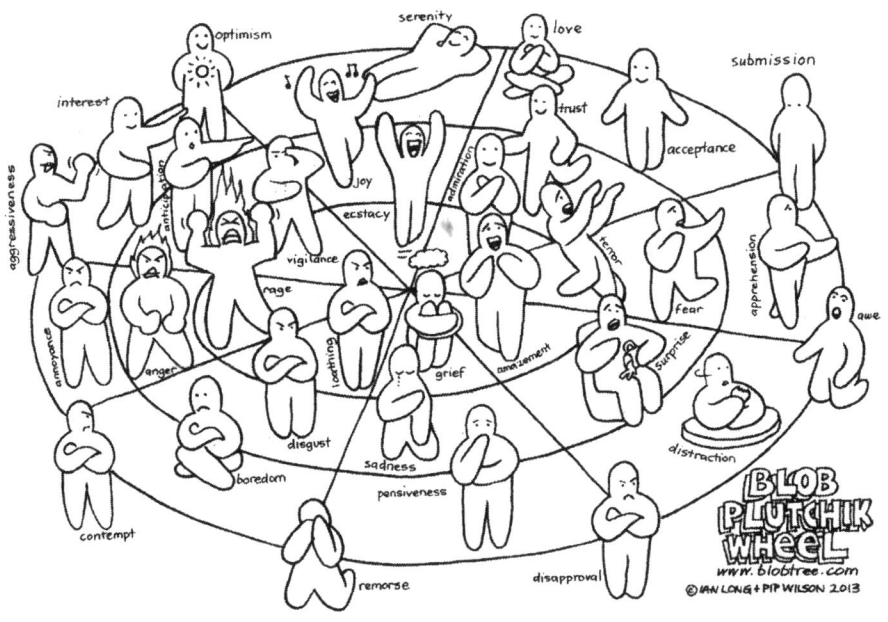

How to use this book

A thesaurus is a collection of words which have a similar meaning (synonyms) or opposite meanings (antonyms). This book is focused upon emotional words and provides visual meanings for them all. There are many words that I have missed out. This is a first edition and will be expanded over time.

One of the challenges when exploring feelings words is to know which are the stronger ones and which are gentler. The 'ranges of feelings' pages provide a visual spectrum which enables even the youngest of writers and explorers to grasp their intensity.

No one agrees upon the correct order. There is no official word order for emotions. This is a first attempt to visualise this idea and responses are welcome.

Opposite pairs are difficult to choose. A traditional thesaurus usually contains a range of words to attempt to provide an antonym. I have tried to choose the one which best fits.

On the 'individual feelings' pages, I have tried to provide two synonyms beneath the main word. They will be either one lesser or one greater in intensity than the middle word. If you are unsure, take a look at the relevant feelings range page. I have also provided one sentence to show how the word might be used in written work. **Some of the words only have two images because they are at the extreme of emotions and only have one word to the side of them rather than a stronger or weaker feeling.**

This book can be used to help writers strengthen their language. As a teacher, I was aware just how many children were told to improve their work using a thesaurus, only to choose inappropriate substitutes because the alternative words were outside their experience. By adding the images, and a visual range, that difficulty should be reduced.

This book can also be used in discussions on feelings, in drama lessons to picture feelings for actors and in reading to strengthen the skills of all levels of reader.

About the author

I have been a youth worker, a primary school teacher and an assistant pastor. Currently, my main role is as a carer. This book, therefore, has been produced in spaces throughout the day.

I first developed visual books with Pip Wilson, the trainer / youth worker / ideas man / beautiful human person, when we created the Blob Tree image together in the 1980s. It was to help all types of people to express their feelings, no matter what age they were or country they were from. The Blobs in these images have no gender or age. They express feelings common to us all.

Pip describes them as signals. He says that feelings are not good or bad, just signs for us to understand. When we are young we often see feelings as instructions. As we get older we choose which feelings to respond to.

It is my desire that this book enables future generations to become more emotionally literate.

Use this book to identify your feelings, to name them and not to be scared of them. Actors are one of the few groups of people who practise their feelings. As we become more emotionally intelligent, feelings will be a part of us that we can more confidently describe and appreciate.

Ian

The Blob Emotional Thesaurus

Ranges of feelings

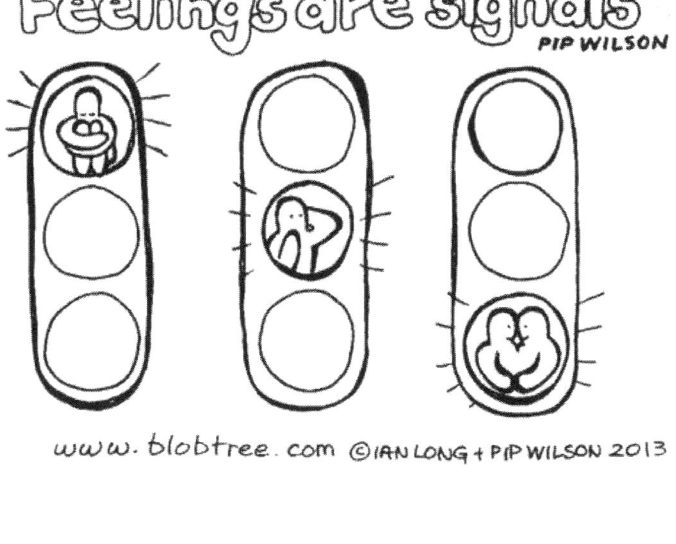

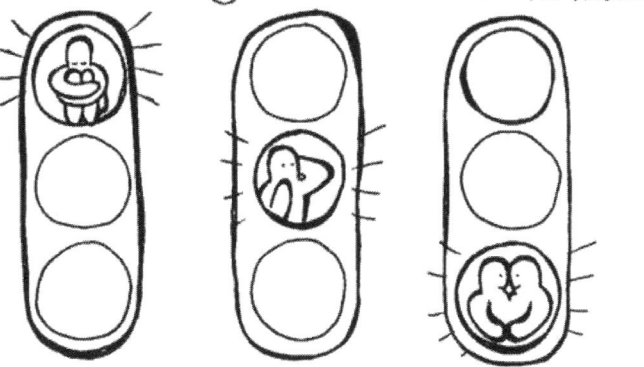

A range of sad feelings

stronger

depressed

down

distraught

hurt

pessimistic

upset

embarrassed

discouraged

moody

sensitive

disappointed

sad

weaker

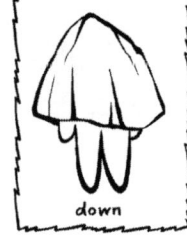

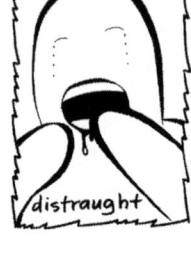

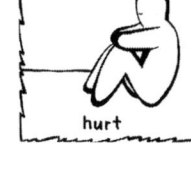
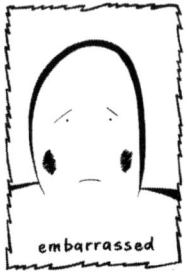

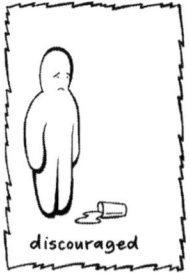
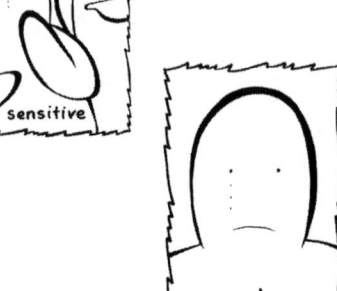

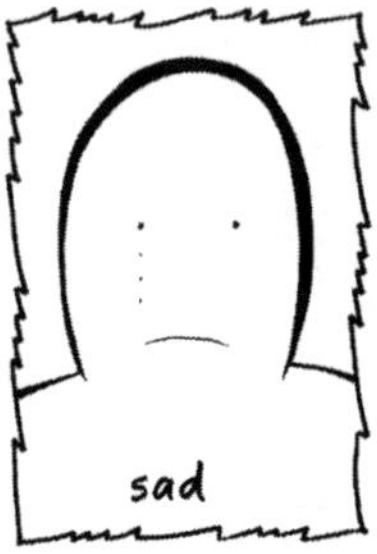

Ranges of feelings

A range of angry feelings

stronger

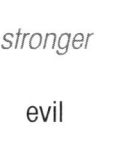

evil

violent

volcanic

incensed

raging

hostile

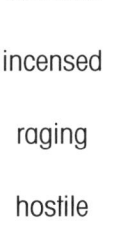

furious

angry

mad

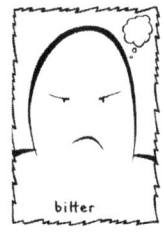
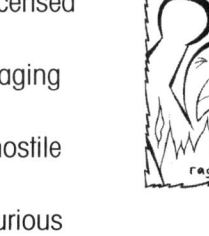

bitter

seething

annoyed

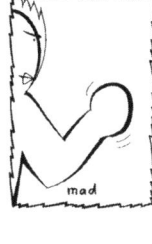

jealous

frustrated

irritated

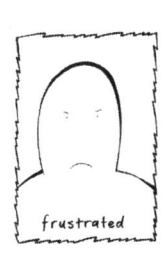
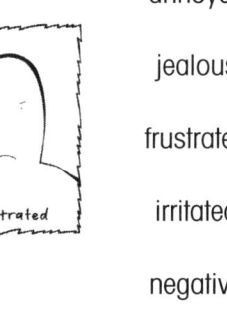
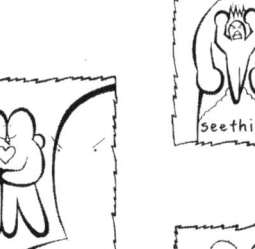
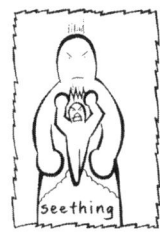
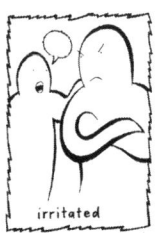

negative

weaker

The Blob Emotional Thesaurus

From **dispirited to obsessed**

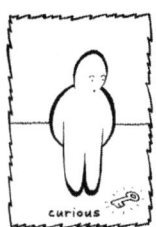

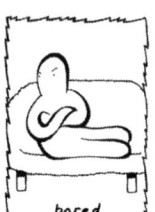
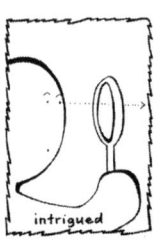
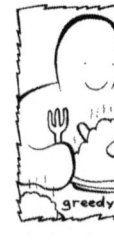

stronger

dispirited

despondent

disillusioned

bored

lazy

neutral

weaker

curious

intrigued

fascinated

enthralled

mesmerised

greedy

compelled

fixated

obsessed

weaker

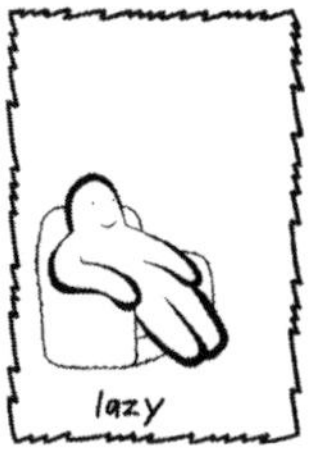

Ranges of feelings

A range of positive feelings

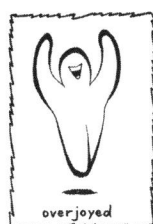

stronger

euphoric

overjoyed

thrilled

bouncy

enthusiastic

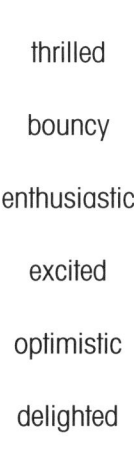

excited

optimistic

delighted

cheerful

happy

encouraged

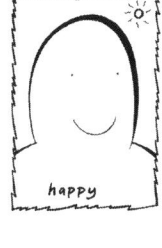
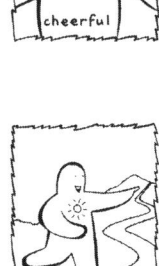

relieved

hopeful

amused

peaceful

patient

calm

weaker

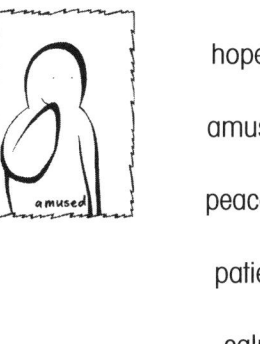

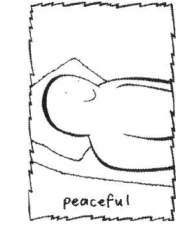

A range of rejection feelings

stronger

worthless

condemned

lost

drowning

wounded

abandoned

hated

empty

rejected

fragile

distant

lonely

cold

isolated

ignored

alone

weaker

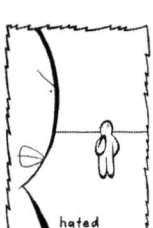

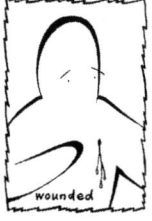

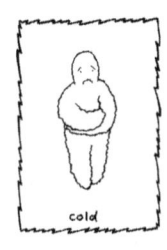

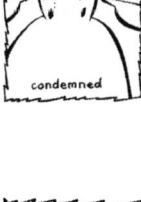

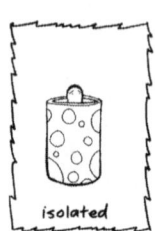

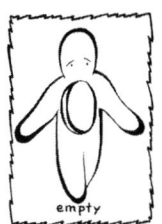

Ranges of feelings

A range of scared feelings

stronger

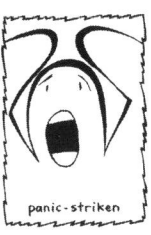

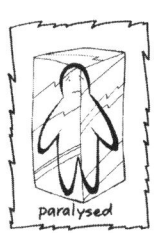

paralysed

panic-stricken

terrified

tormented

paranoid

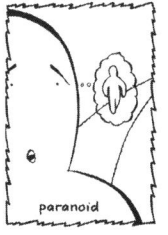

stressed

shocked

frightened

dreading

scared

trapped

uncomfortable

worried

nervous

anxious

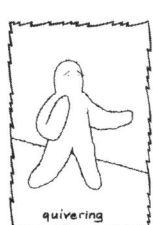

quivering

concerned

confused

bothered

weaker

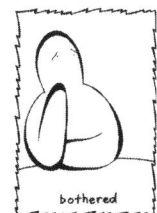

A range of close feelings

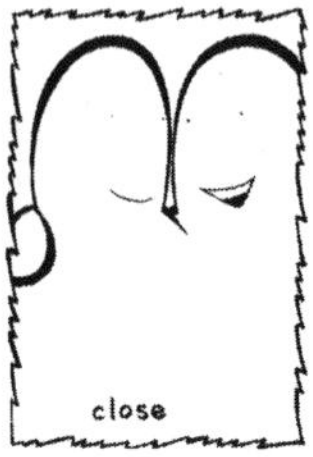

stronger

open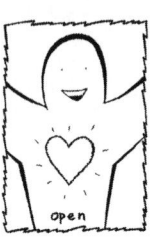

  purposeful

loved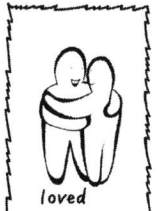

confident

 safe

satisfied

 strong

close

 touched

empowered

trusting

 nurtured

accepted

calm

weaker

Individual feeling words

Individual feeling words

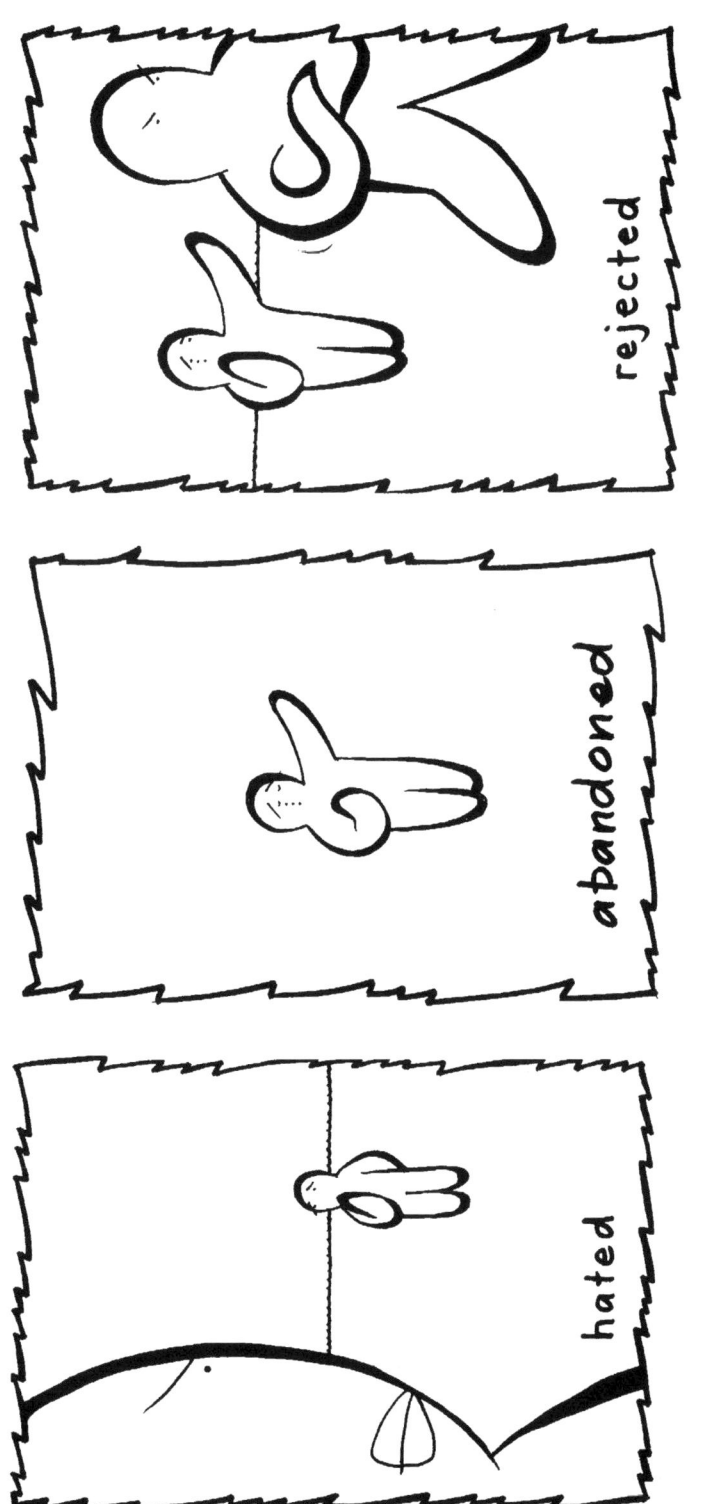

Charlie felt abandoned when all his family went shopping, leaving him to finish his work.

Individual feeling words

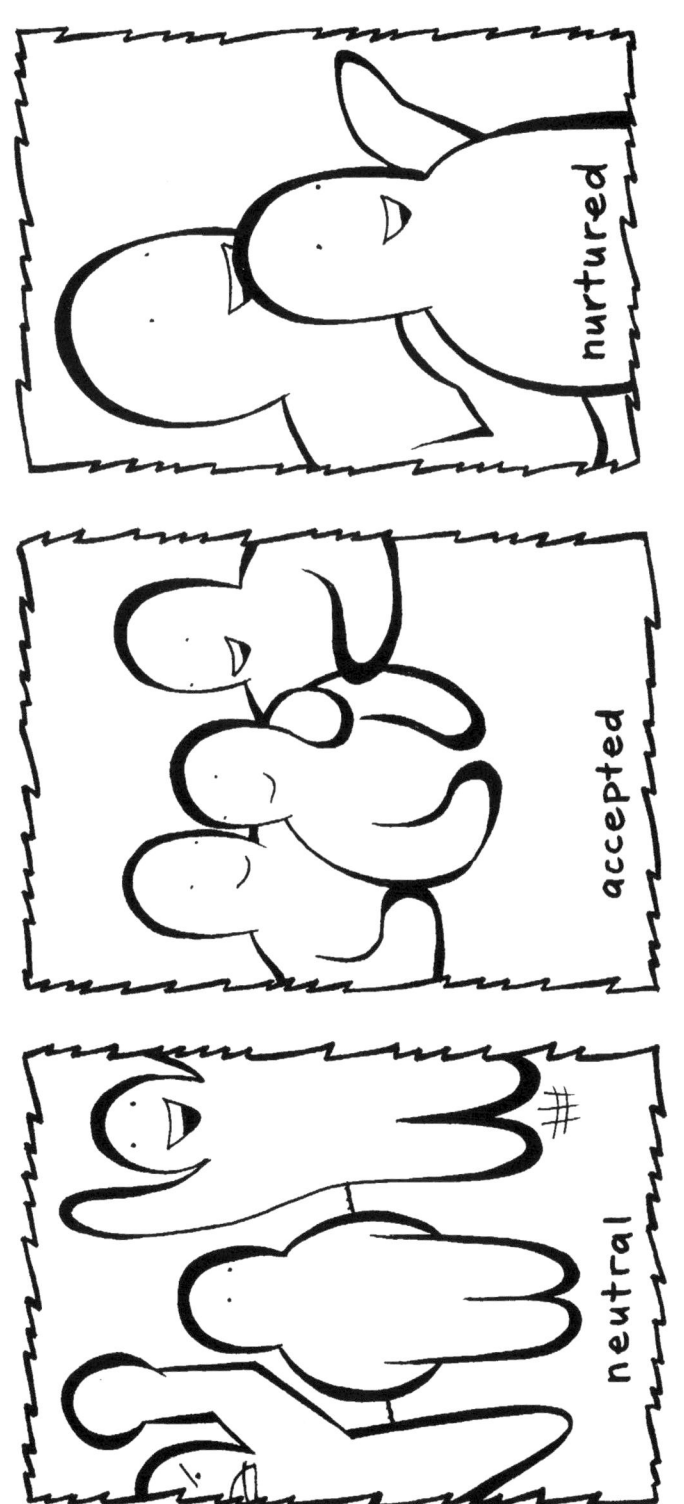

Lewis always felt **accepted** by his friends and family.

Individual feeling words

Jacqui felt alone when her best friend was off sick.

Individual feeling words

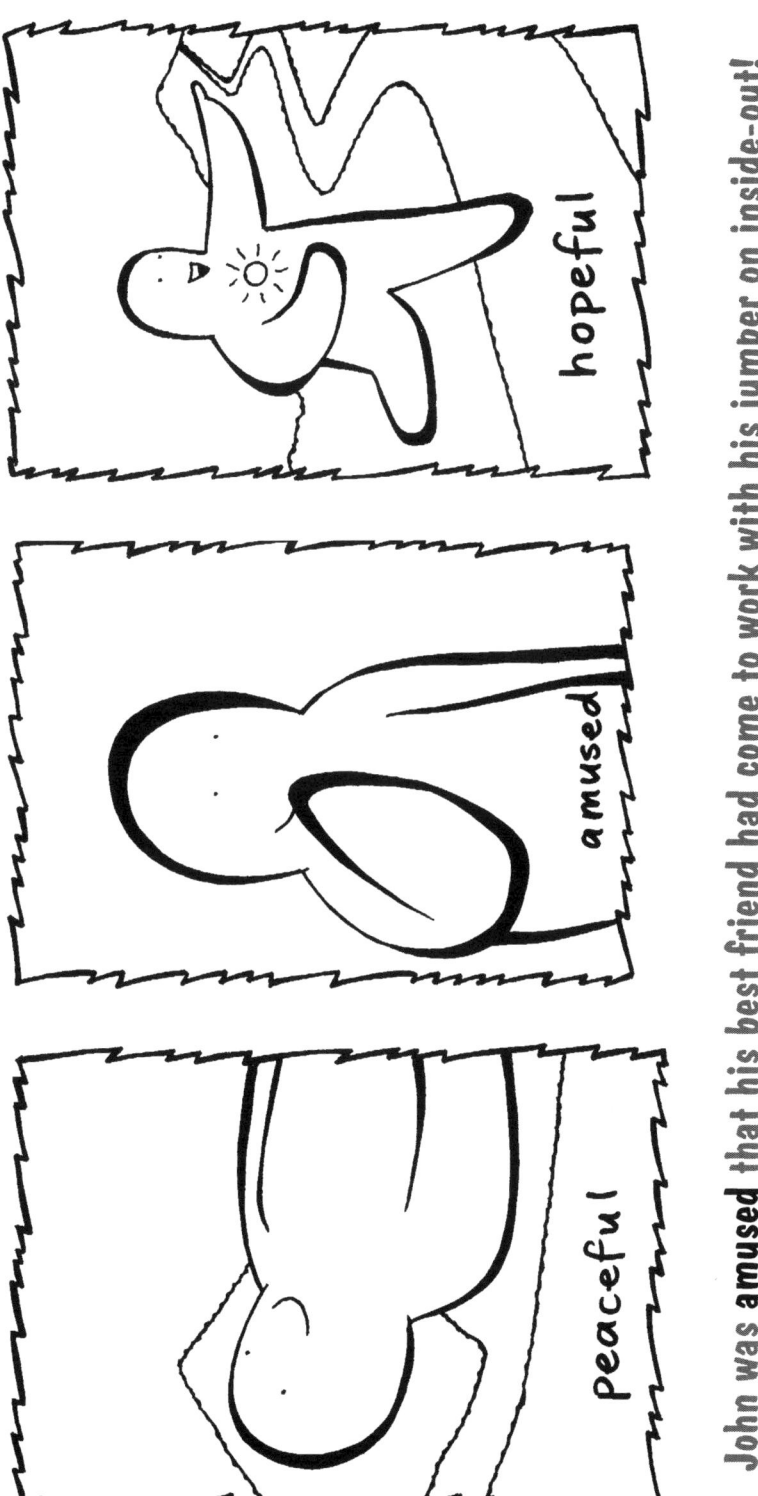

John was amused that his best friend had come to work with his jumper on inside-out!

Individual feeling words

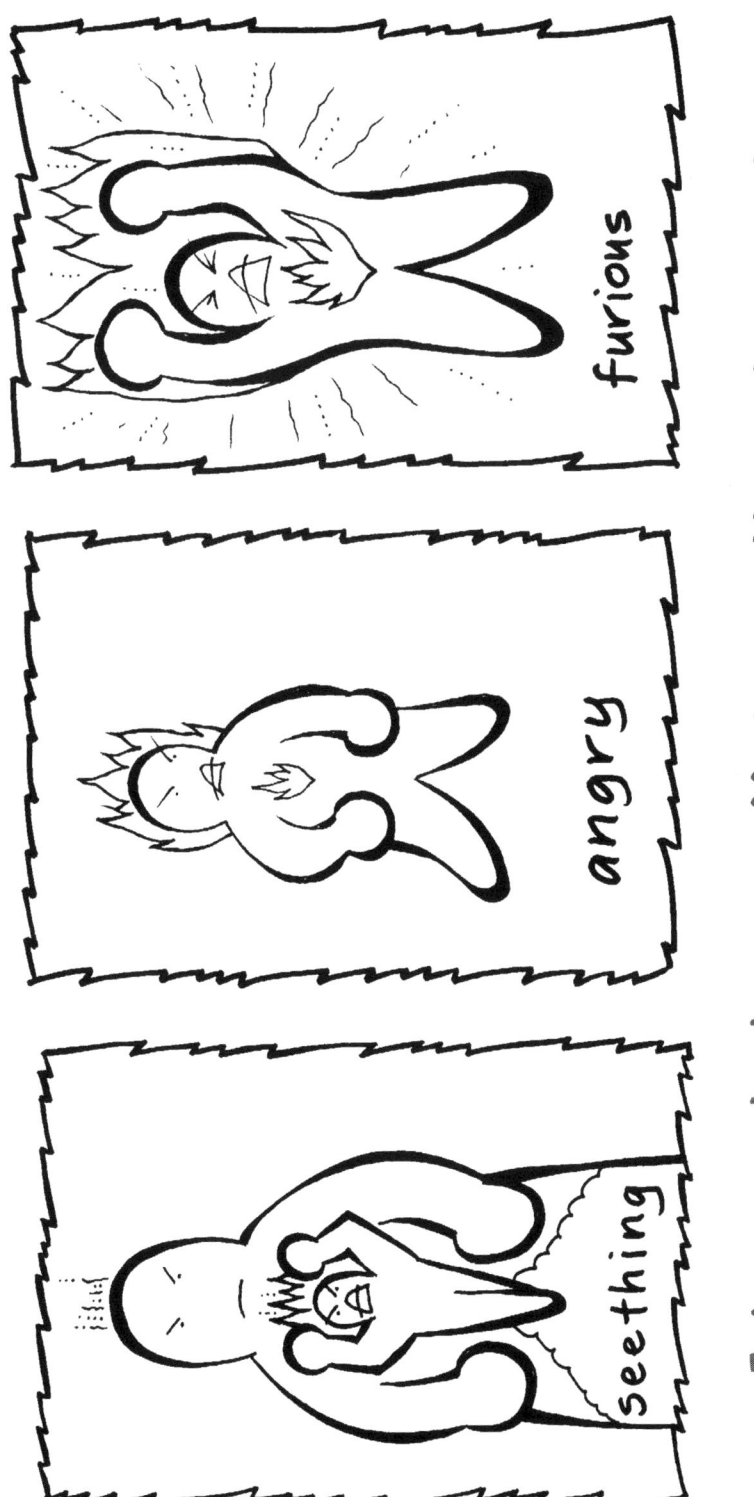

Toni was angry that the message of forgiveness and love was being ignored.

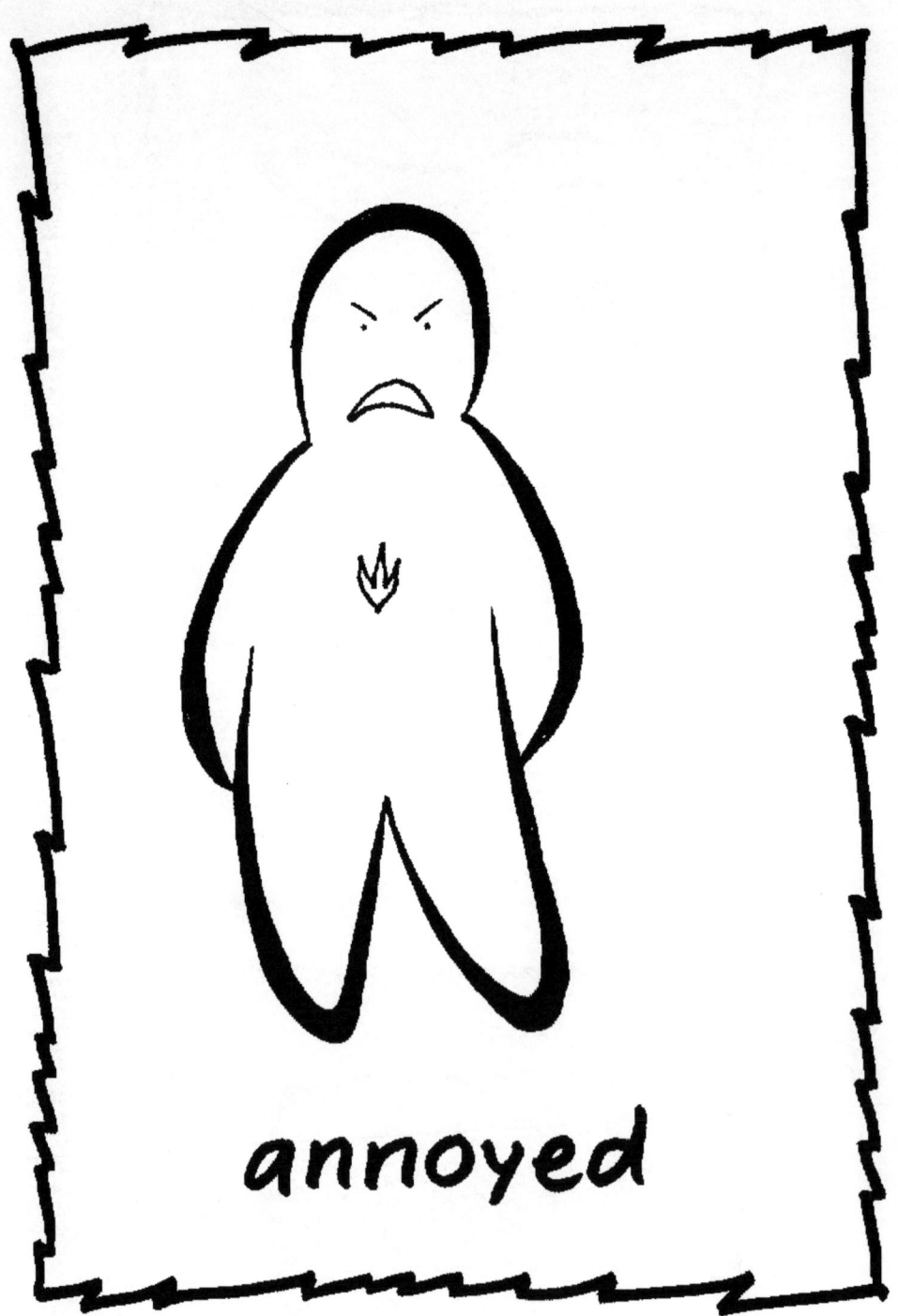

Individual feeling words

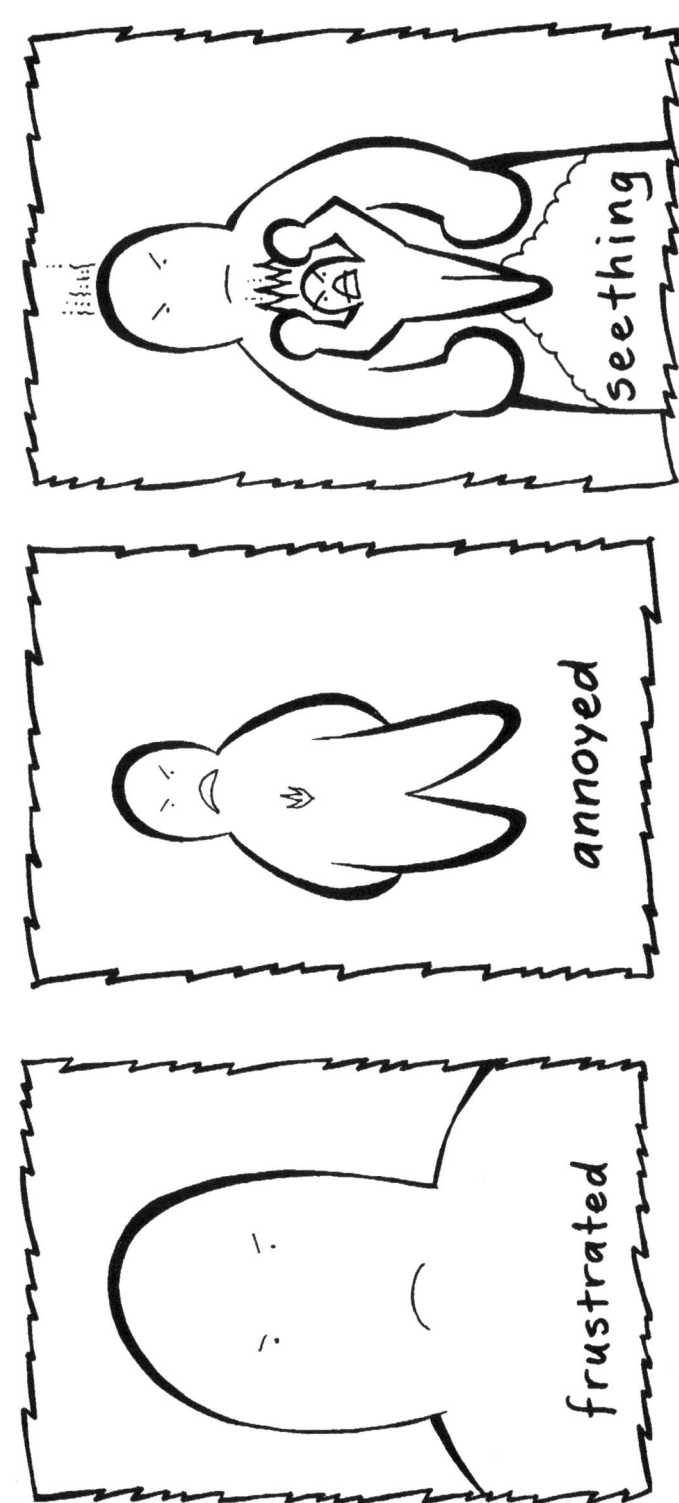

Wendy was annoyed by the constant barking of the dog in the middle of the night.

Individual feeling words

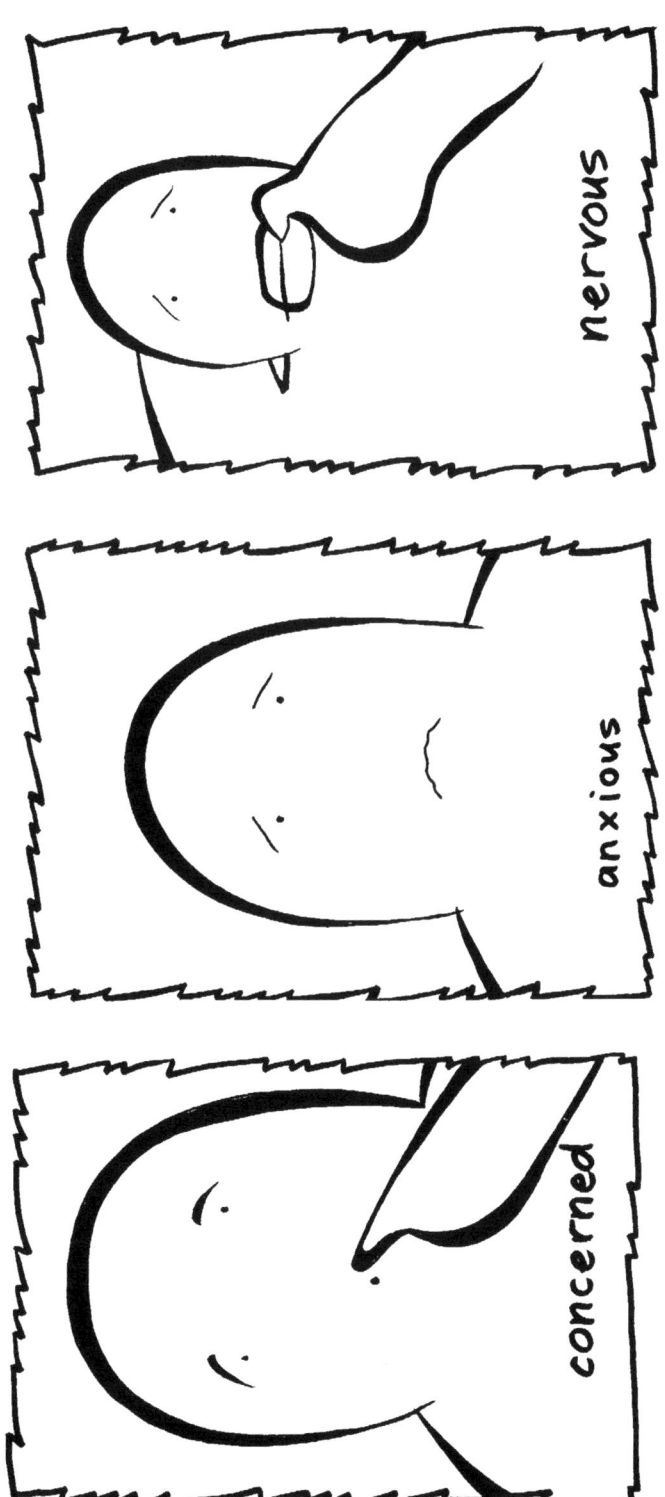

Patrycja was **anxious** as the hours ticked by and there was no sign of her friend.

Individual feeling words

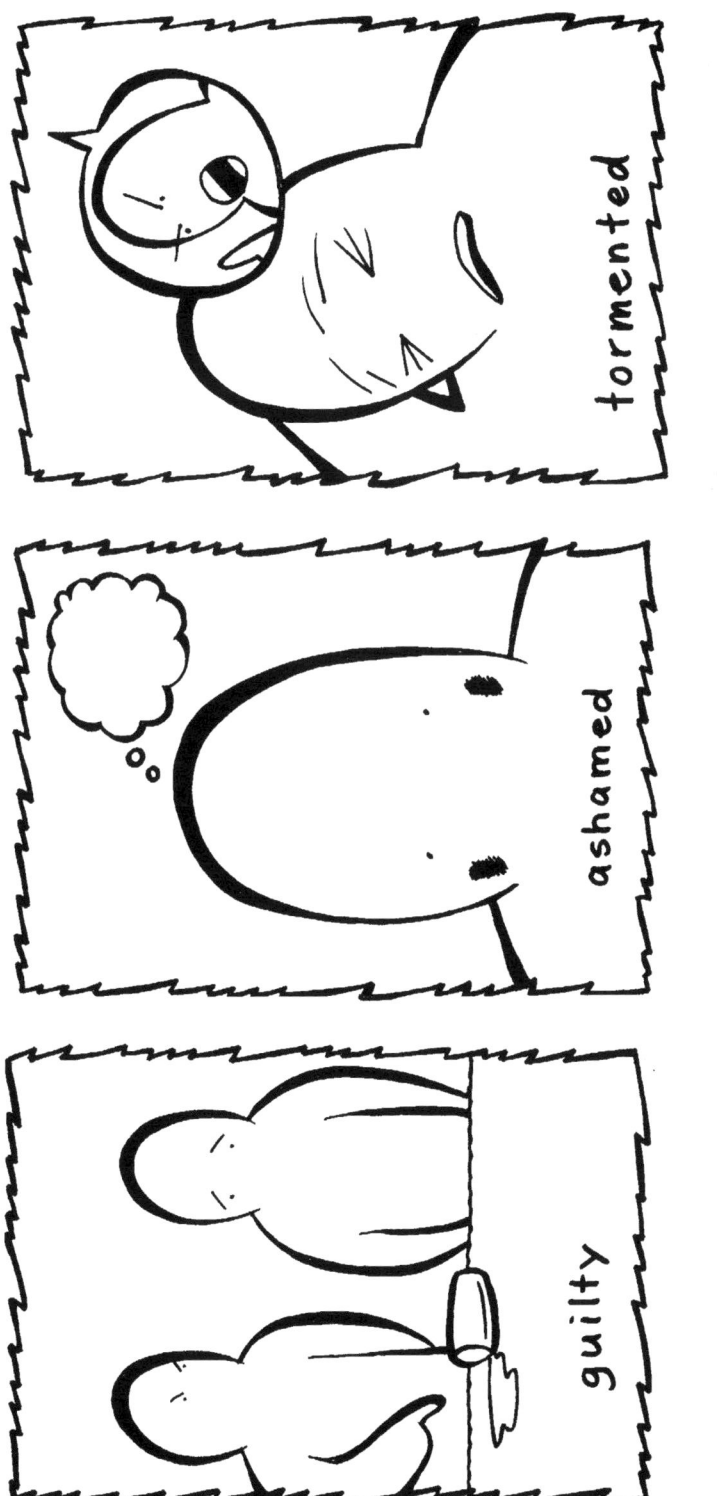

Rob felt ashamed by what he had said and couldn't stop thinking about the incident.

tormented ashamed guilty

Individual feeling words

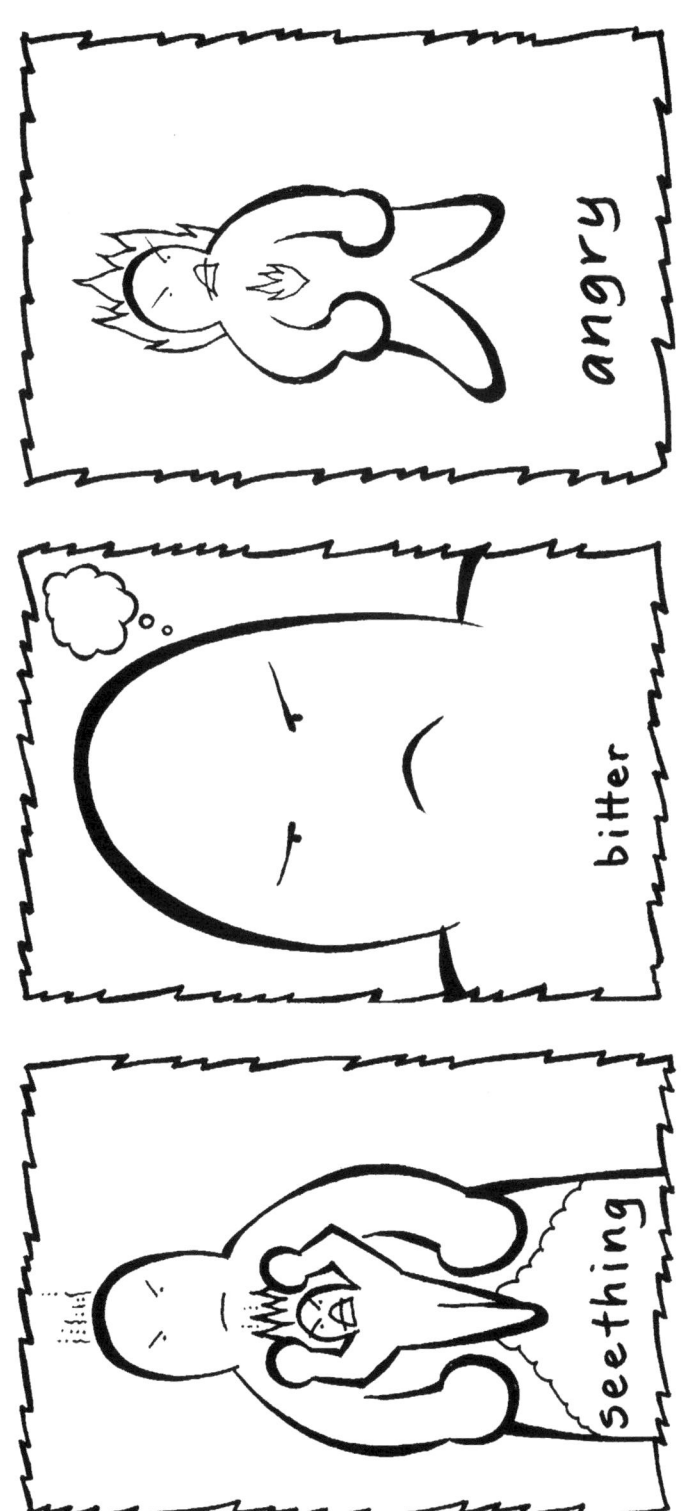

Fern was **bitter** that after six years of marriage, he didn't appreciate her more.

The Blob Emotional Thesaurus

Individual feeling words

Simone felt **bold** for the first time in her life as she ate her least favourite food – raw fish.

The Blob Emotional Thesaurus

Individual feeling words

disillusioned

bored

lazy

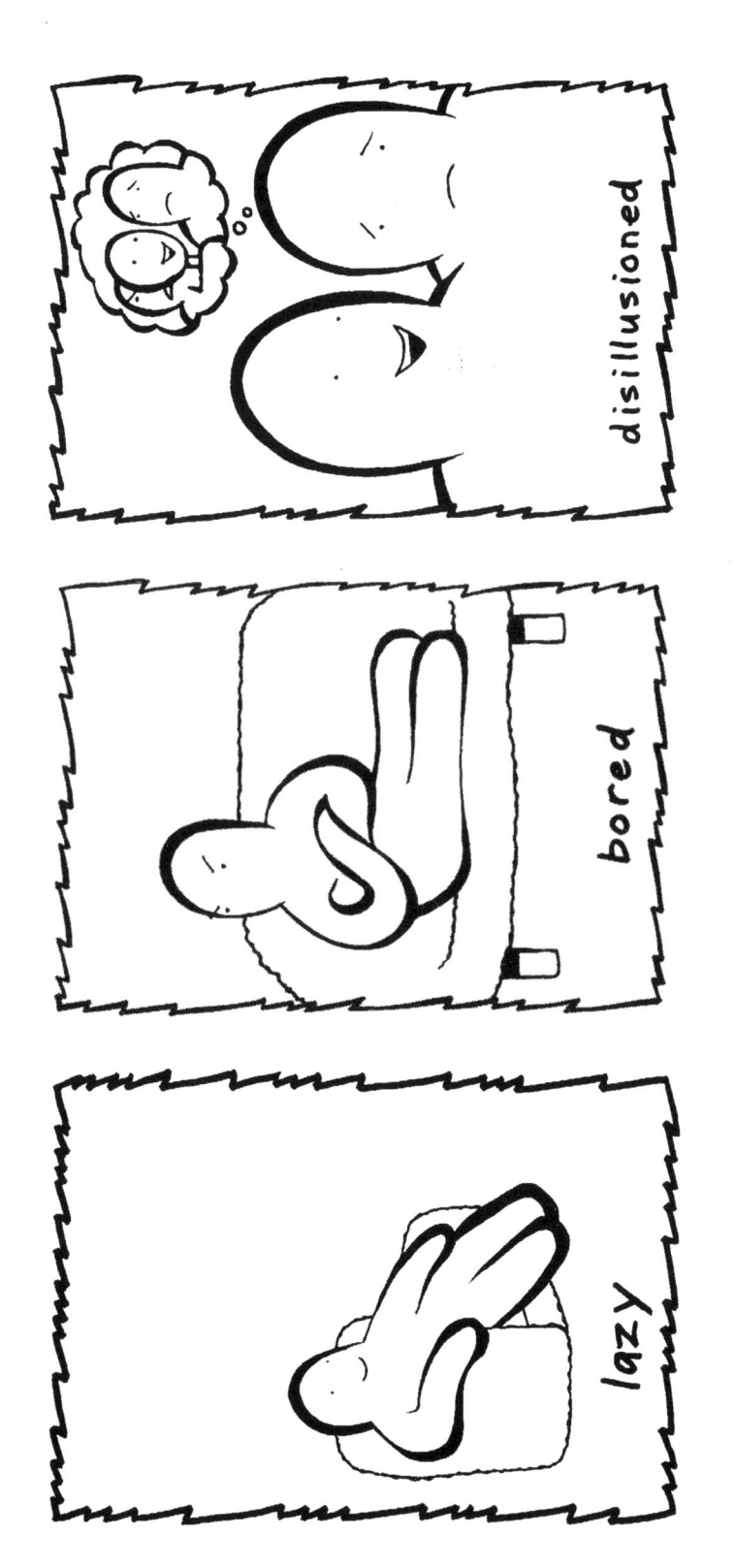

Ever since her phone had broken, Teri had been bored beyond description.

The Blob Emotional Thesaurus

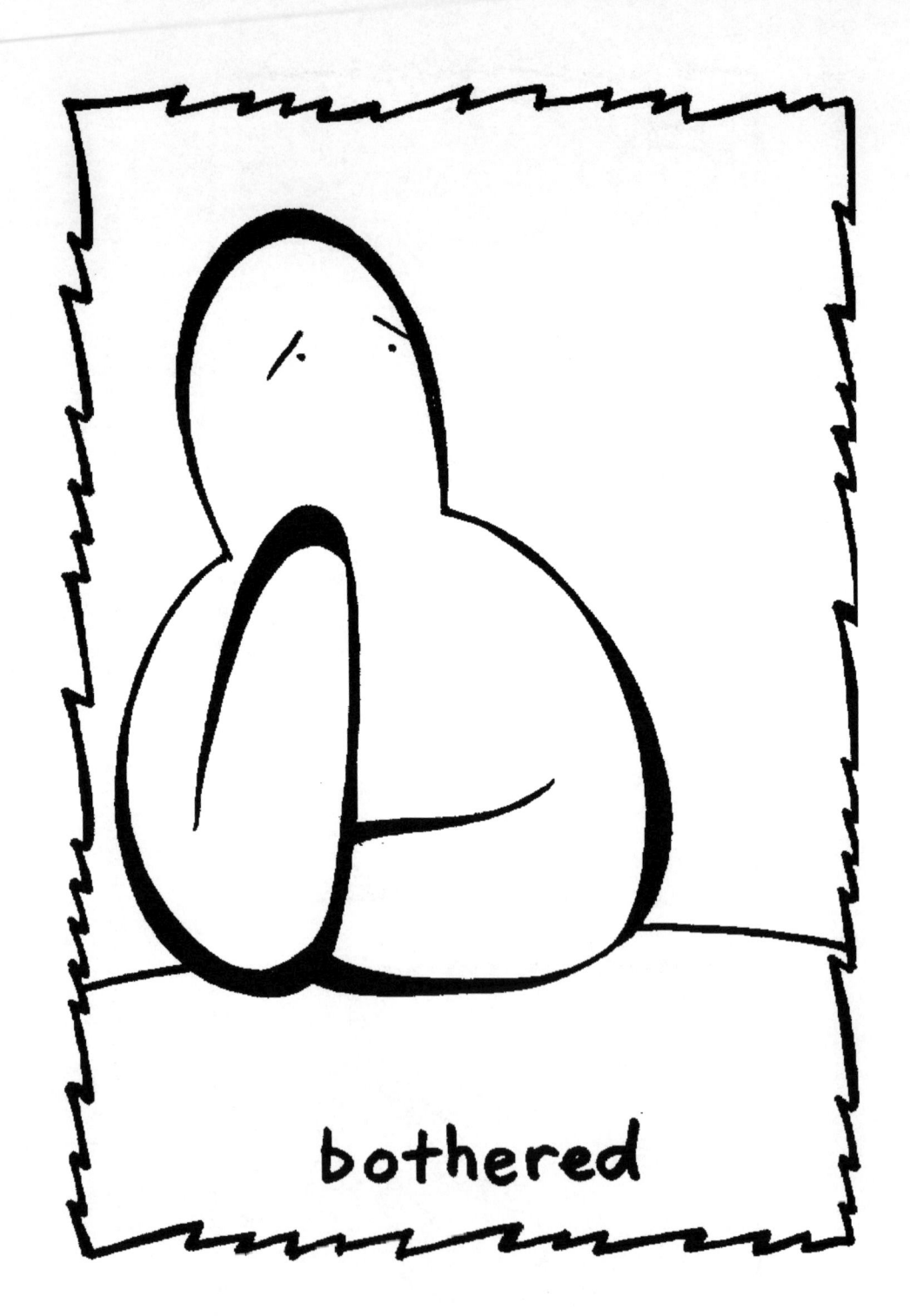

bothered

Individual feeling words

tense

bothered

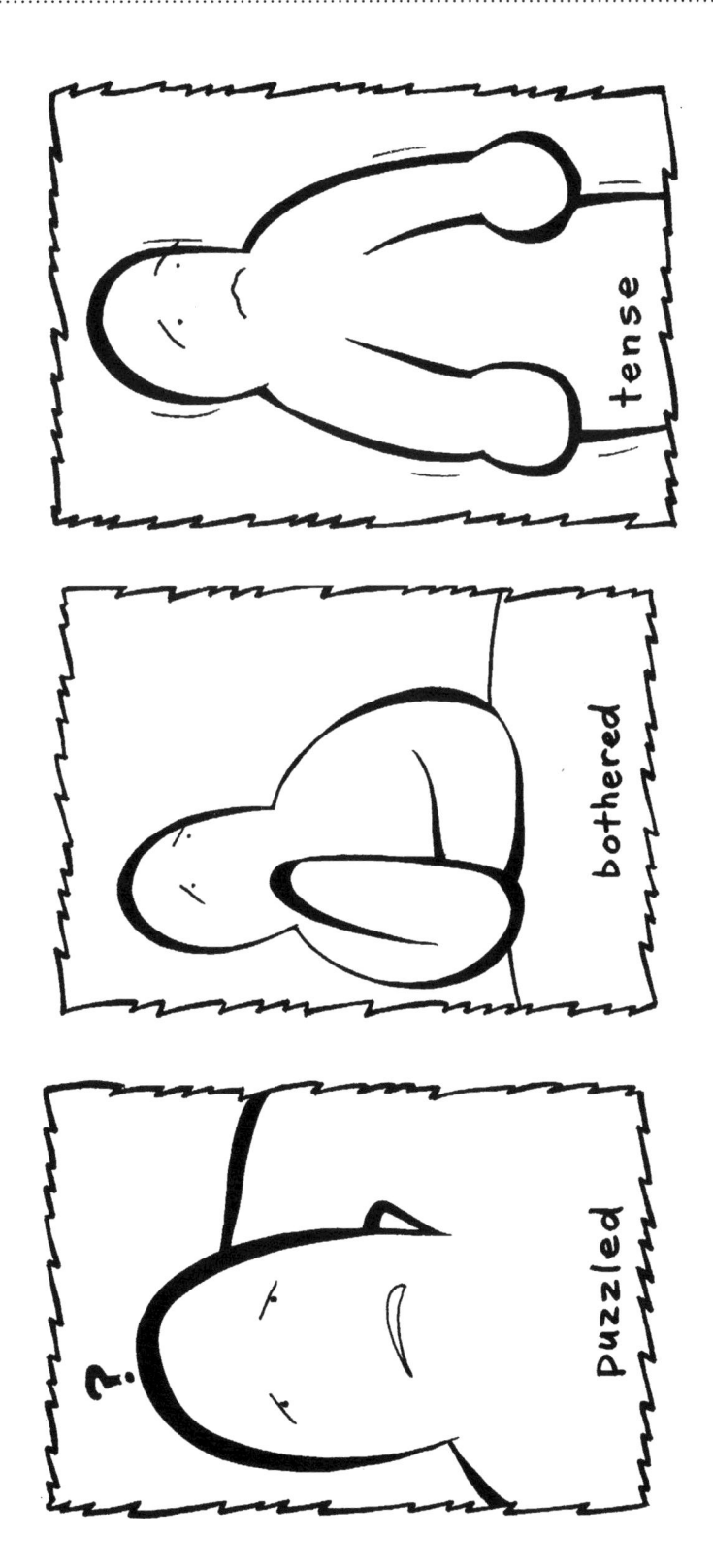

puzzled

The sound of crying each night *bothered* Ben all day.

The Blob Emotional Thesaurus

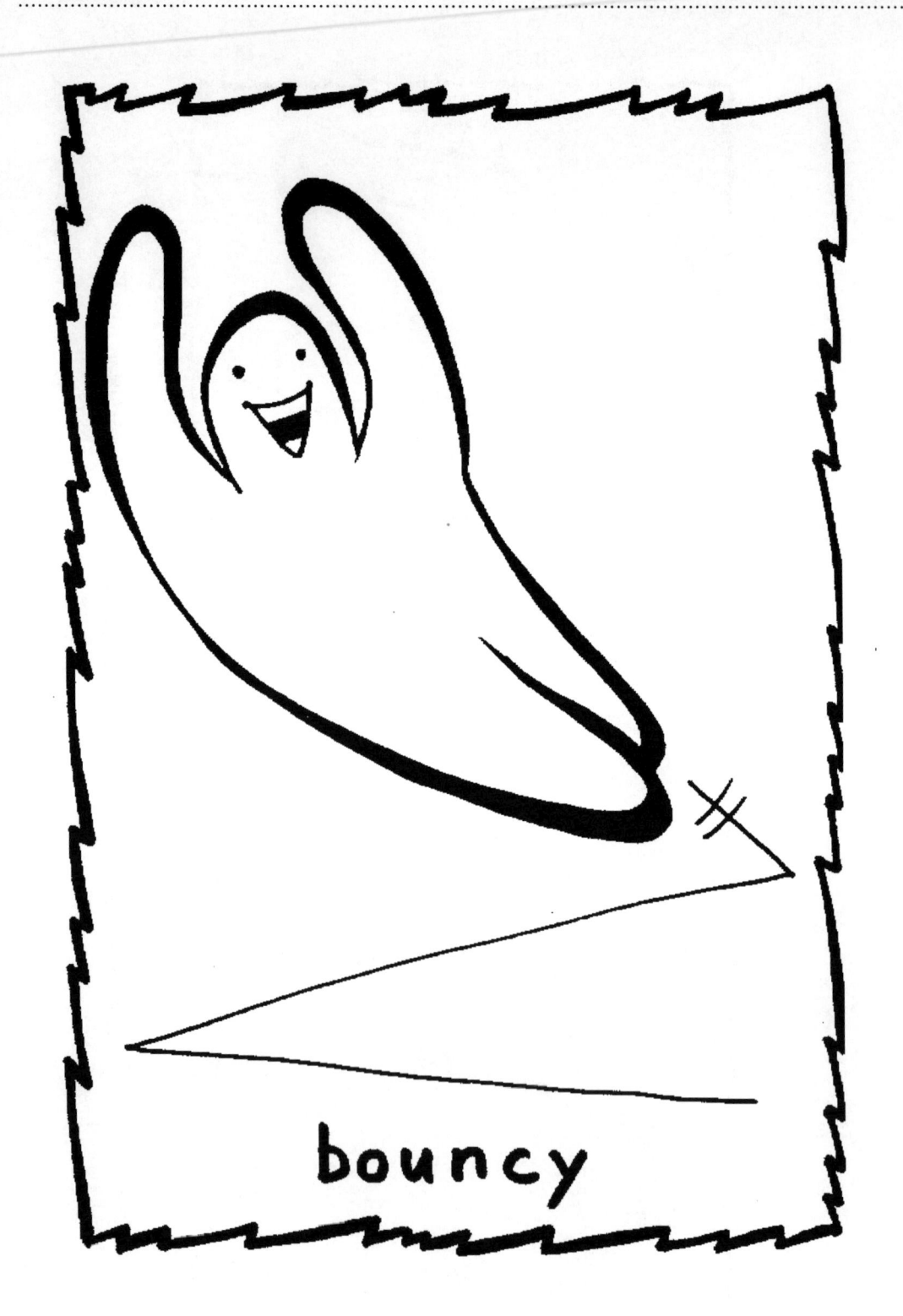

bouncy

Individual feeling words

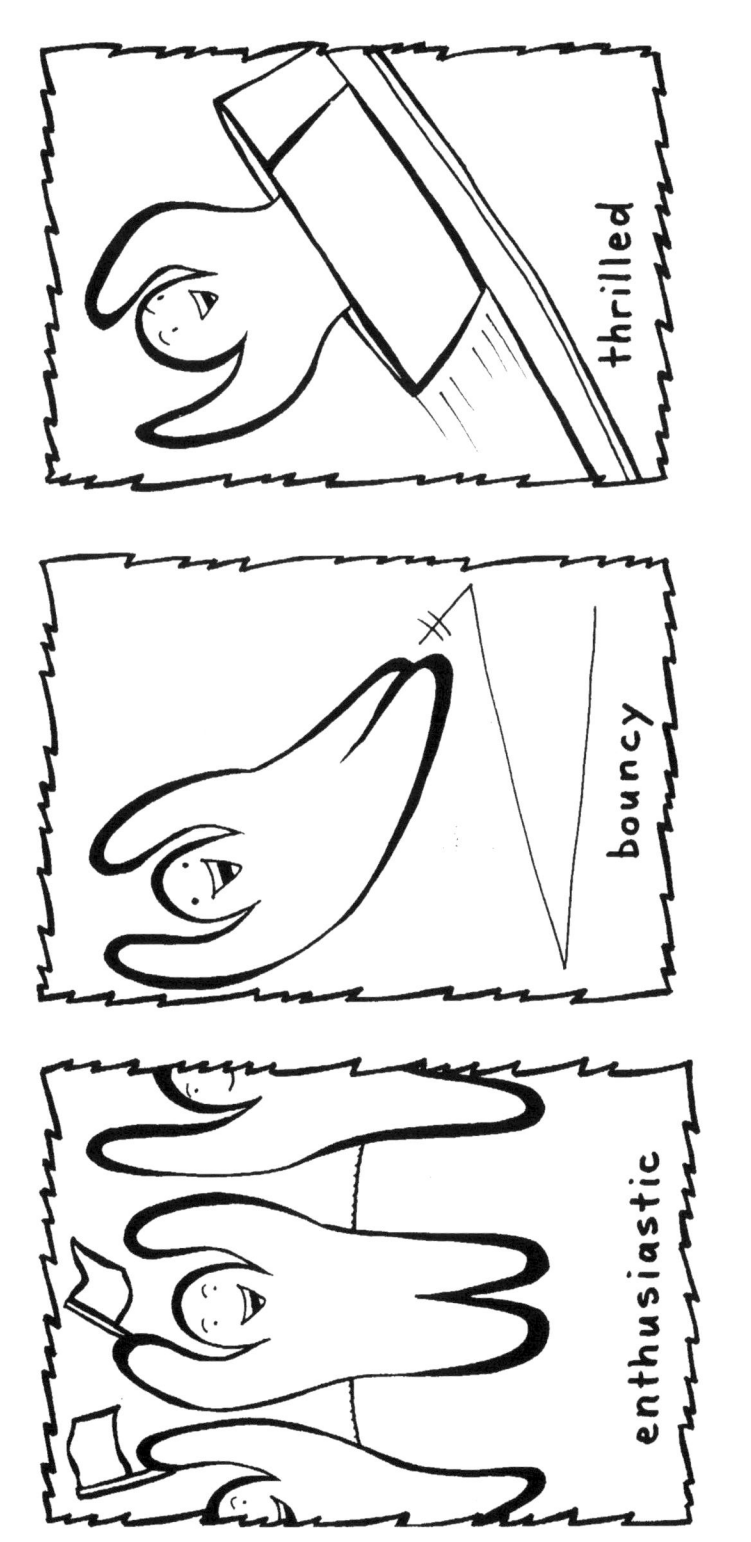

After arriving at the disco, Jo felt decidedly **bouncy**

thrilled

bouncy

enthusiastic

The Blob Emotional Thesaurus

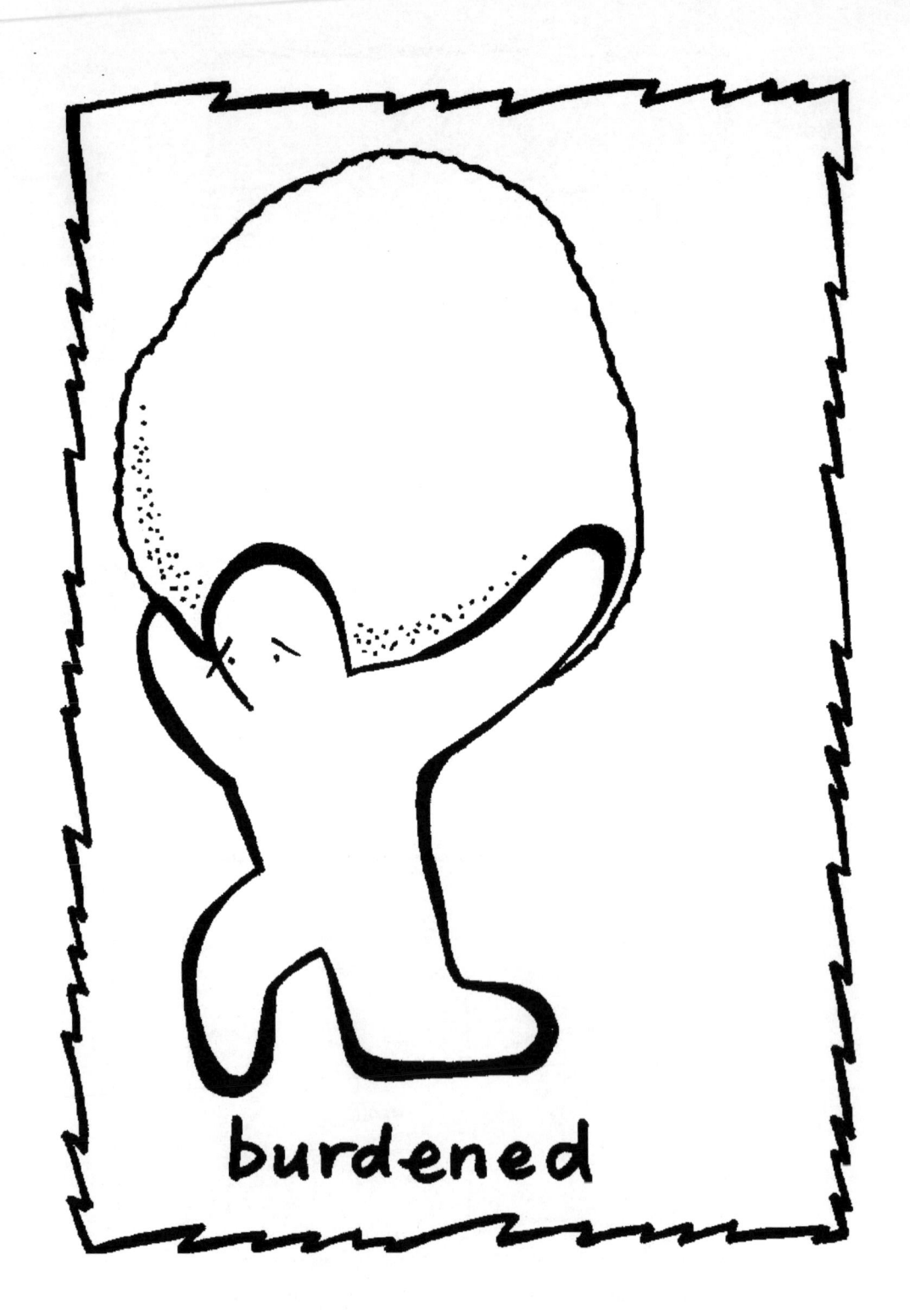

burdened

Individual feeling words

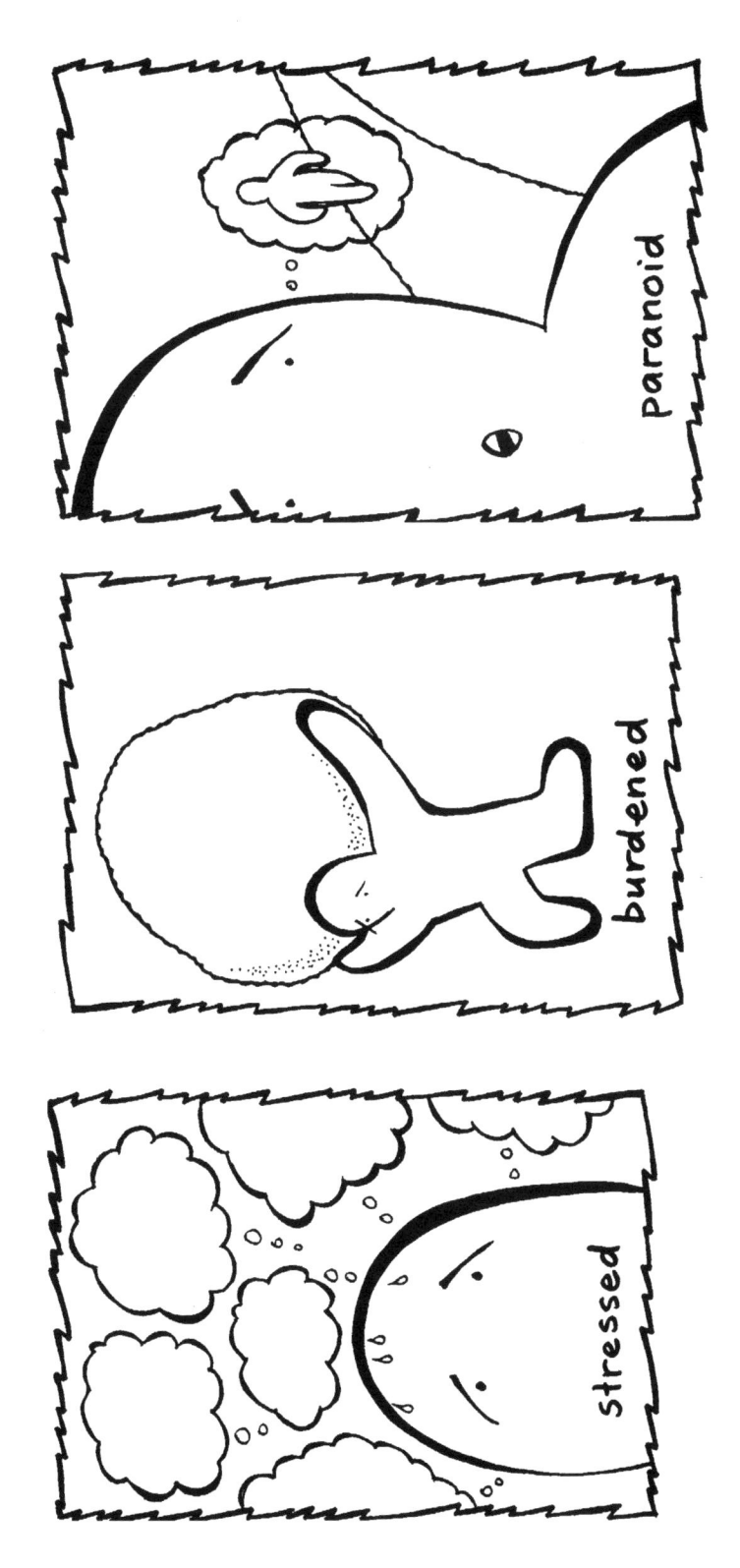

Vinnie felt **burdened** by having to look after her sick mother, even though she wanted to.

calm

Individual feeling words

As he sipped his mug of coffee, Ravi felt **calm** once more.

accepted

calm

neutral

The Blob Emotional Thesaurus

cheerful

Individual feeling words

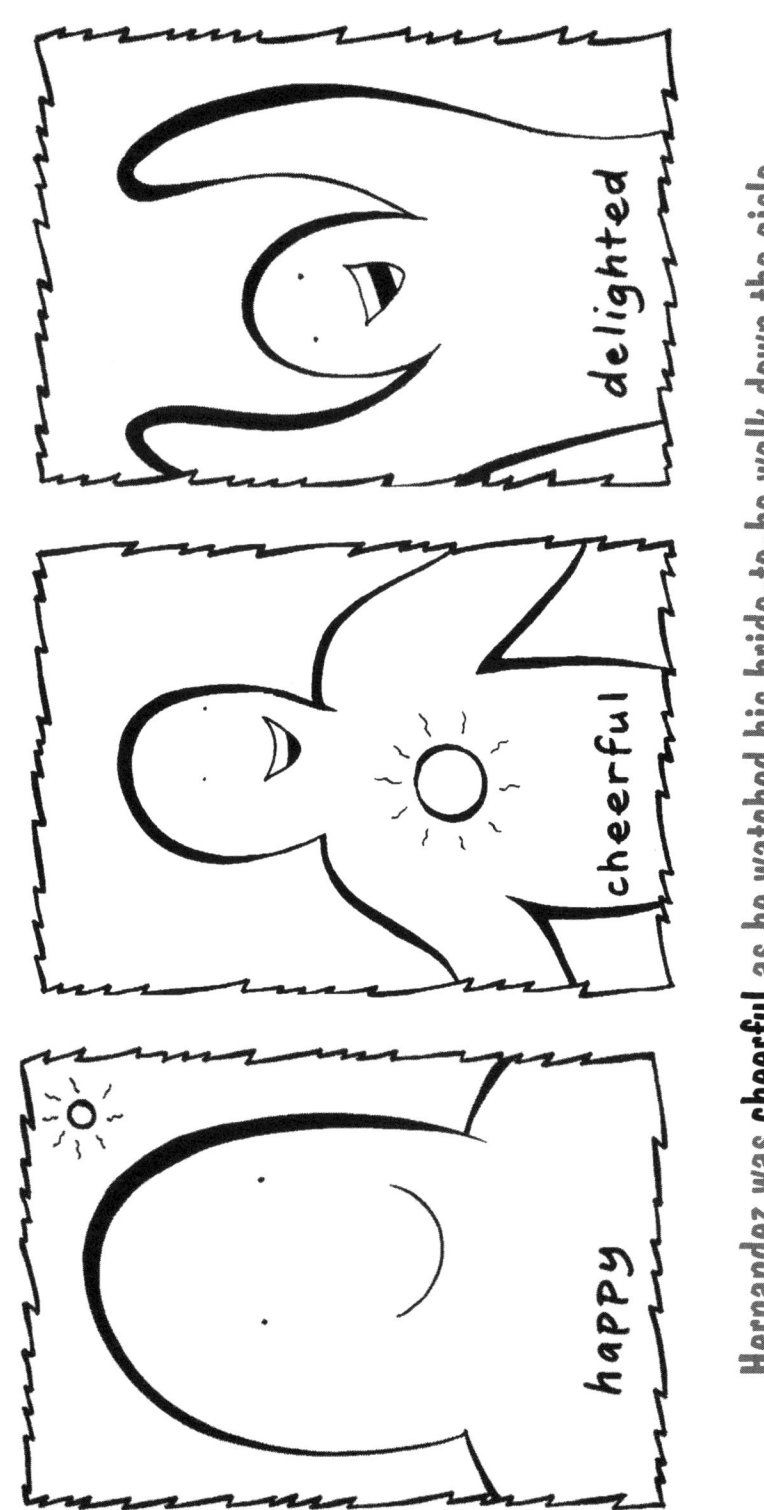

Hernandez was **cheerful** as he watched his bride-to-be walk down the aisle towards him, smiling.

The Blob Emotional Thesaurus

close

Individual feeling words

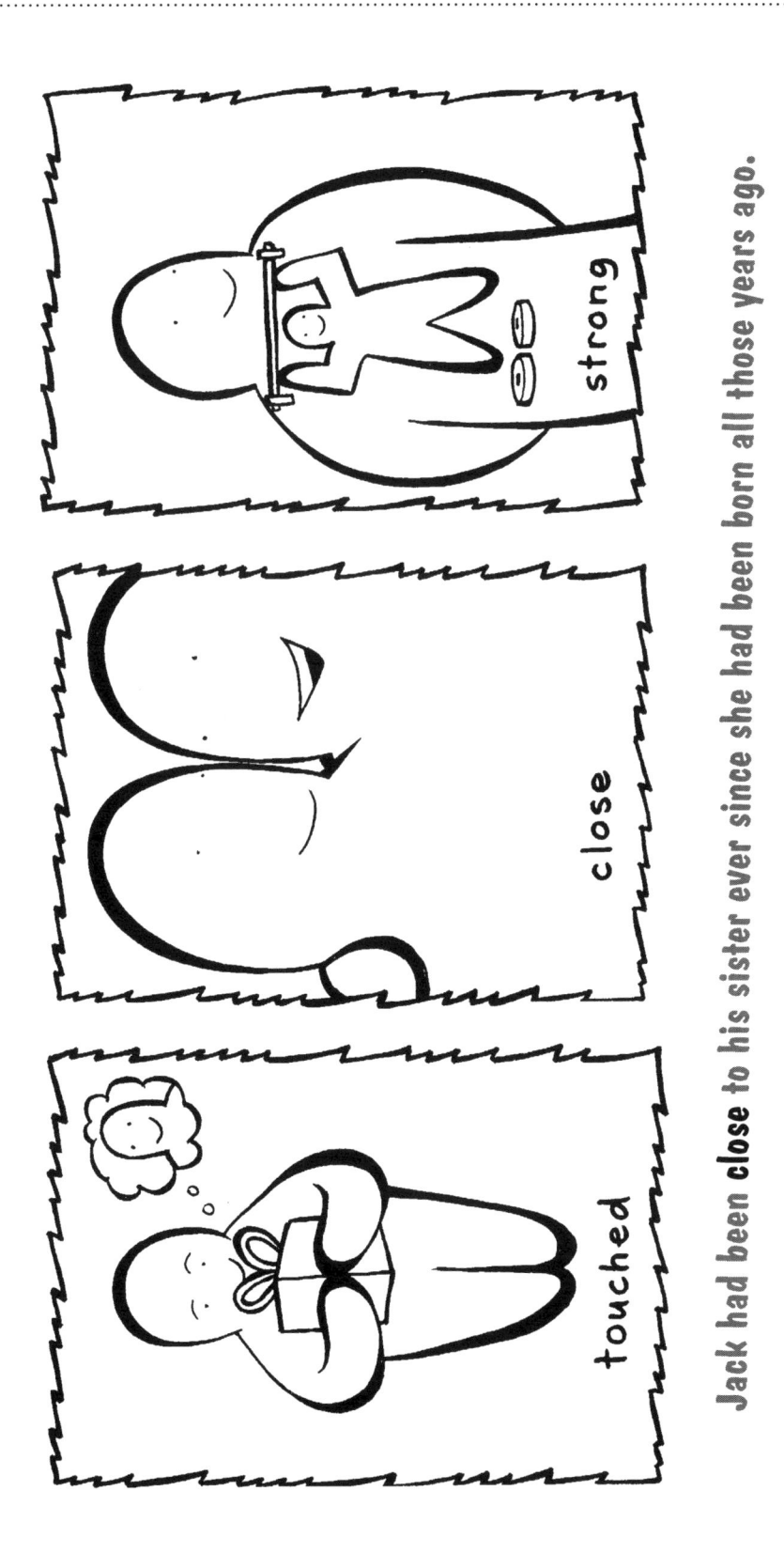

strong

close

touched

Jack had been **close** to his sister ever since she had been born all those years ago.

The Blob Emotional Thesaurus

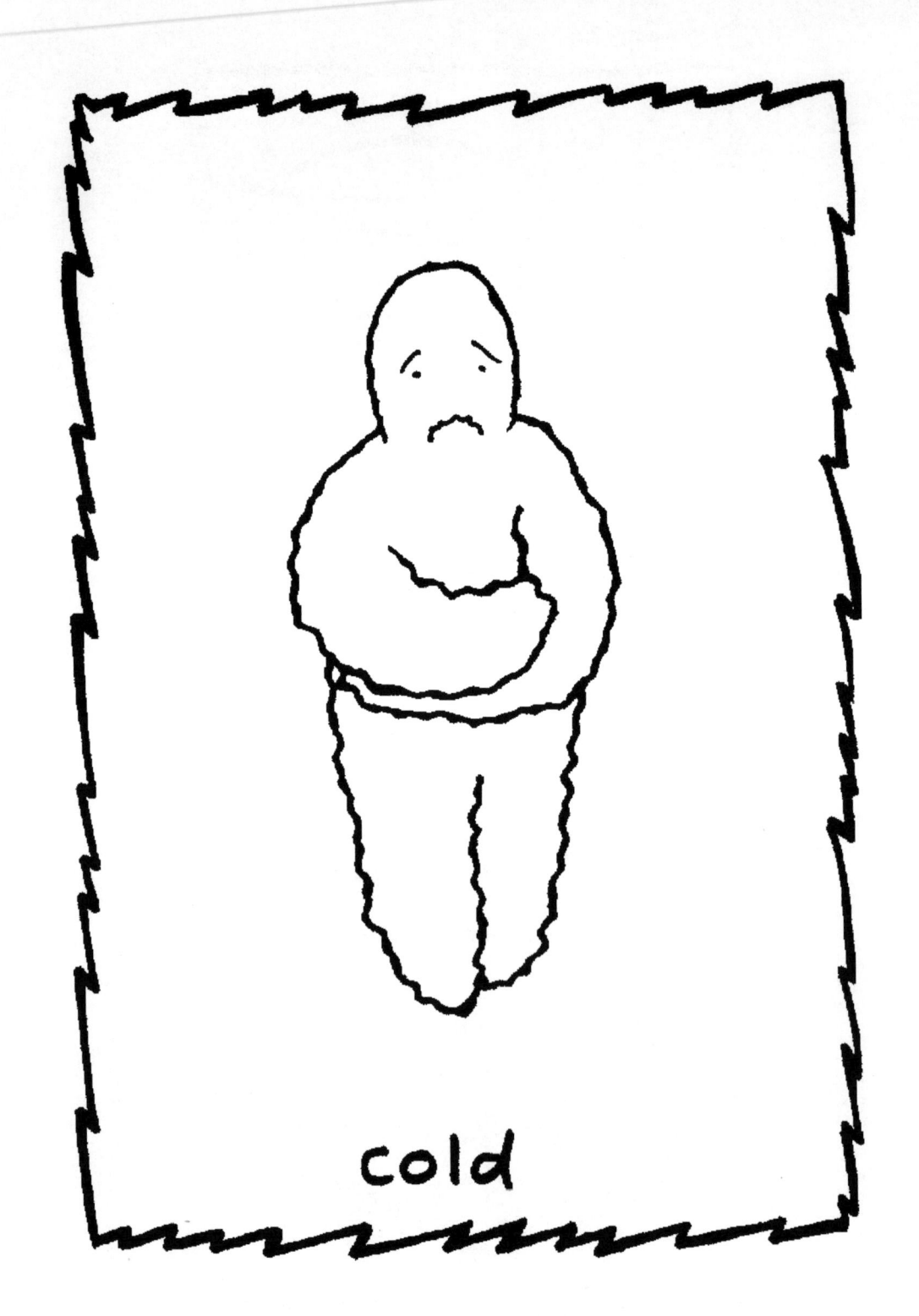

cold

Individual feeling words

lonely

cold

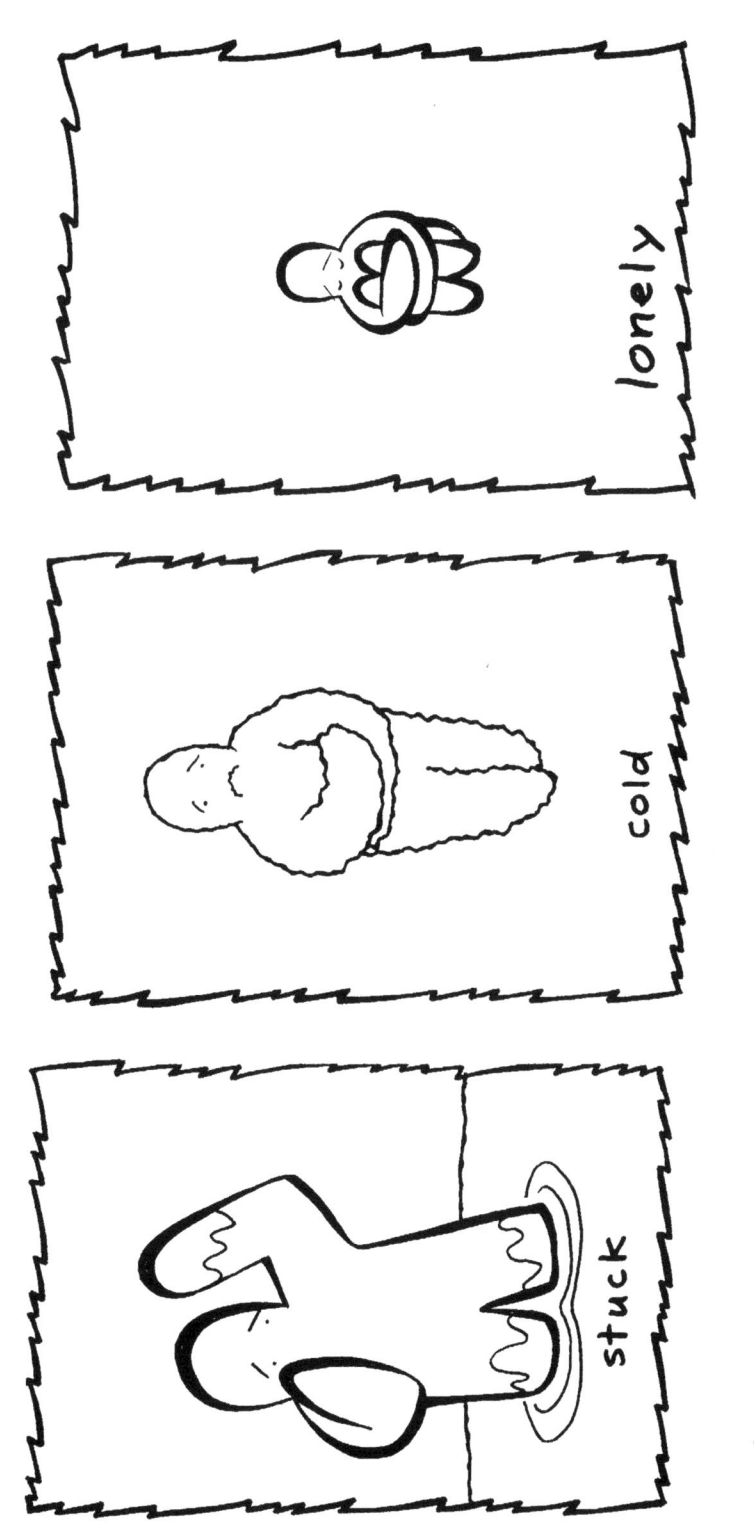

stuck

His reaction to her question made Lucy immediately feel **cold** throughout her being.

45

The Blob Emotional Thesaurus

compelled

Individual feeling words

mesmerised

compelled

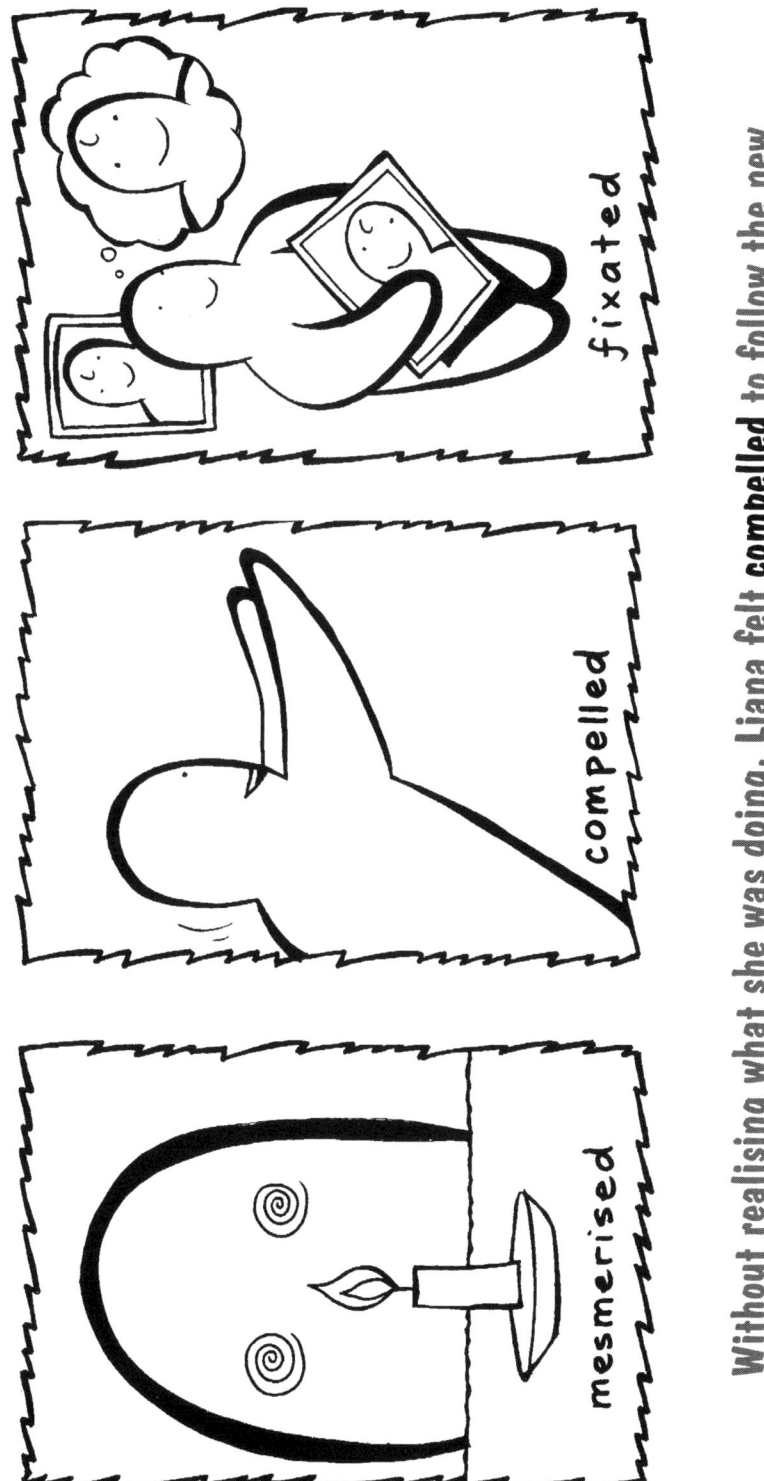

fixated

Without realising what she was doing, Liana felt **compelled** to follow the new boy around the playground.

47

concerned

Individual feeling words

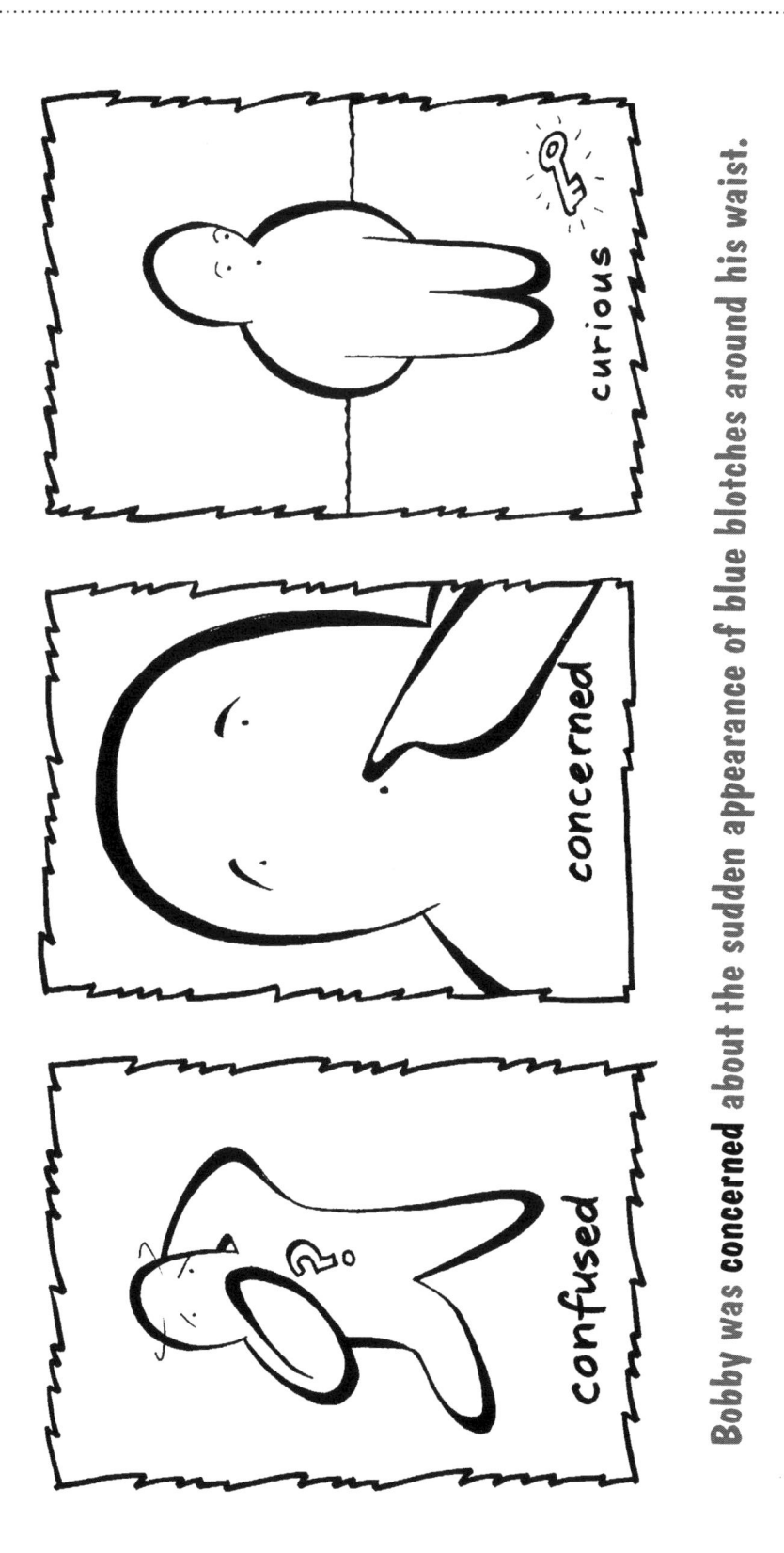

curious

concerned

confused

Bobby was concerned about the sudden appearance of blue blotches around his waist.

The Blob Emotional Thesaurus

condemned

Individual feeling words

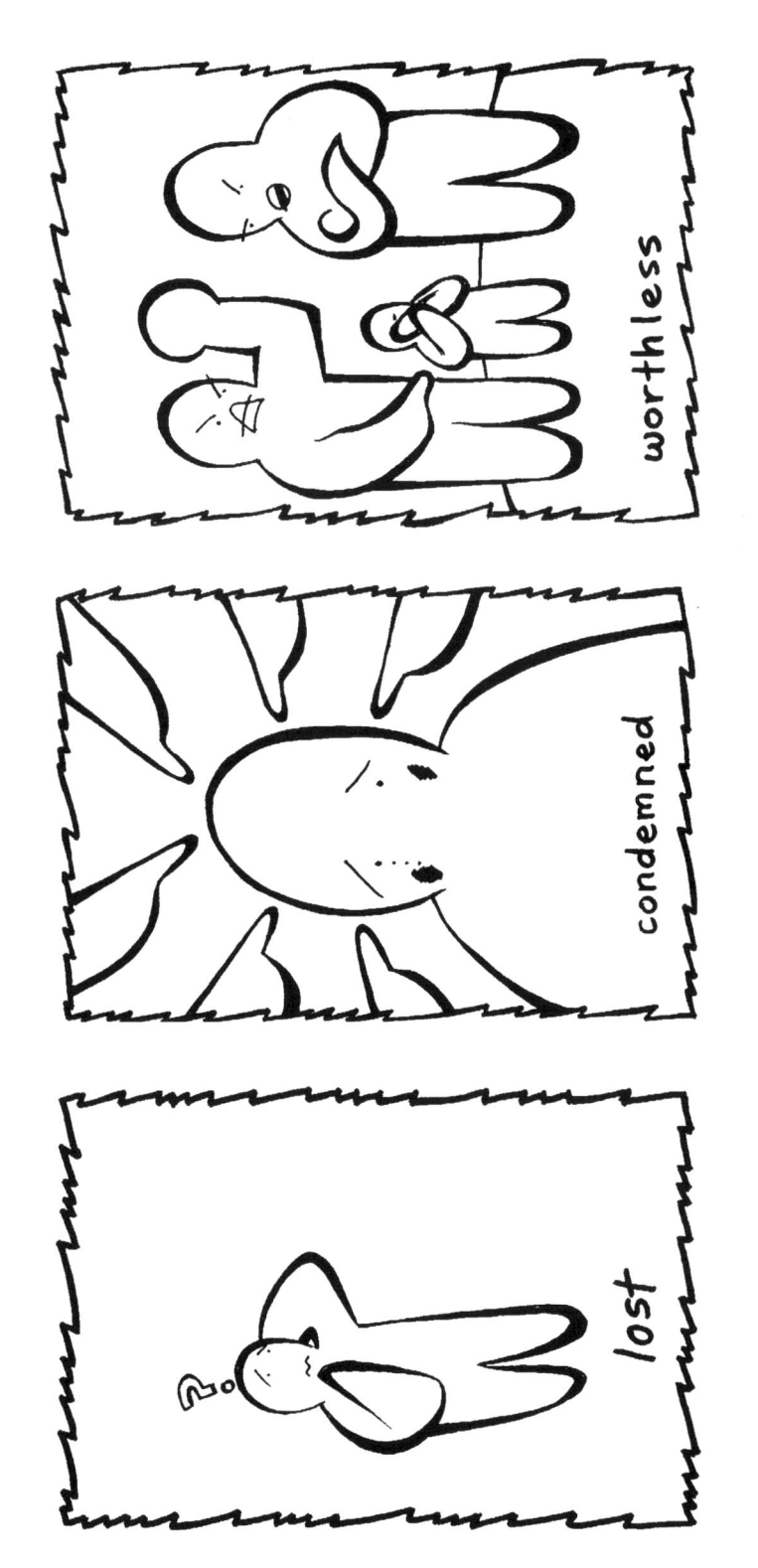

Heidi felt condemned for standing up for her own opinions on clothing.

The Blob Emotional Thesaurus

confident

Individual feeling words

loved

confident

safe

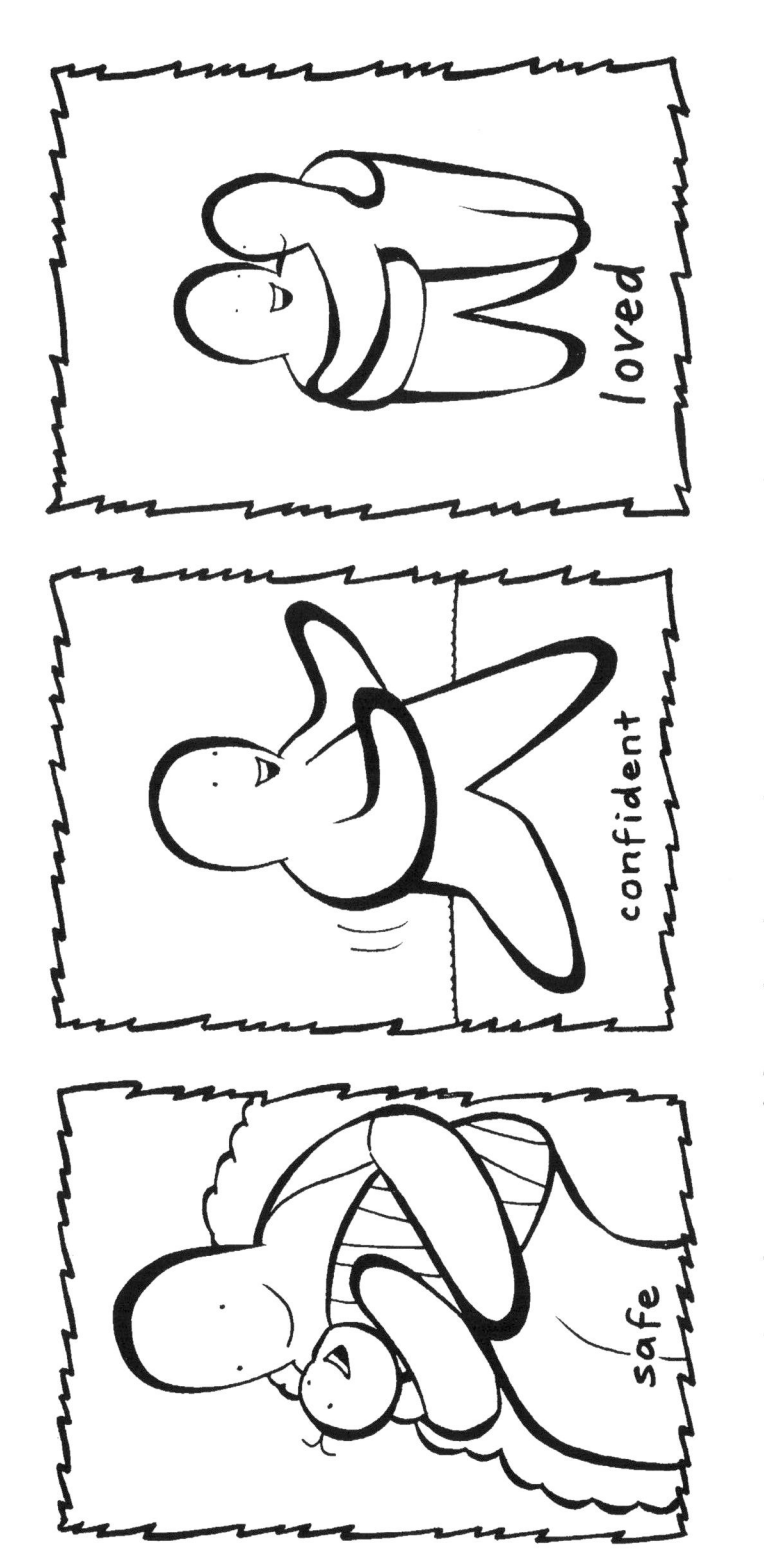

Ahmed was **confident** that he could climb to the top of the mountain!

The Blob Emotional Thesaurus

confused

Individual feeling words

concerned

confused

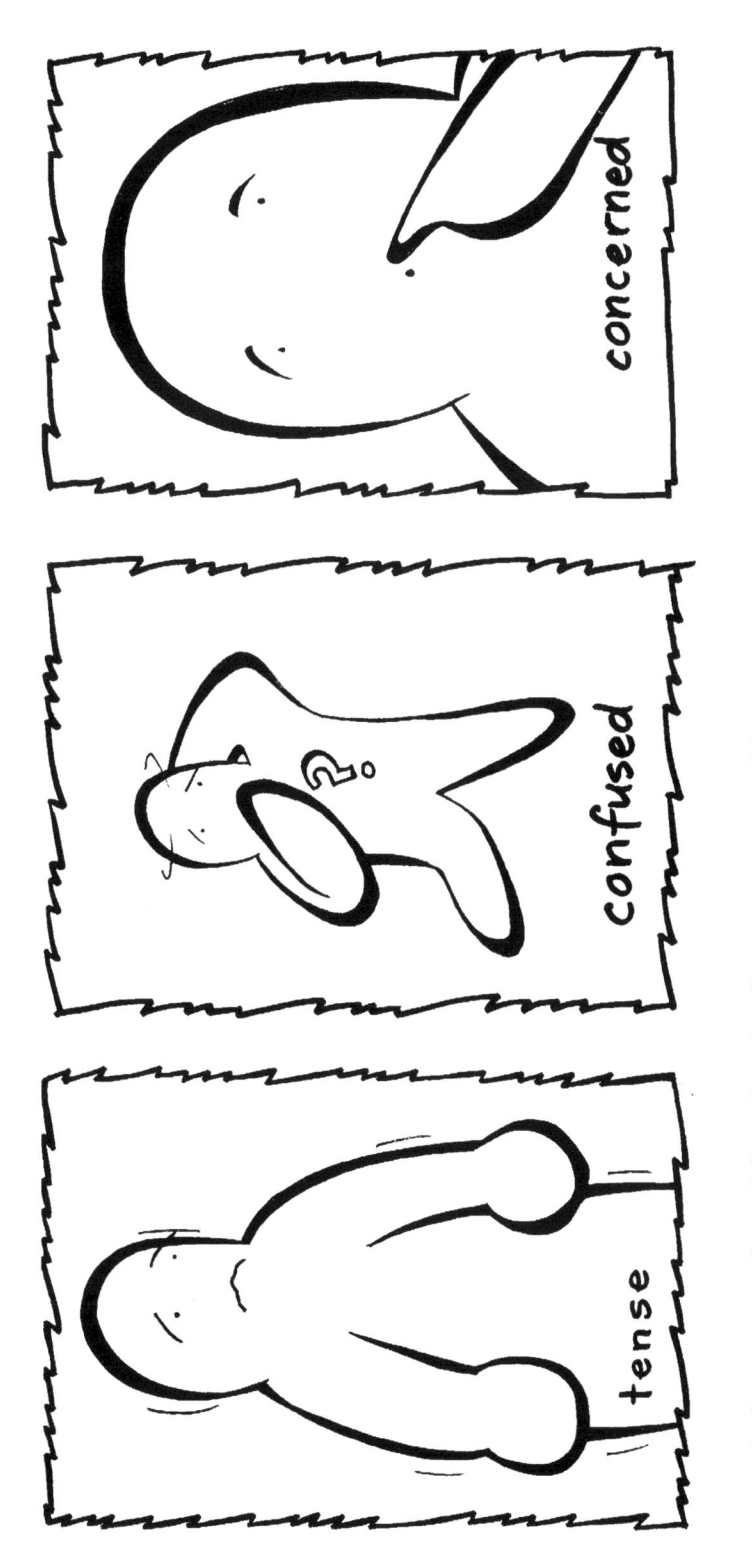

tense

Sid was **confused** by the deafening noise of banging coming from behind the wall.

The Blob Emotional Thesaurus

constant

Individual feeling words

peaceful

constant

calm

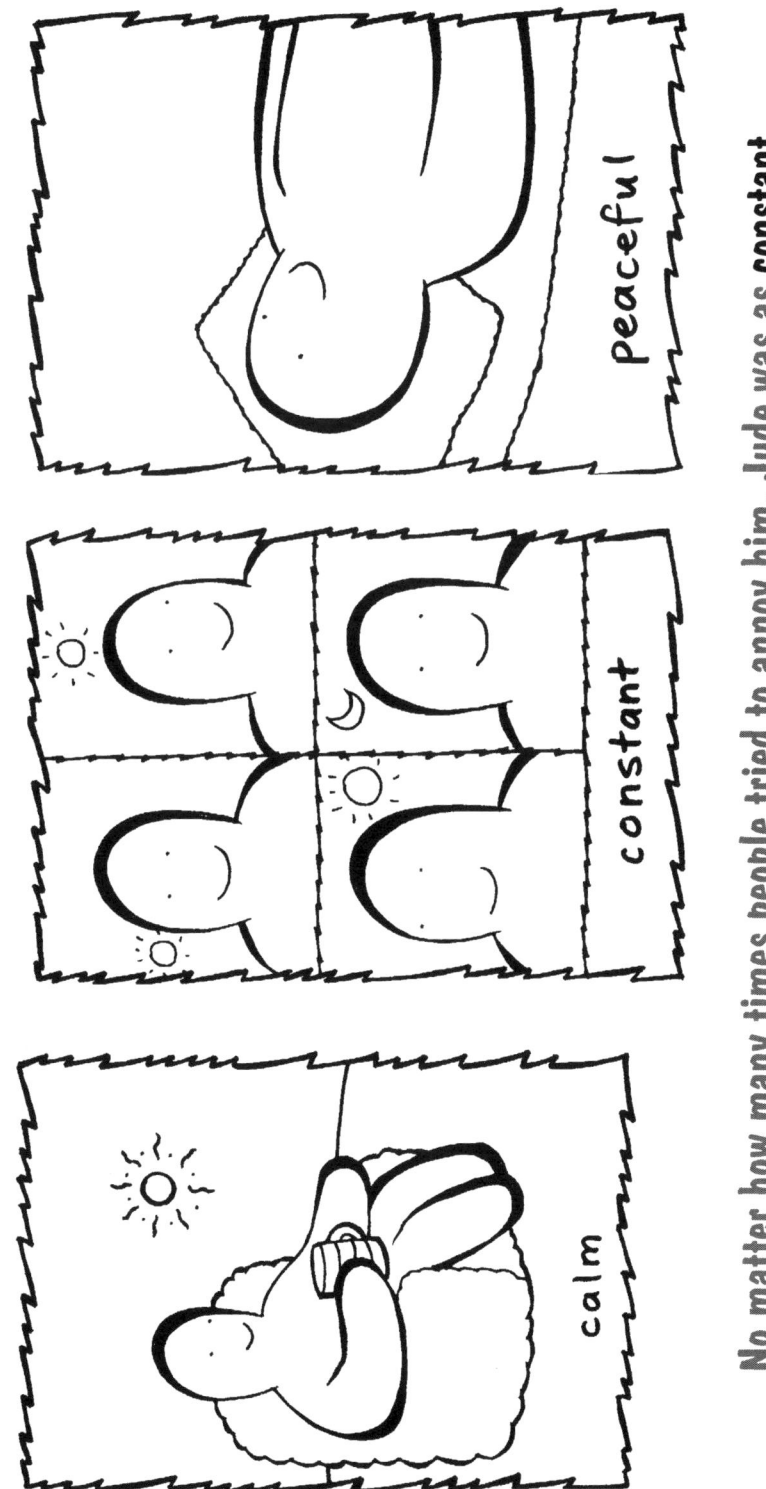

No matter how many times people tried to annoy him, Jude was as **constant** as the march of time.

The Blob Emotional Thesaurus

controlled

Individual feeling words

restrained	controlled	weak

Whenever Joy was with friends, she felt **controlled**, as if the decisions were made by everyone else.

The Blob Emotional Thesaurus

courageous

Individual feeling words

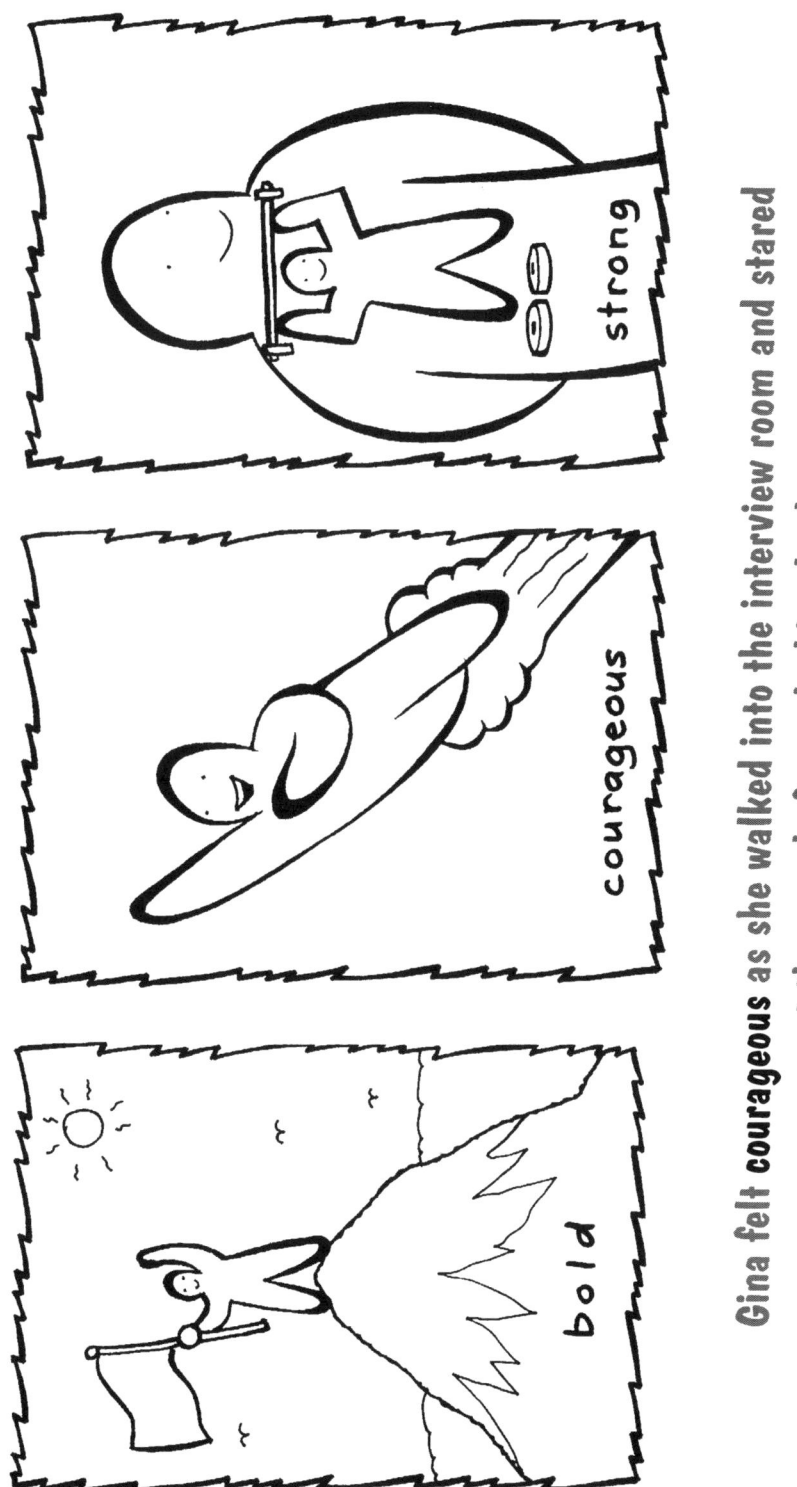

Gina felt *courageous* as she walked into the interview room and stared at the crowd of eyes looking back.

strong

courageous

bold

The Blob Emotional Thesaurus

cowardly

Individual feeling words

crushed

cowardly

weak

Herbert felt **cowardly** as he walked away from the bully who was threatening him, but it was the right thing to do.

crushed

Individual feeling words

crushed

trapped

Kyle felt crushed when everybody laughed at his performance in the talent show, even the teachers.

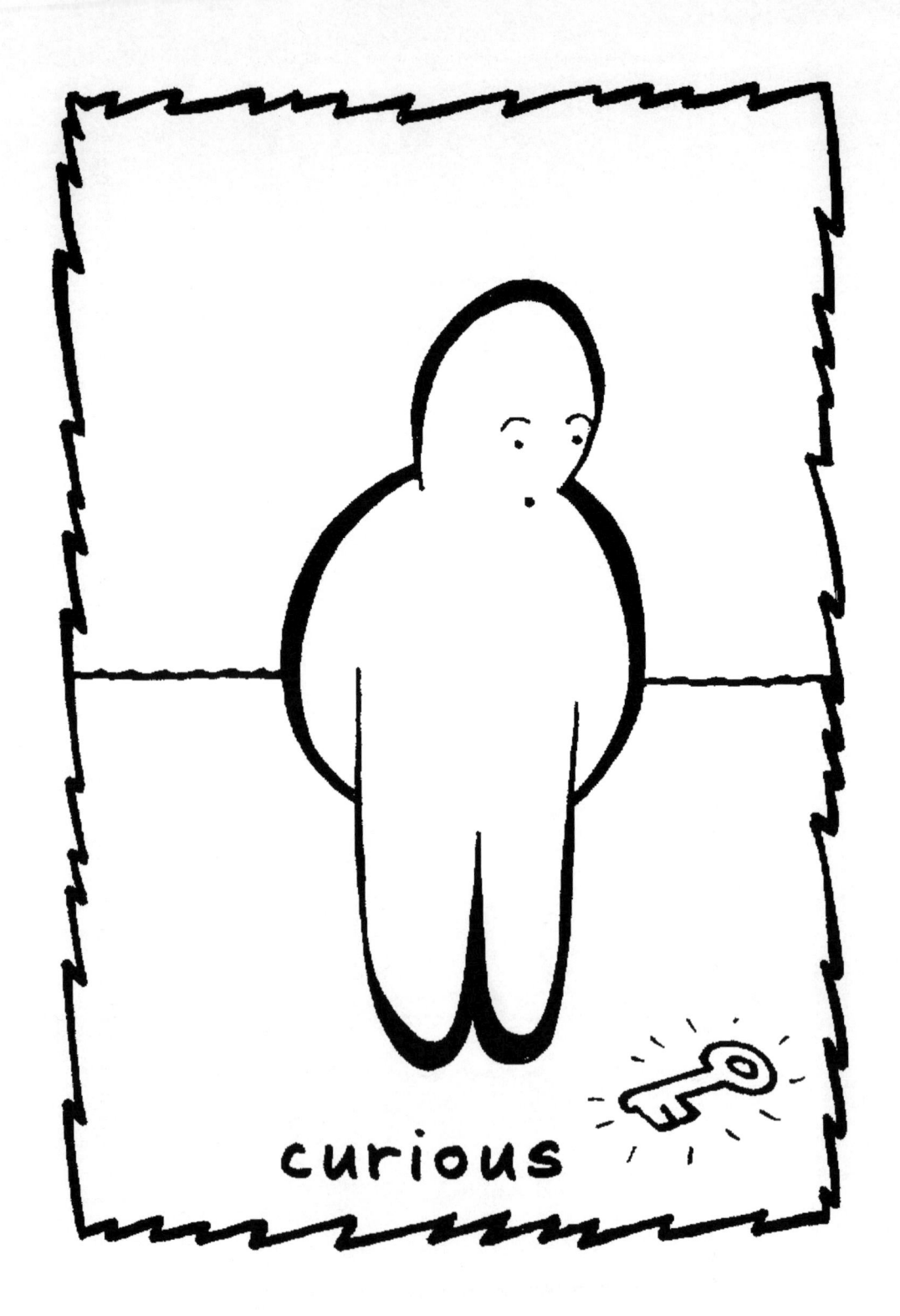

curious

Individual feeling words

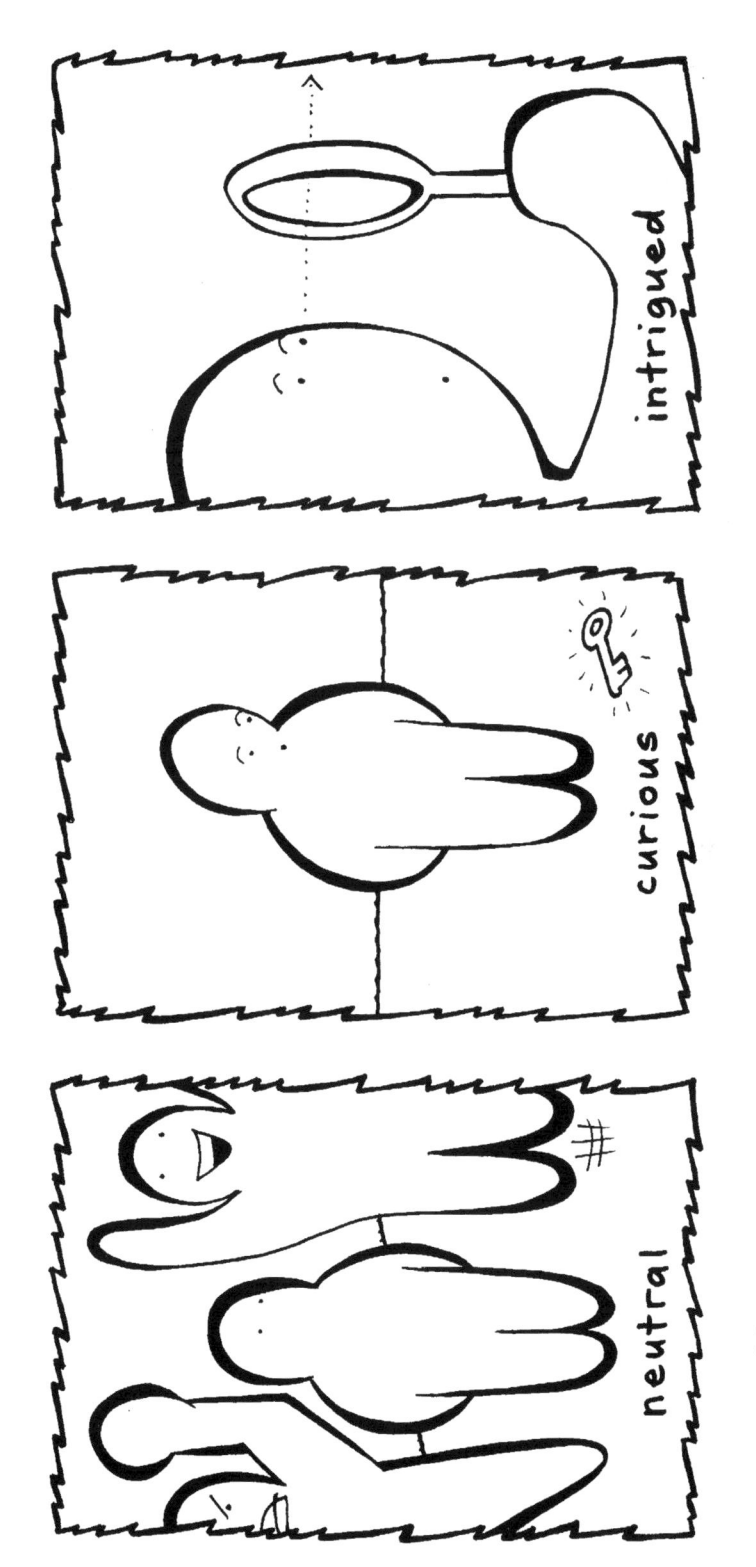

Maddie was **curious** about which door the key that she had found may open.

intrigued

curious

neutral

The Blob Emotional Thesaurus

delighted

Individual feeling words

optimistic

delighted

happy

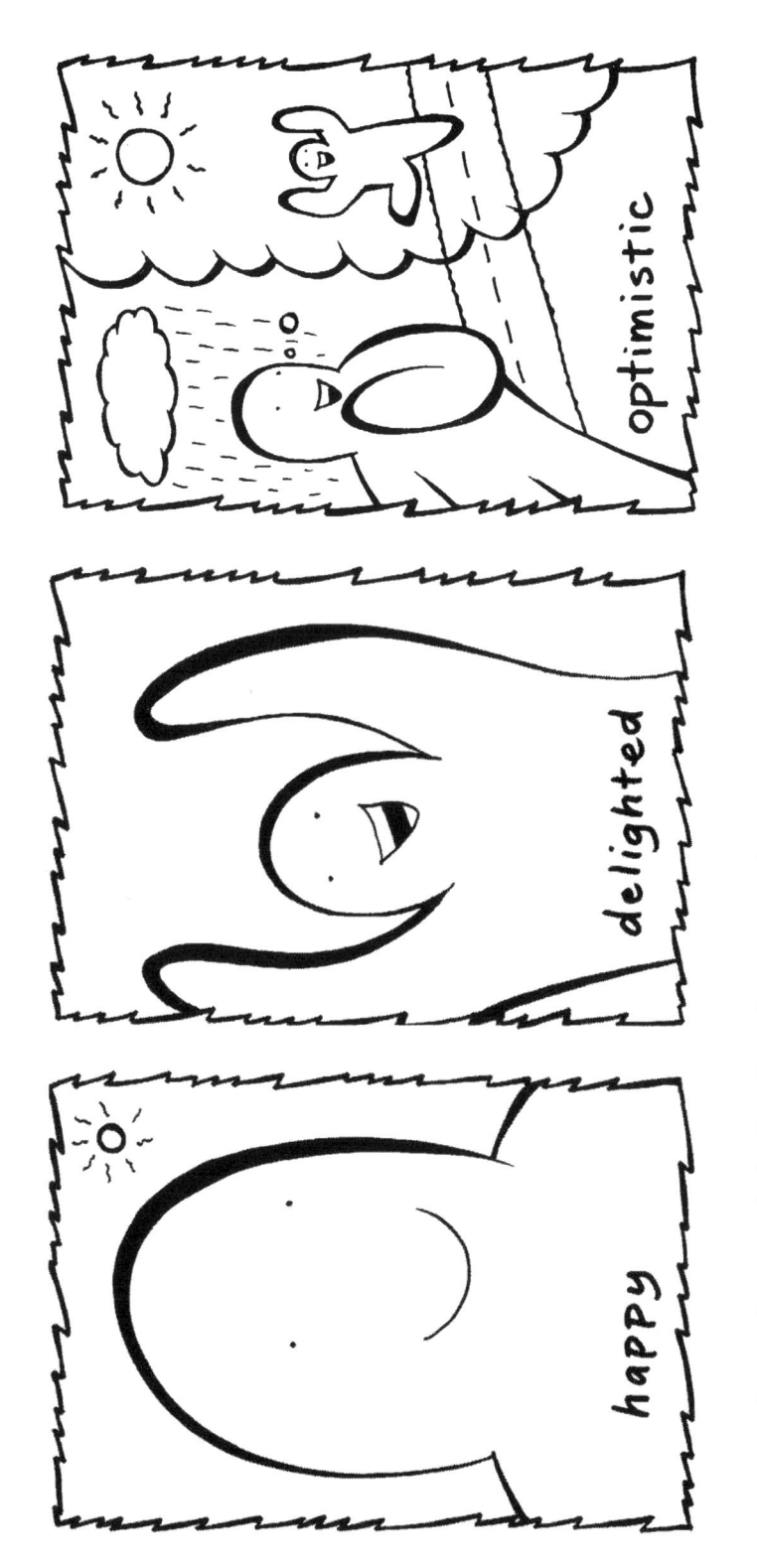

Joseph was **delighted** to be invited to see the Queen at Buckingham Palace.

The Blob Emotional Thesaurus

depressed

Individual feeling words

depressed

down

After a year of being bullied, Jake felt **depressed** every time he went to work.

The Blob Emotional Thesaurus

deprived

Individual feeling words

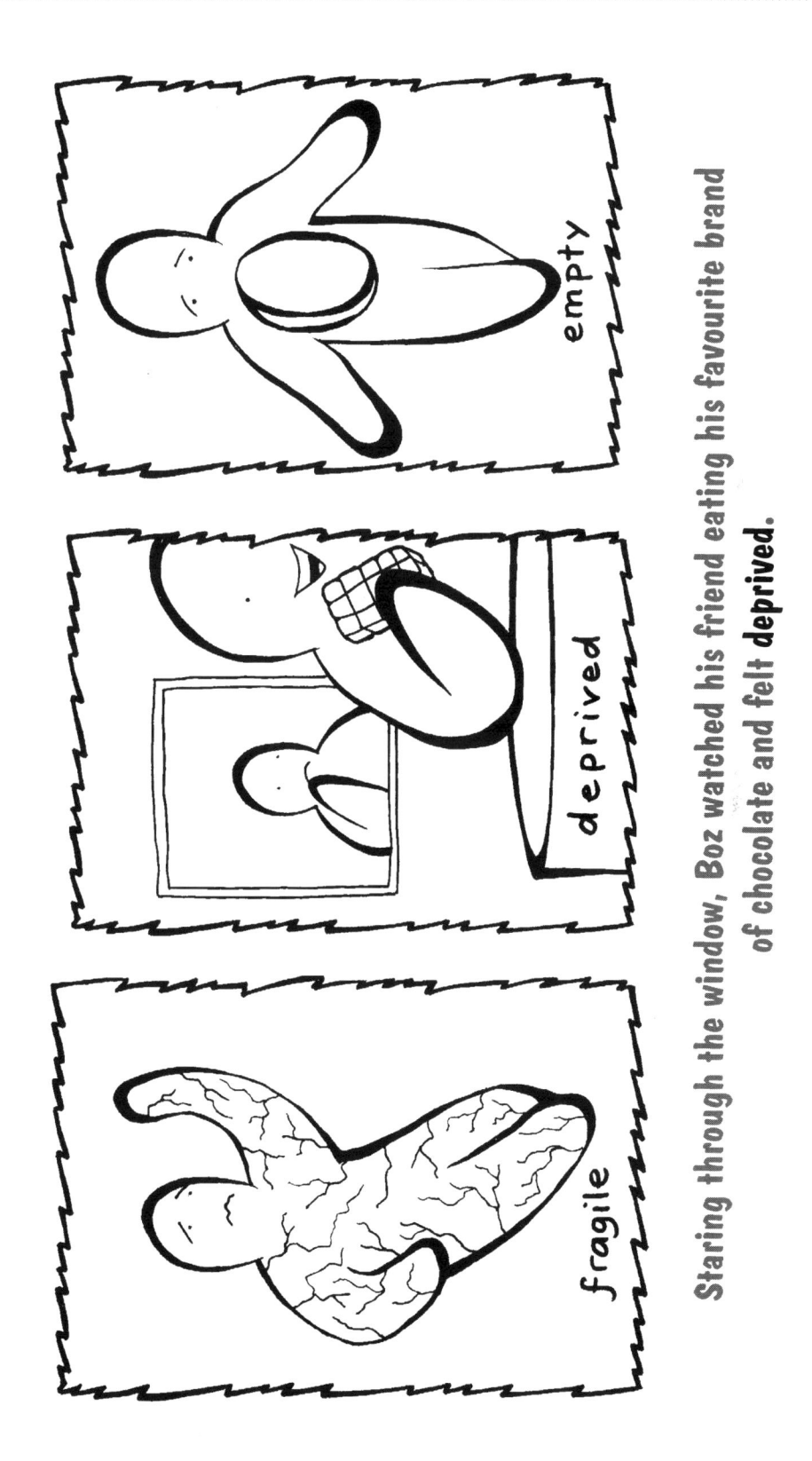

empty

deprived

fragile

Staring through the window, Boz watched his friend eating his favourite brand of chocolate and felt **deprived**.

The Blob Emotional Thesaurus

desperate

Individual feeling words

dreading

desperate

scared

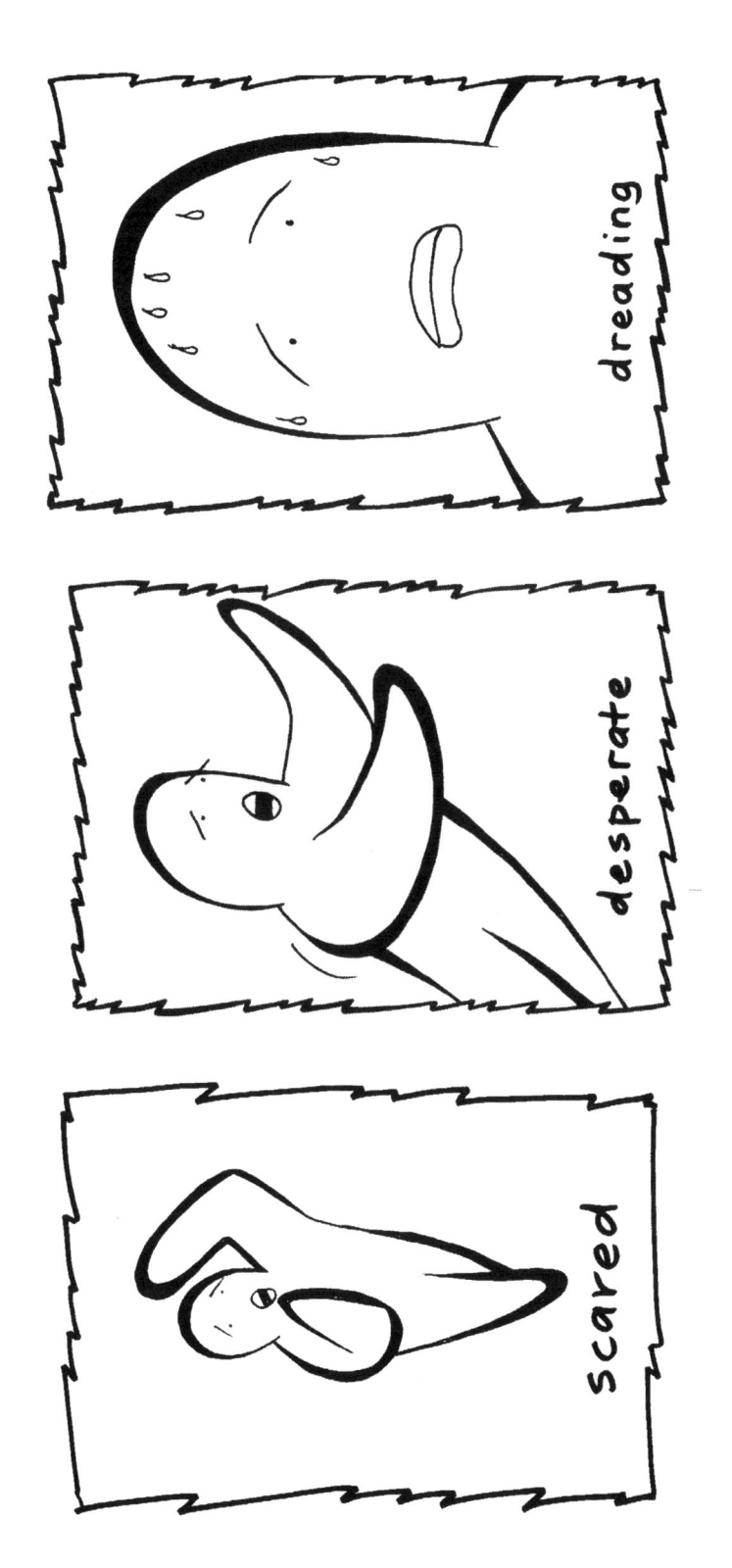

Standing outside his home, without any keys, Grant was desperate to find a way in!

The Blob Emotional Thesaurus

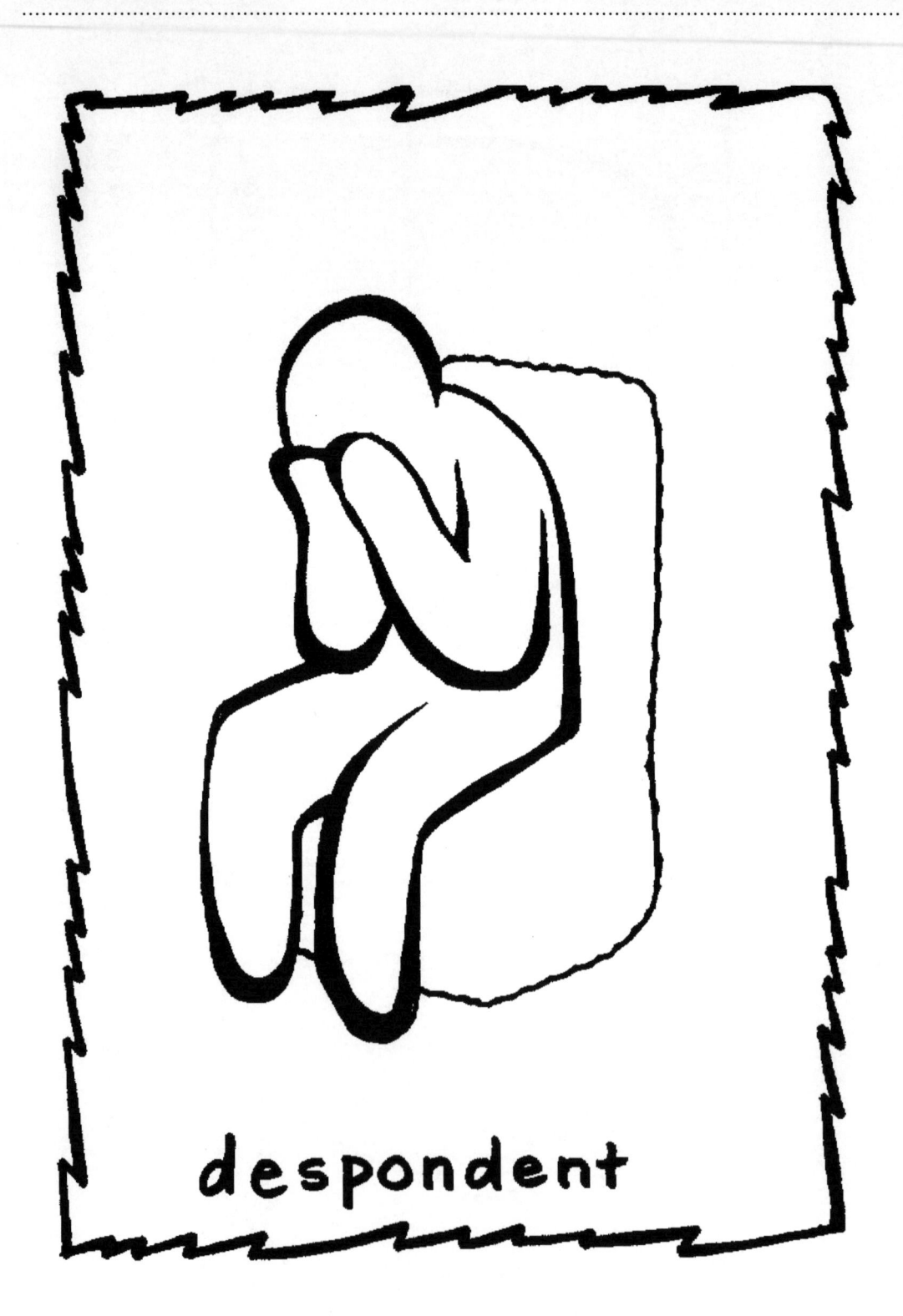

despondent

Individual feeling words

disspirited

despondent

disillusioned

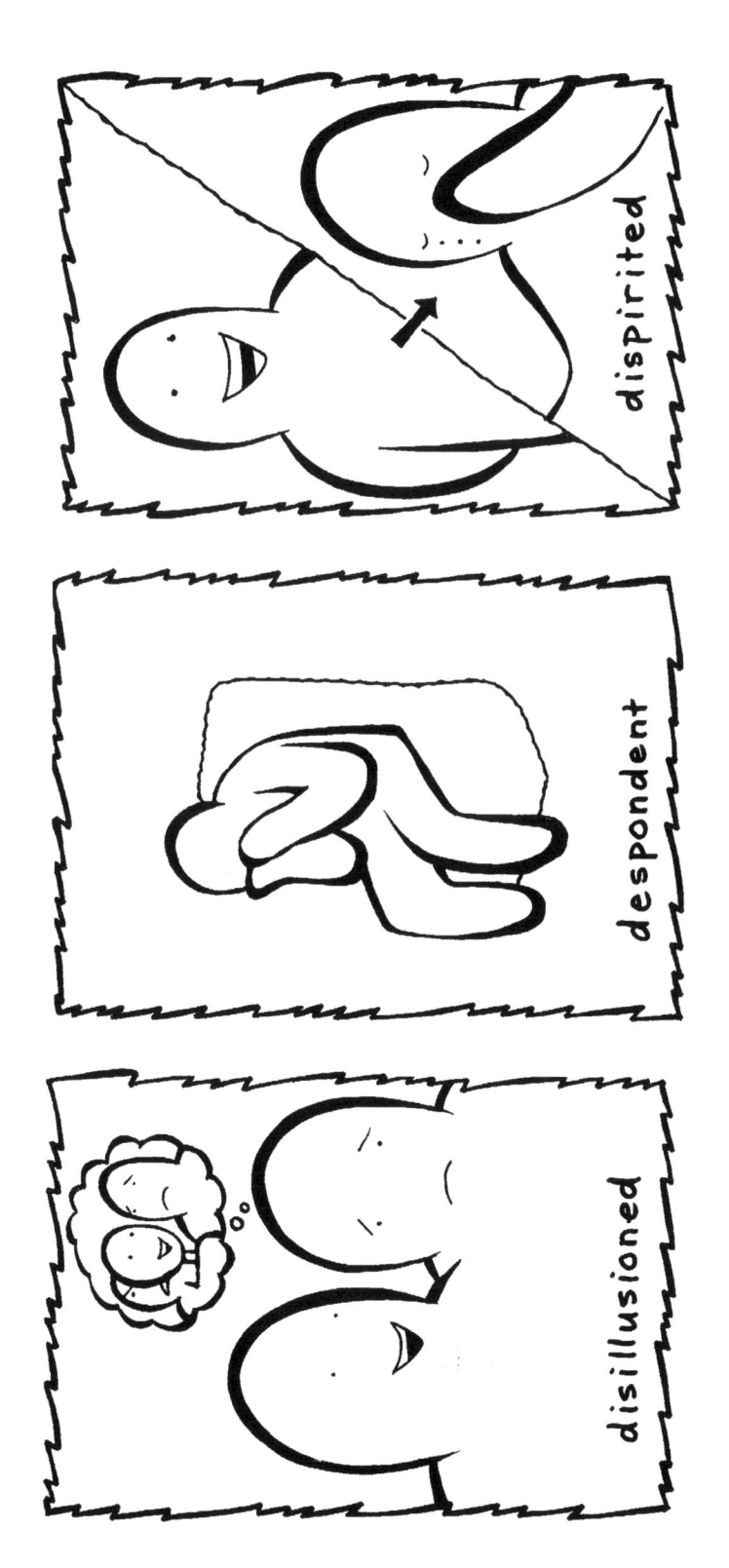

Jack was despondent after his girlfriend decided to leave him.

The Blob Emotional Thesaurus

dirty

Individual feeling words

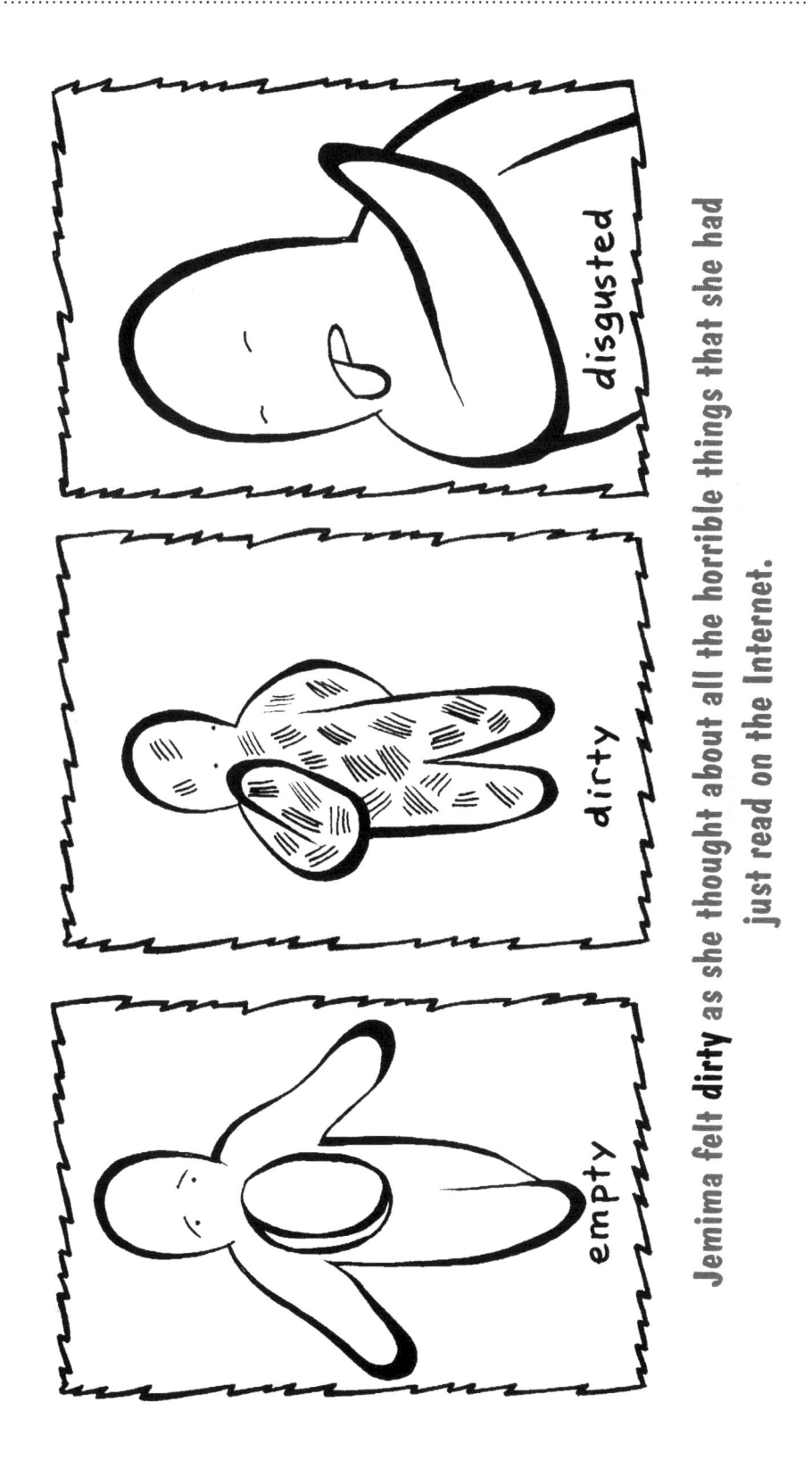

Jemima felt dirty as she thought about all the horrible things that she had just read on the Internet.

disgusted

dirty

empty

The Blob Emotional Thesaurus

disappointed

Individual feeling words

sad

disappointed

discouraged

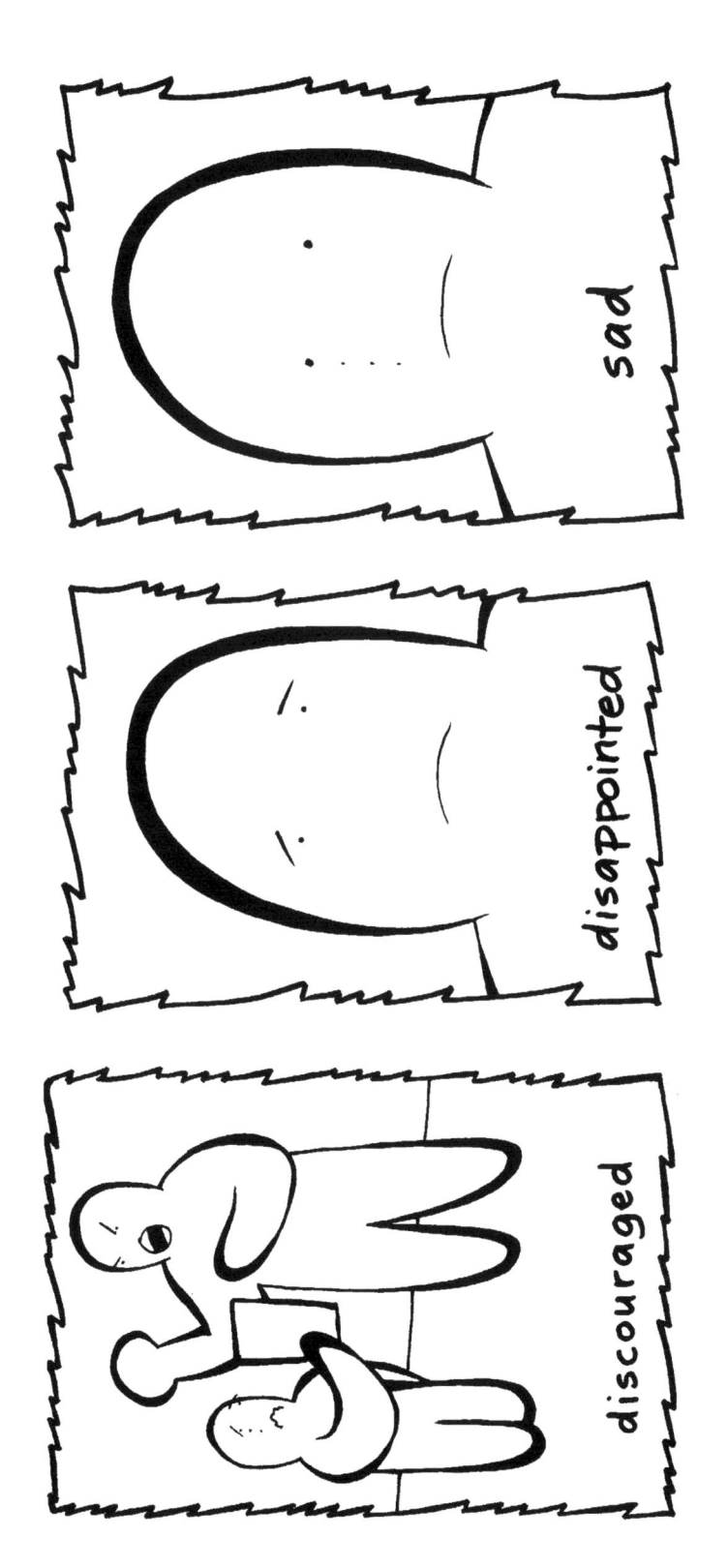

Mia was disappointed when she realised that she had failed to get full marks in the test.

The Blob Emotional Thesaurus

discouraged

82

Individual feeling words

embarrassed

discouraged

disappointed

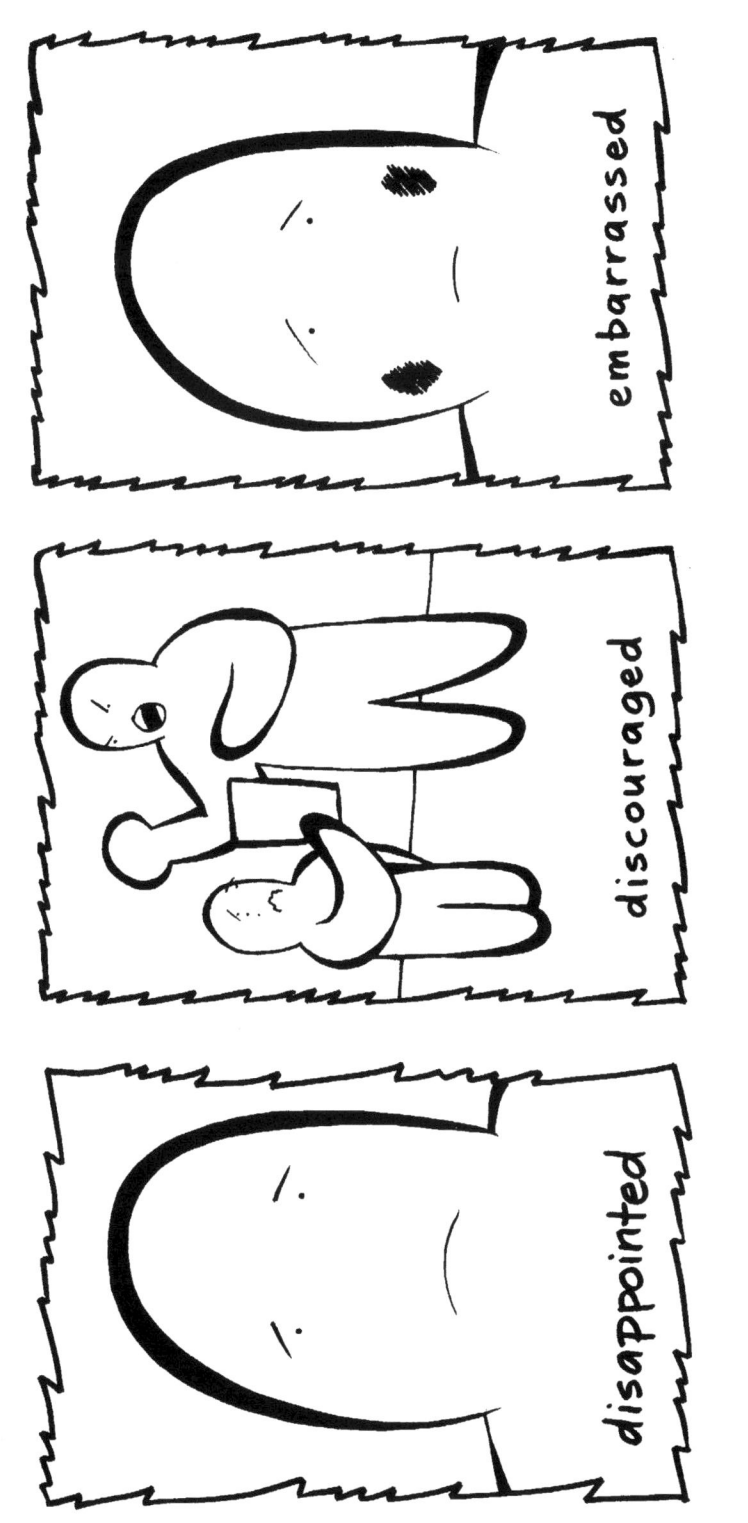

Paul was discouraged by the lack of enthusiasm in his class for chess.

The Blob Emotional Thesaurus

disgusted

Individual feeling words

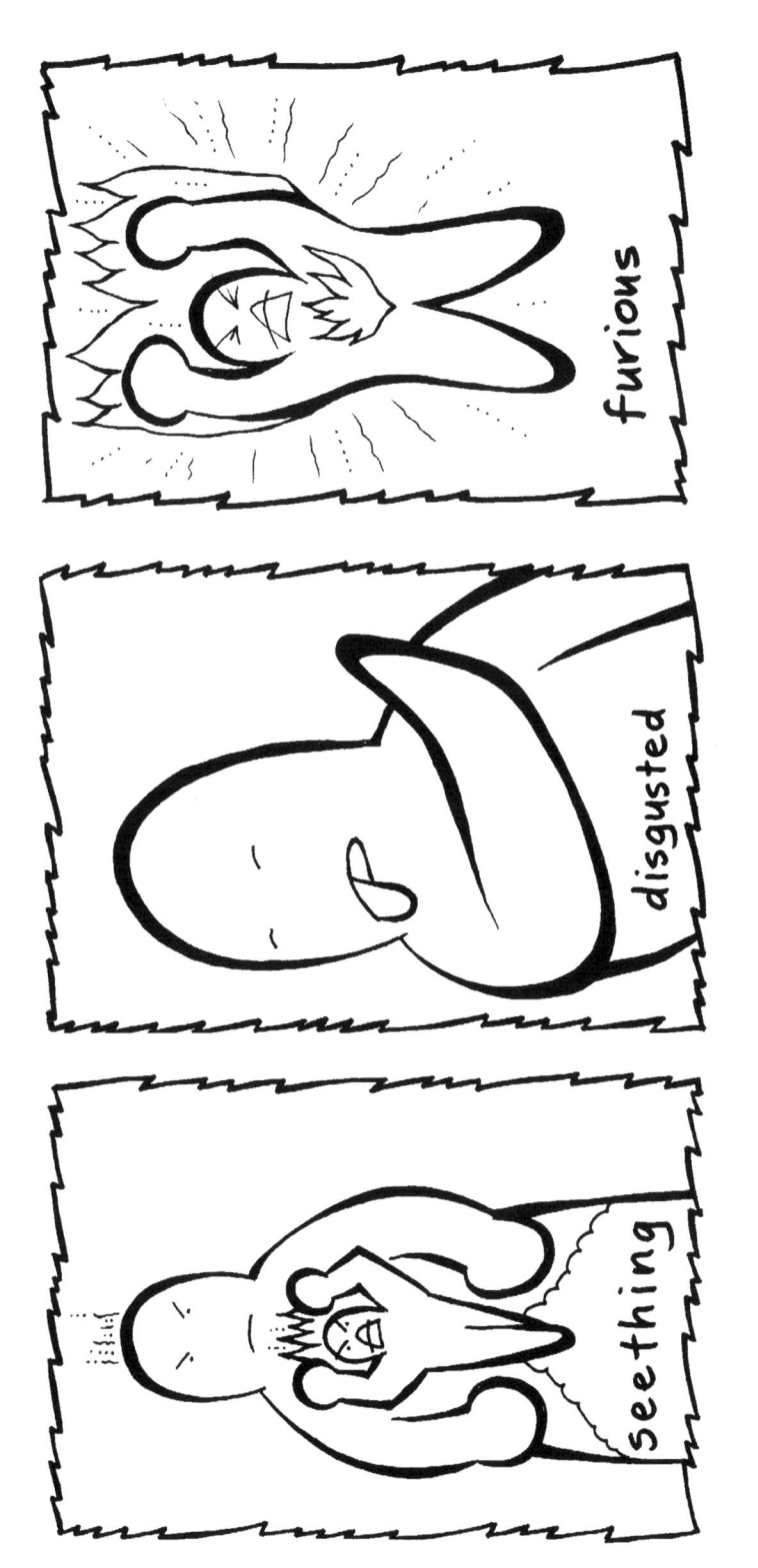

seething   *disgusted*   *furious*

Ali was disgusted by the gruesome images he could see upon his computer.

The Blob Emotional Thesaurus

disillusioned

Individual feeling words

furious

disillusioned

bored

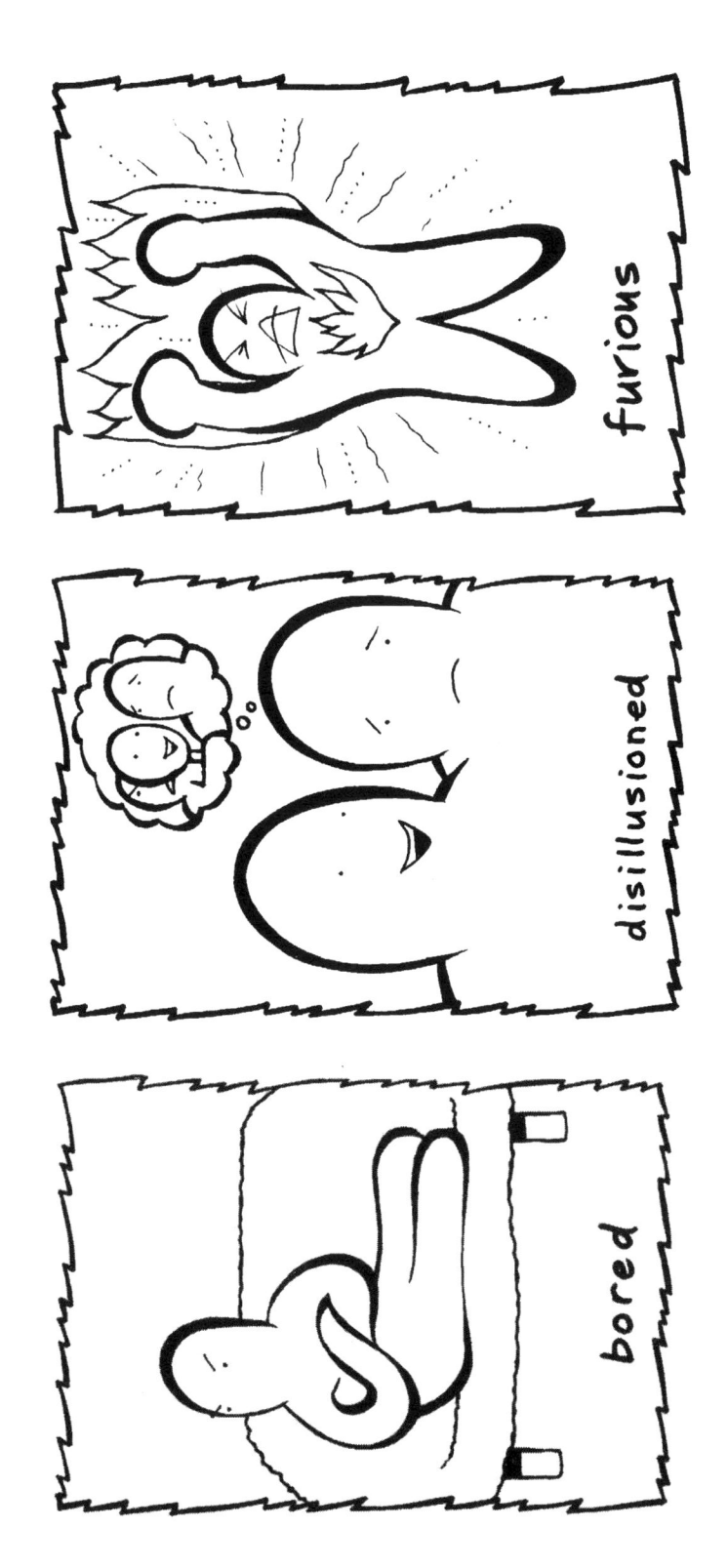

Twenty minutes after agreeing to be friends with Josie, Natalie was feeling disillusioned by her choice.

The Blob Emotional Thesaurus

dispirited

Individual feeling words

dispirited

despondent

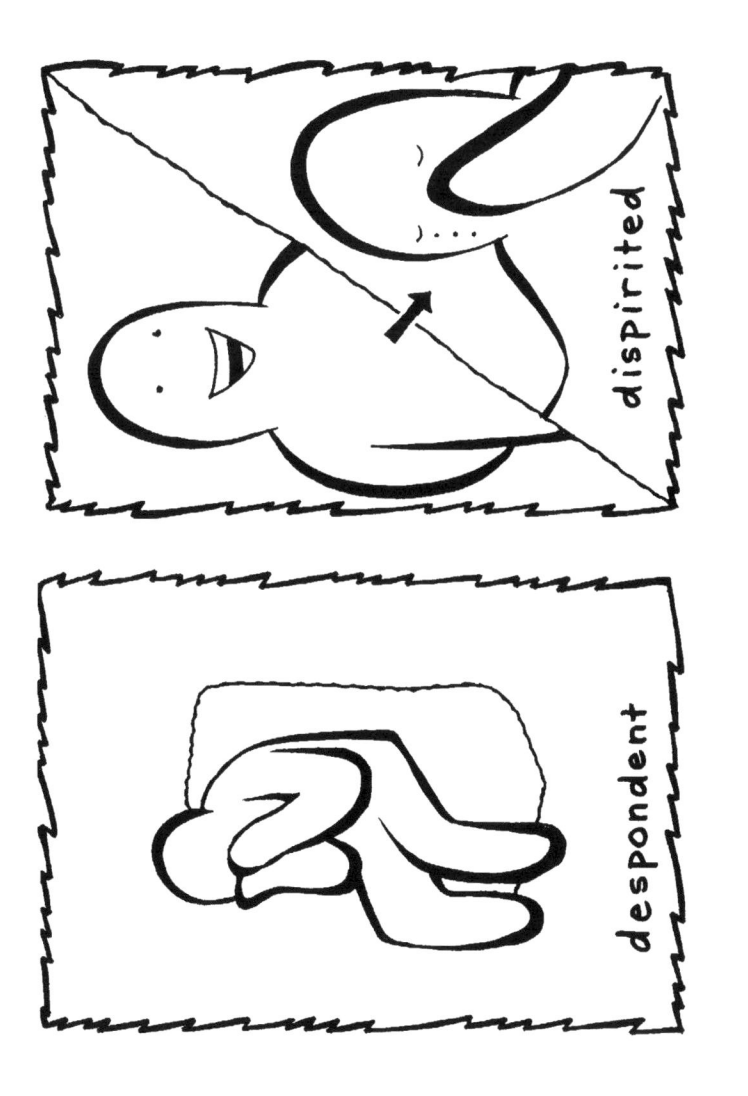

Omar was dispirited after twenty days of being left on his own at playtime.

The Blob Emotional Thesaurus

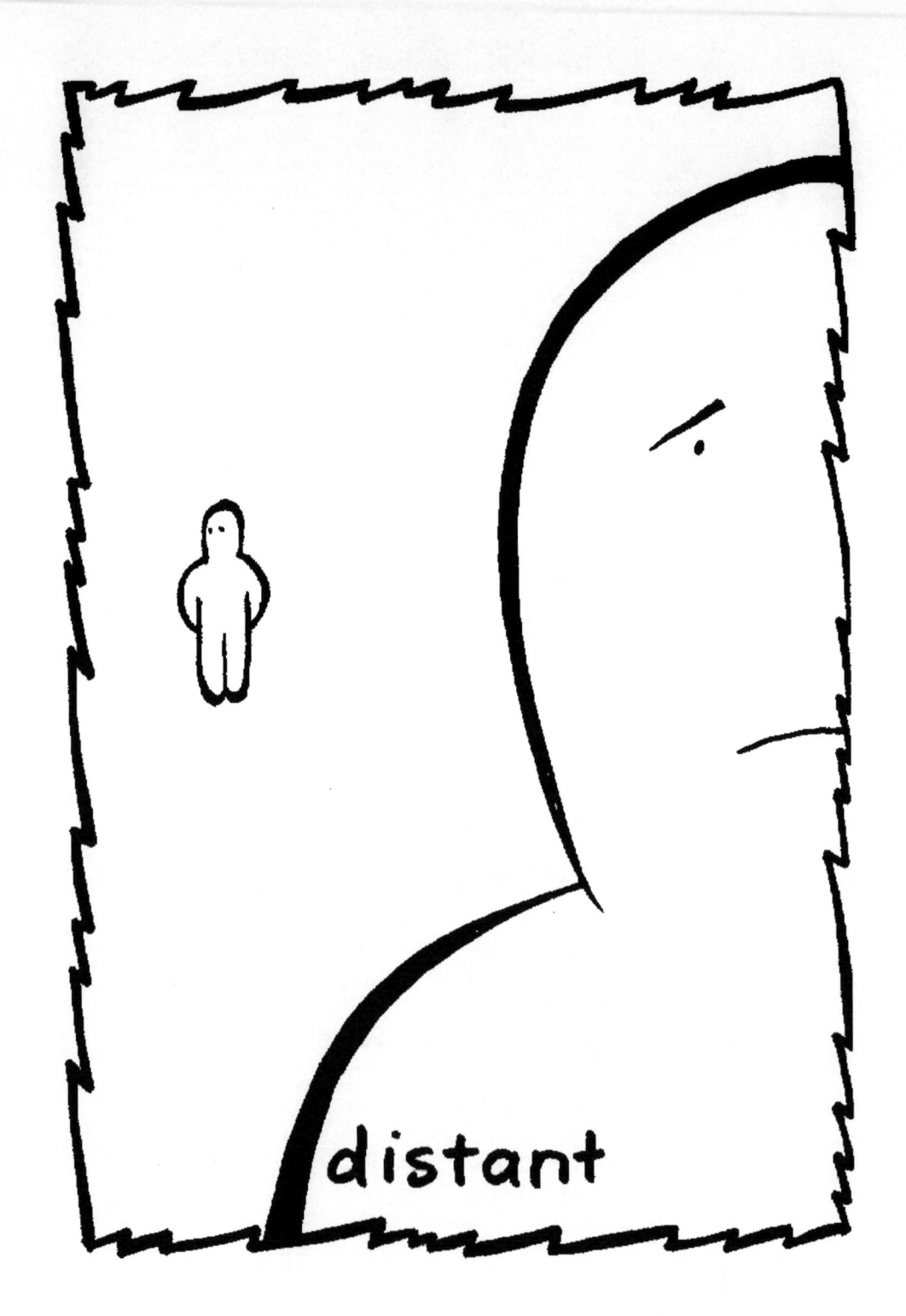

distant

Individual feeling words

fragile

distant

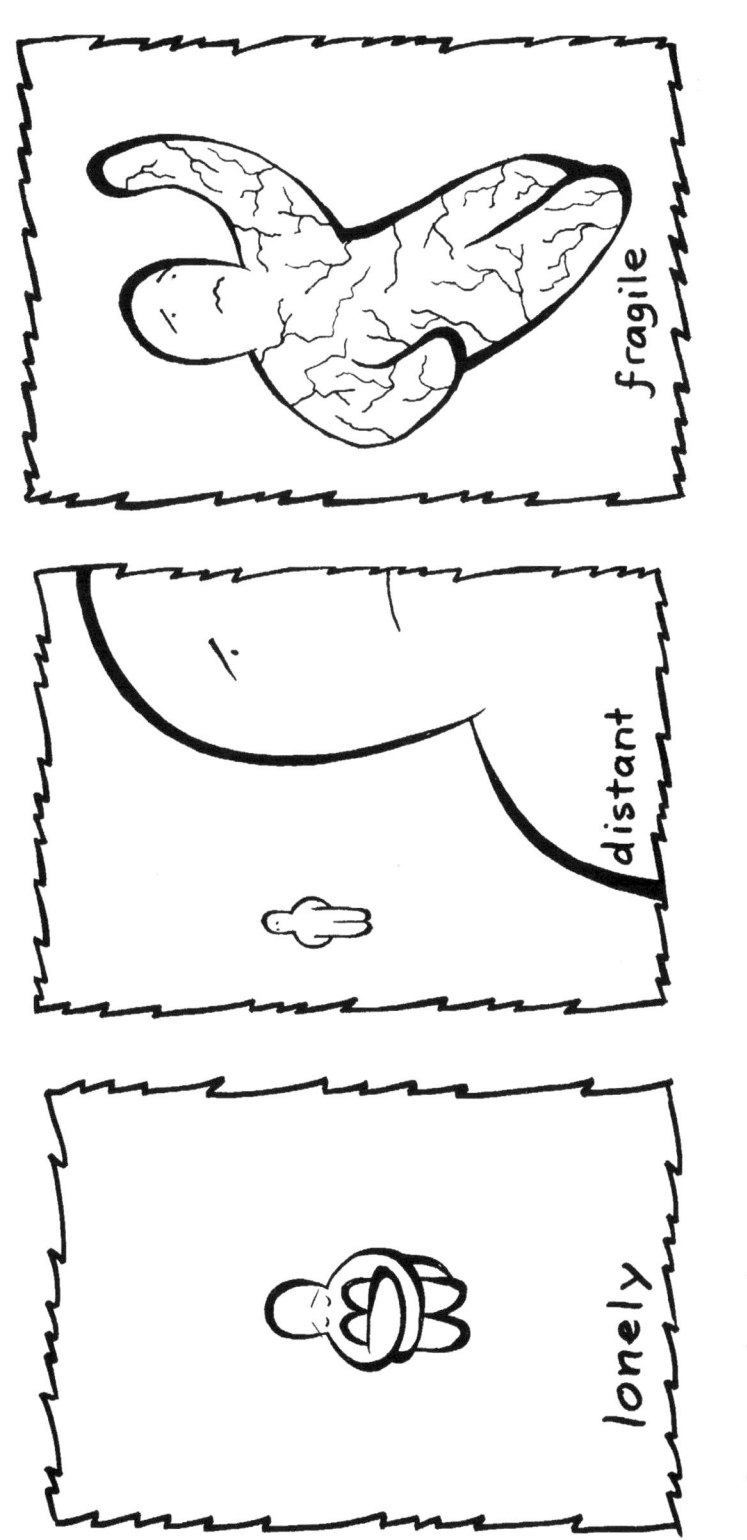

lonely

Heather felt distant from her friend when she refused to speak to her for several days.

The Blob Emotional Thesaurus

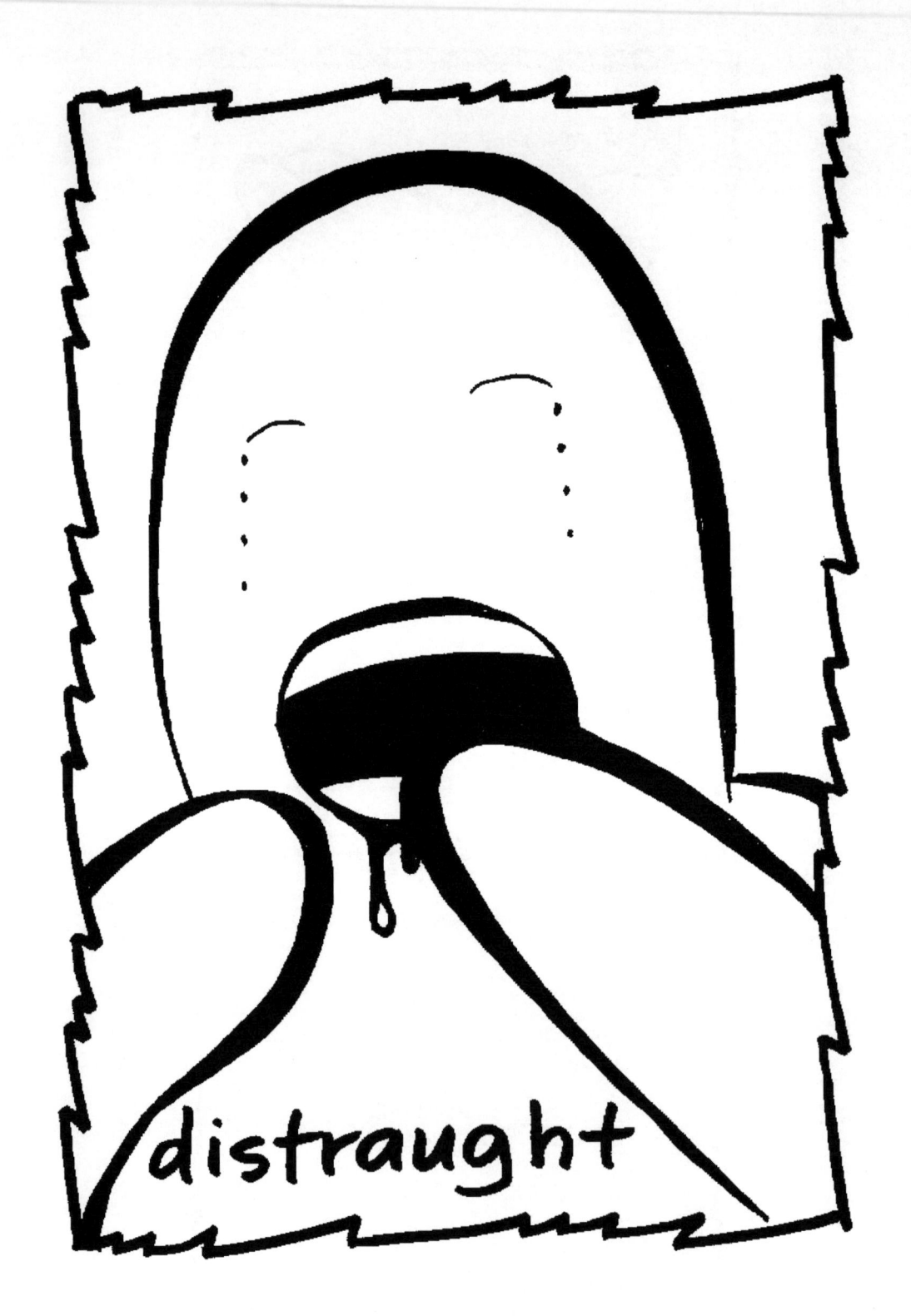

distraught

Individual feeling words

hurt

distraught

down

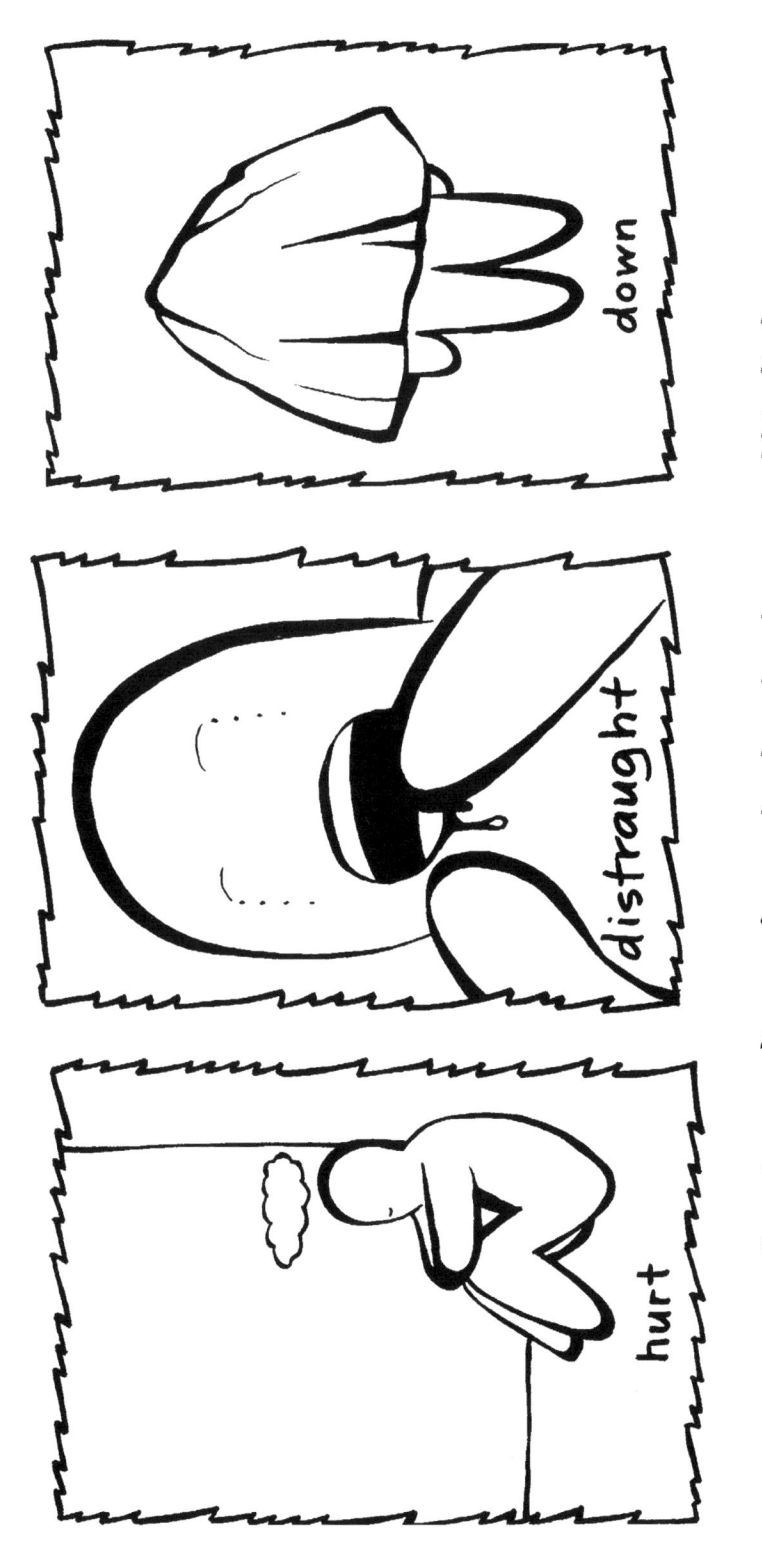

Bonnie was distraught on the day that her pet rabbit died.

The Blob Emotional Thesaurus

domineering

Individual feeling words

strong

domineering

Bruce smiled at the quivering minions … he felt domineering and loved it.

The Blob Emotional Thesaurus

down

Individual feeling words

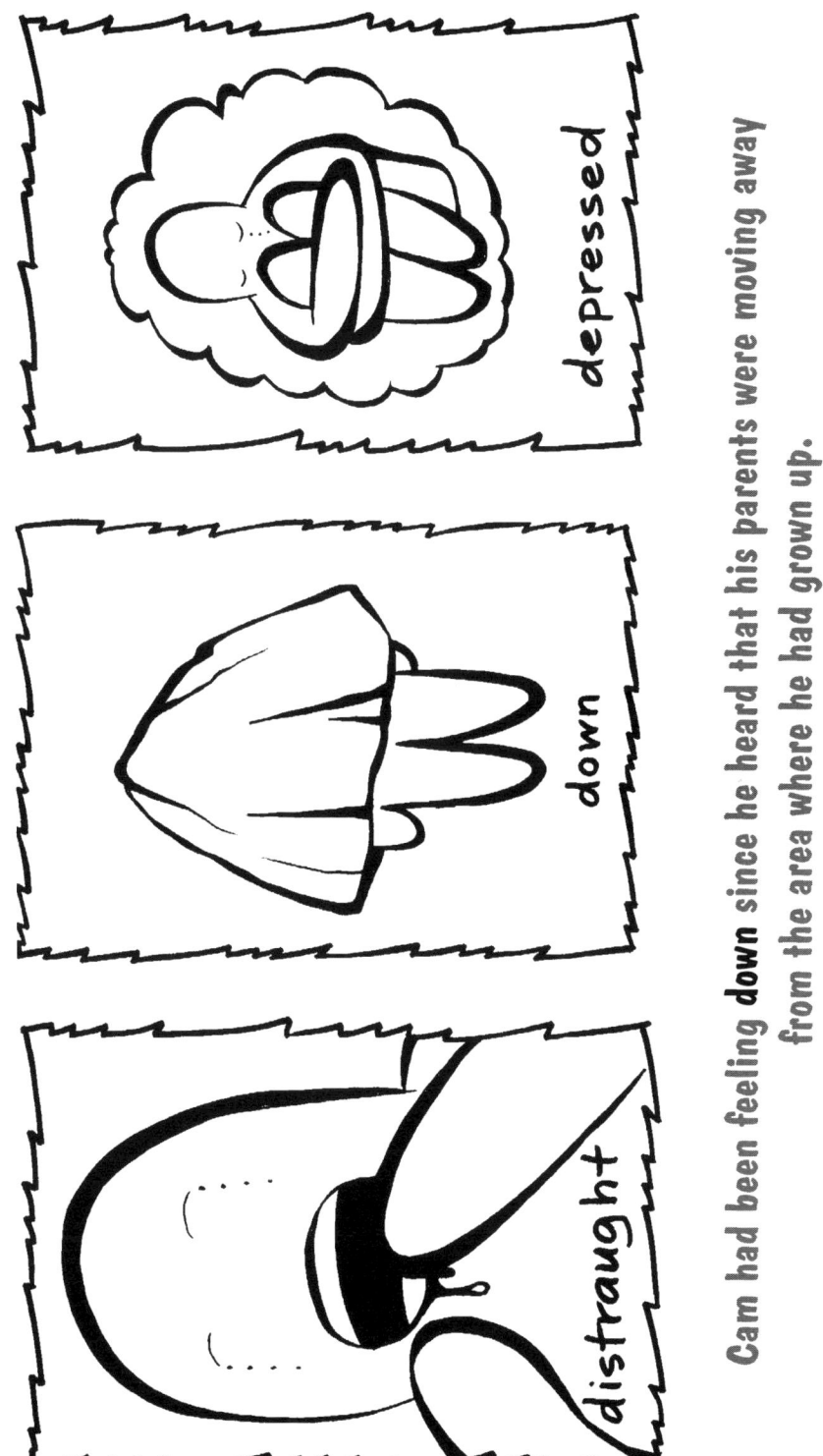

depressed

down

distraught

Cam had been feeling **down** since he heard that his parents were moving away from the area where he had grown up.

The Blob Emotional Thesaurus

drained

Individual feeling words

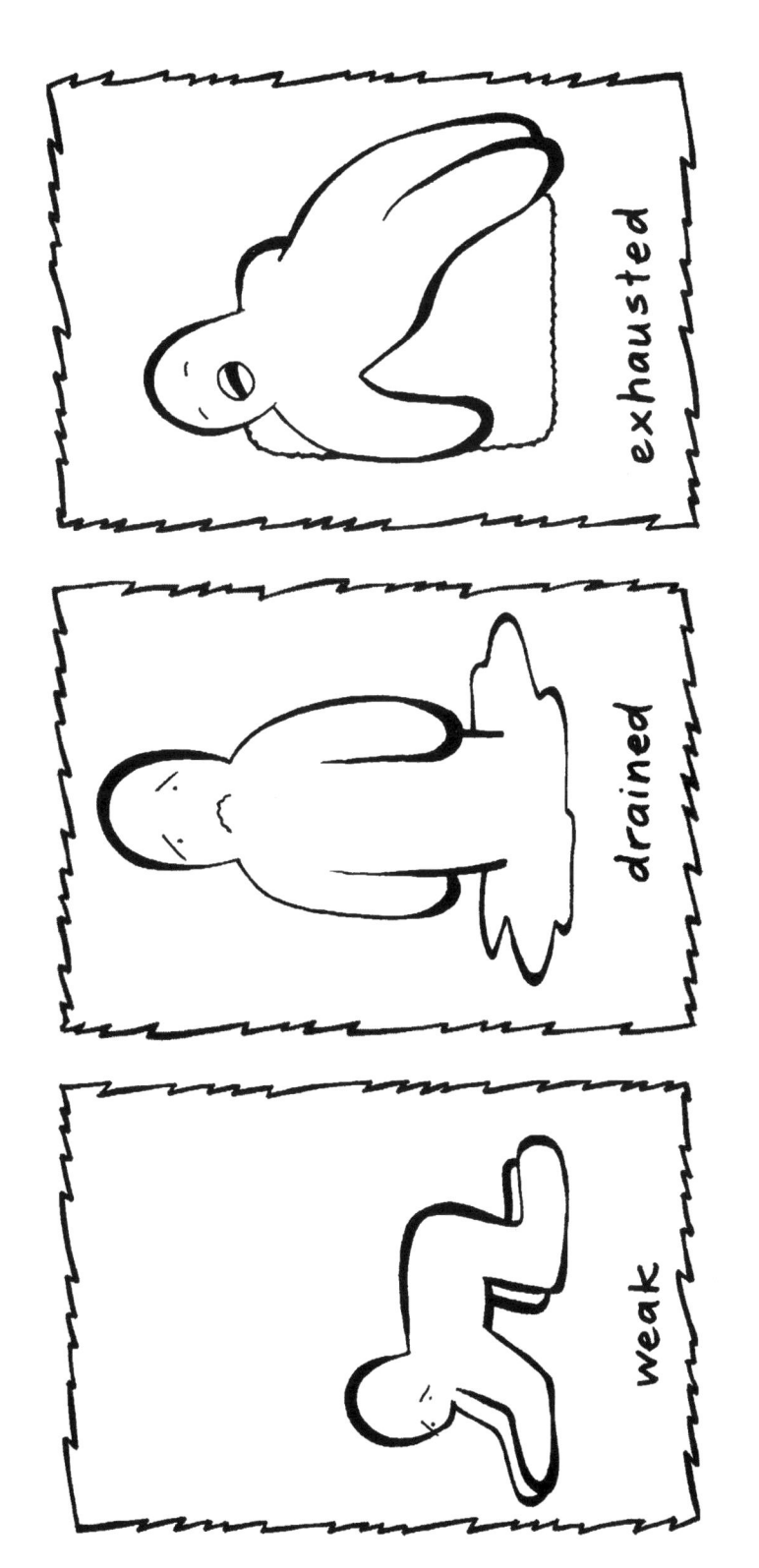

exhausted

drained

weak

Kissing her family goodbye before setting off to university had drained Suzanna.

The Blob Emotional Thesaurus

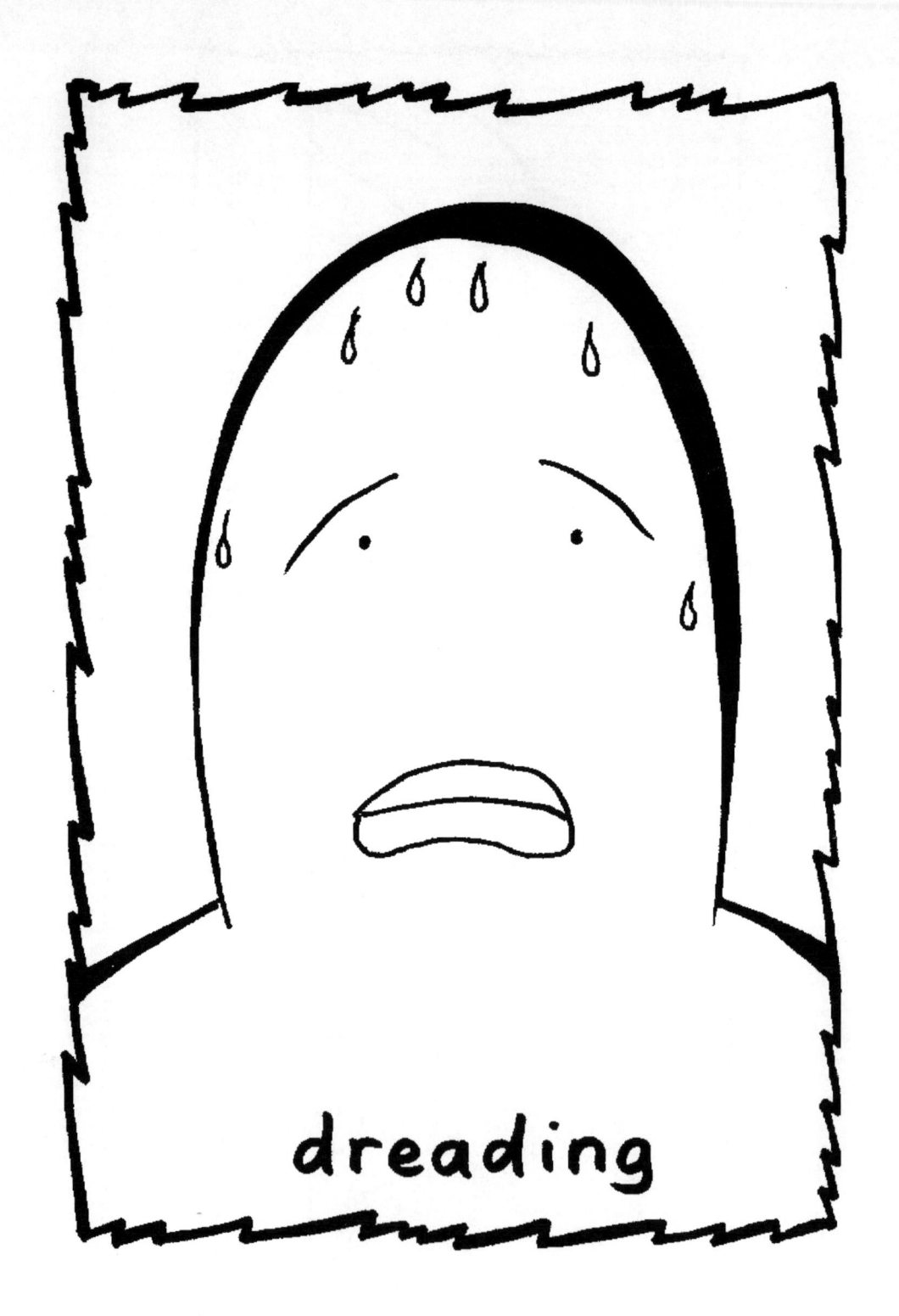

dreading

Individual feeling words

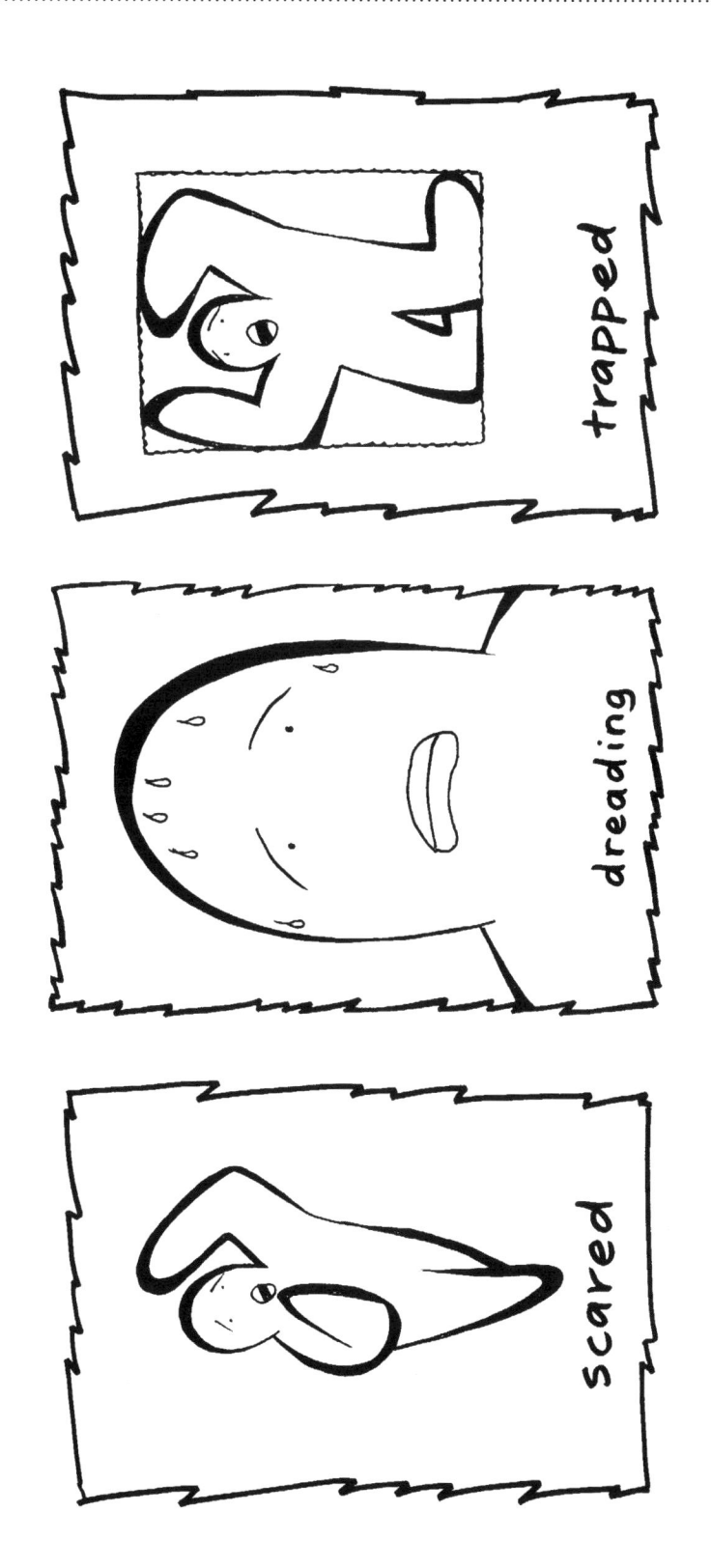

| scared | dreading | trapped |

Ella was dreading the moment when they all realised that she was a secret princess.

The Blob Emotional Thesaurus

drowning

Individual feeling words

lost

drowning

wounded

Left to manage the shop on her own, Bella felt like she was drowning after only a few minutes.

The Blob Emotional Thesaurus

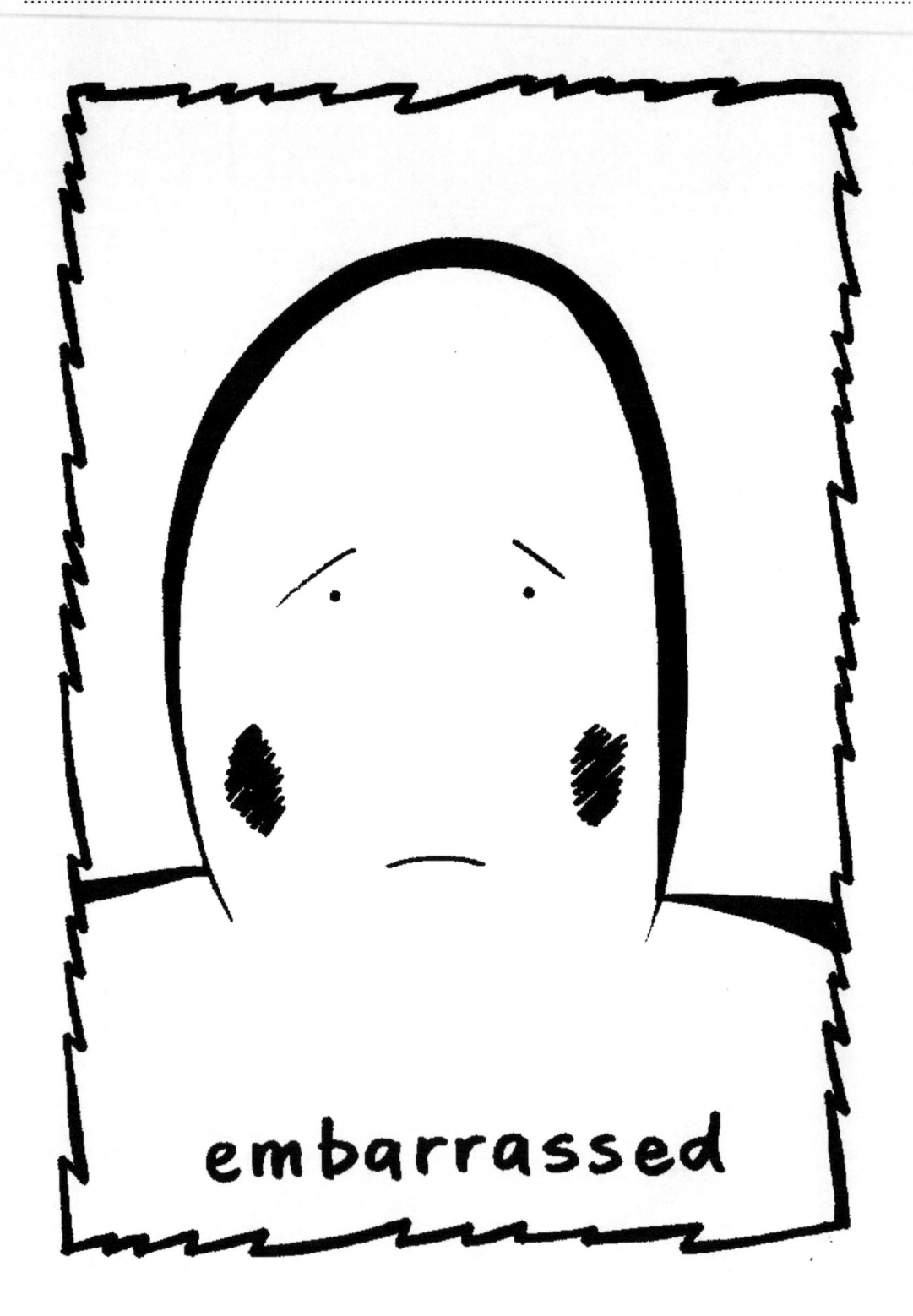

embarrassed

Individual feeling words

upset

embarrassed

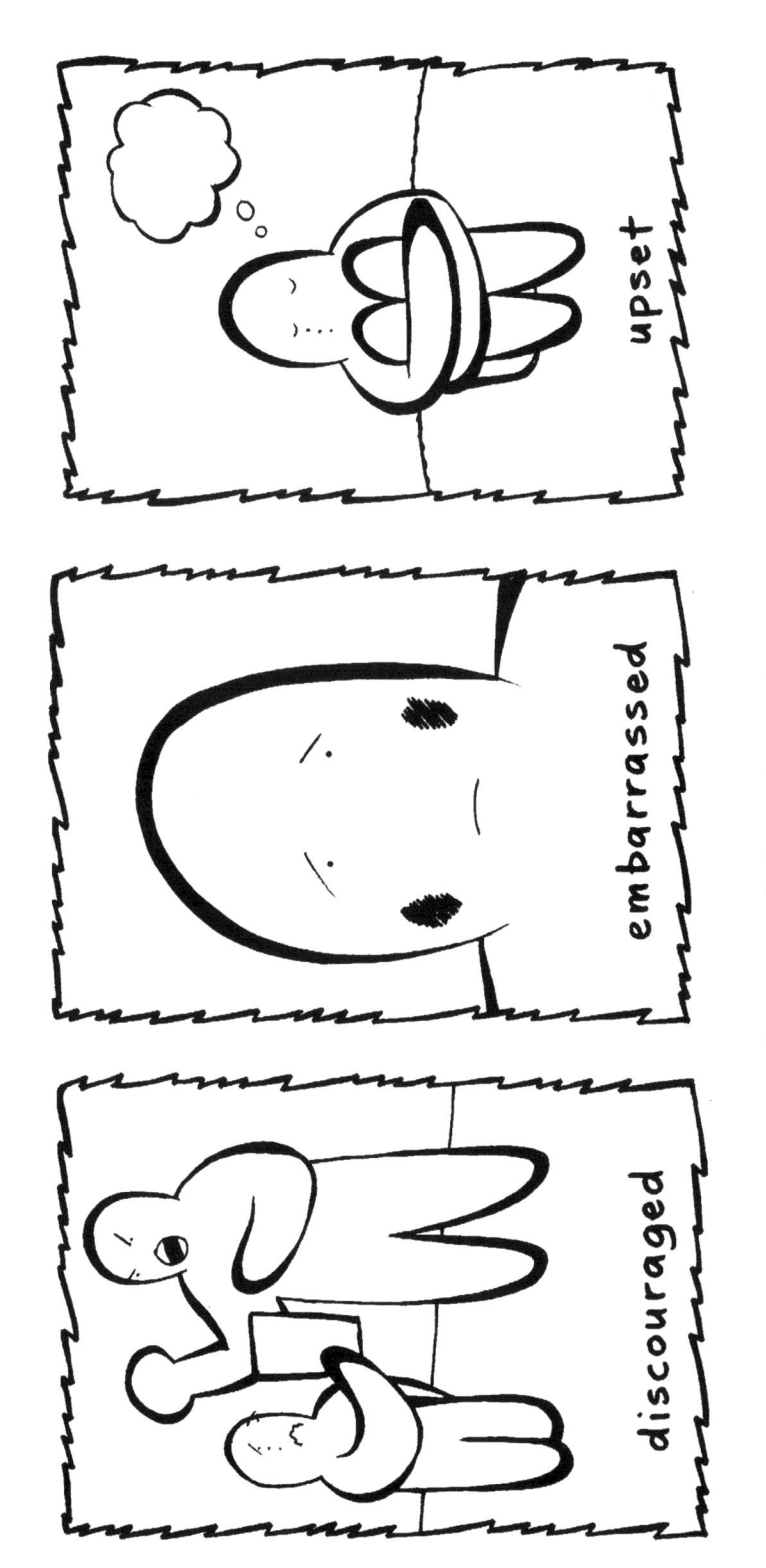

discouraged

Jane was embarrassed that she had lost her keys again!

The Blob Emotional Thesaurus

empowered

Individual feeling words

trusting

empowered

touched

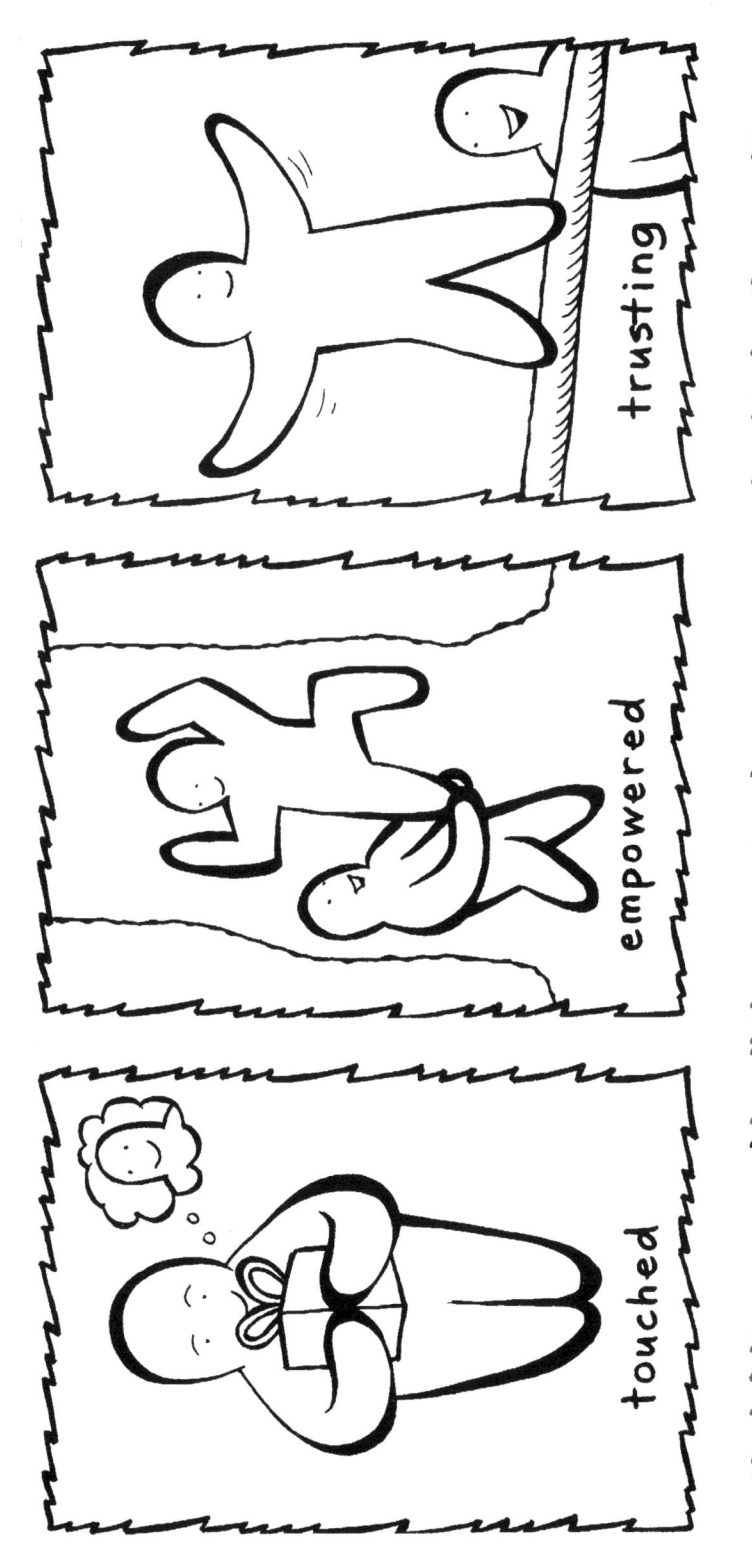

Mark felt empowered by all the support and encouragement that his family gave him.

The Blob Emotional Thesaurus

empty

Individual feeling words

deprived

empty

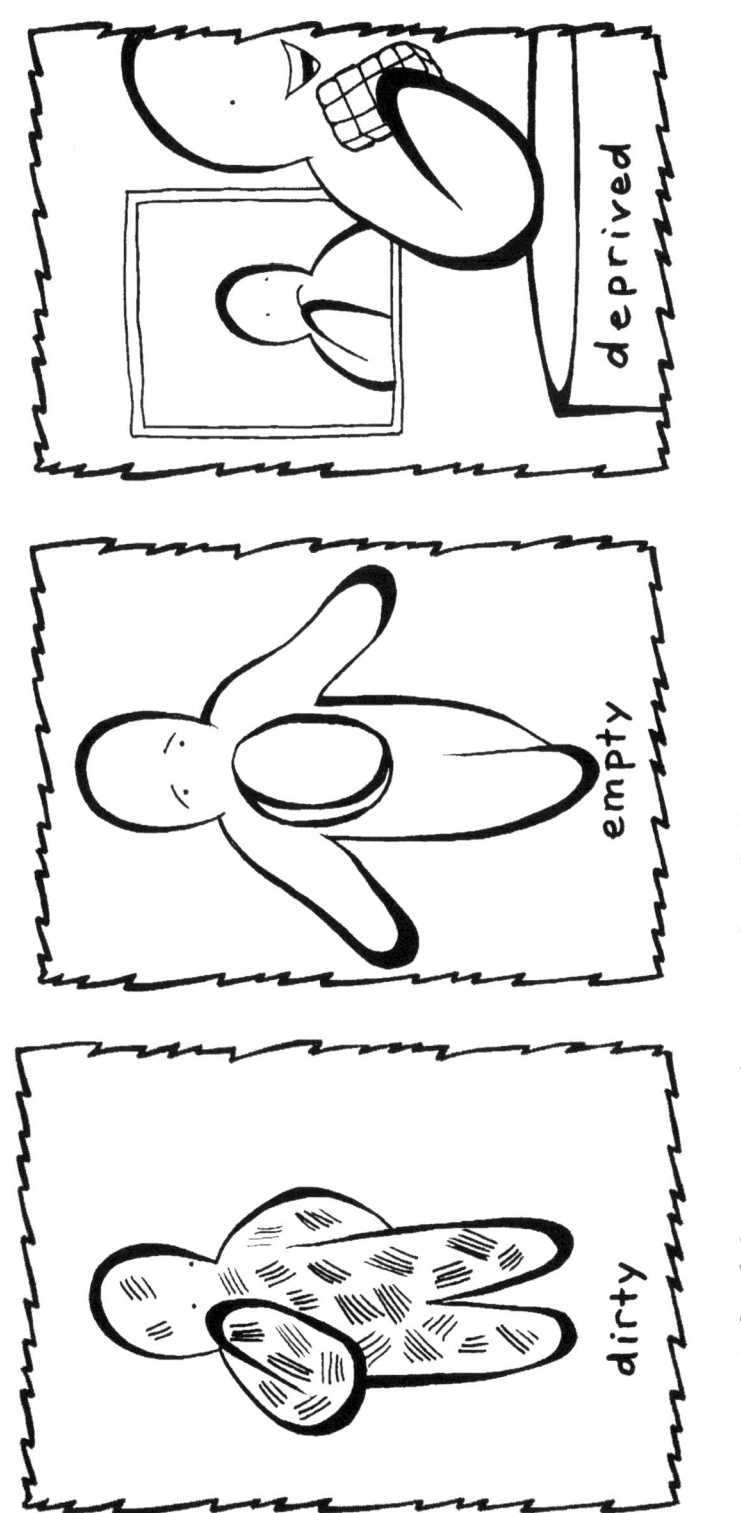

dirty

Jake felt **empty** after another dull night out with the 'girl of his dreams'.

The Blob Emotional Thesaurus

encouraged

Individual feeling words

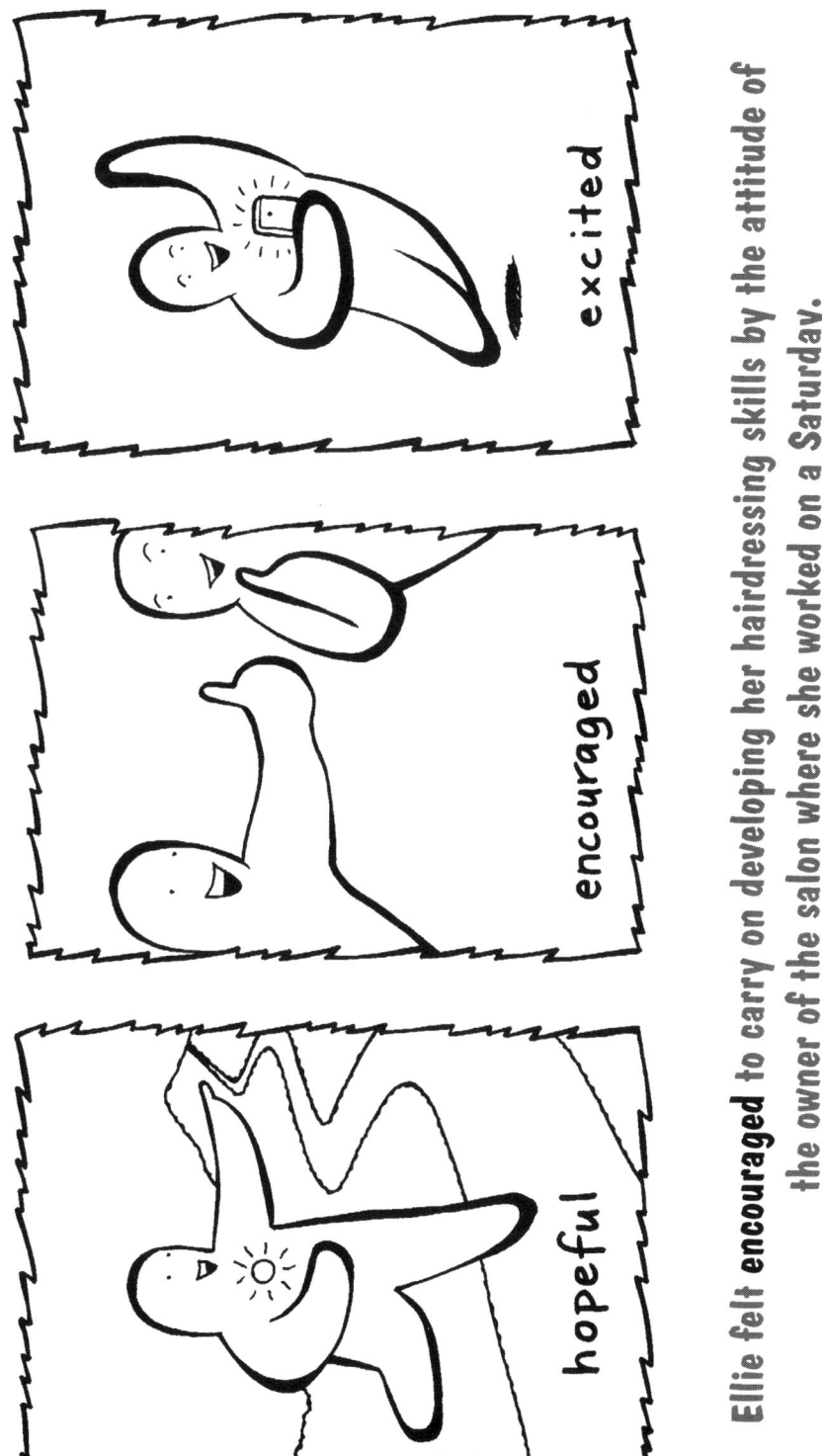

excited

encouraged

hopeful

Ellie felt **encouraged** to carry on developing her hairdressing skills by the attitude of the owner of the salon where she worked on a Saturday.

The Blob Emotional Thesaurus

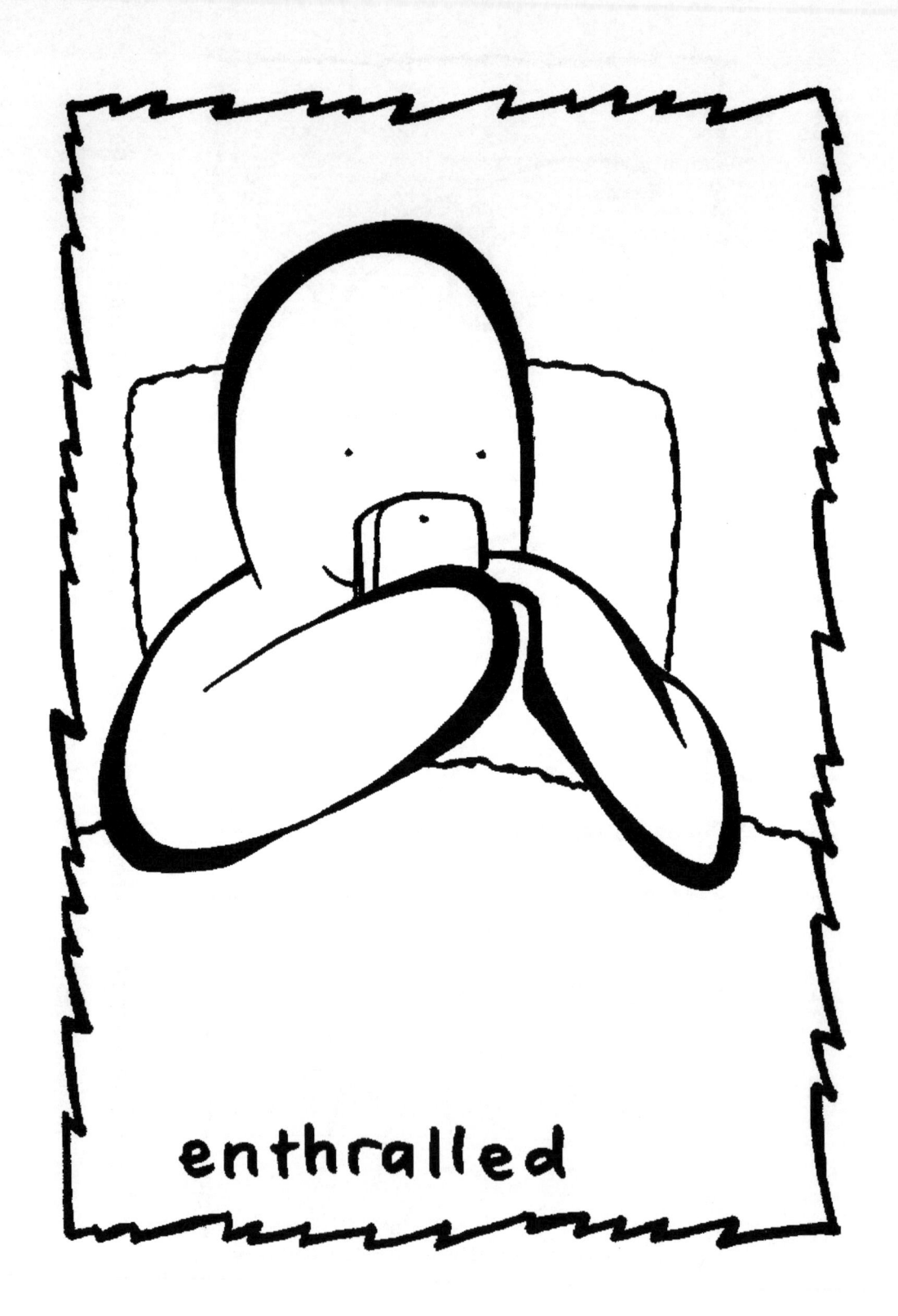

enthralled

Individual feeling words

mesmerised

enthralled

fascinated

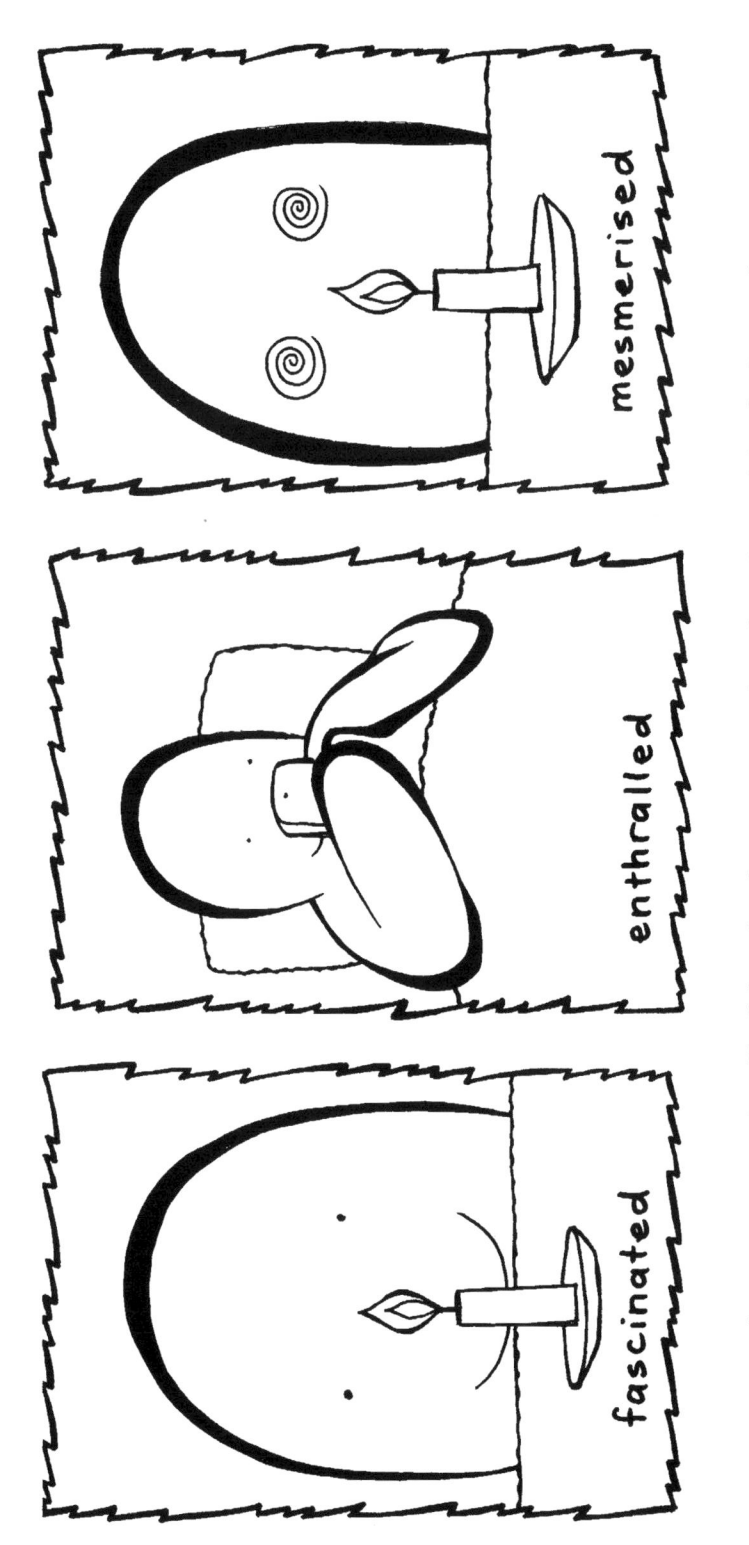

Claire was **enthralled** by the latest app that her friend had shown her.

The Blob Emotional Thesaurus

enthusiastic

Individual feeling words

bouncy

enthusiastic

excited

Harry was much more **enthusiastic** when he knew that there was the promise of chocolate eggs at the end of the journey to *Canterbury Cathedral!*

The Blob Emotional Thesaurus

euphoric

Individual feeling words

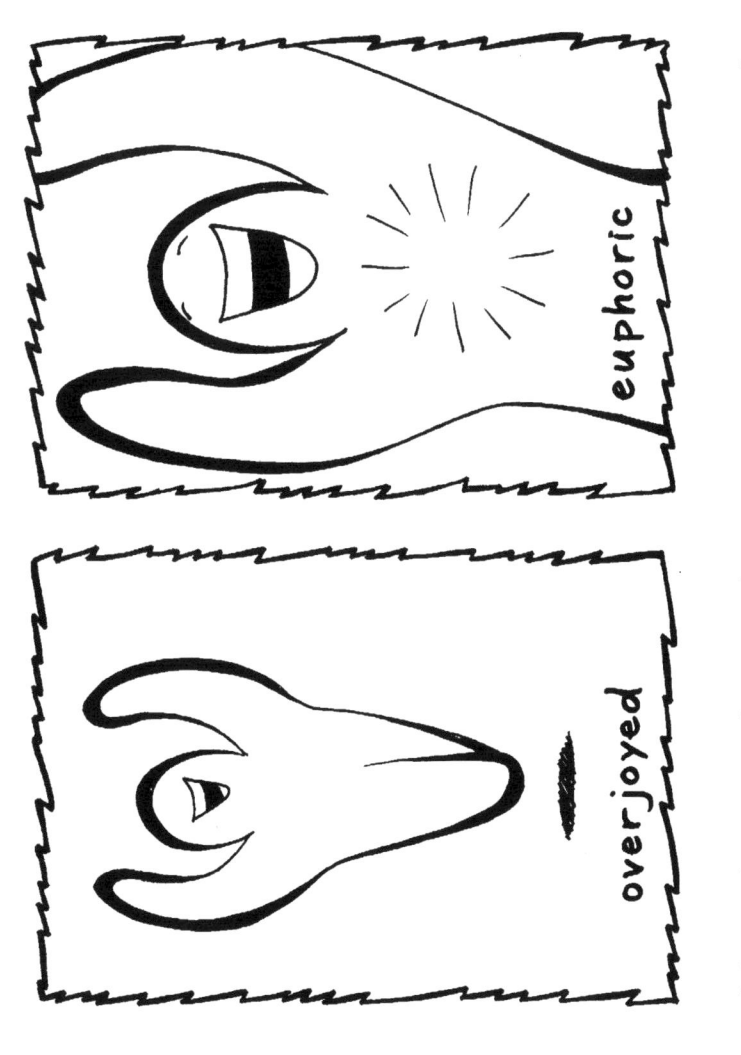

overjoyed

euphoric

Mia felt euphoric as she won the 100m sprint race in a record time.

The Blob Emotional Thesaurus

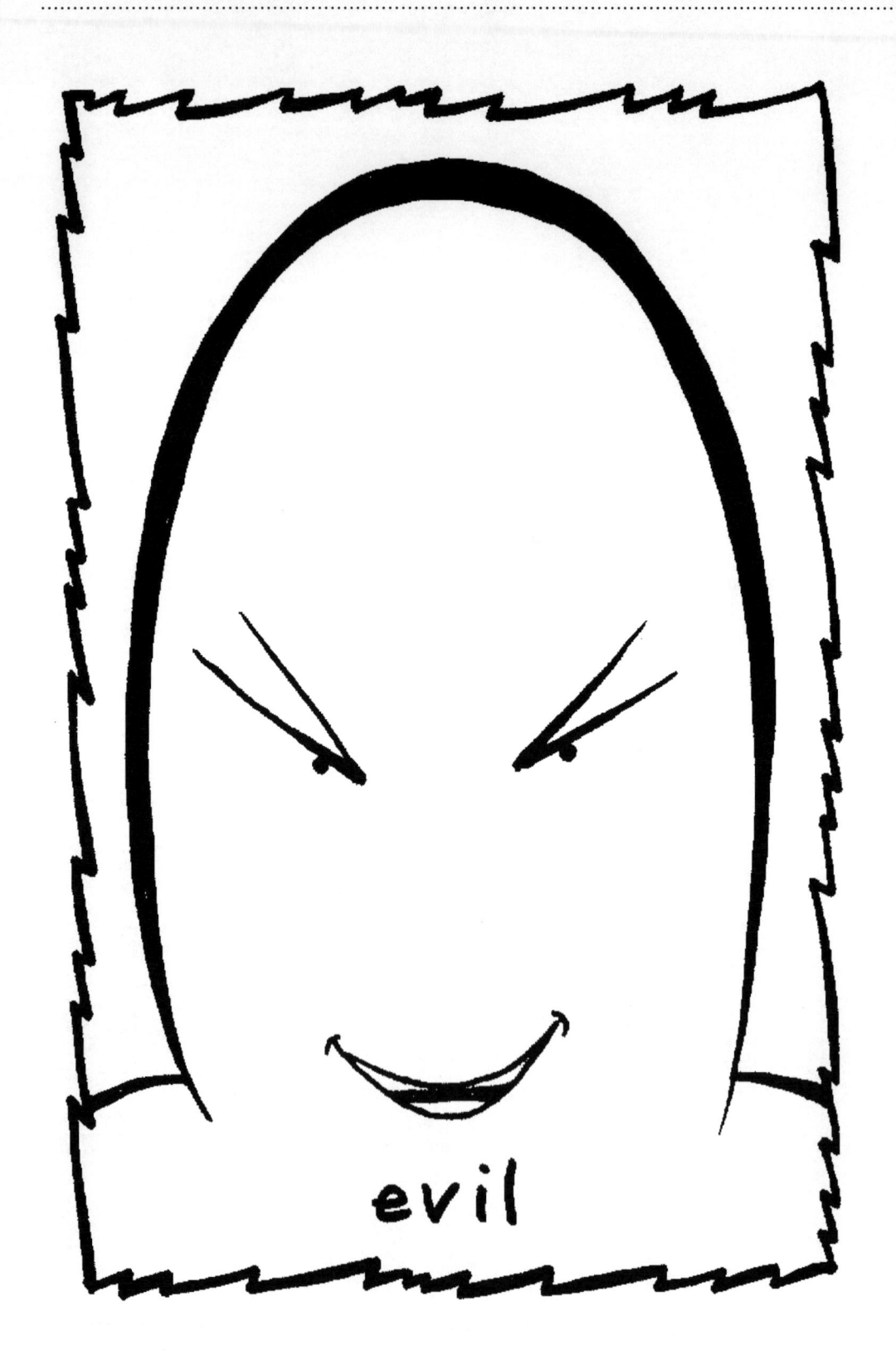

evil

Individual feeling words

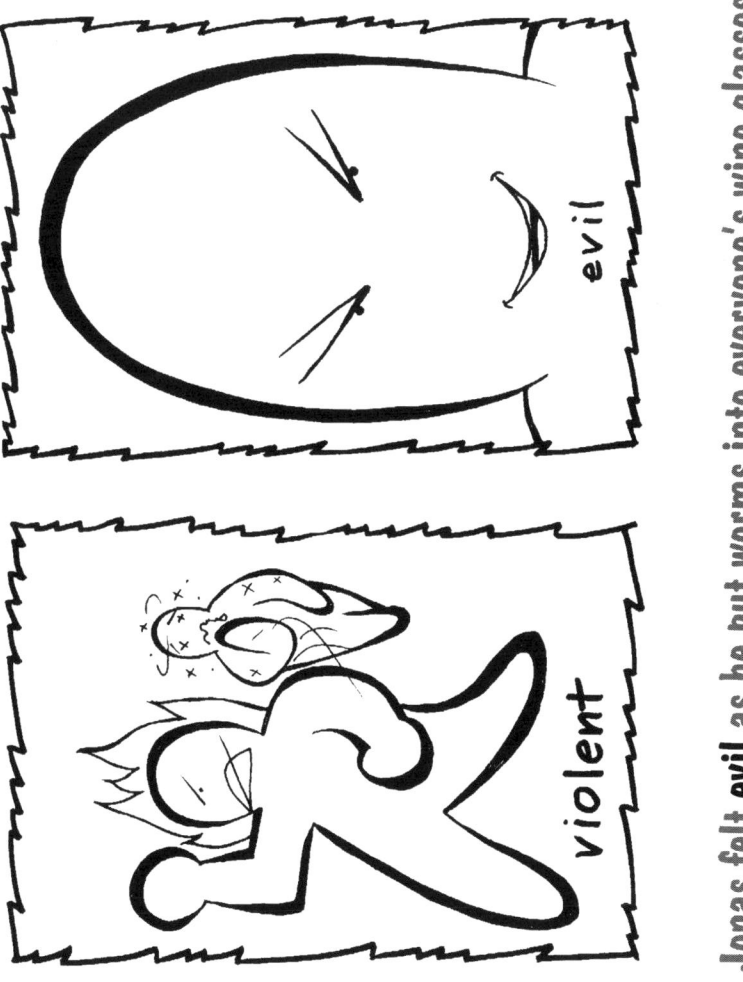

evil

violent

Jonas felt evil as he put worms into everyone's wine glasses.

The Blob Emotional Thesaurus

excited

Individual feeling words

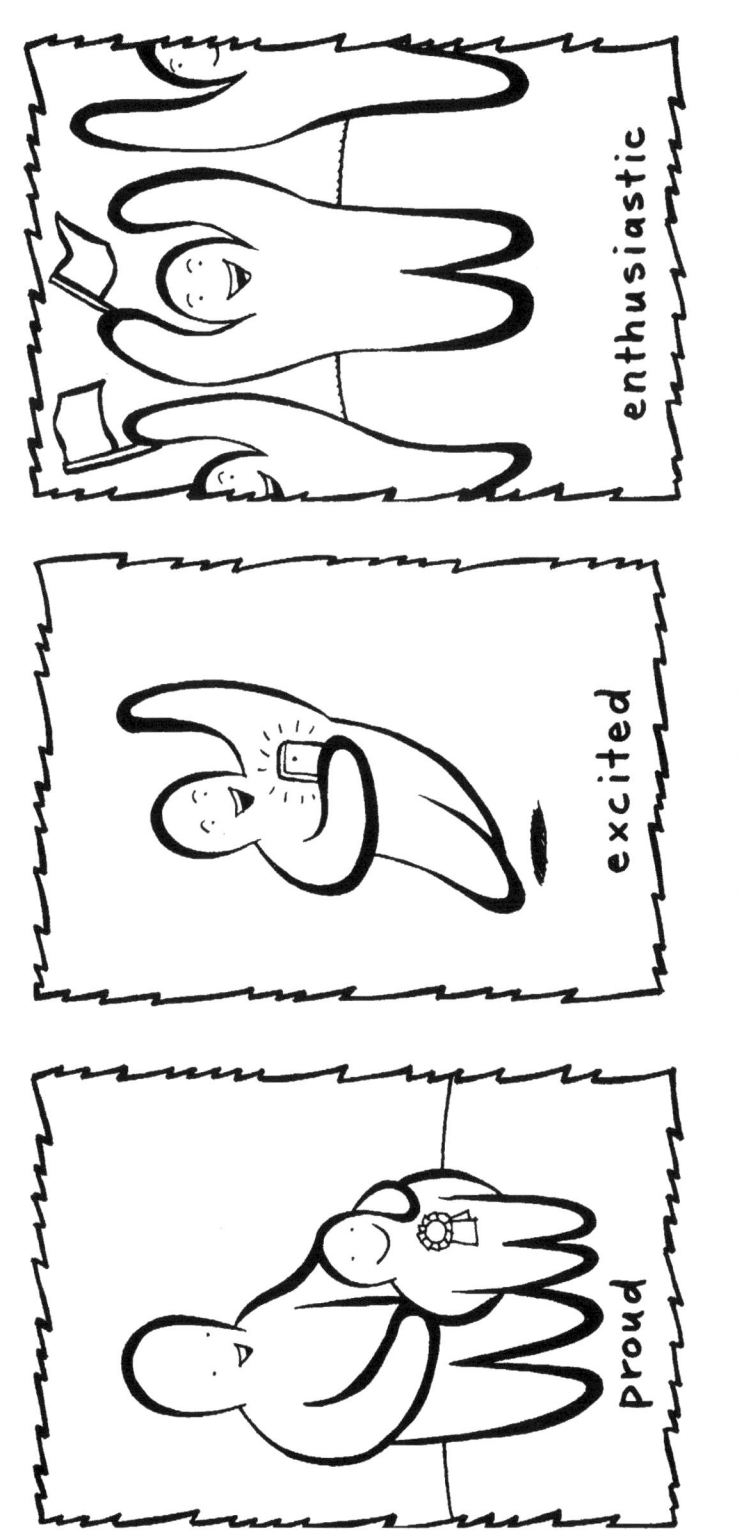

enthusiastic

excited

Proud

Kirsty was **excited** to use her first mobile phone!

121

The Blob Emotional Thesaurus

exhausted

Individual feeling words

drained

exhausted

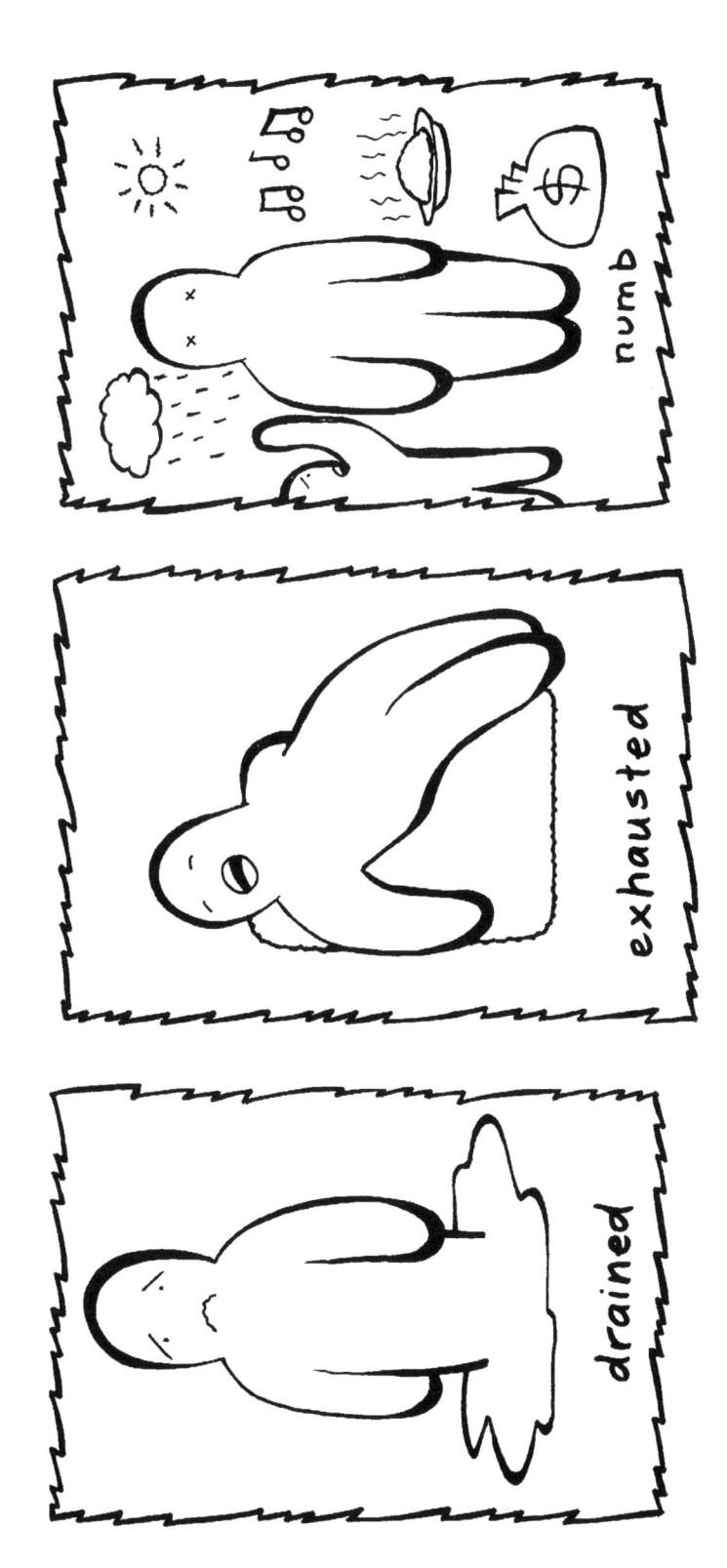

numb

Fi was exhausted because her new baby was screaming throughout the night.

The Blob Emotional Thesaurus

fascinated

Individual feeling words

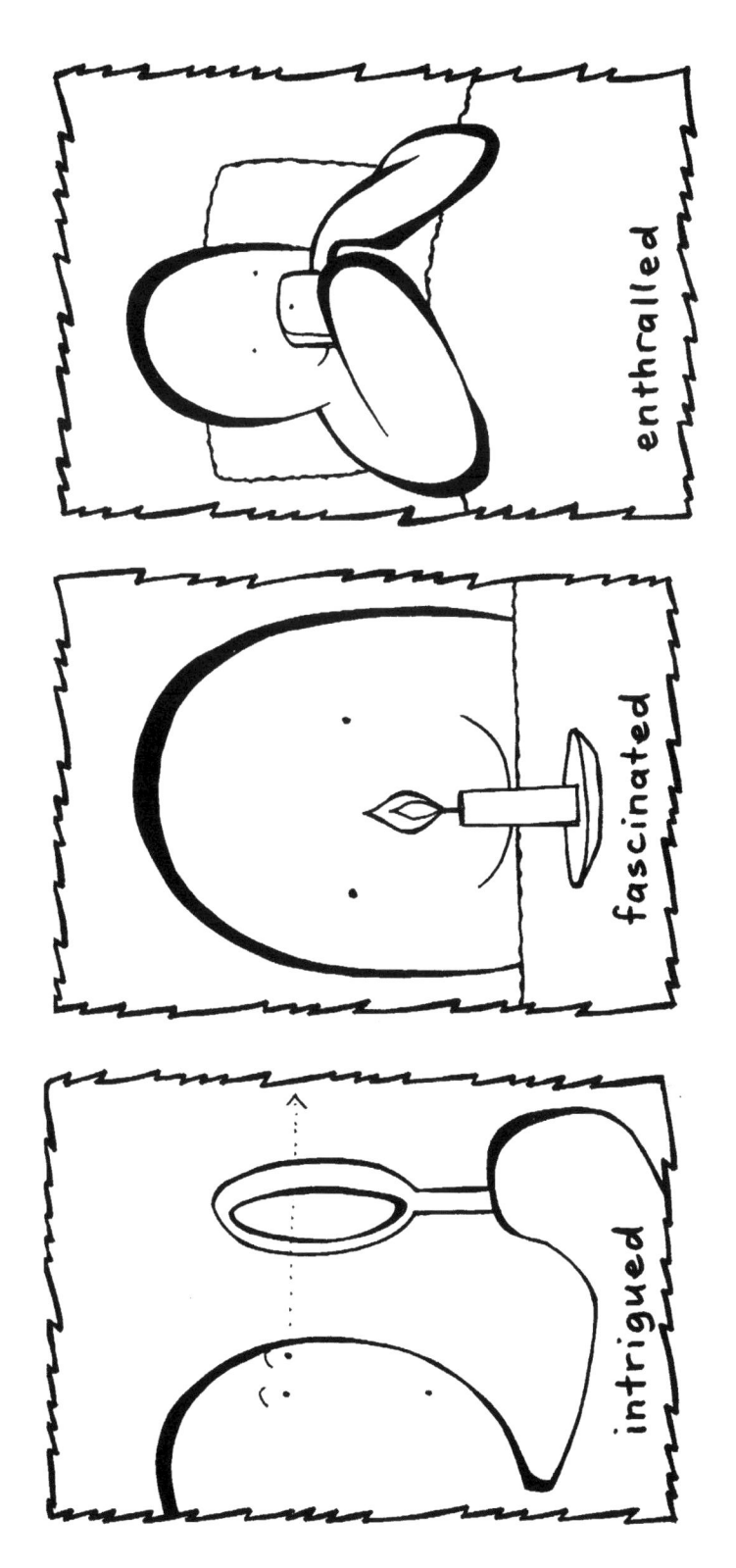

Nadia was fascinated by the flickering light of the Christmas candle.

enthralled

fascinated

intrigued

fixated

Individual feeling words

obsessed

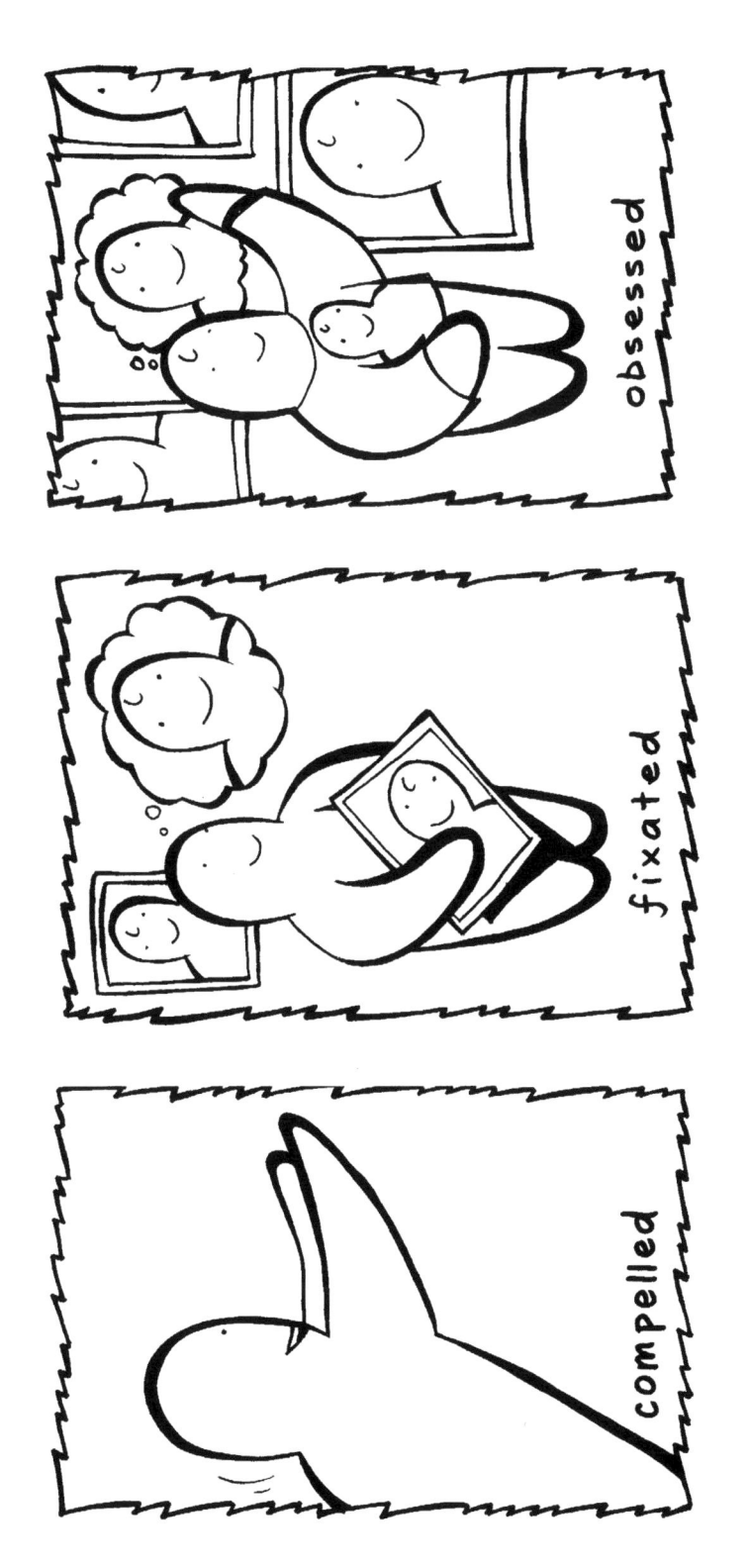

fixated

compelled

Chris was fixated upon the lead singer of her favourite 'boy-band'.

The Blob Emotional Thesaurus

forgiving

Individual feeling words

loved

forgiving

accepted

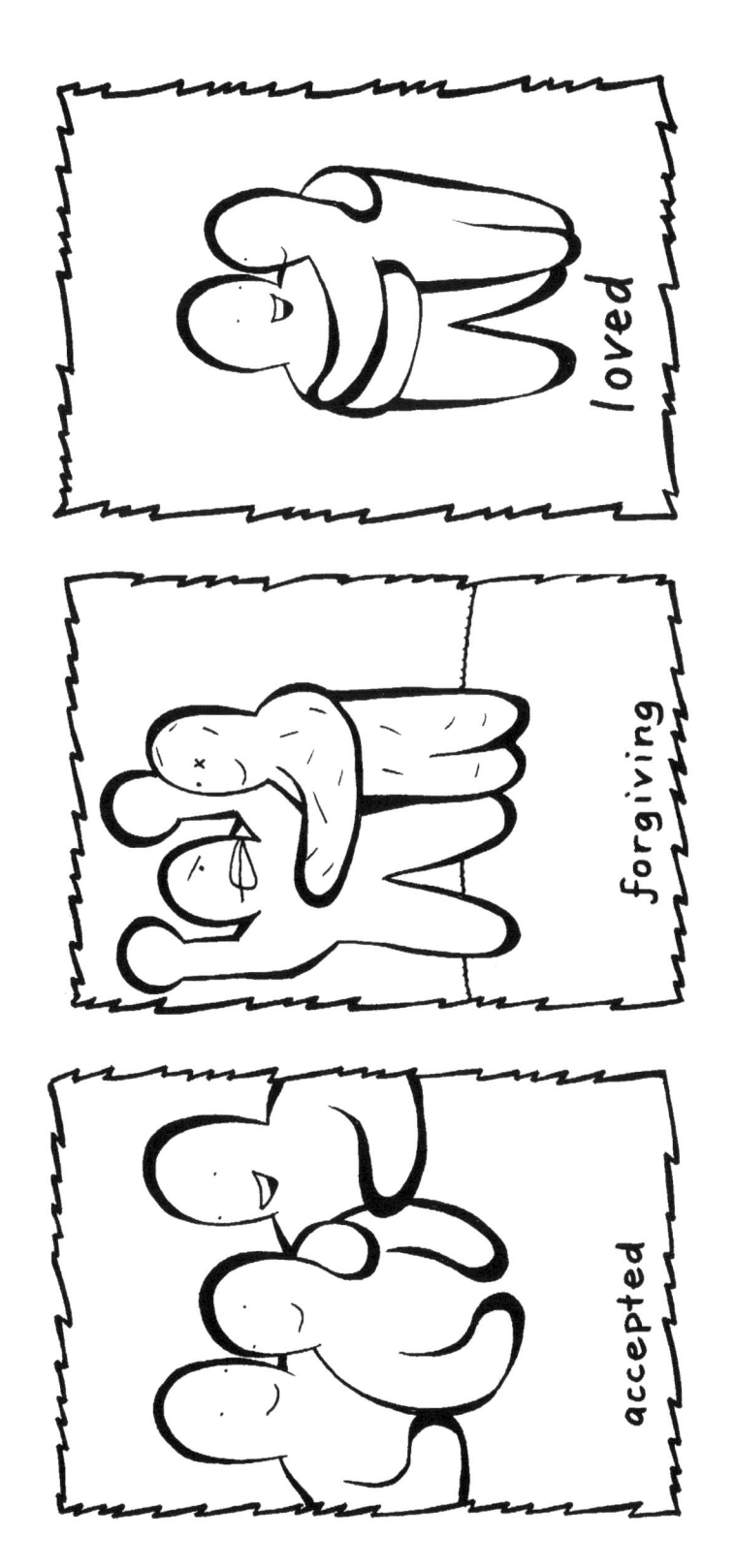

Even though he didn't feel like **forgiving** the bully, he chose to do it.

The Blob Emotional Thesaurus

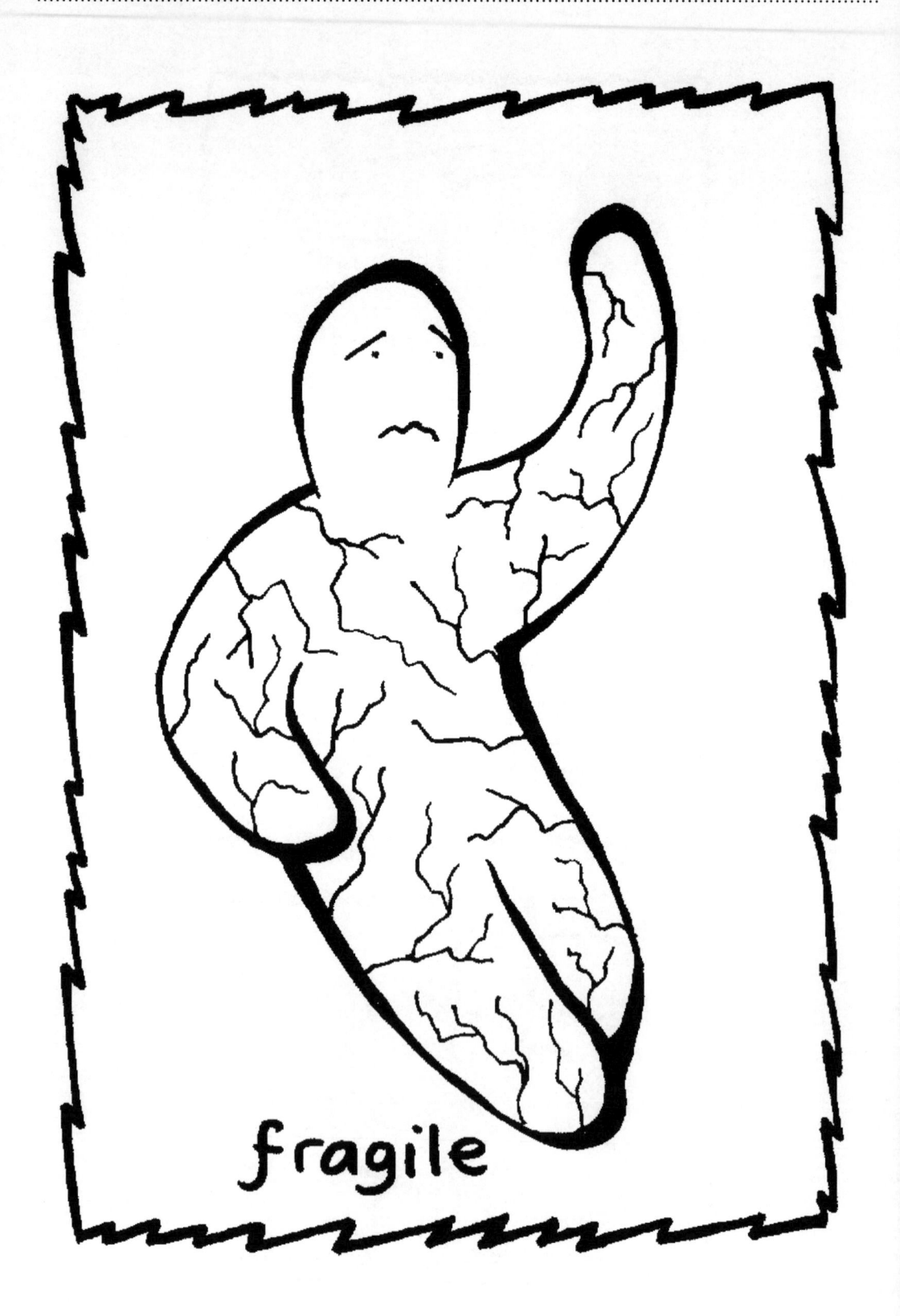

fragile

Individual feeling words

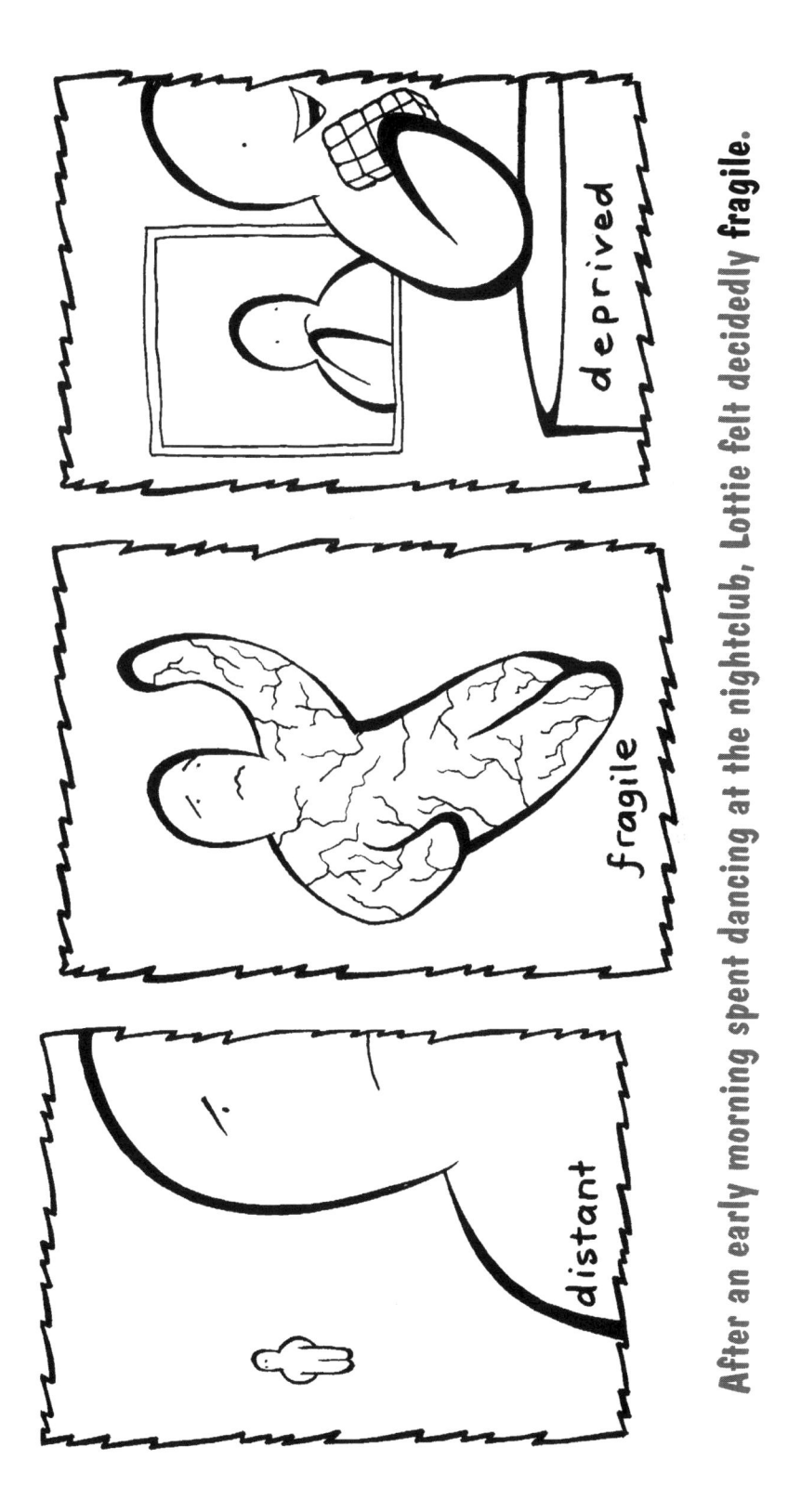

After an early morning spent dancing at the nightclub, Lottie felt decidedly **fragile.**

free

Individual feeling words

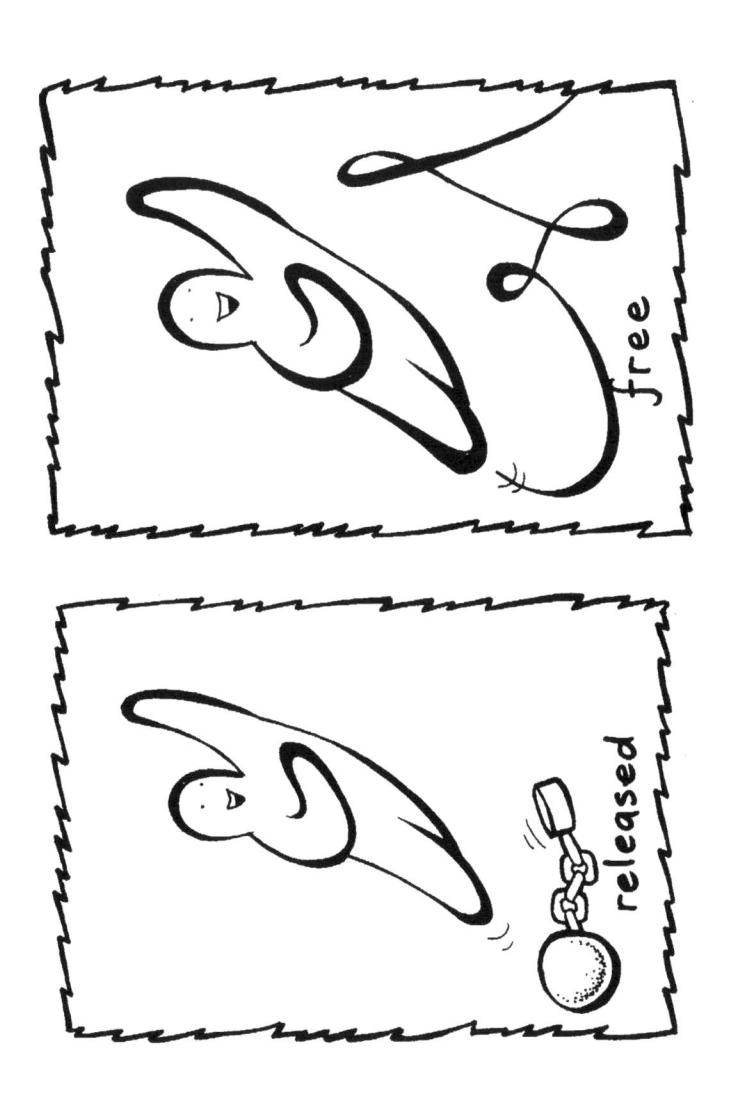

Matt danced across the field, feeling free now that the holiday was about to begin!

The Blob Emotional Thesaurus

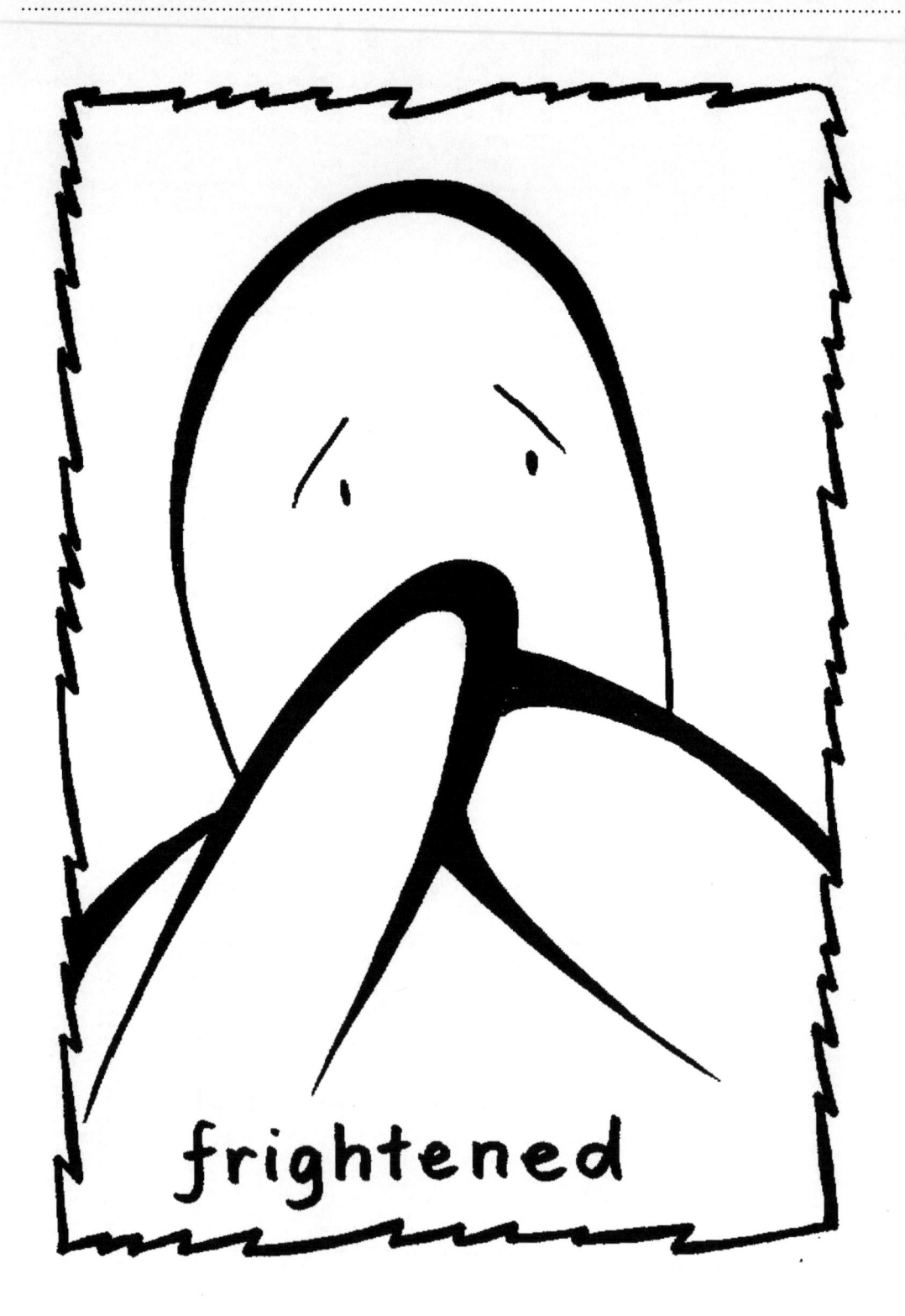

frightened

Individual feeling words

shocked

frightened

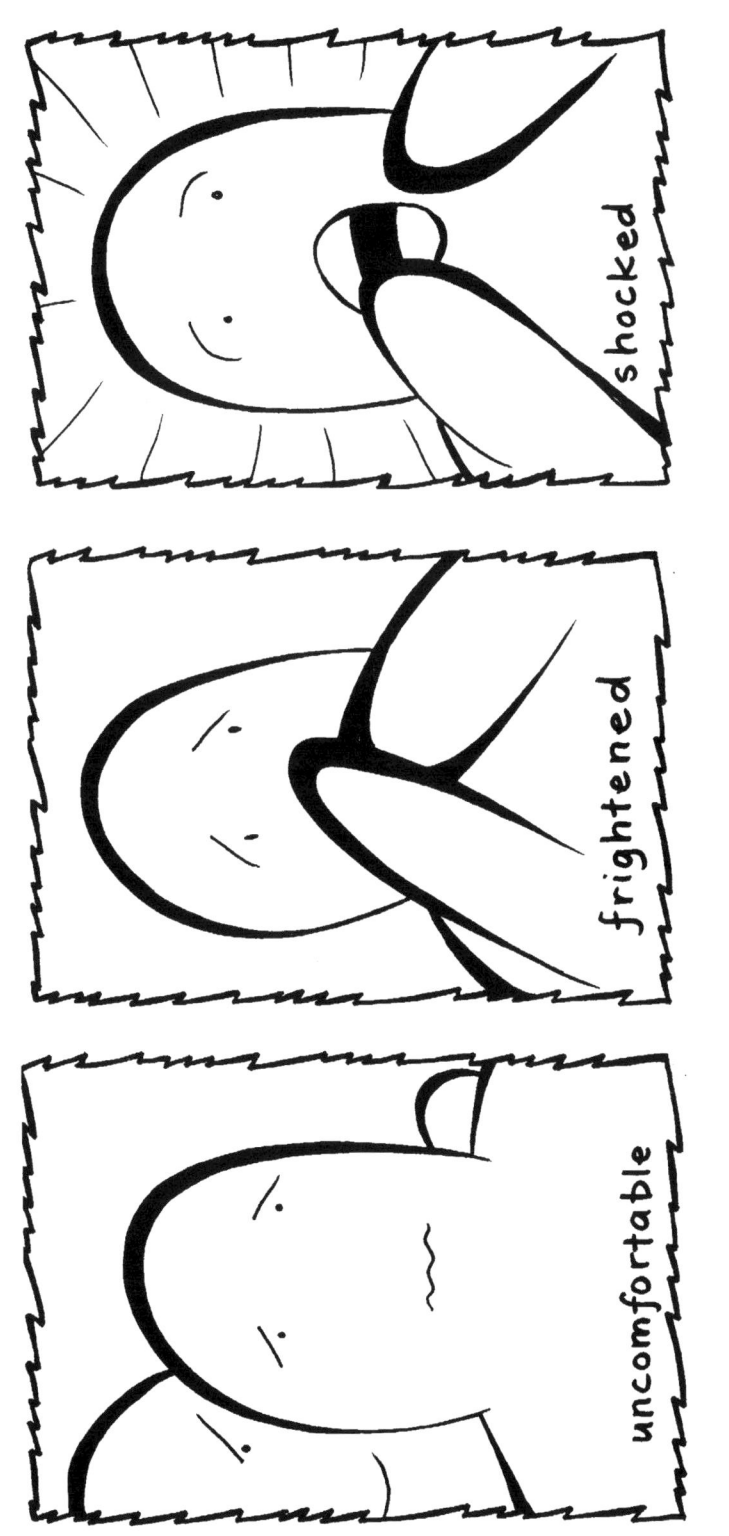

uncomfortable

Peter was frightened of what he had seen in the darkened science lab.

The Blob Emotional Thesaurus

frustrated

Individual feeling words

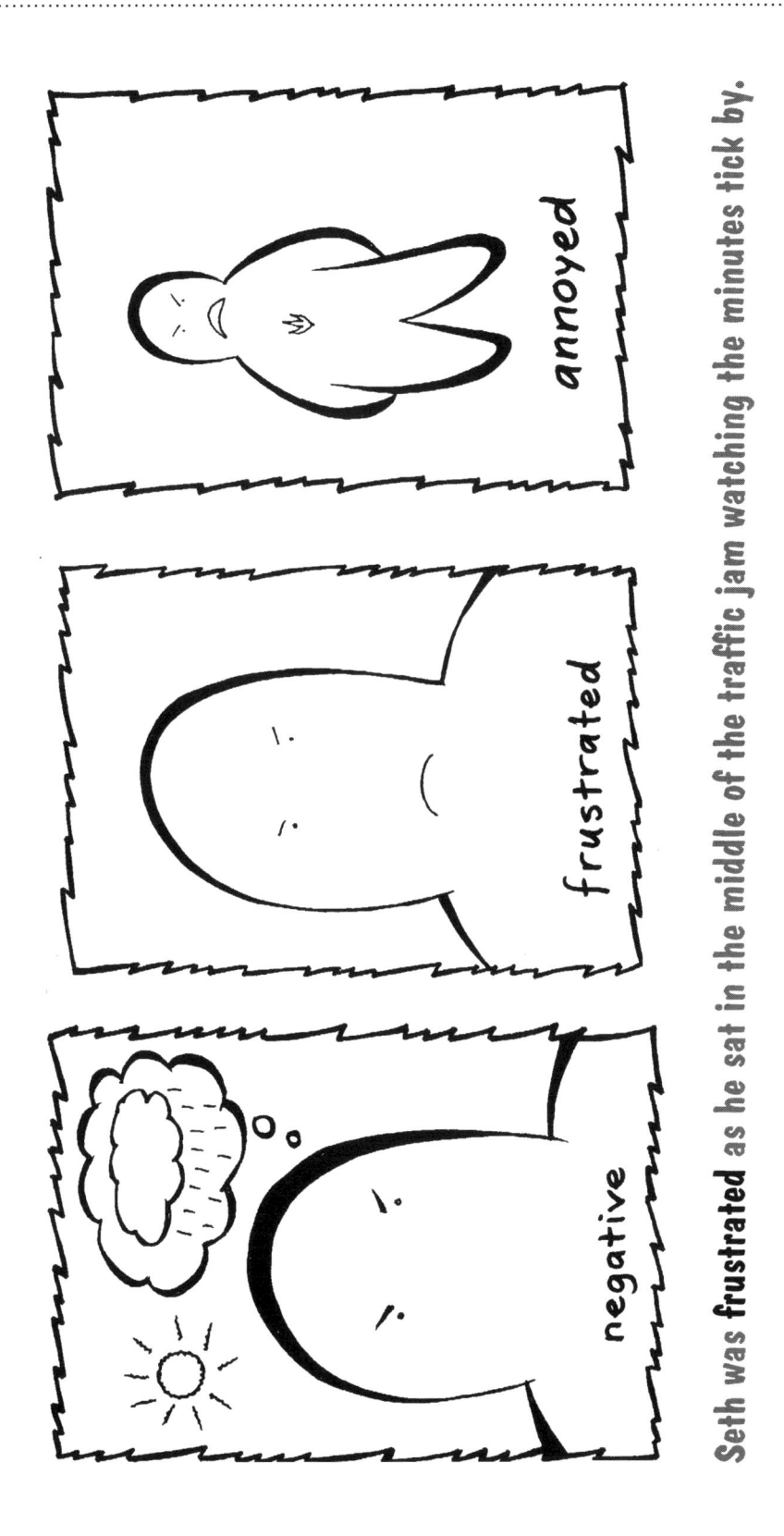

annoyed

frustrated

negative

Seth was frustrated as he sat in the middle of the traffic jam watching the minutes tick by.

137

The Blob Emotional Thesaurus

furious

Individual feeling words

angry

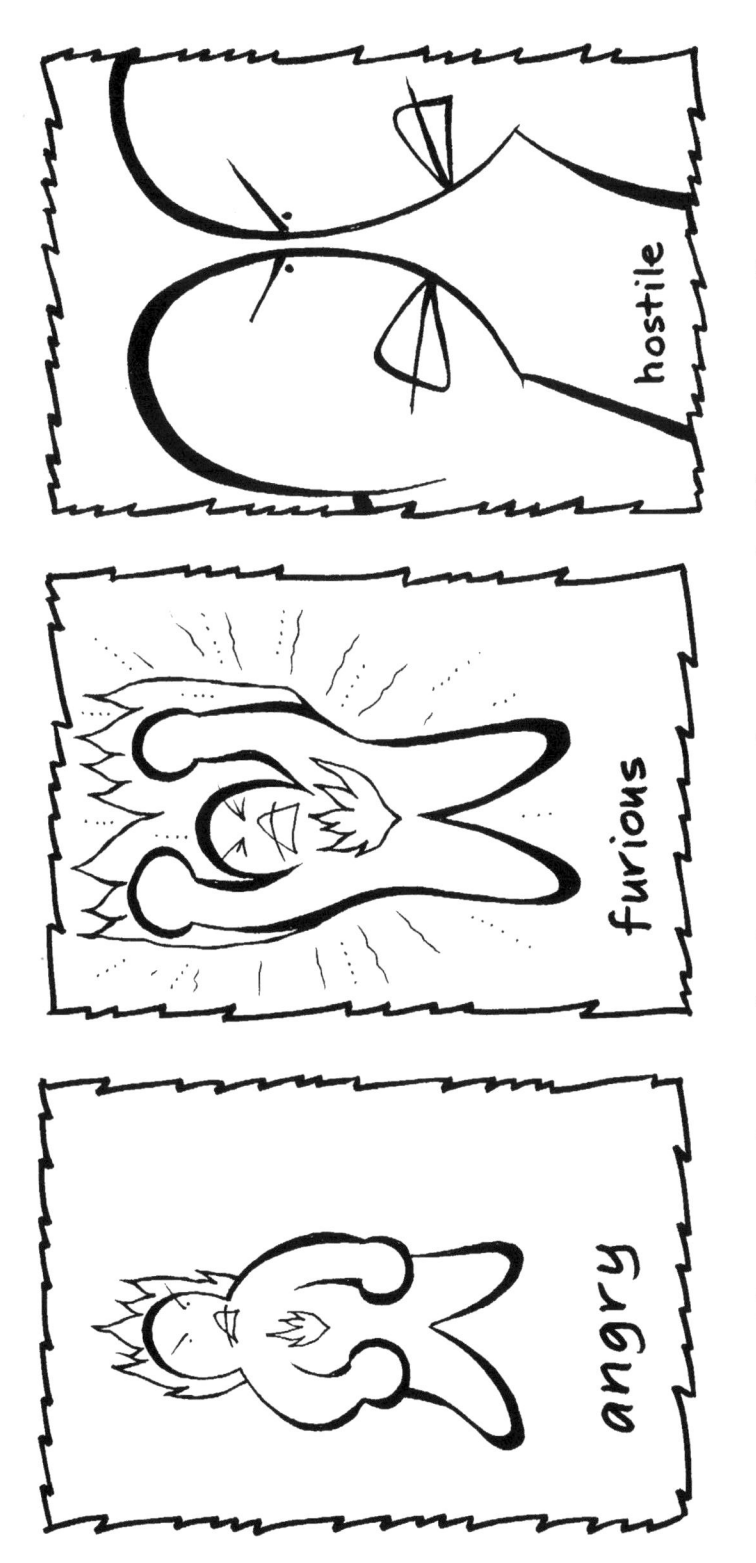

furious

hostile

Alexis was furious that her request for a sweet had been rejected!

The Blob Emotional Thesaurus

generous

Individual feeling words

With the sun shining in a summer sky, Stephan felt **generous** as he gave away sweets!

The Blob Emotional Thesaurus

good

Individual feeling words

patient

good

forgiving

Ruby felt **good** after helping her father do the tidying around the house.

grateful

Individual feeling words

close

grateful

touched

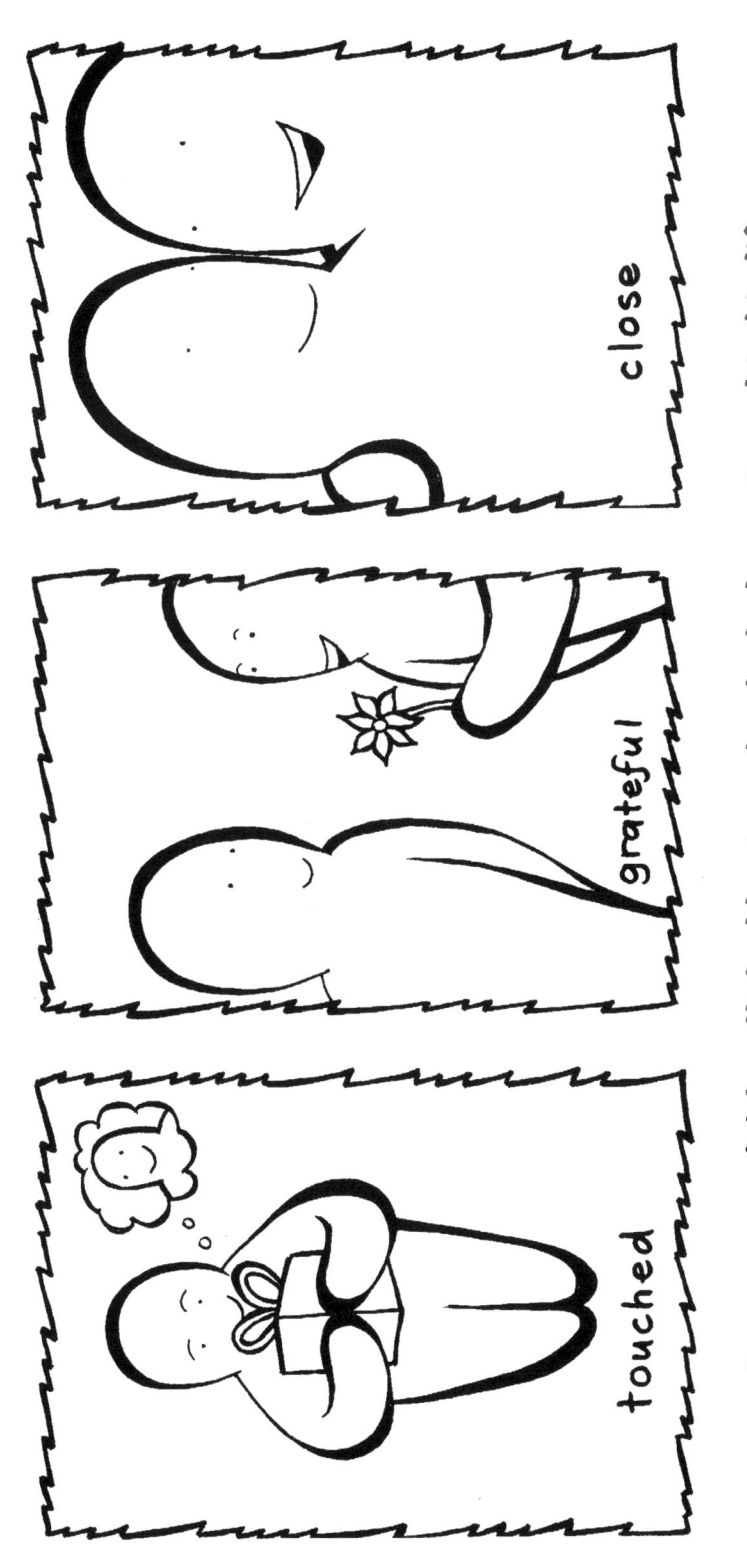

Joe was grateful for all the blessings that he had experienced in his life.

The Blob Emotional Thesaurus

greedy

Individual feeling words

compelled

greedy

mesmerised

Every time a meal was served before Solomon, he felt *greedy* for more and more!

The Blob Emotional Thesaurus

guilty

Individual feeling words

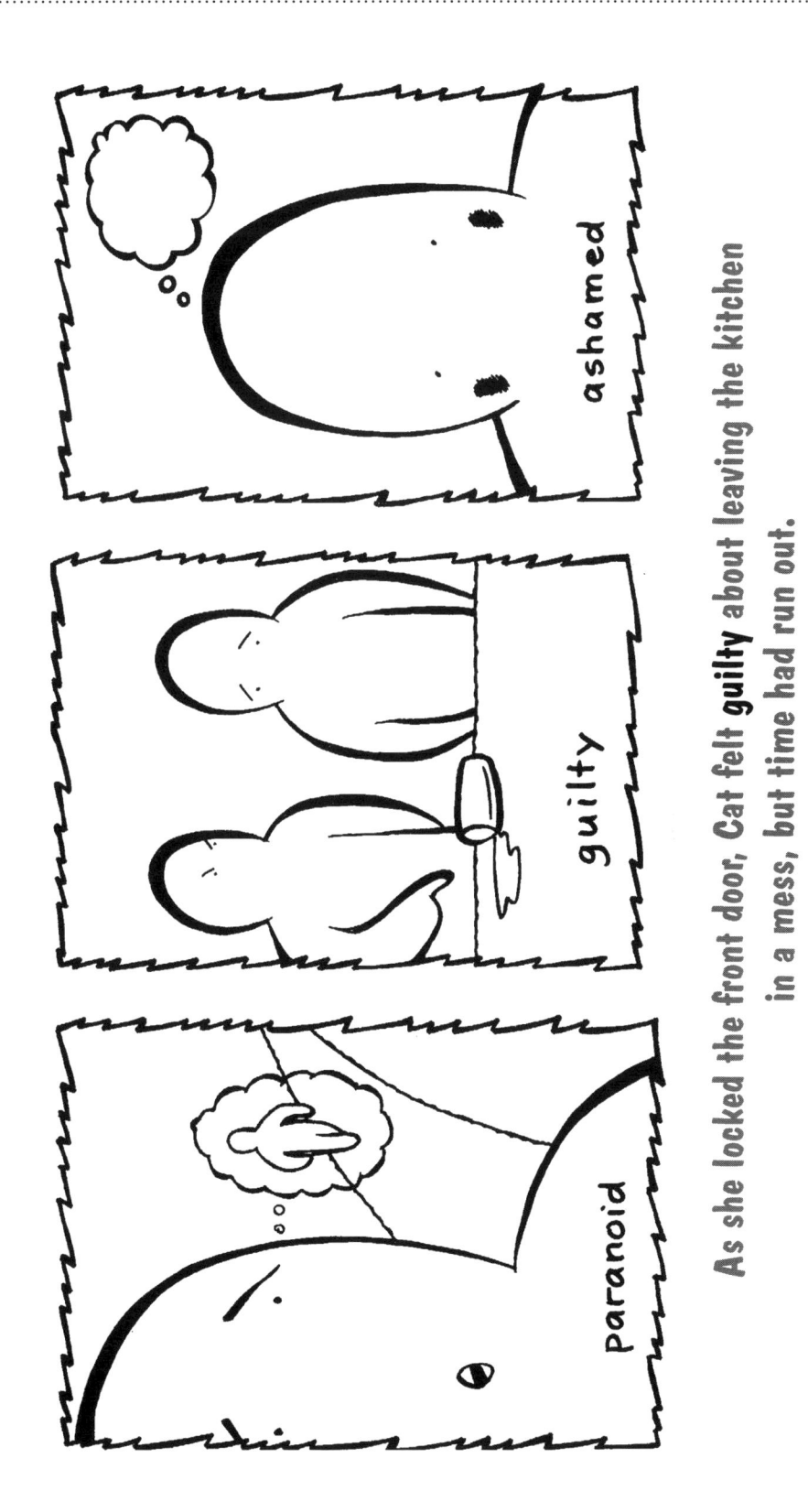

ashamed

guilty

paranoid

As she locked the front door, Cat felt **guilty** about leaving the kitchen in a mess, but time had run out.

The Blob Emotional Thesaurus

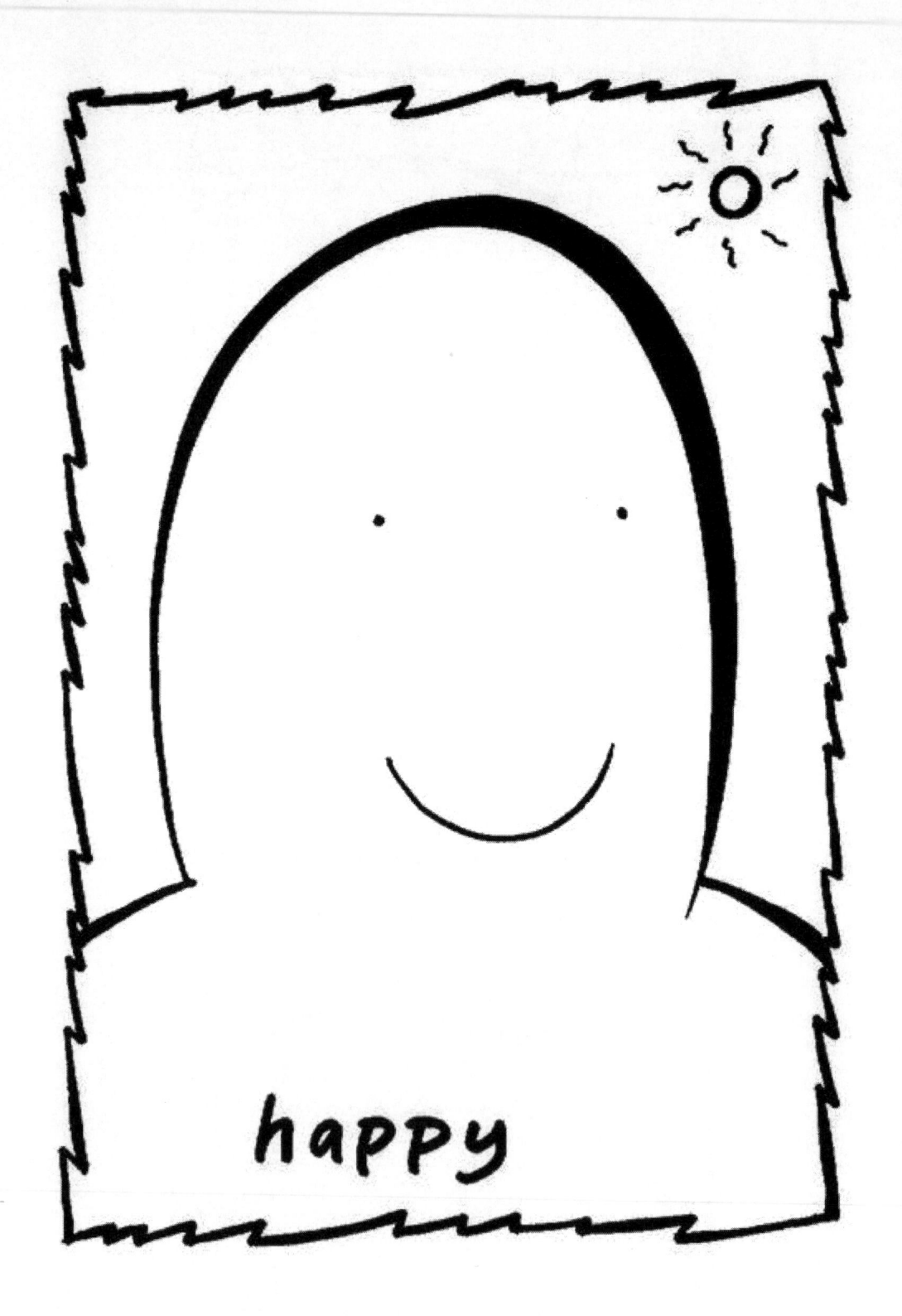

happy

Individual feeling words

encouraged

happy

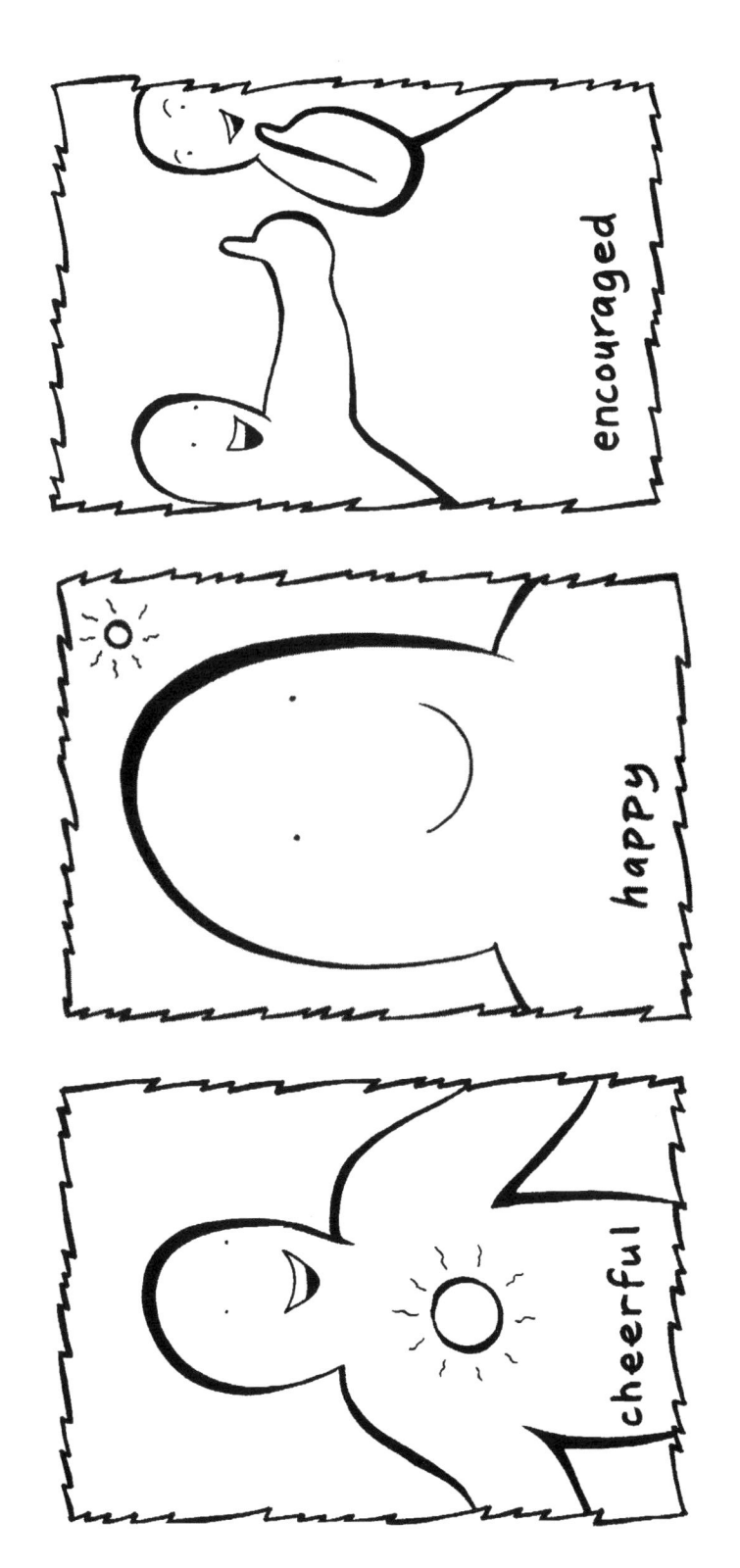

cheerful

Hernandez was happy to be at work, because he loved the people in his team.

The Blob Emotional Thesaurus

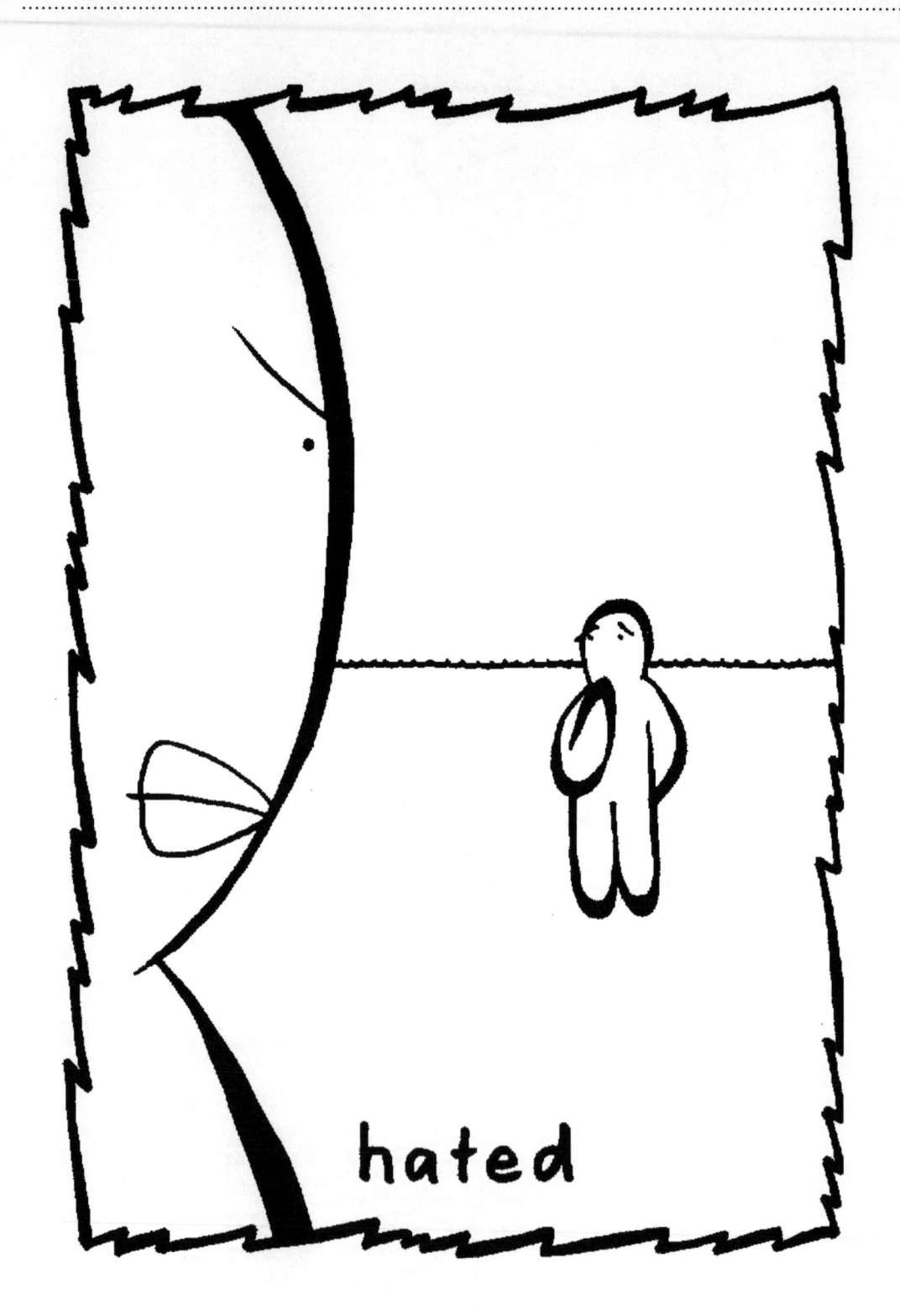

hated

Individual feeling words

abandoned

hated

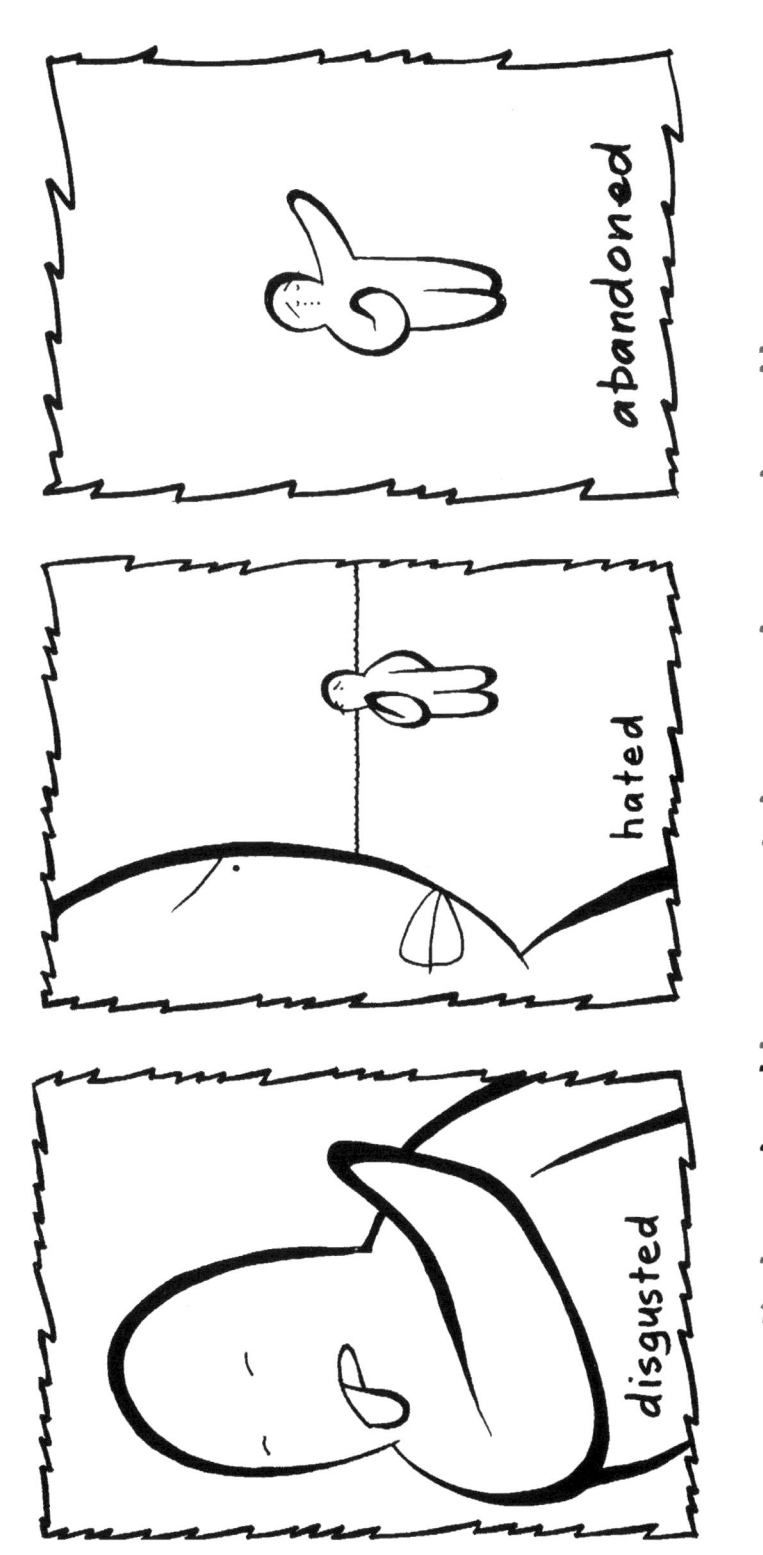

disgusted

Kayla was **hated** by everyone in her street because she could never keep a secret and gossiped dreadfully.

The Blob Emotional Thesaurus

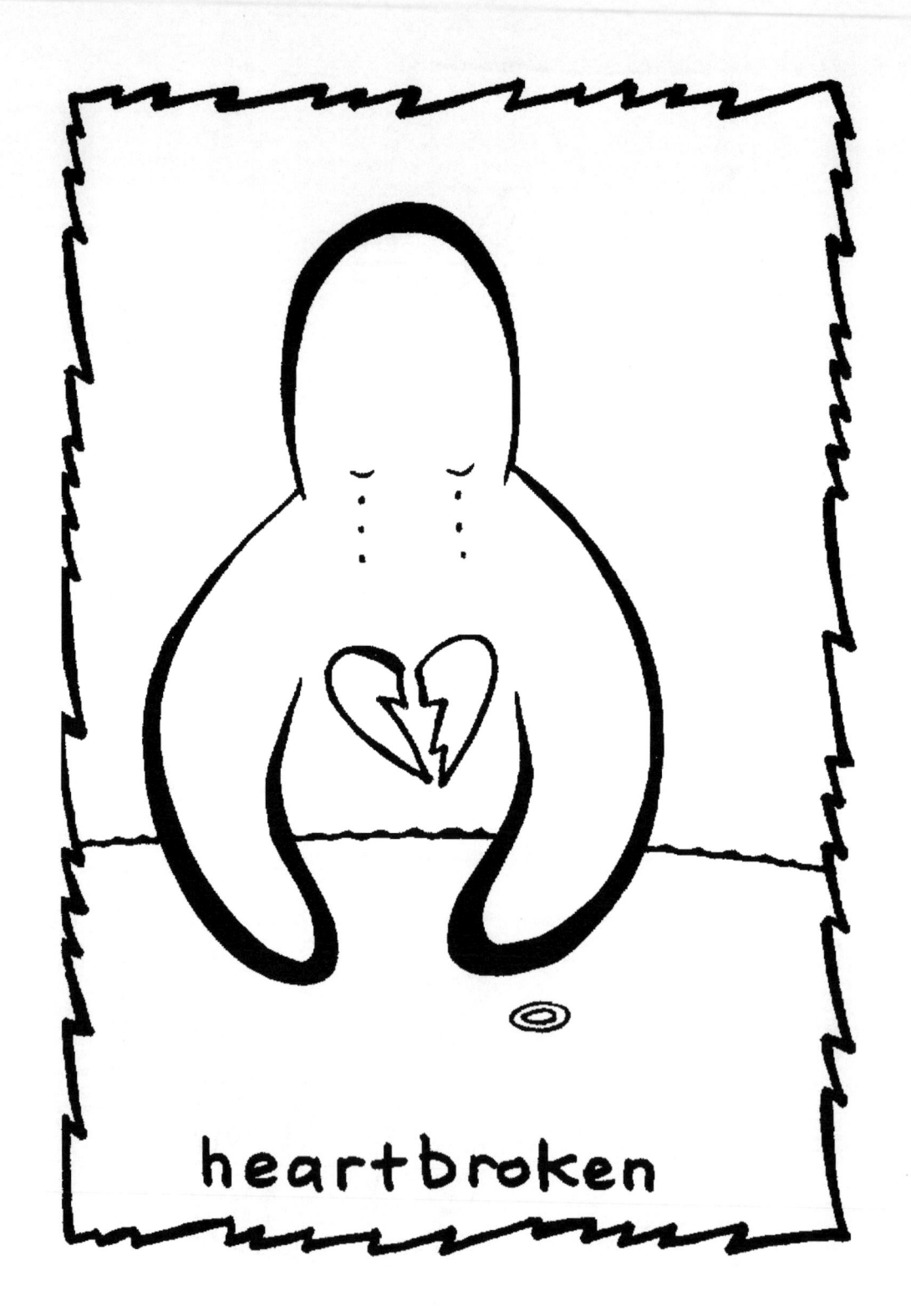

heartbroken

Individual feeling words

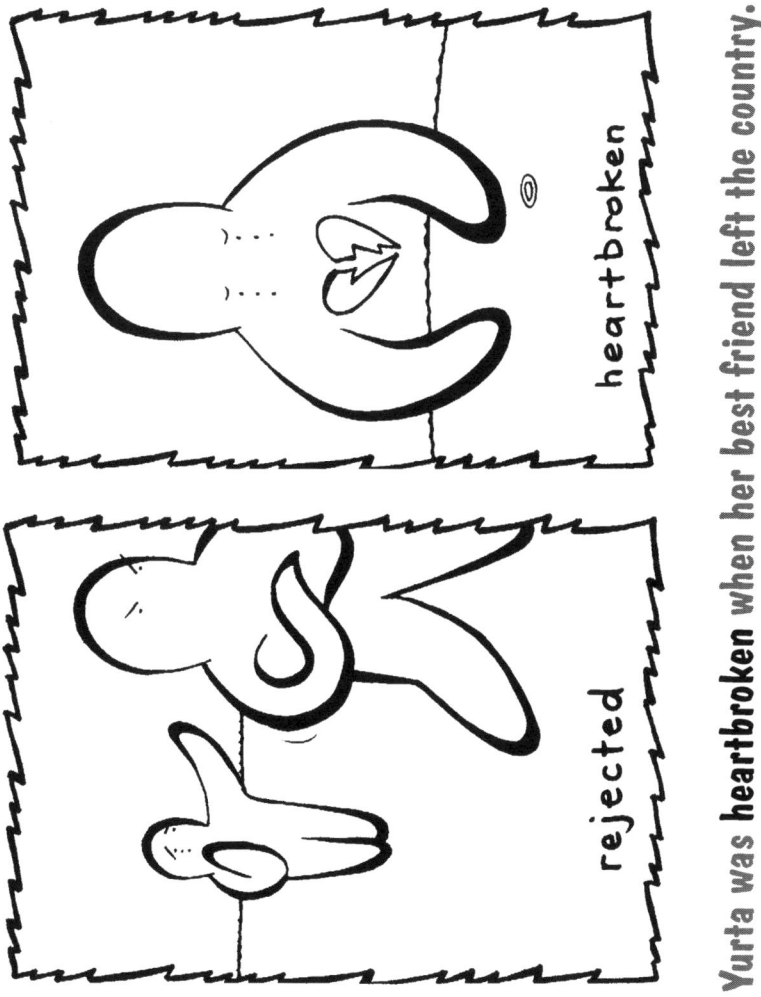

heartbroken

rejected

Yurta was heartbroken when her best friend left the country.

The Blob Emotional Thesaurus

hesitant

Individual feeling words

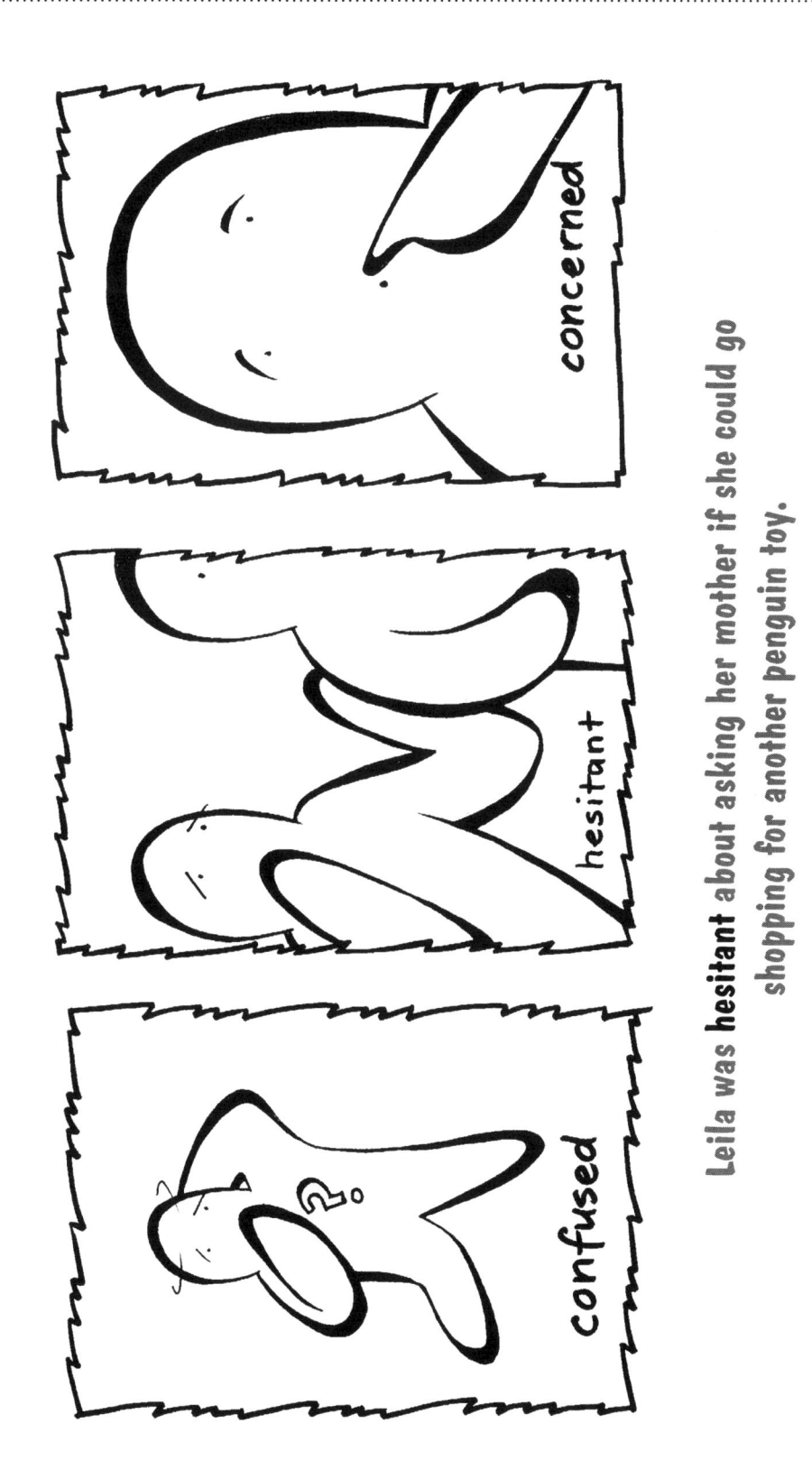

concerned

hesitant

confused

Leila was hesitant about asking her mother if she could go shopping for another penguin toy.

The Blob Emotional Thesaurus

hopeful

Individual feeling words

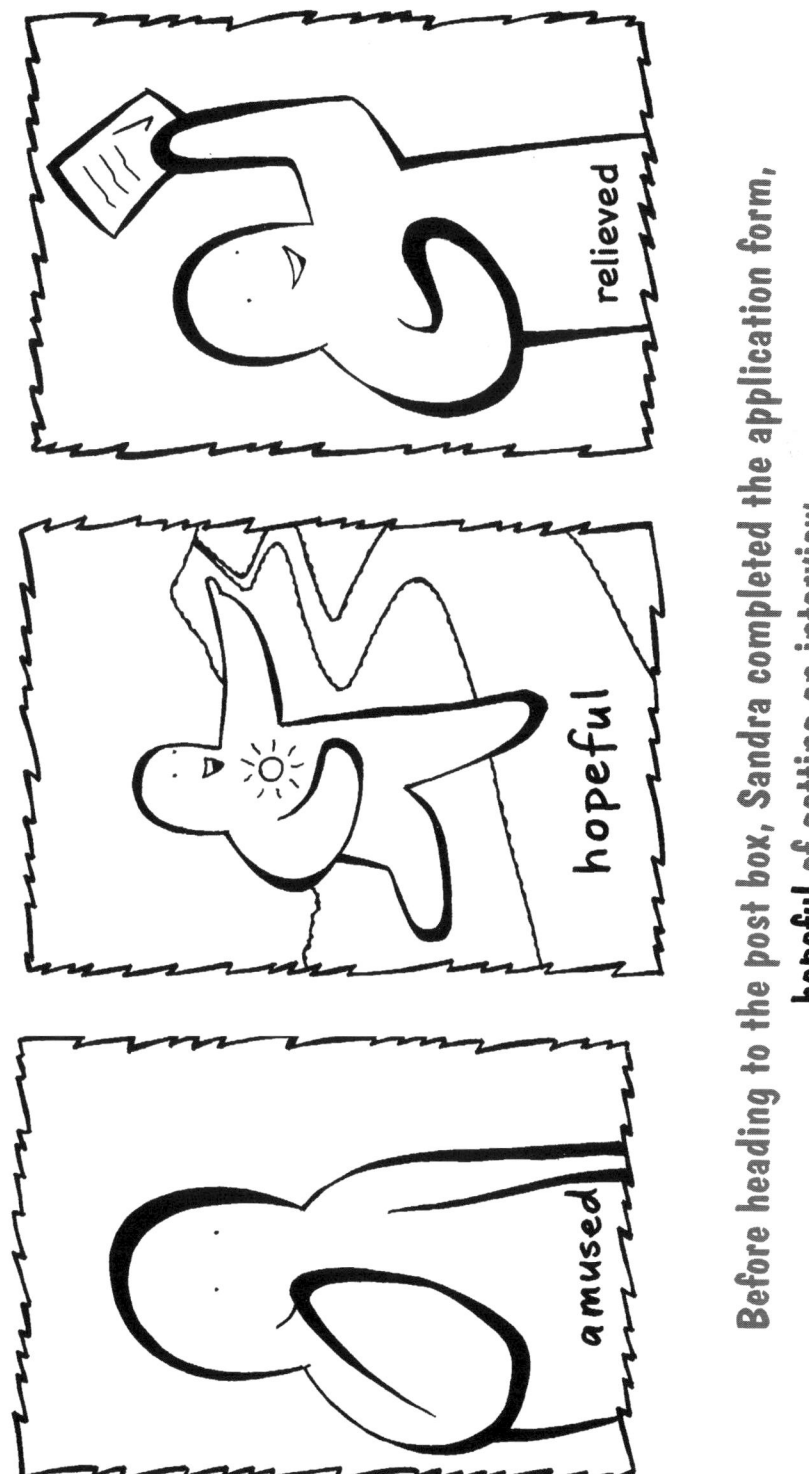

relieved

hopeful

amused

Before heading to the post box, Sandra completed the application form, **hopeful** of getting an interview.

159

The Blob Emotional Thesaurus

hostile

Individual feeling words

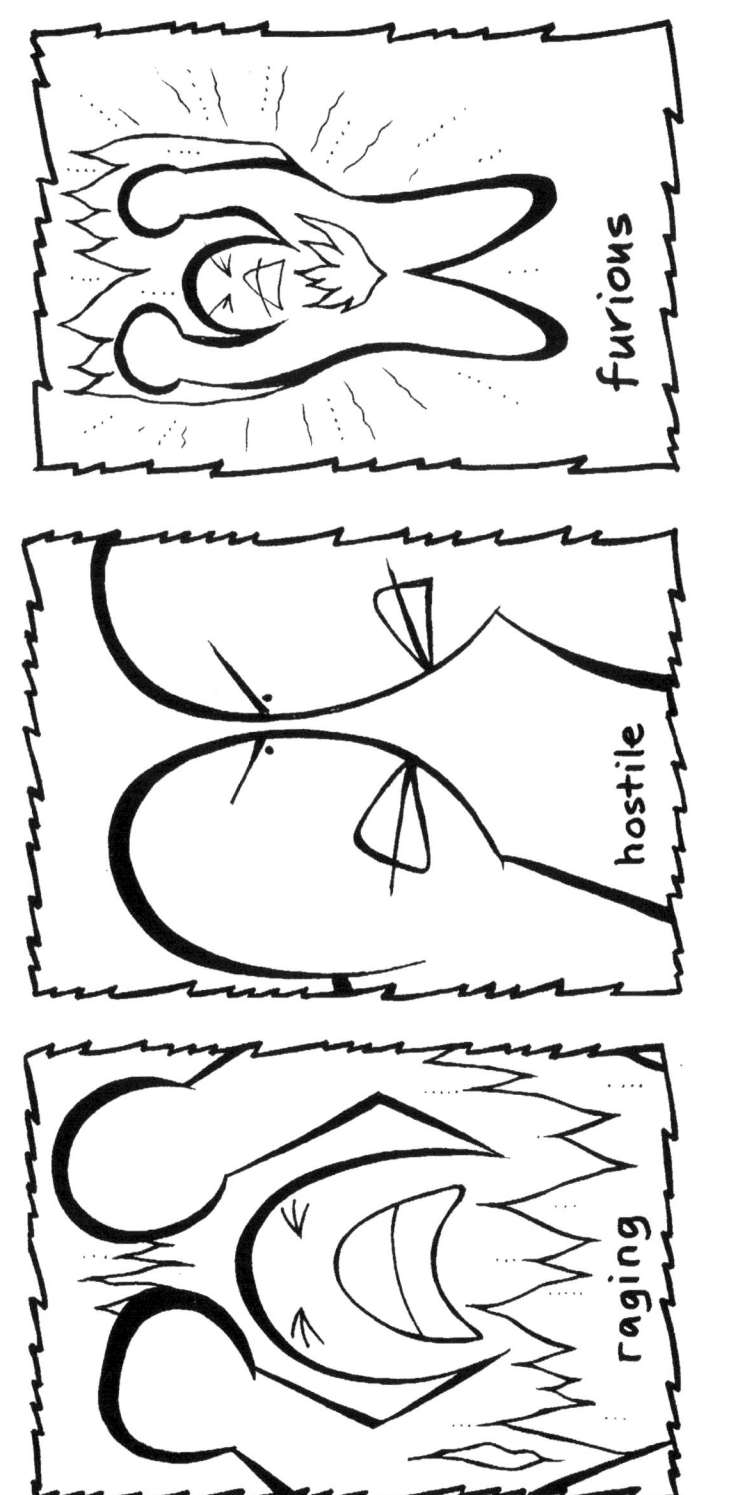

furious

hostile

raging

Rachel felt very **hostile** when her latest boyfriend suggested that she should pay for all their holiday to Spain.

The Blob Emotional Thesaurus

hurt

Individual feeling words

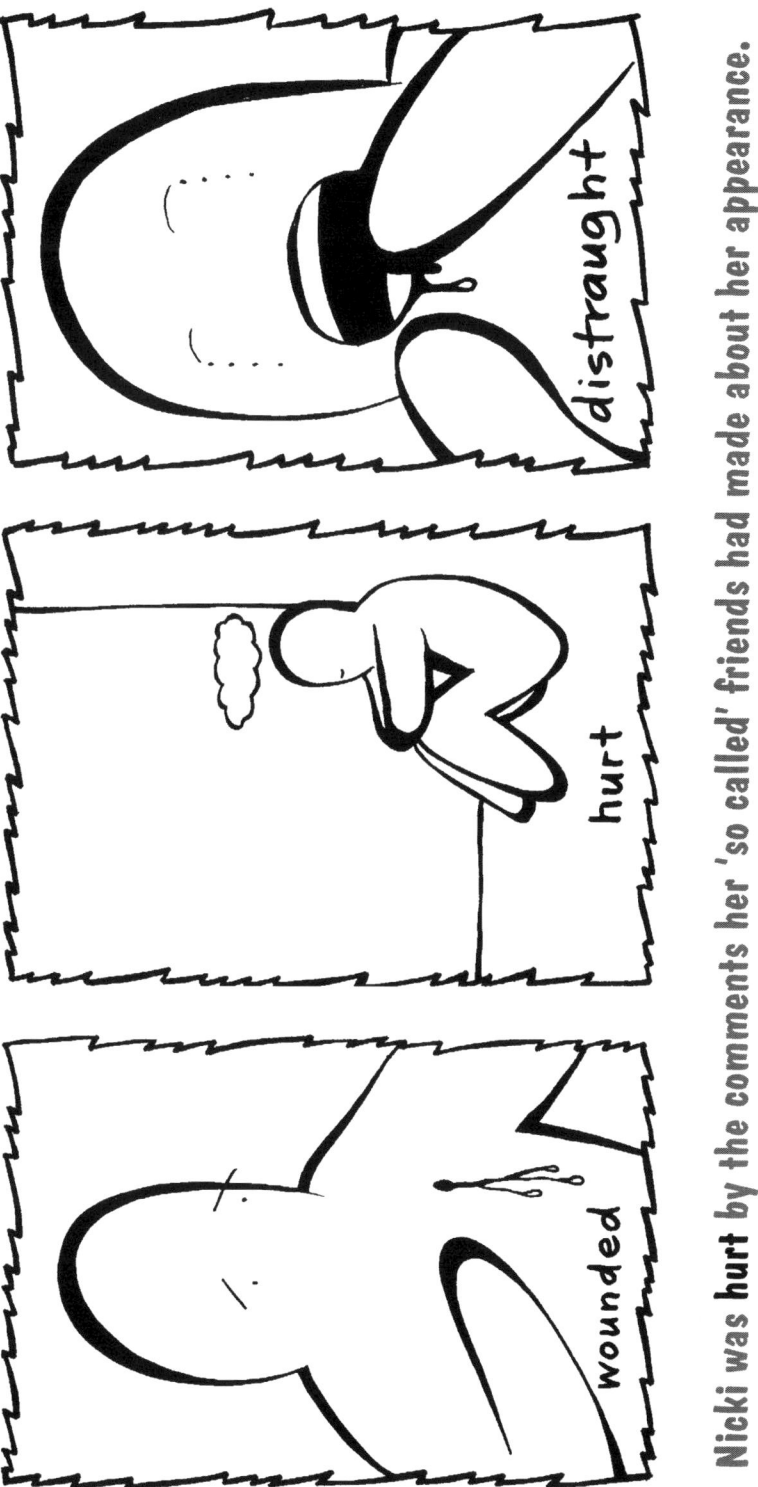

distraught | hurt | wounded

Nicki was hurt by the comments her 'so called' friends had made about her appearance.

The Blob Emotional Thesaurus

ignored

Individual feeling words

lonely

ignored

isolated

Lyn was ignored by the teacher whenever she put up her hand.

incensed

Individual feeling words

volcanic

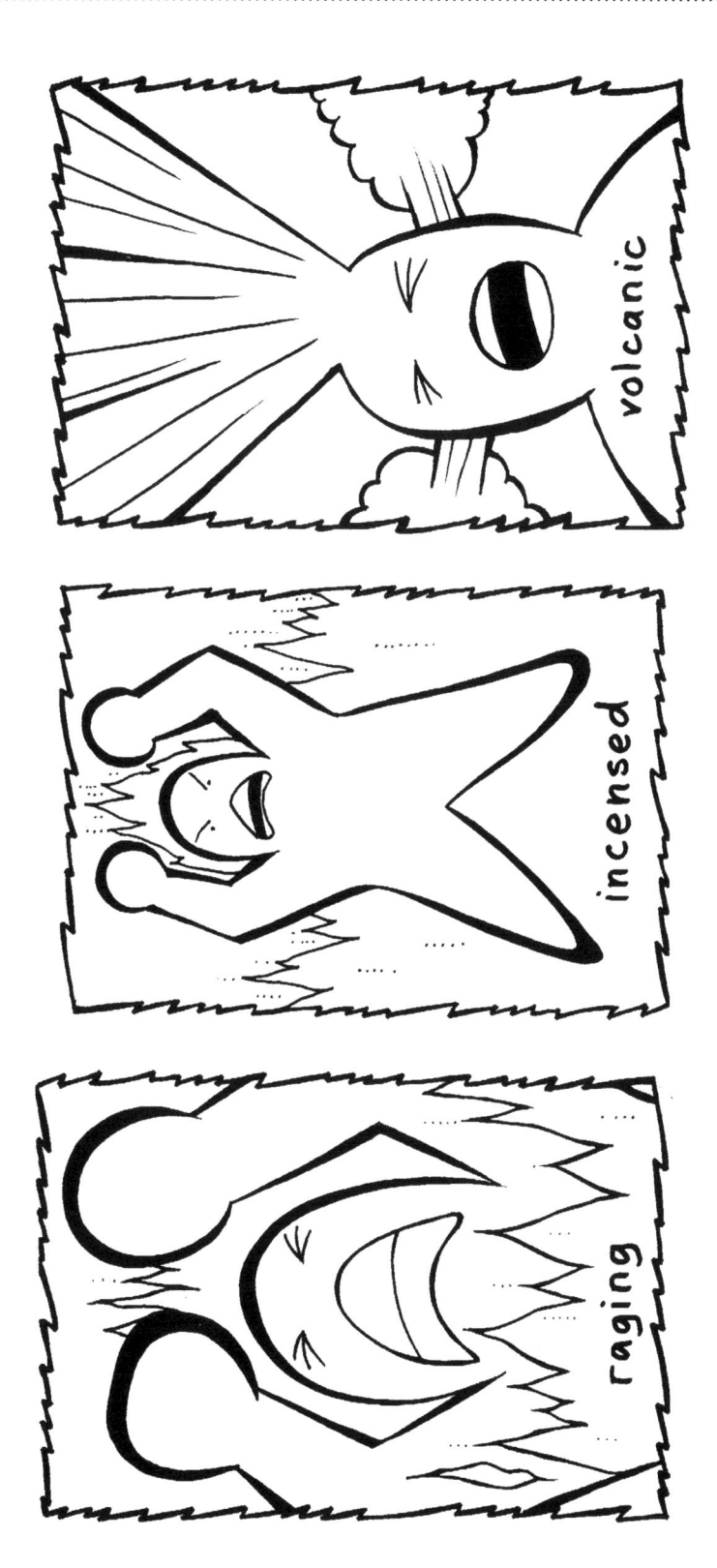

incensed

raging

Wallace was incensed that someone had eaten all of his cheese up!

The Blob Emotional Thesaurus

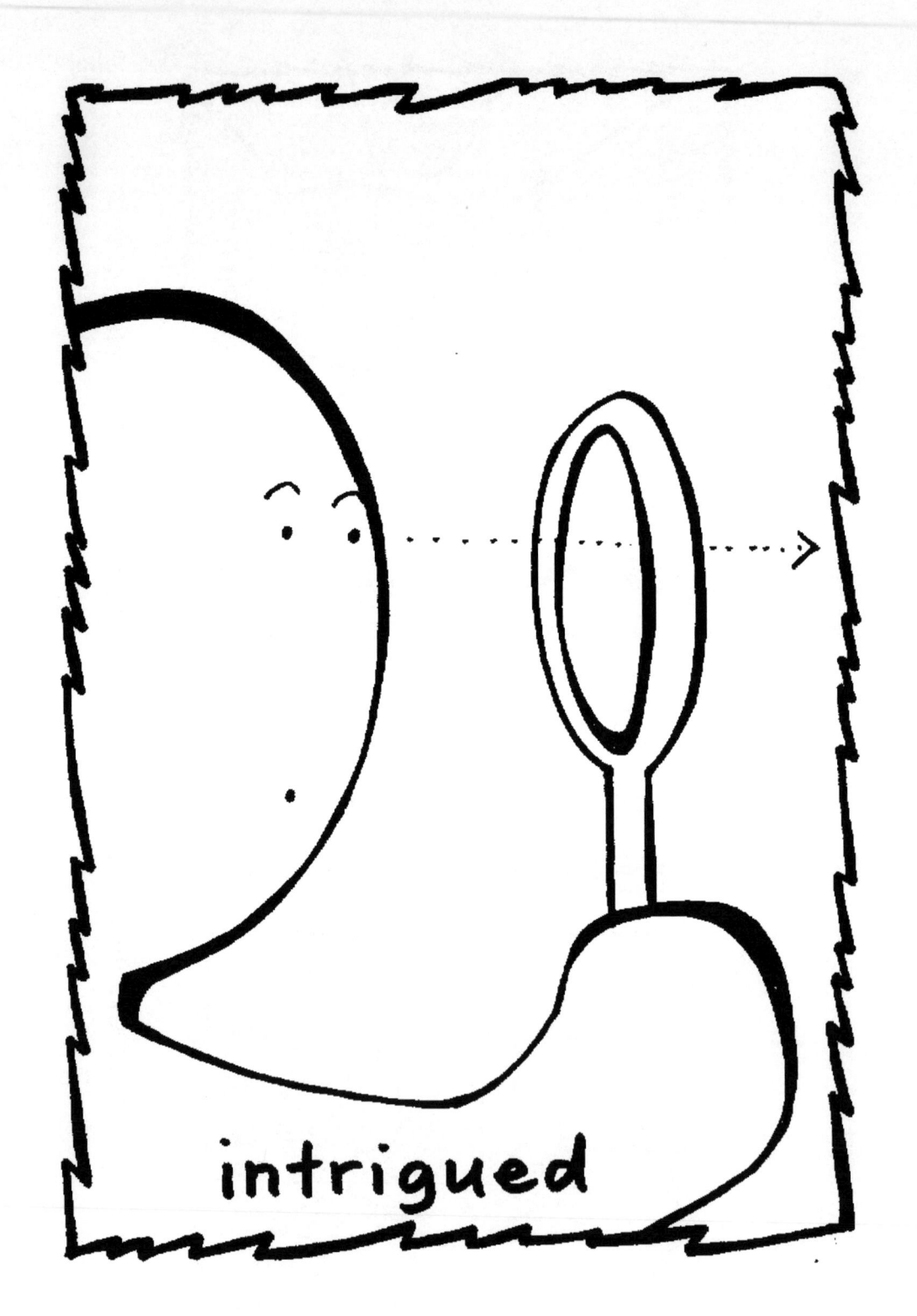

intrigued

Individual feeling words

fascinated

intrigued

curious

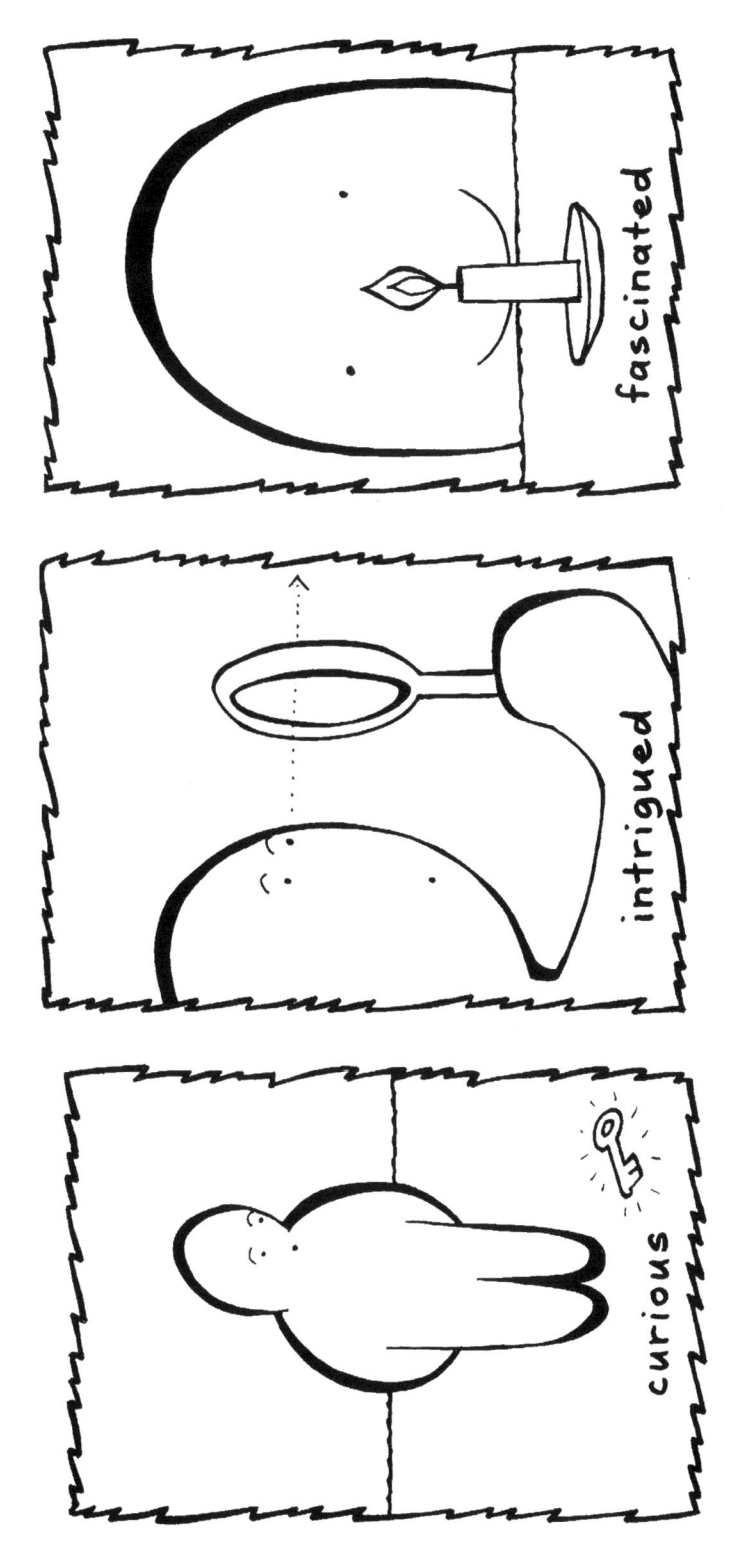

Max was intrigued by the appearance of a large pot of honey on the kitchen table.

irritated

Individual feeling words

annoyed

irritated

negative

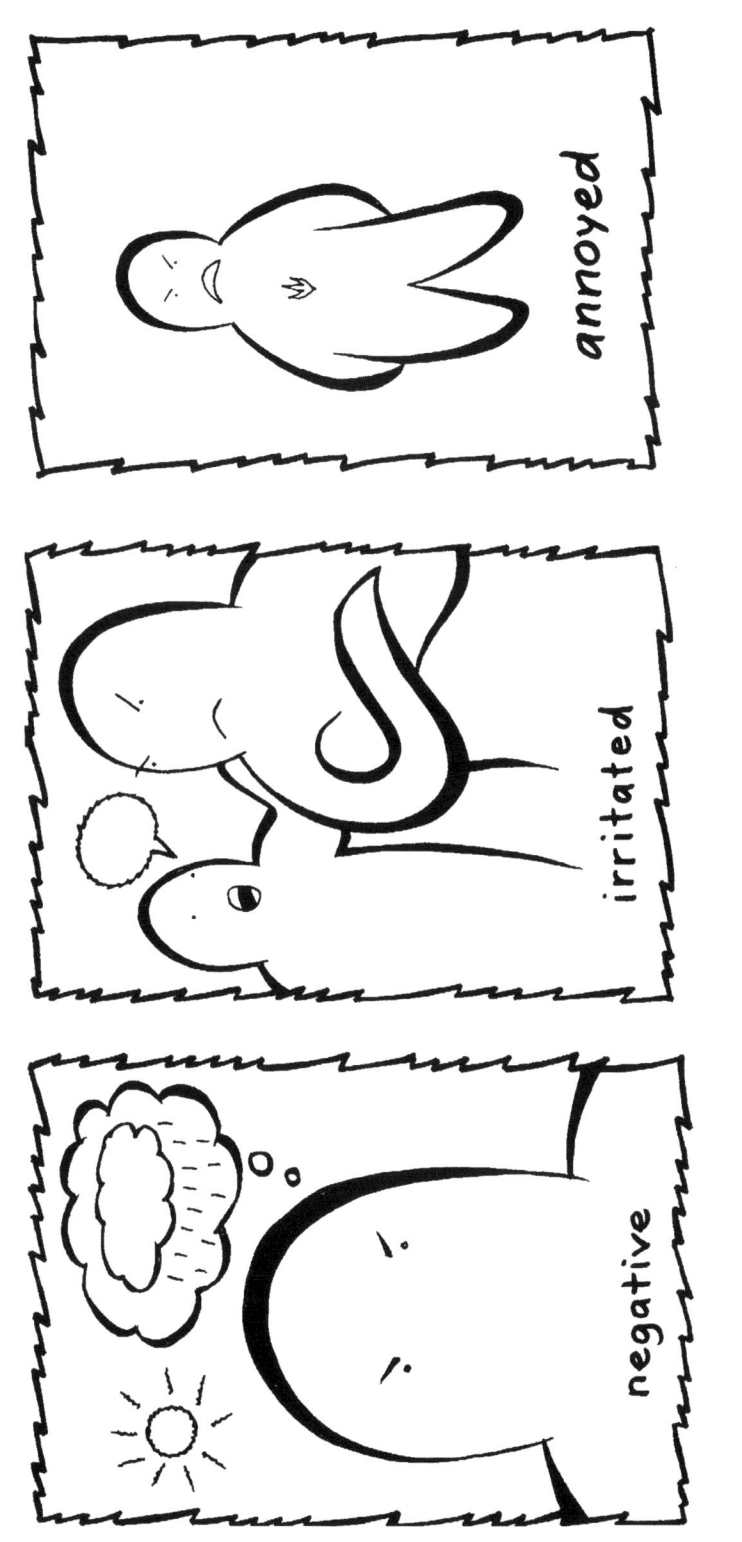

James was irritated by her constant whining about his interest in football.

The Blob Emotional Thesaurus

isolated

Individual feeling words

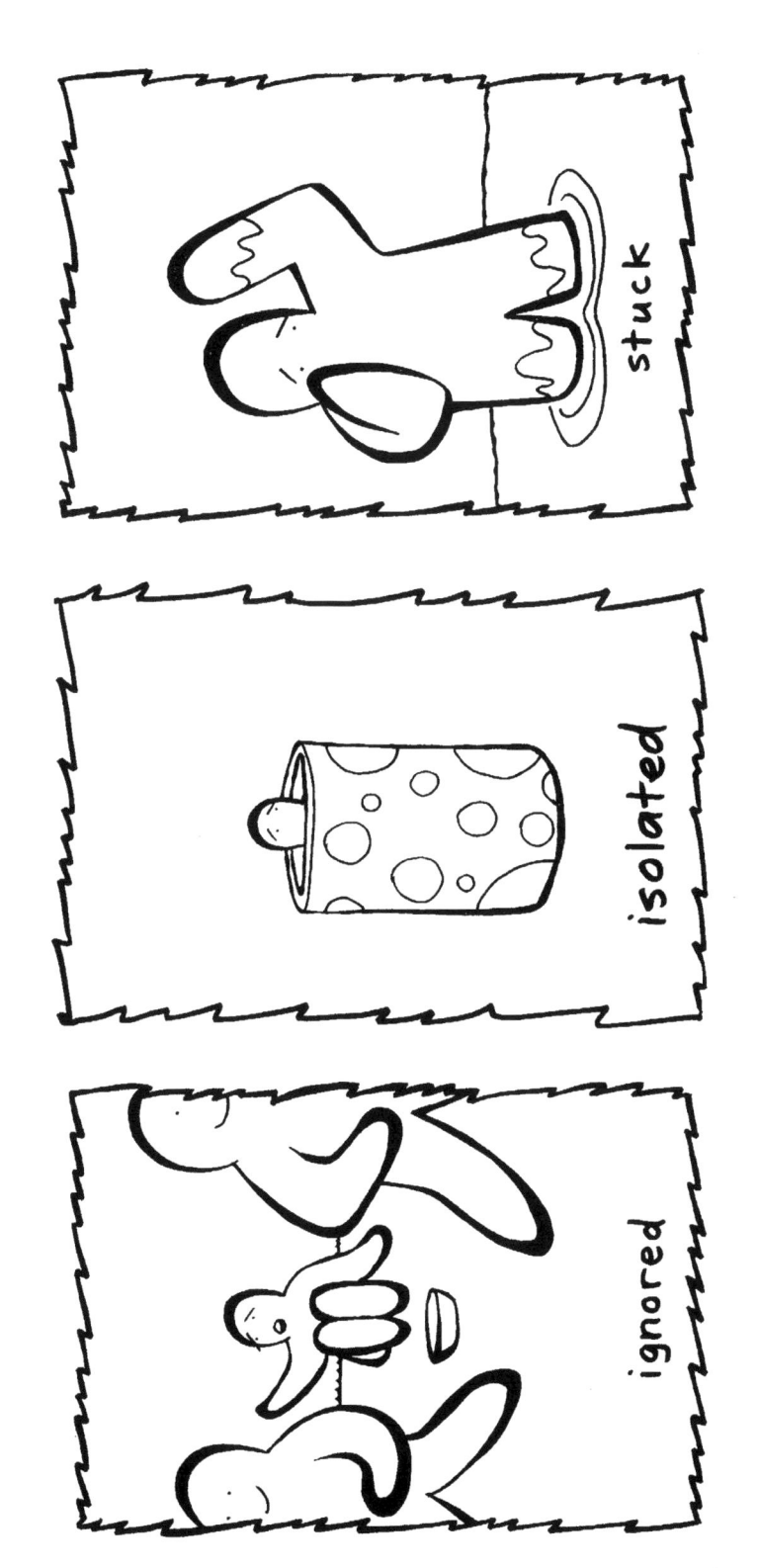

ignored	isolated	stuck

Romeo felt isolated when all of his friends told him they didn't like his opinions.

The Blob Emotional Thesaurus

jealous

Individual feeling words

frustrated

jealous

negative

Keira was jealous of the love her best friend had found with the new boy.

The Blob Emotional Thesaurus

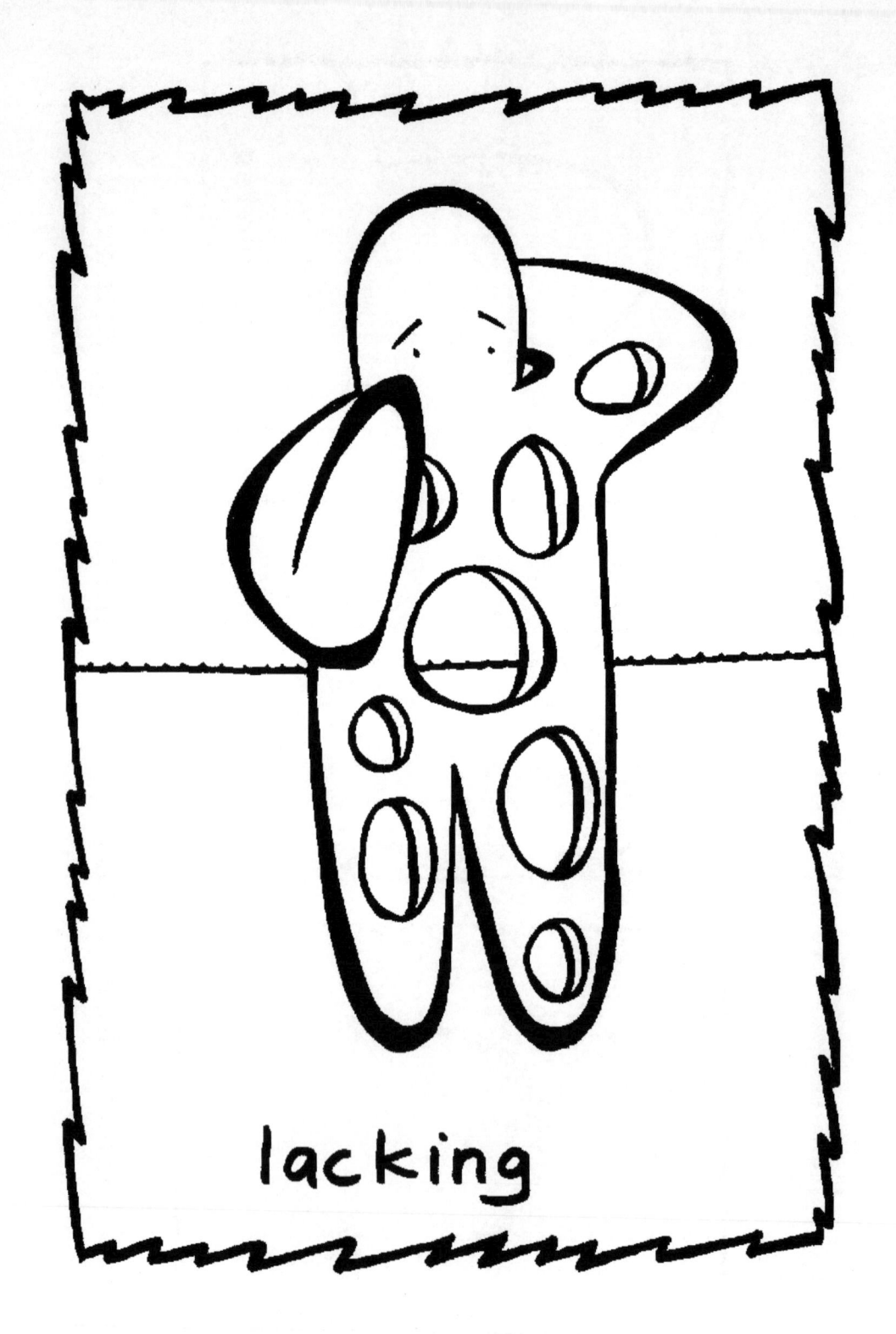

lacking

Individual feeling words

empty

lacking

fragile

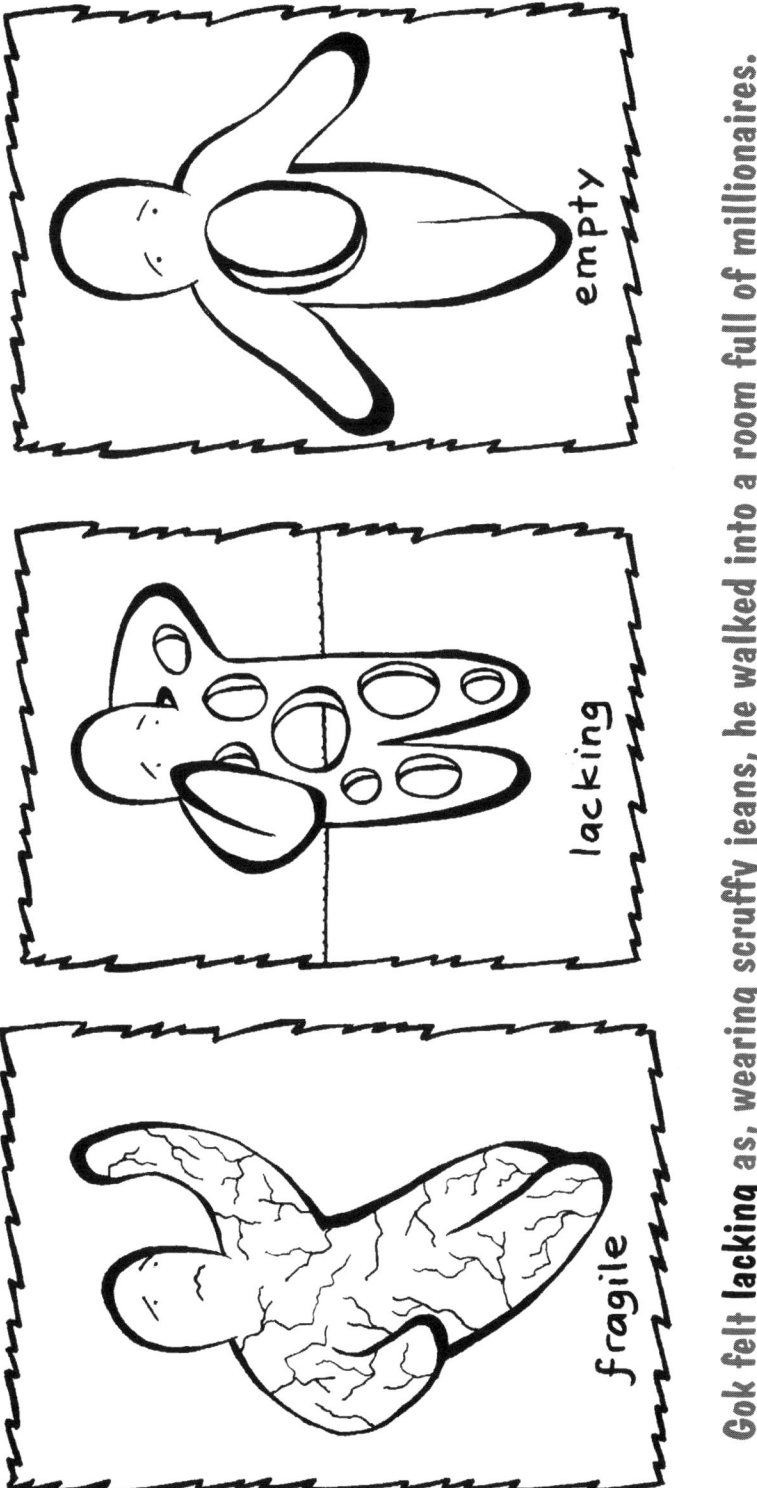

Gok felt lacking as, wearing scruffy jeans, he walked into a room full of millionaires.

The Blob Emotional Thesaurus

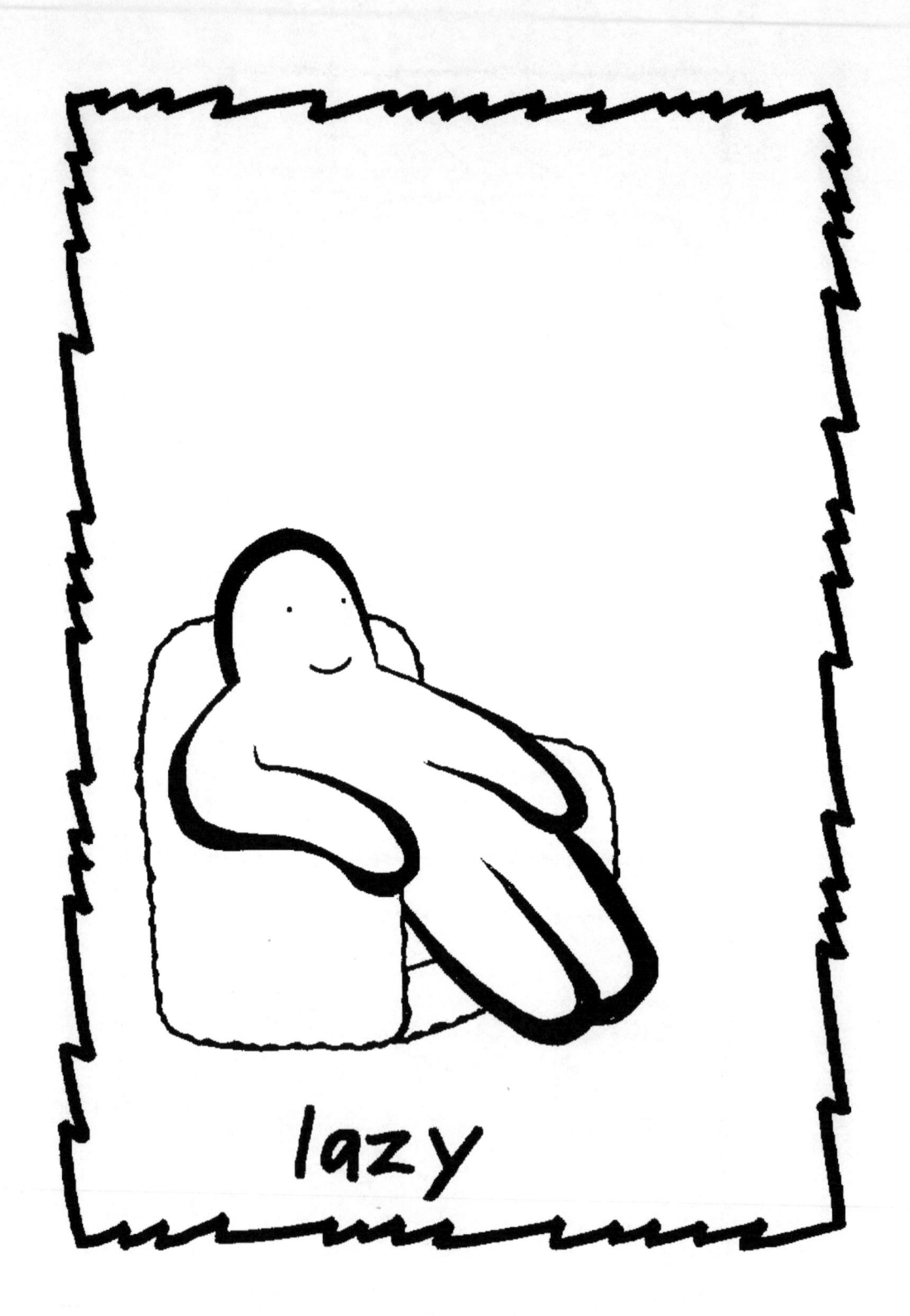

lazy

Individual feeling words

bored

lazy

neutral

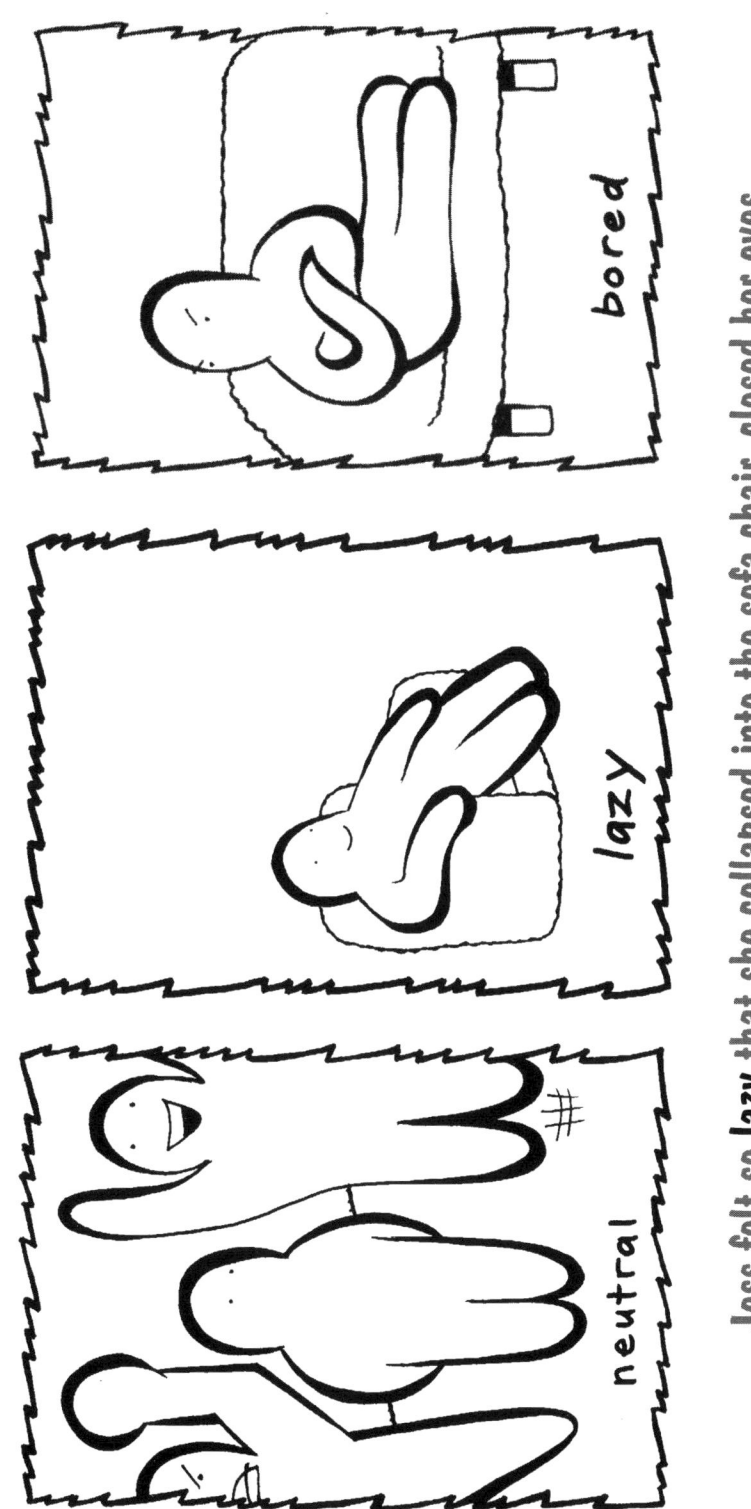

Jess felt so lazy that she collapsed into the sofa chair, closed her eyes and listened to the music.

The Blob Emotional Thesaurus

lonely

Individual feeling words

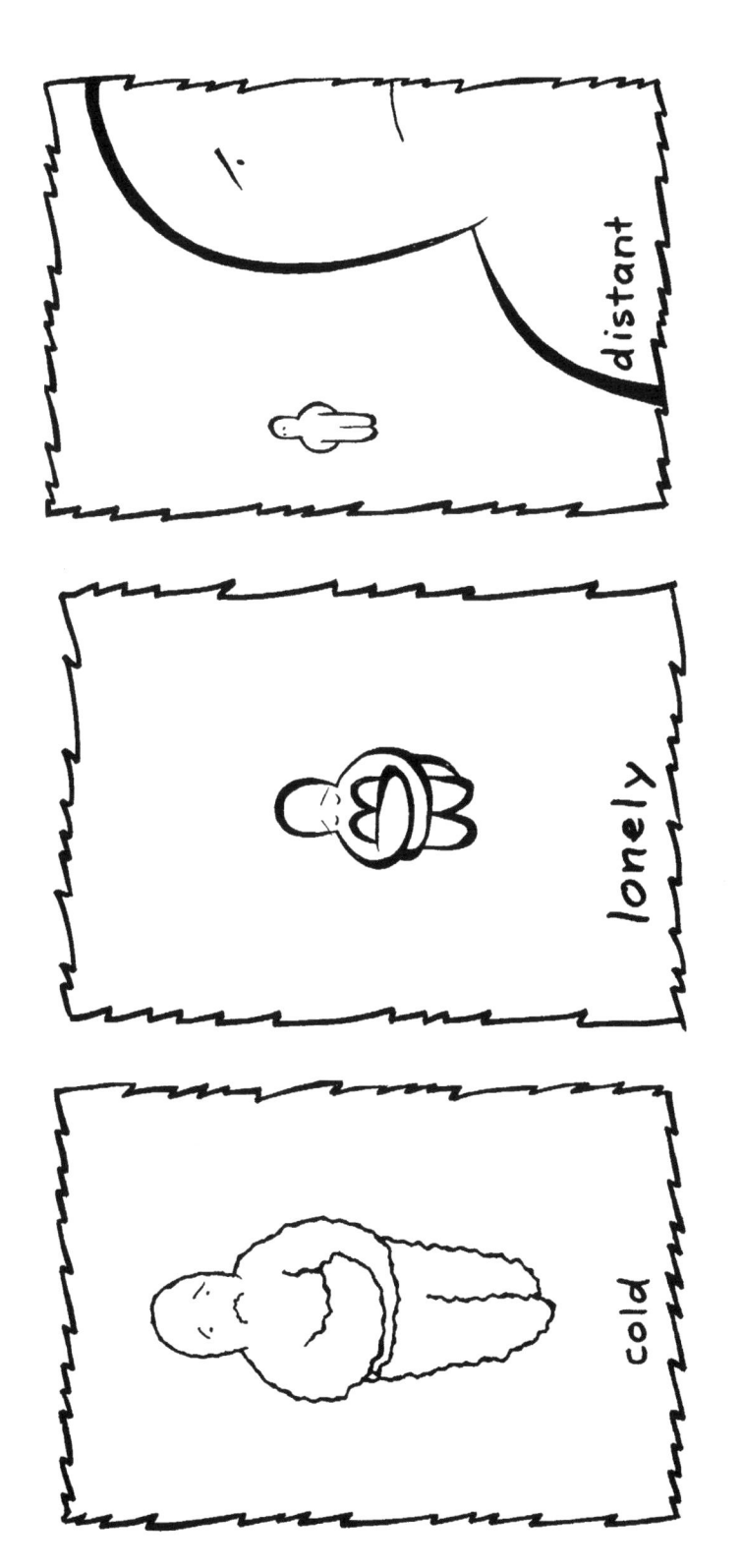

cold | lonely | distant

Tash felt desperately **lonely** when her best friend changed schools.

The Blob Emotional Thesaurus

lost

Individual feeling words

condemned

lost

Without her best friend, Penny felt **lost** all day.

The Blob Emotional Thesaurus

loved

Individual feeling words

open

loved

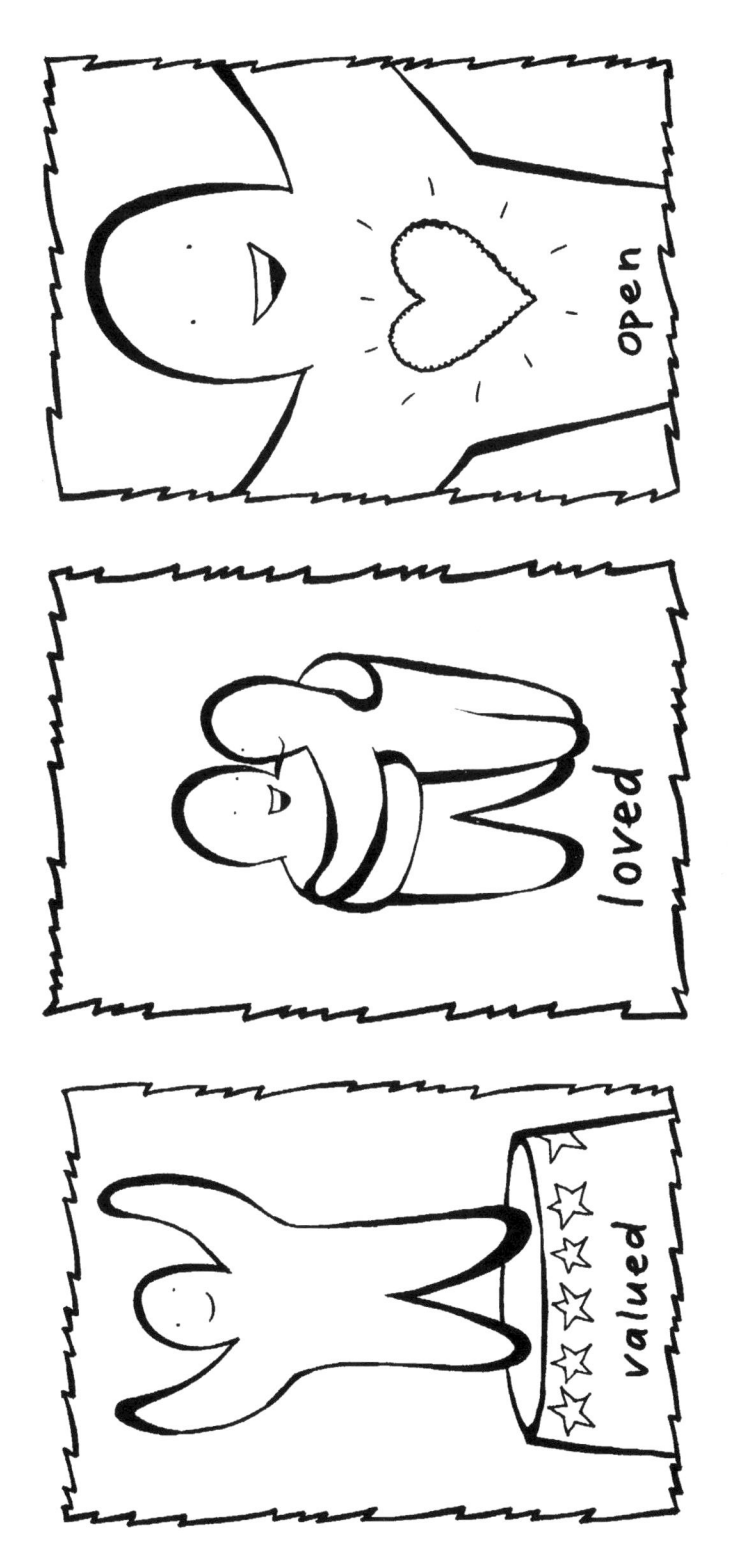

valued

Being home once more, Trudi felt truly loved.

185

The Blob Emotional Thesaurus

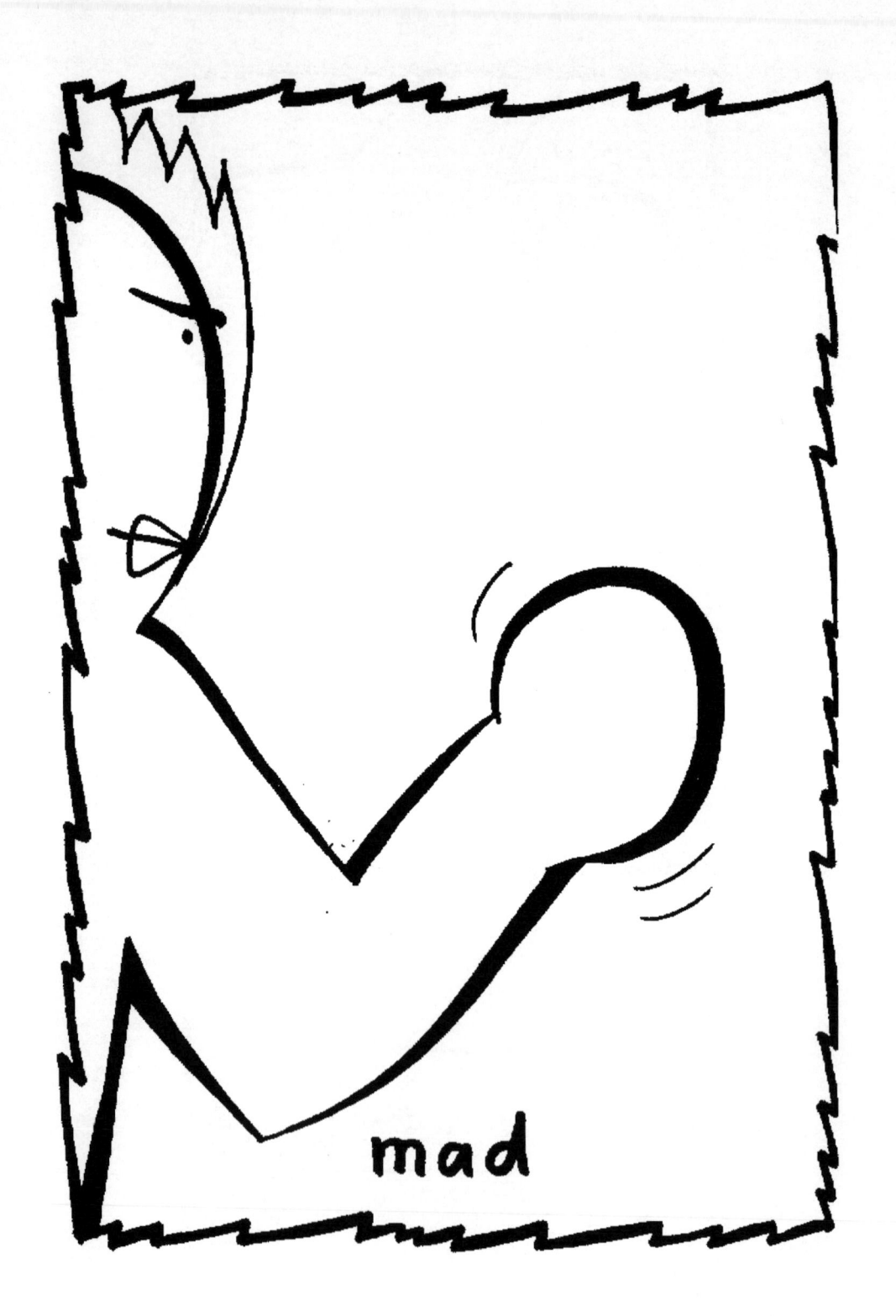

mad

Individual feeling words

angry

mad

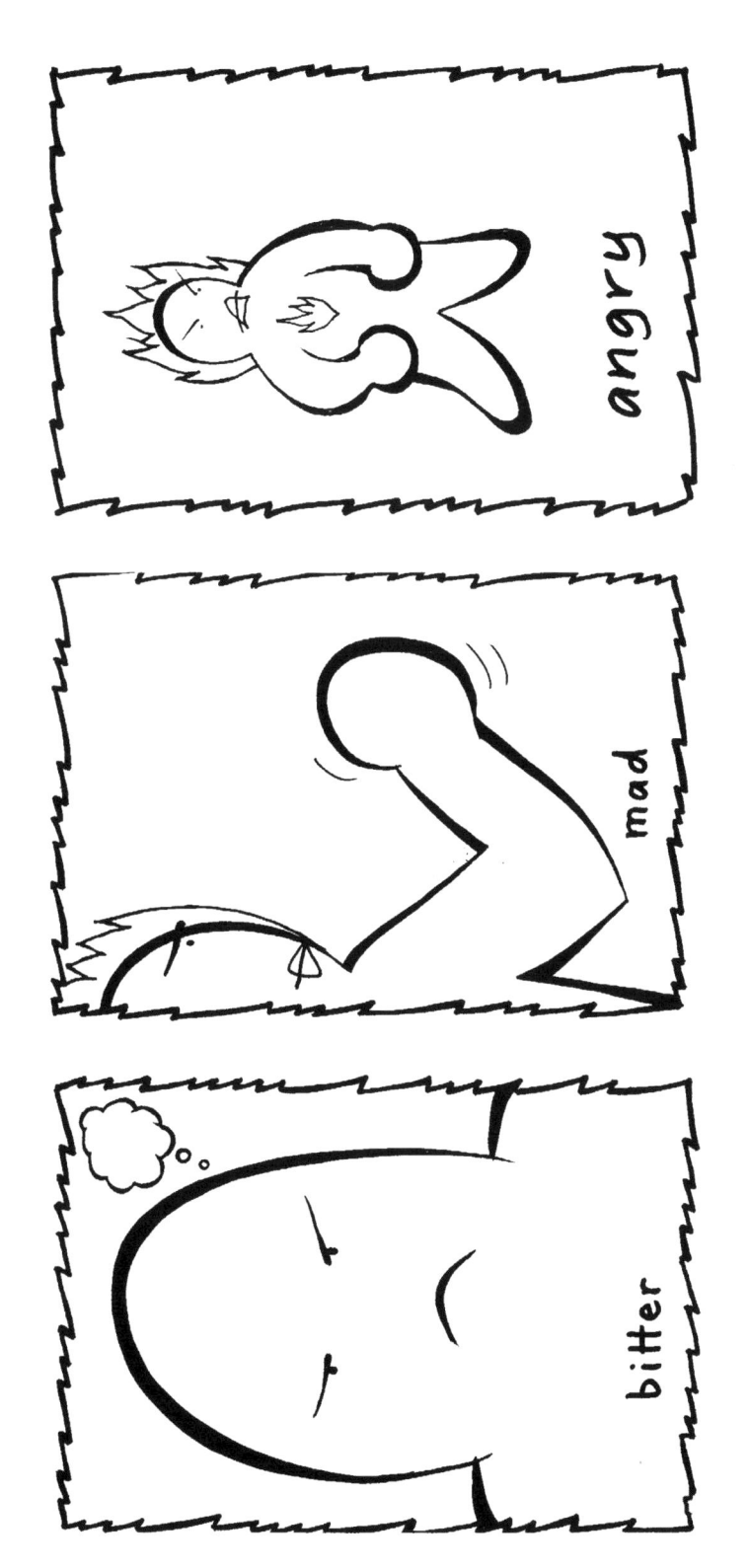

bitter

Freddy was mad with his football team because they had lost once again.

The Blob Emotional Thesaurus

mesmerised

Individual feeling words

fixated

mesmerised

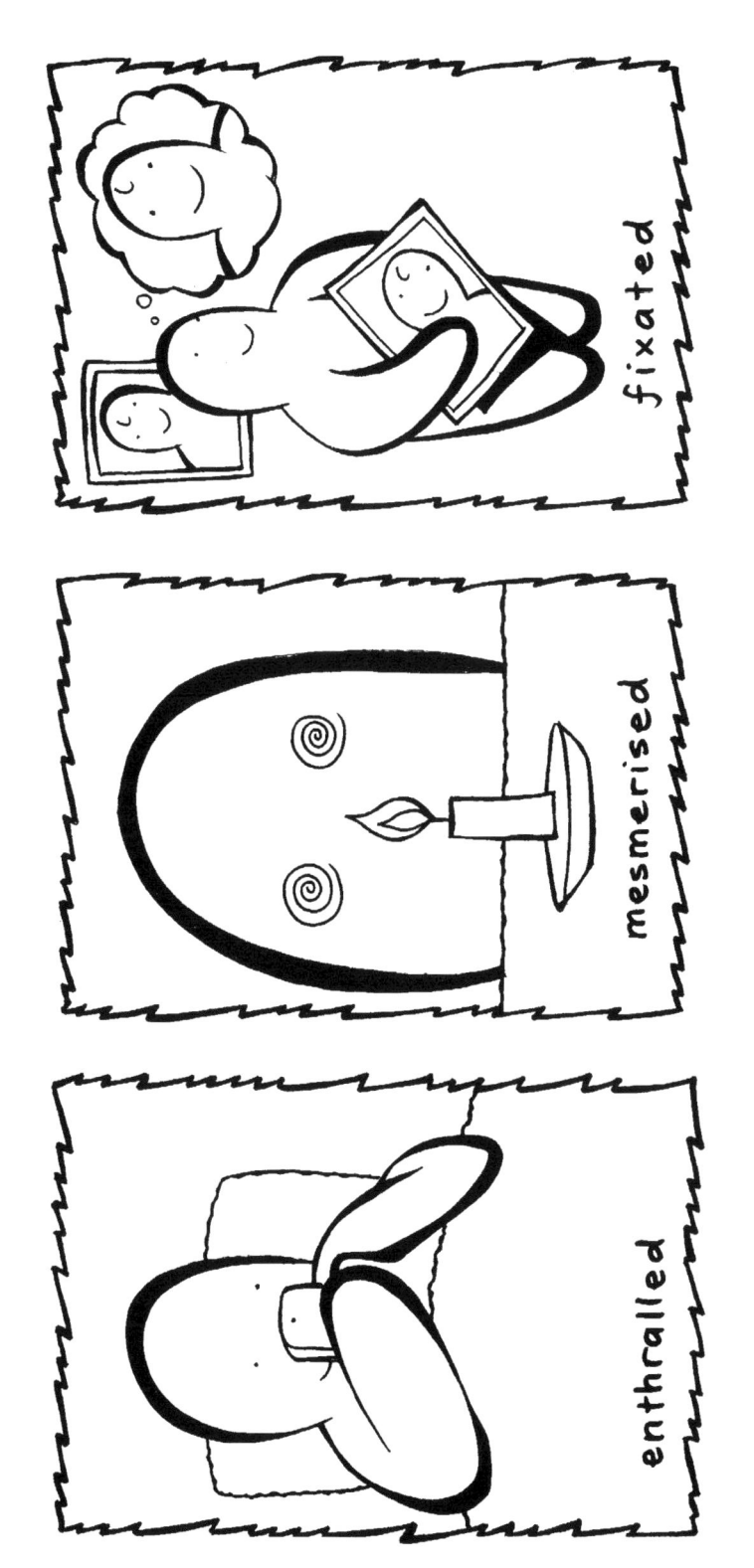

enthralled

Ali was mesmerised by the cat following the moving torchlight.

The Blob Emotional Thesaurus

moody

Individual feeling words

discouraged

moody

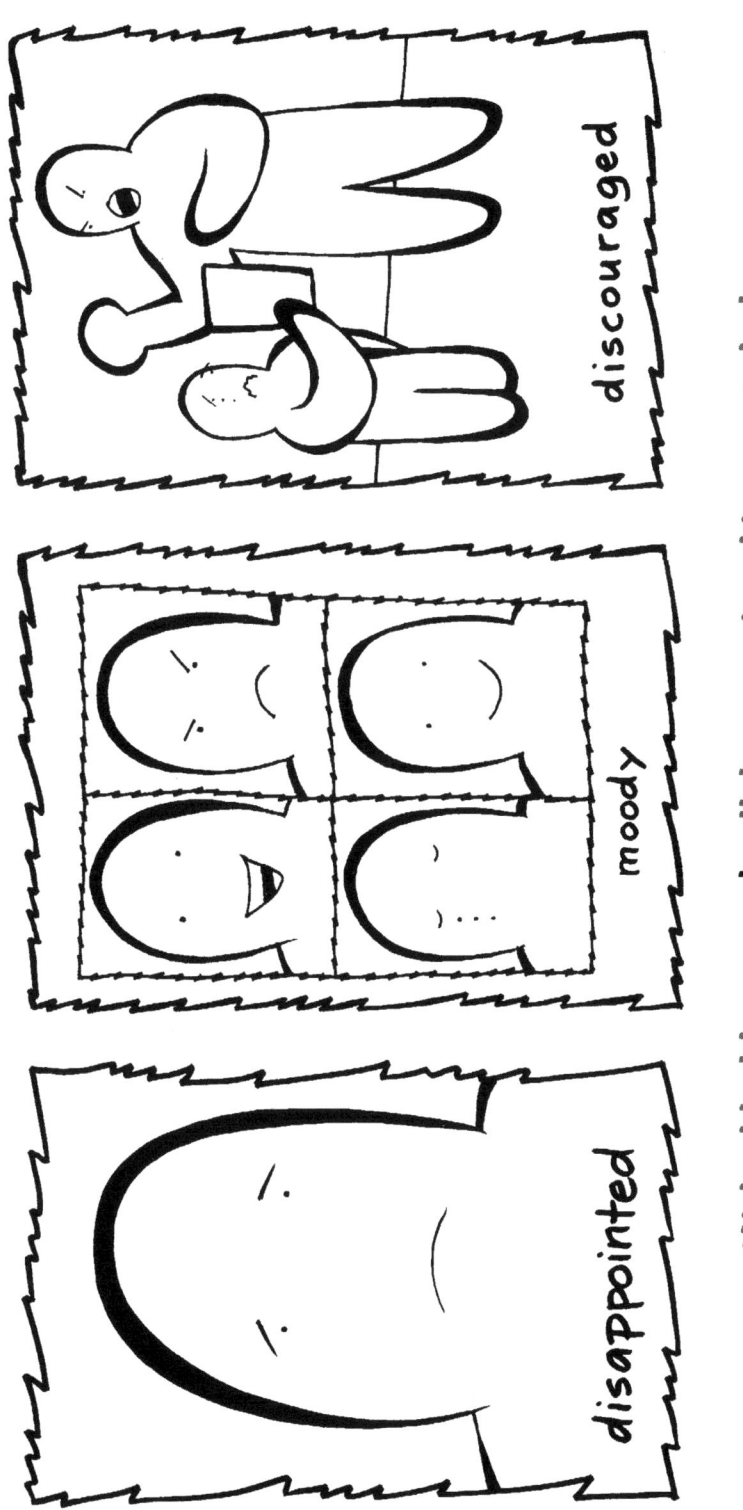

disappointed

Michael had been **moody** all day ever since his parents had broken their promise to him.

The Blob Emotional Thesaurus

negative

Individual feeling words

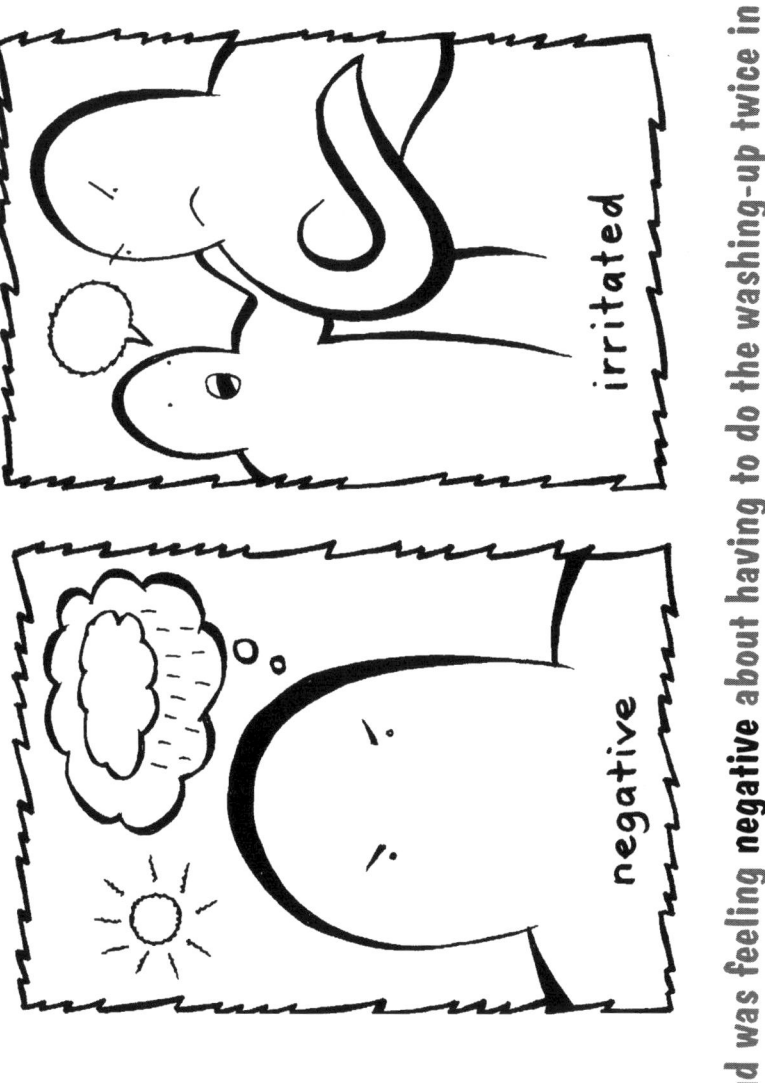

| negative | irritated |

Bud was feeling negative about having to do the washing-up twice in a day.

The Blob Emotional Thesaurus

nervous

Individual feeling words

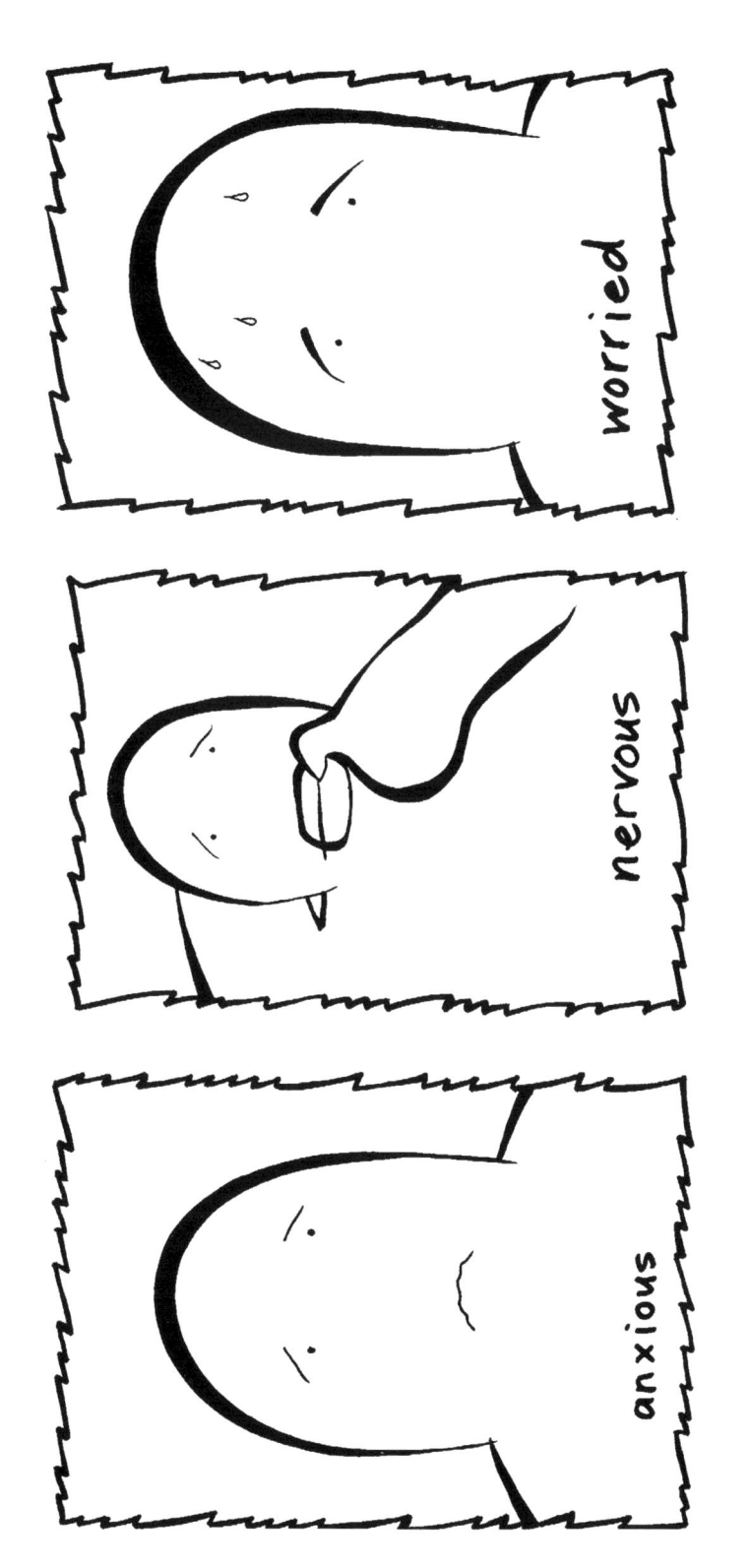

worried

nervous

anxious

Don was **nervous** as he watched the rugby squad get close to the try line.

The Blob Emotional Thesaurus

neutral

Individual feeling words

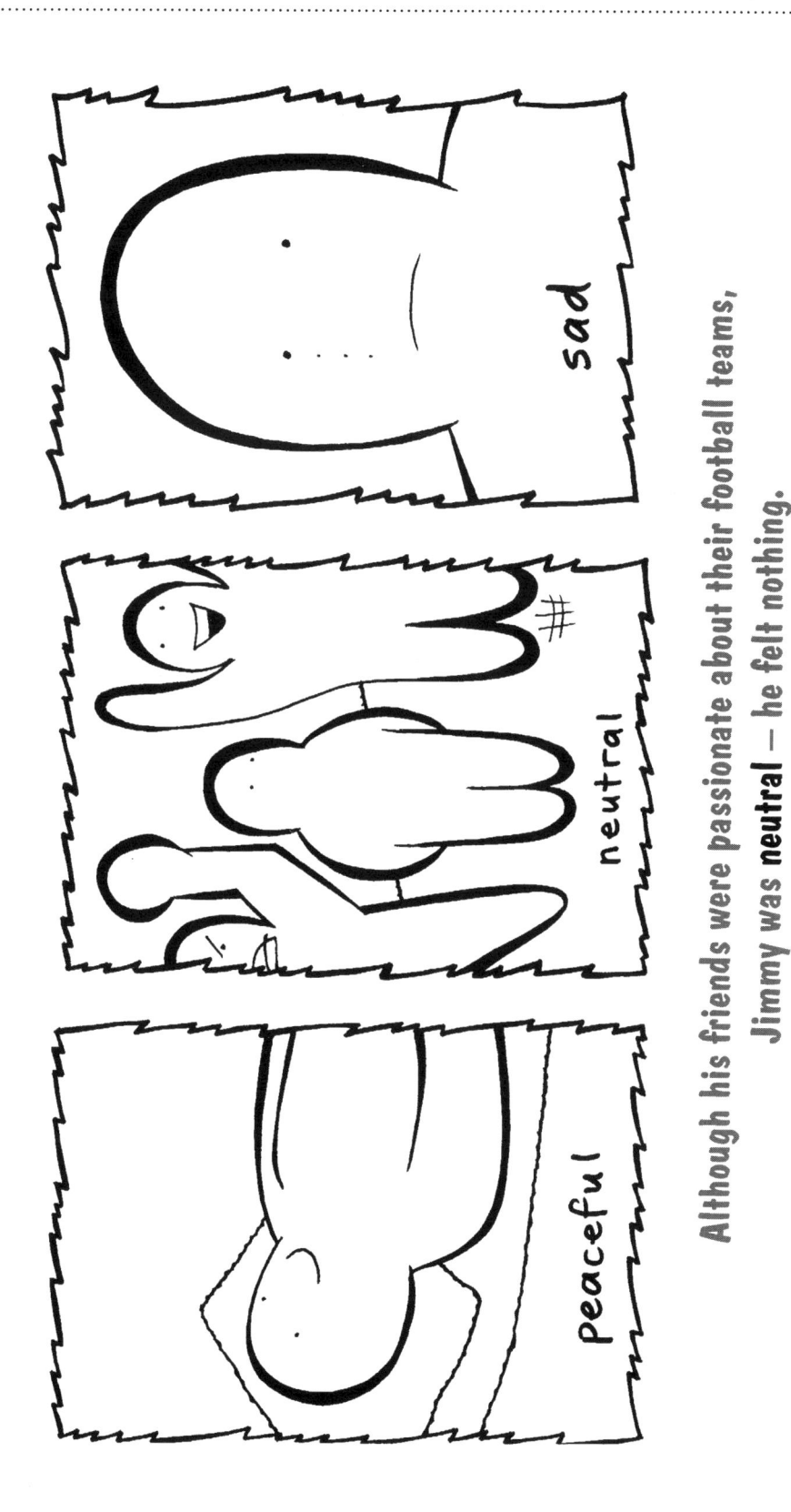

Although his friends were passionate about their football teams, Jimmy was **neutral** – he felt nothing.

sad | neutral | Peaceful

The Blob Emotional Thesaurus

numb

Individual feeling words

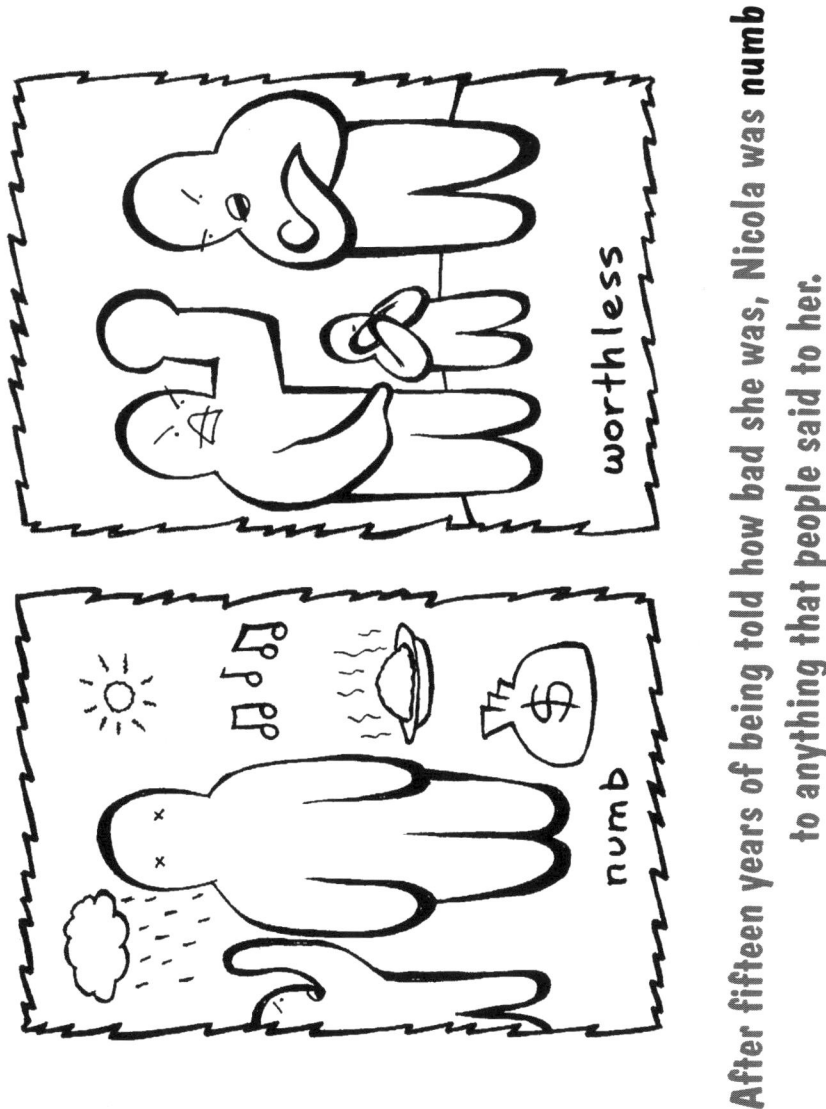

After fifteen years of being told how bad she was, Nicola was *numb* to anything that people said to her.

199

The Blob Emotional Thesaurus

nurtured

Individual feeling words

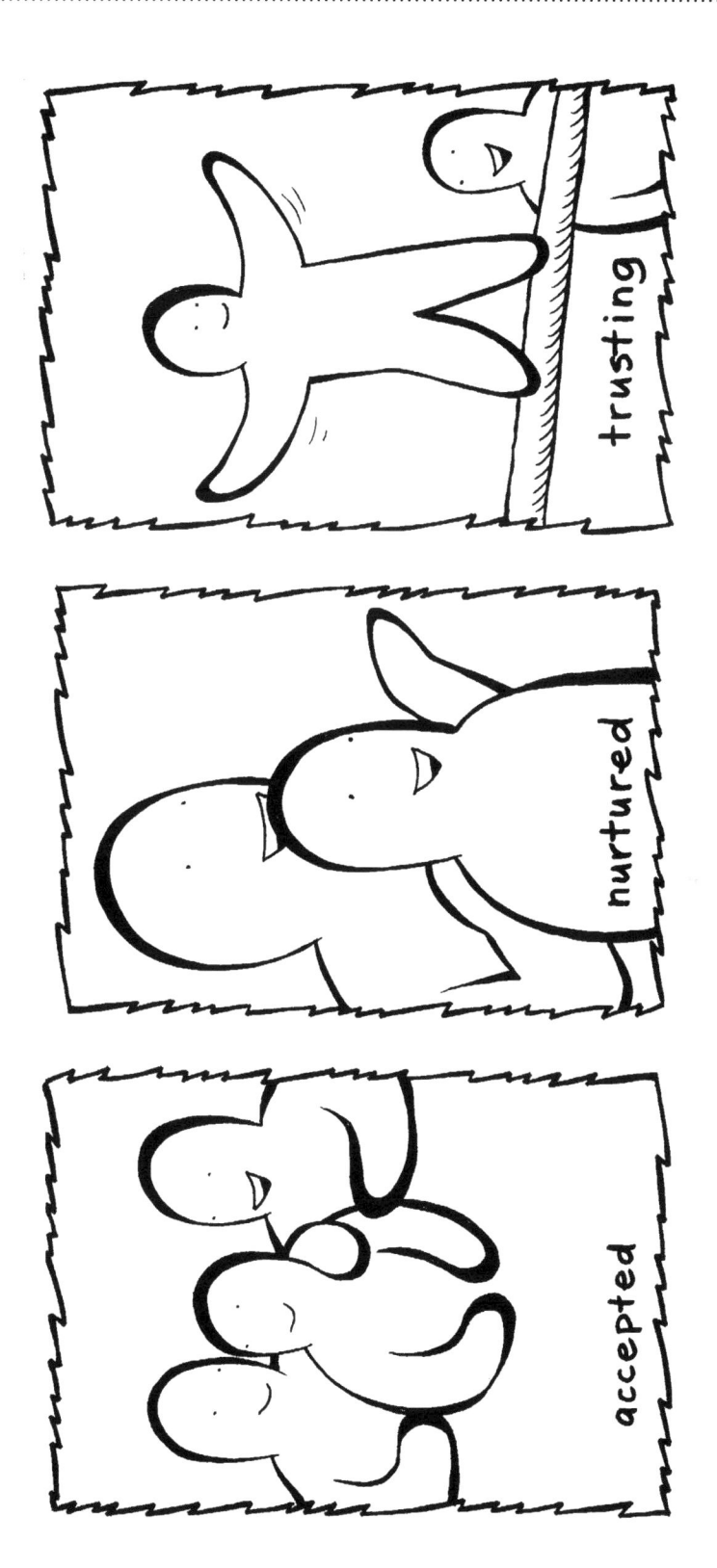

Nadia felt nurtured in her skills and attitude by her sensitive teacher.

trusting

nurtured

accepted

The Blob Emotional Thesaurus

obsessed

Individual feeling words

obsessed

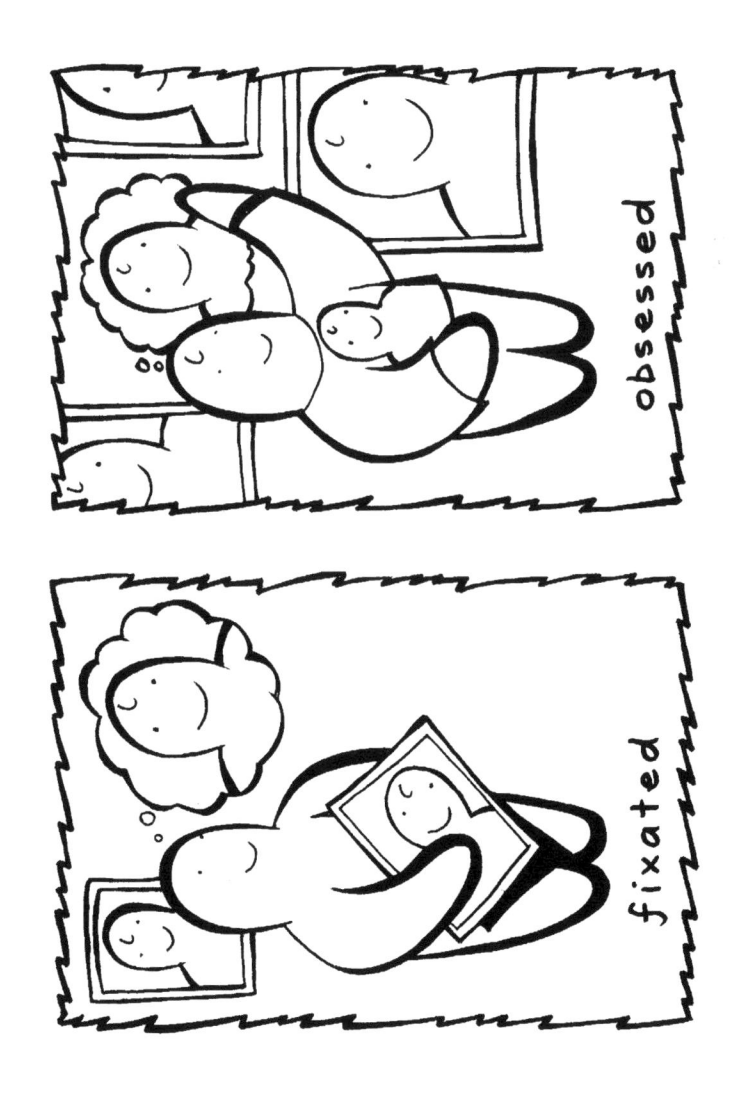

fixated

Tim was **obsessed** by the woman who starred in his favourite film series.

The Blob Emotional Thesaurus

odd

Individual feeling words

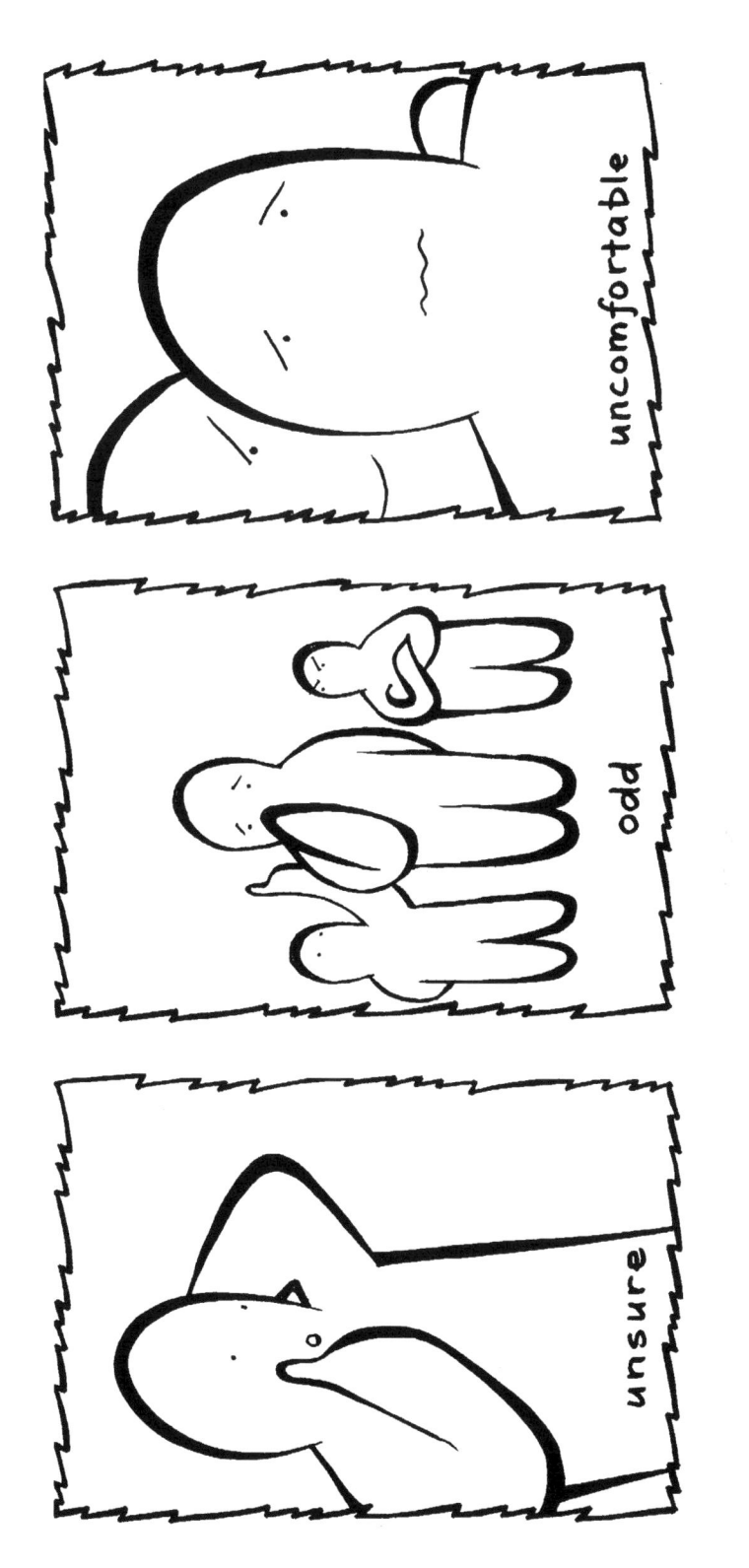

uncomfortable

odd

unsure

Gil always felt **odd** whilst standing next to his friends because he was seven feet tall.

The Blob Emotional Thesaurus

open

Individual feeling words

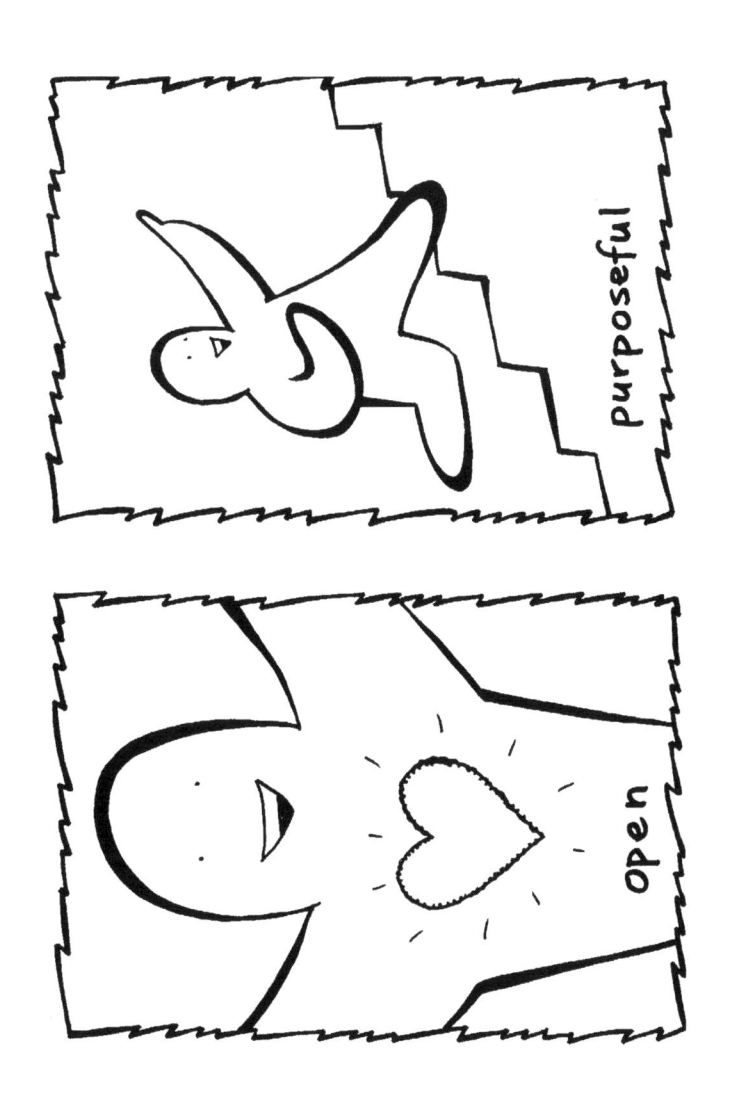

open   **purposeful**

Tina was **open** to all sorts of possibilities as she walked into the adventure park.

optimistic

Individual feeling words

delighted

optimistic

Proud

David was optimistic about his future career in politics.

The Blob Emotional Thesaurus

organised

Individual feeling words

purposeful

organised

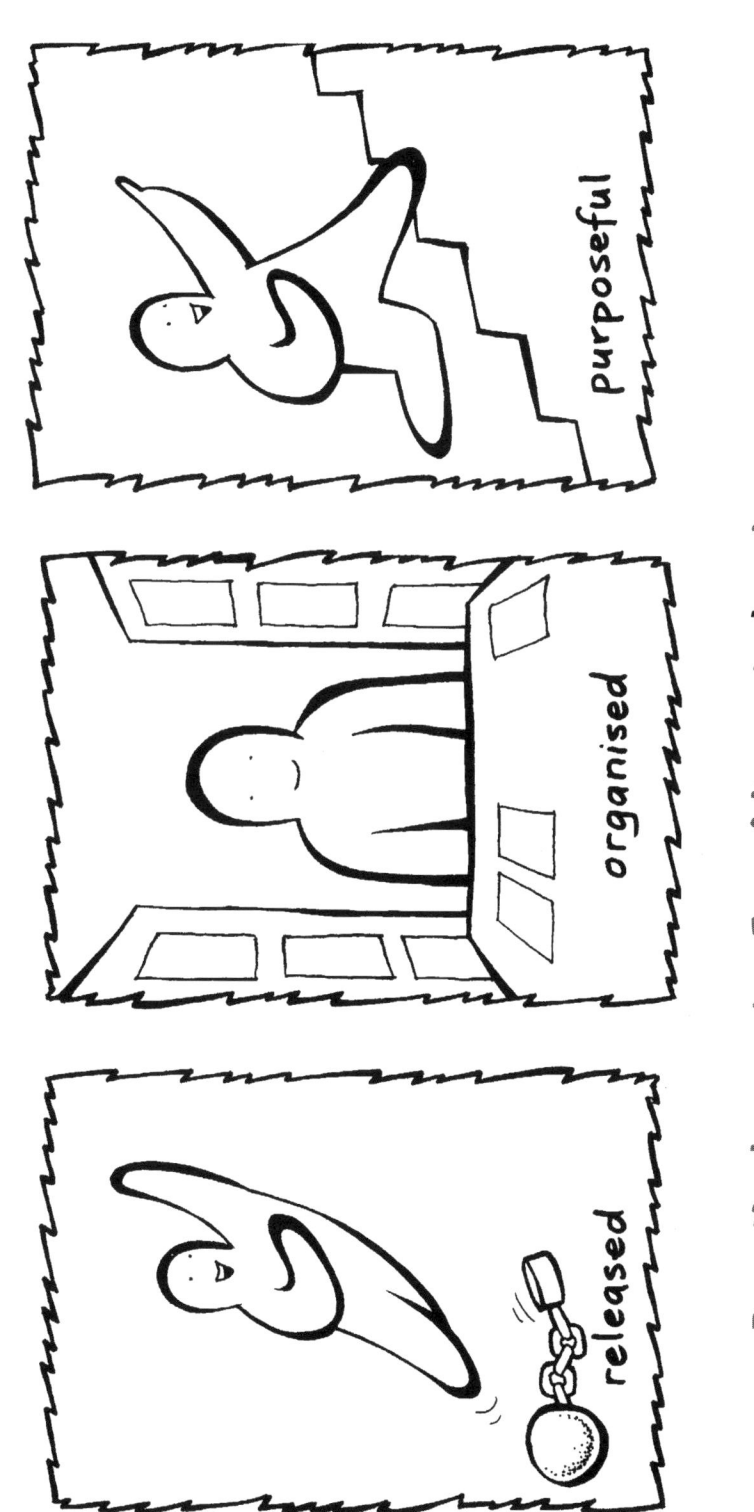

released

Every Monday morning, Tanya felt **organised** as she sat at an empty desk before work began.

The Blob Emotional Thesaurus

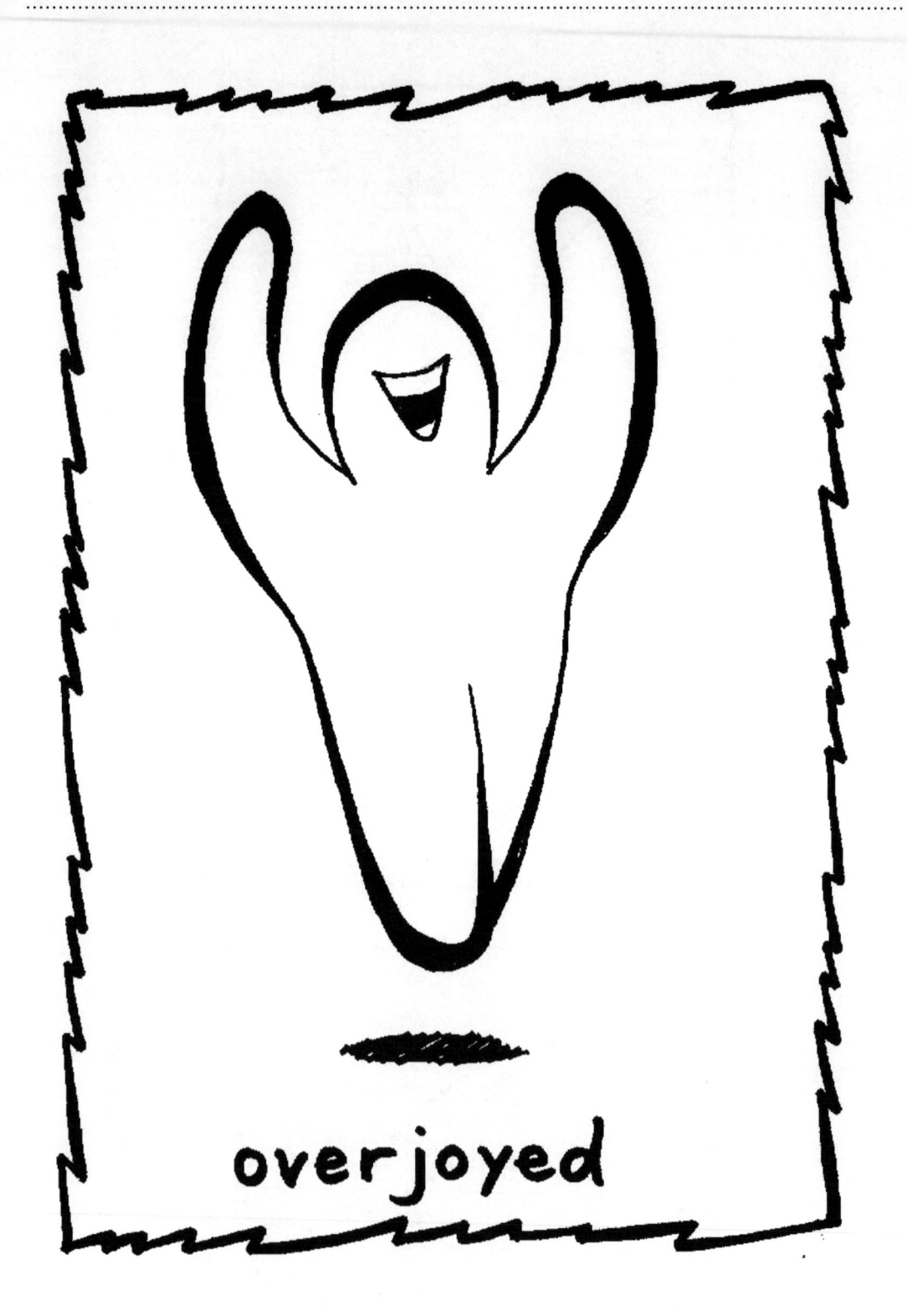

overjoyed

Individual feeling words

thrilled

overjoyed

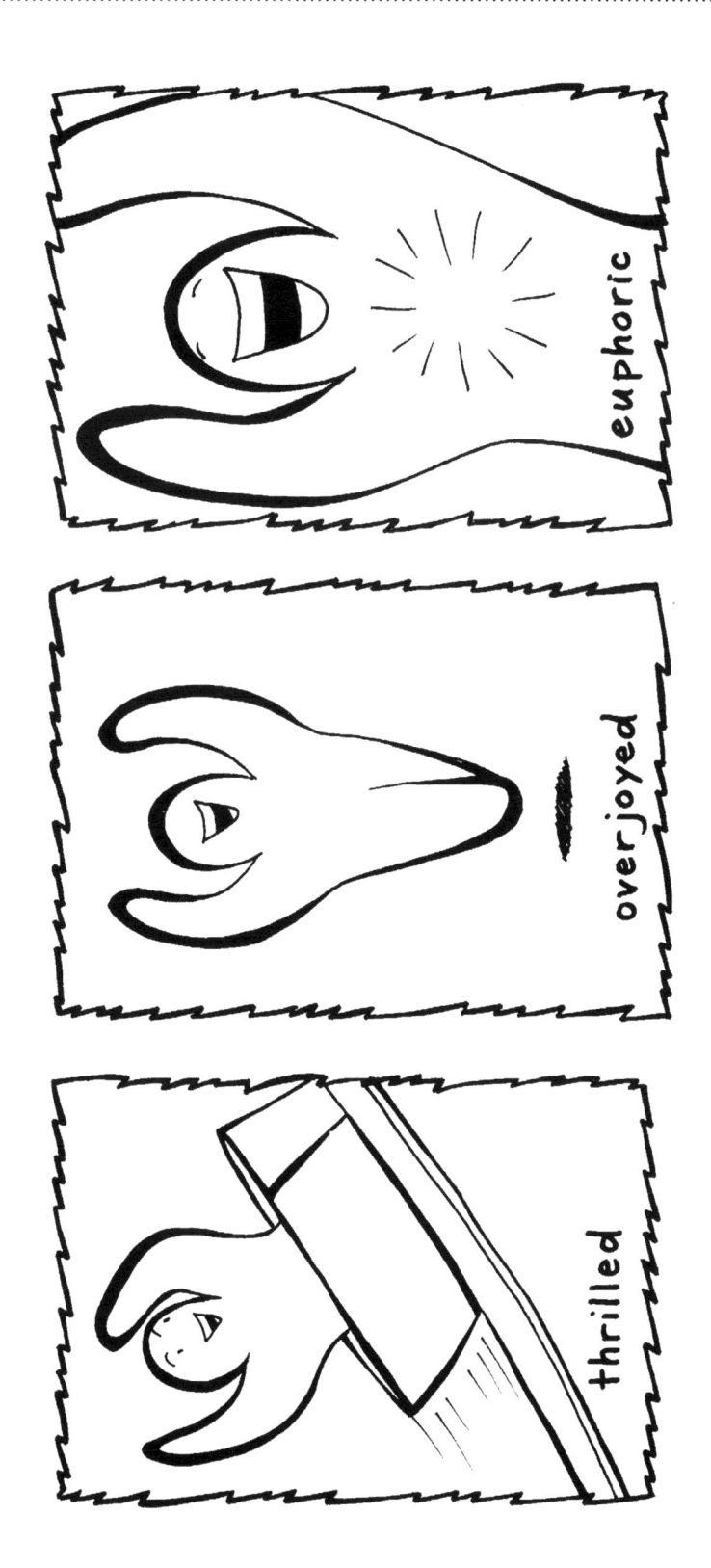

euphoric

Hannah was overjoyed when she heard her first song being played on the radio!

213

The Blob Emotional Thesaurus

panic-stricken

Individual feeling words

terrified · panic-stricken · paralysed

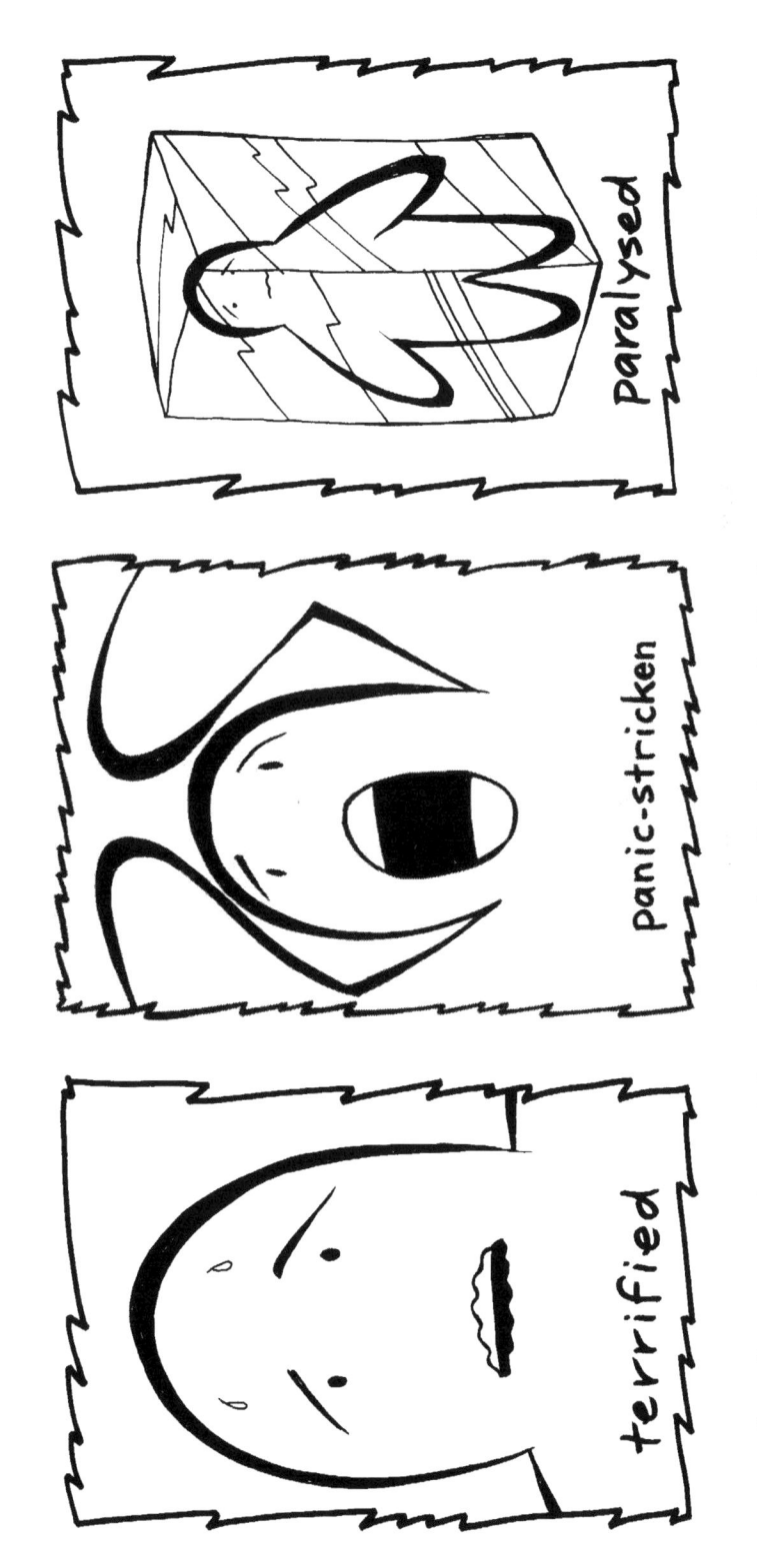

Jacob was panic-stricken when the shadow in the bedroom moved towards him.

The Blob Emotional Thesaurus

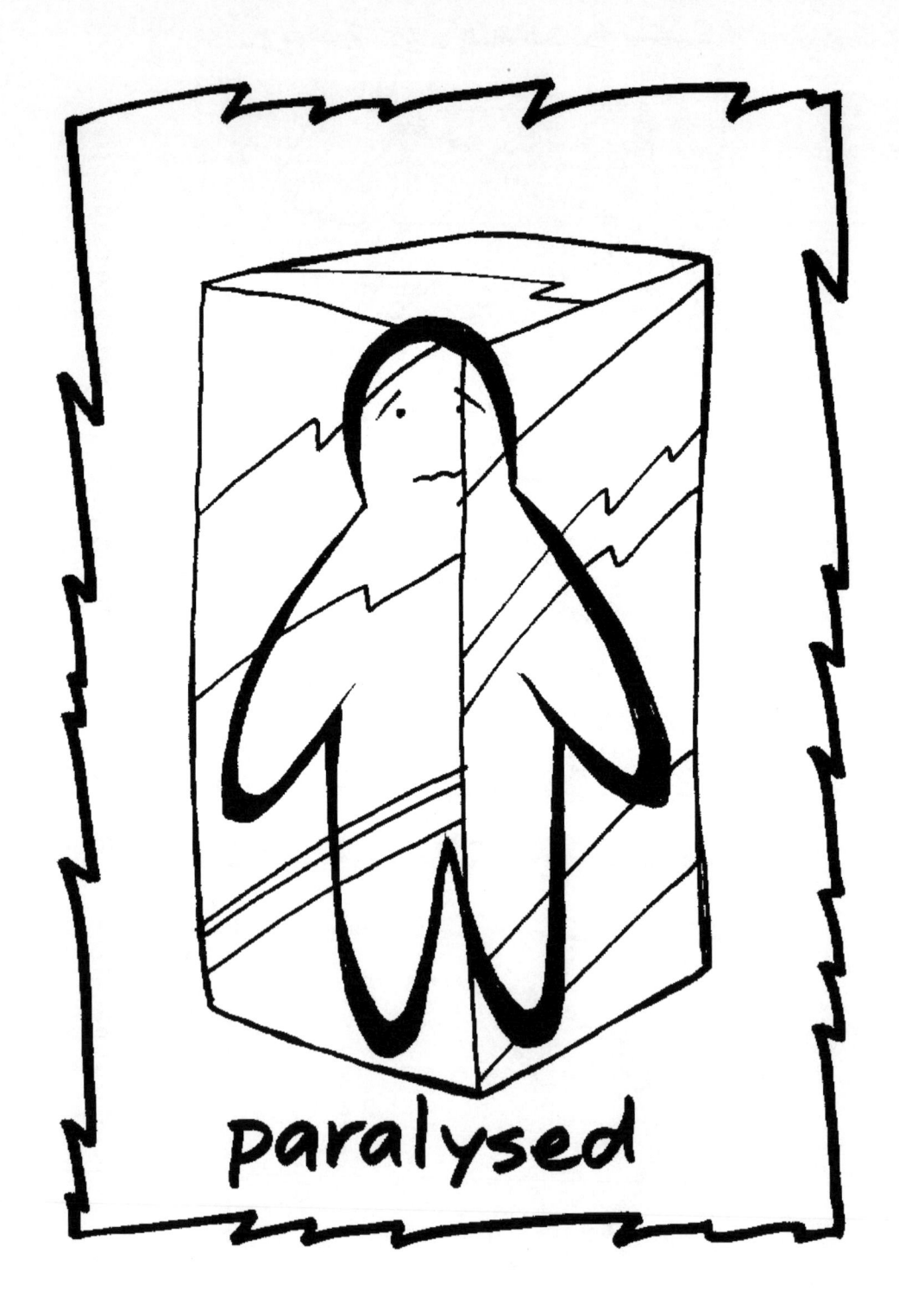

paralysed

Individual feeling words

panic-stricken

paralysed

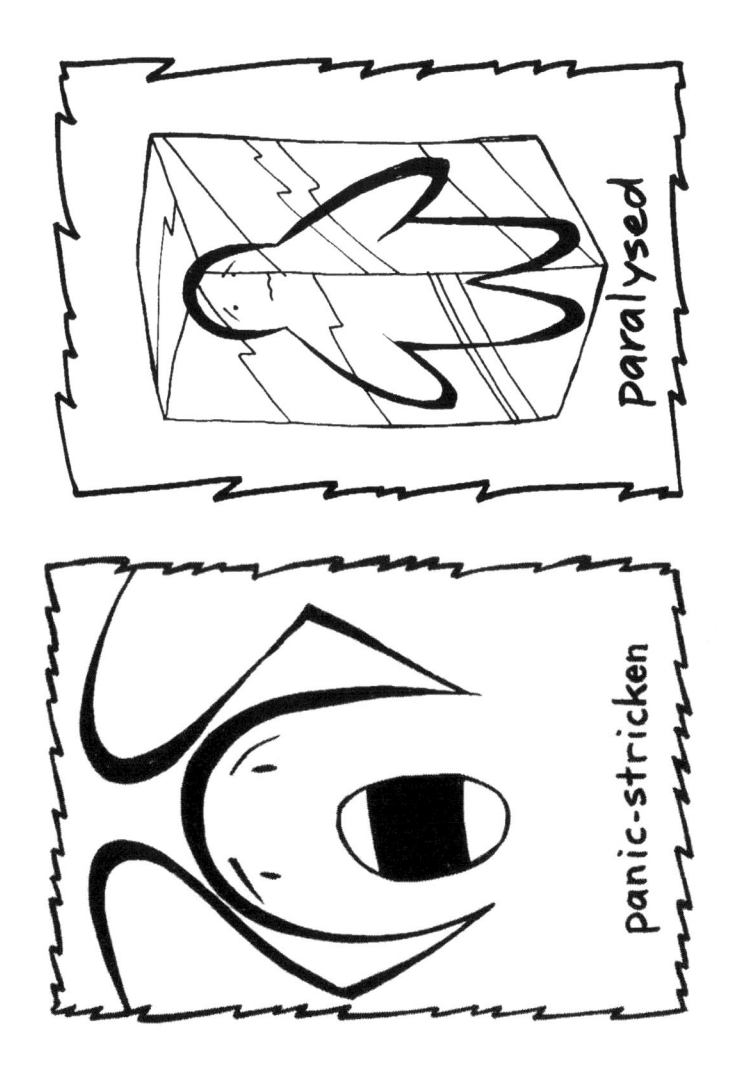

Ben was paralysed with fear as the spider crawled across his stomach!

The Blob Emotional Thesaurus

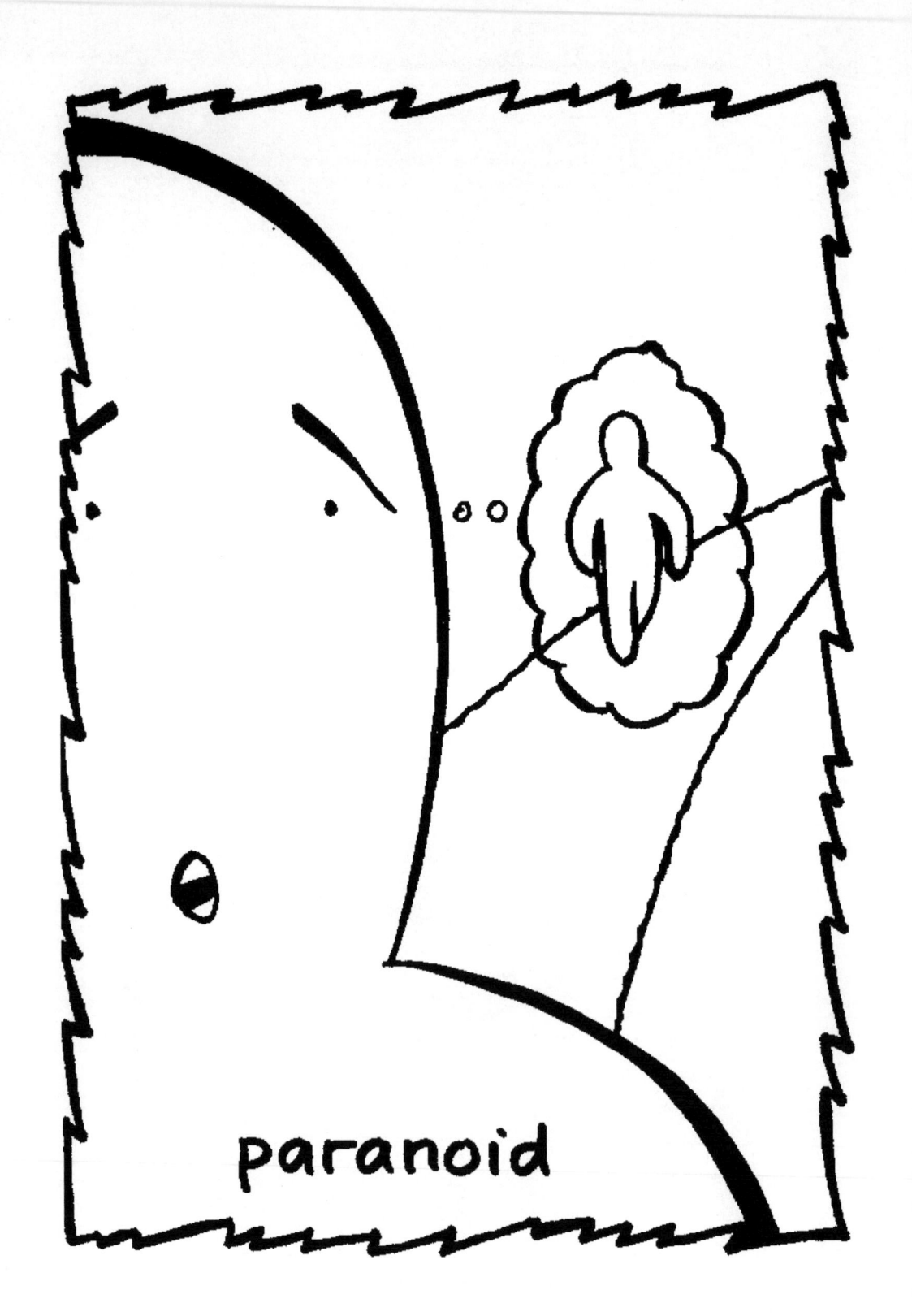

paranoid

Individual feeling words

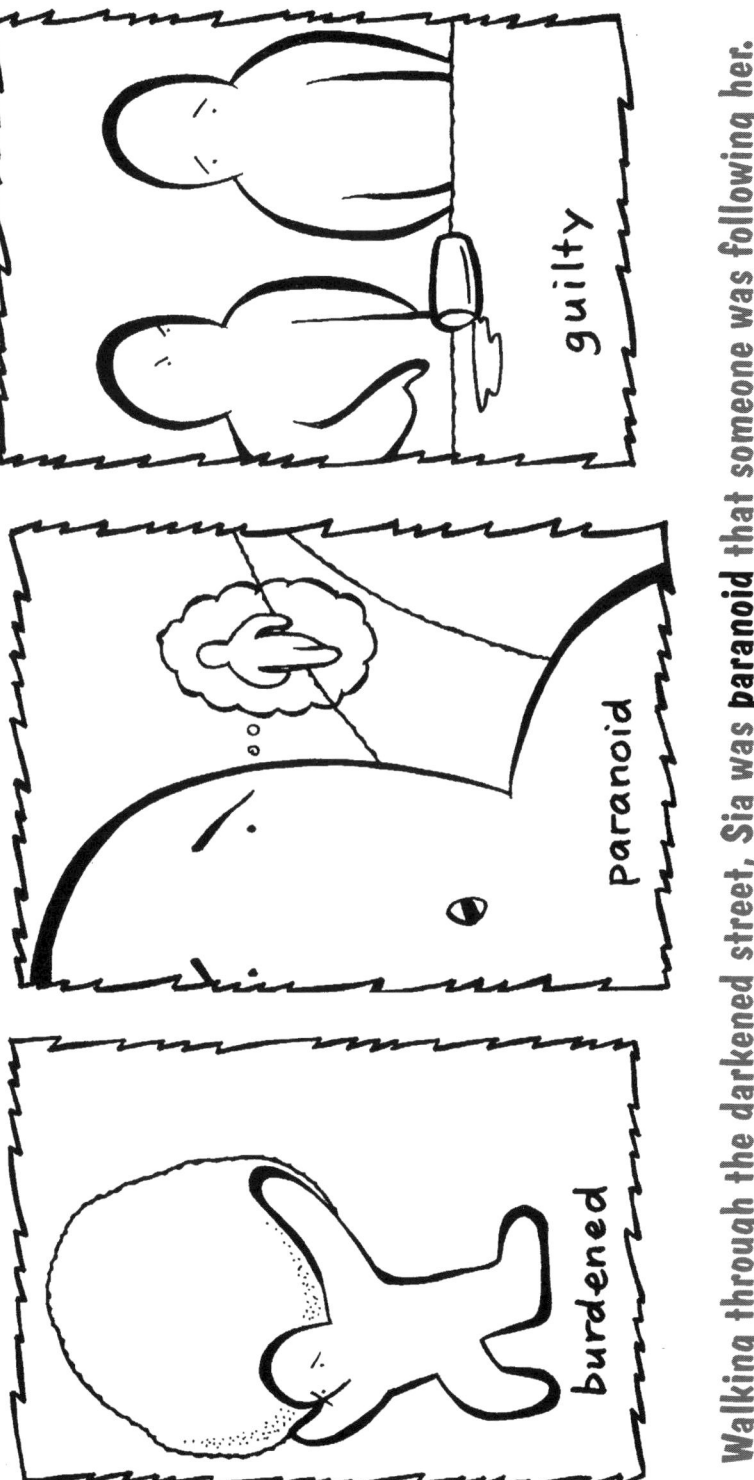

guilty

paranoid

burdened

Walking through the darkened street, Sia was **paranoid** that someone was following her.

The Blob Emotional Thesaurus

patient

Individual feeling words

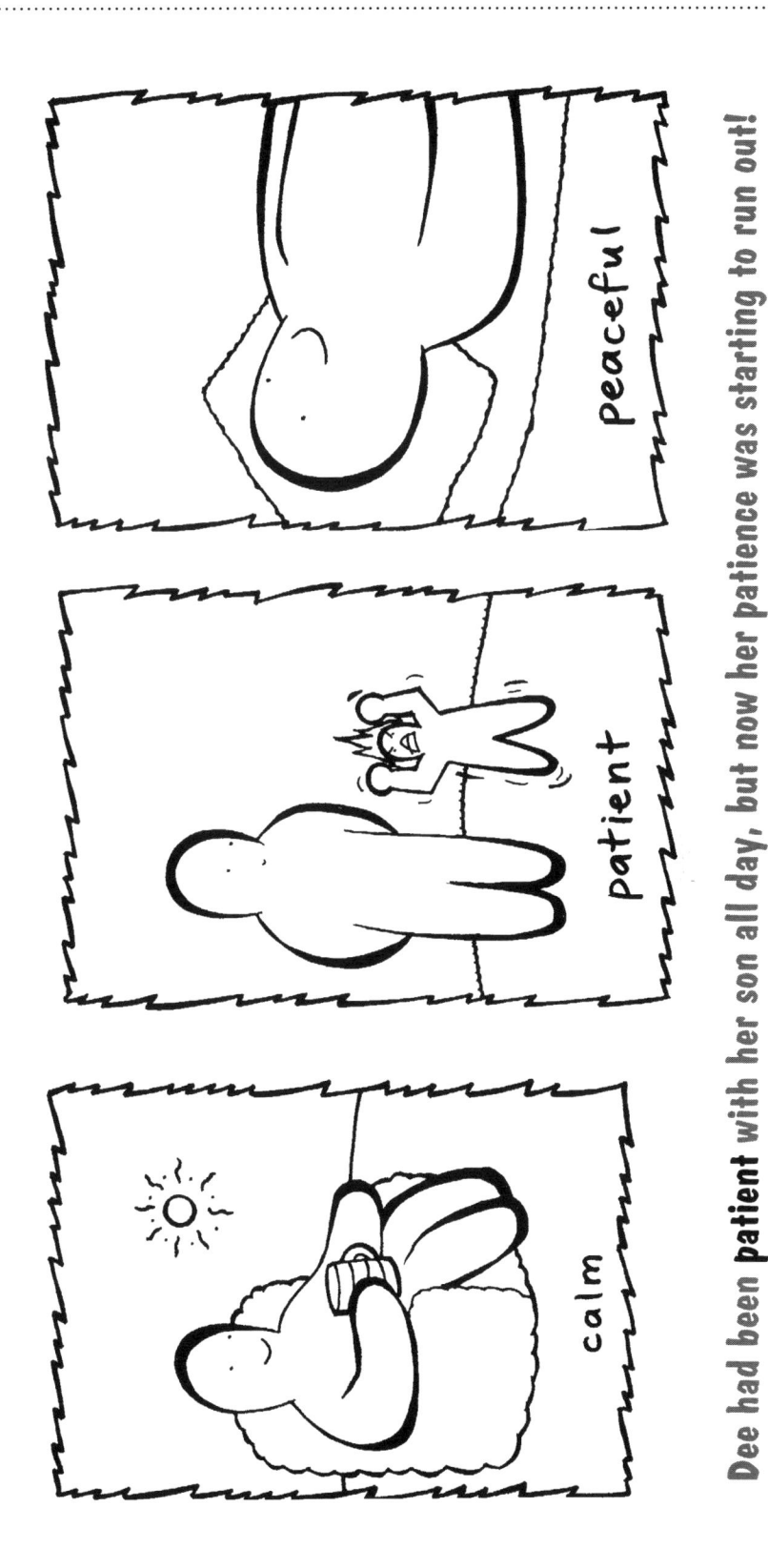

calm

patient

peaceful

Dee had been **patient** with her son all day, but now her patience was starting to run out!

The Blob Emotional Thesaurus

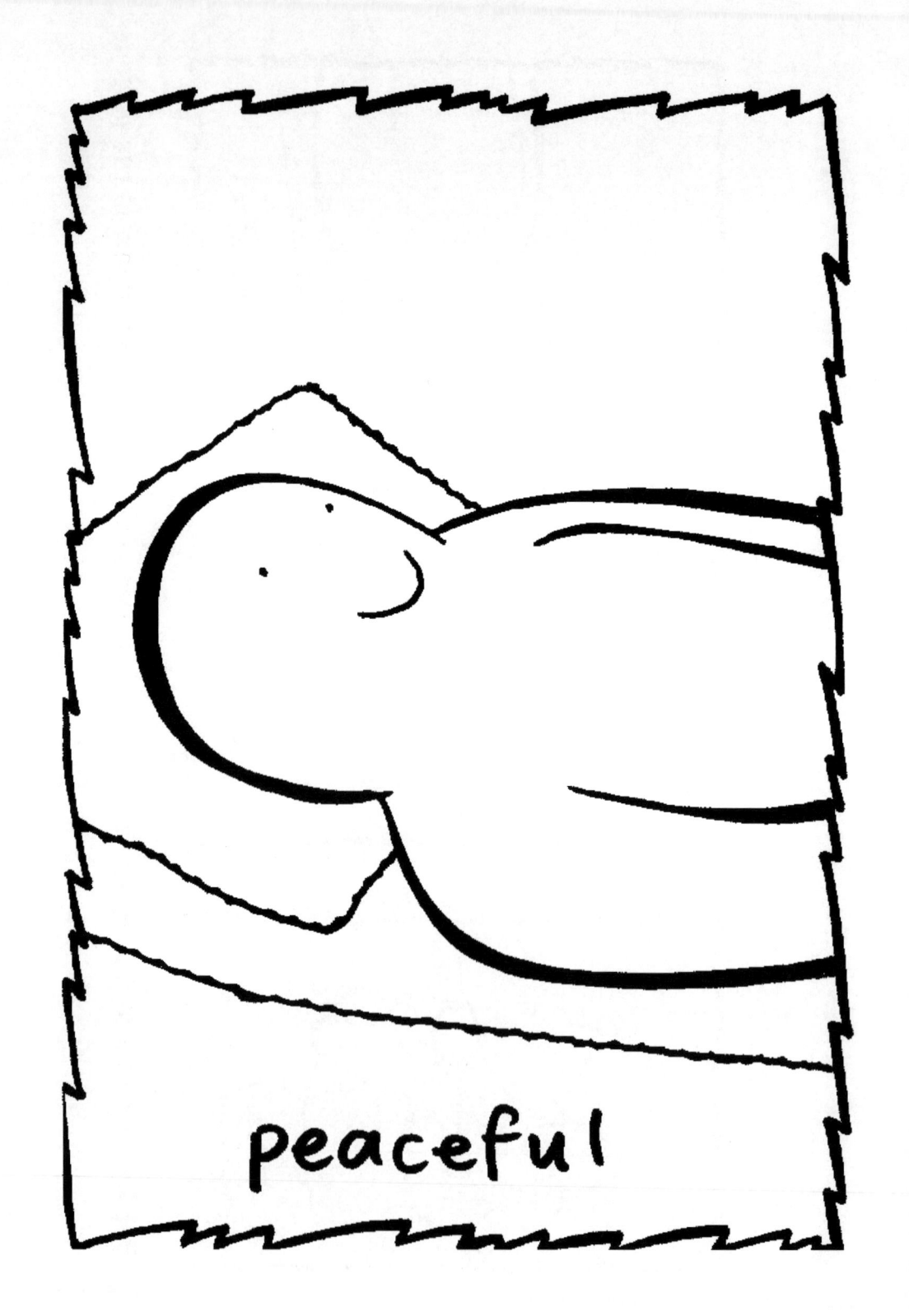

peaceful

Individual feeling words

amused

peaceful

patient

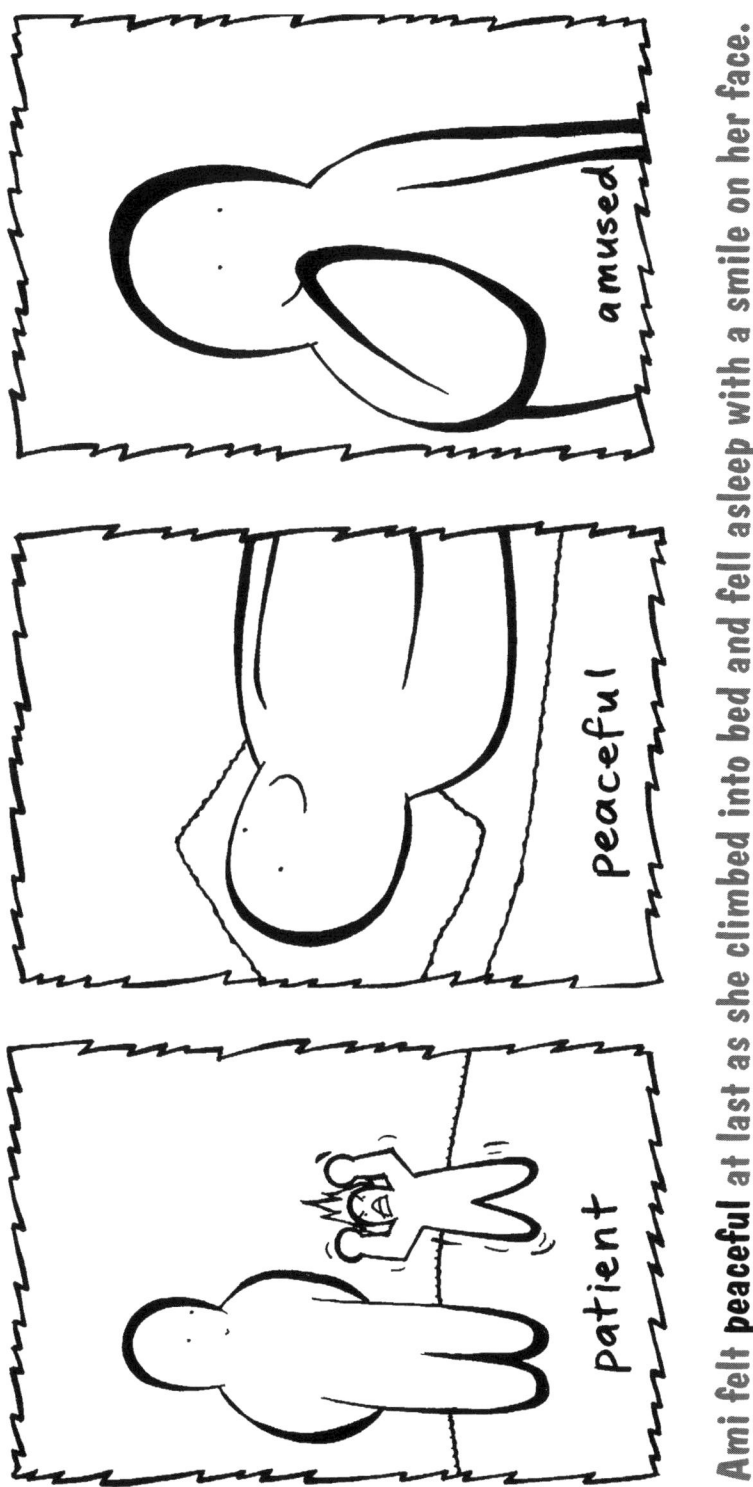

Ami felt **peaceful** at last as she climbed into bed and fell asleep with a smile on her face.

The Blob Emotional Thesaurus

pessimistic

Individual feeling words

upset

pessimistic

hurt

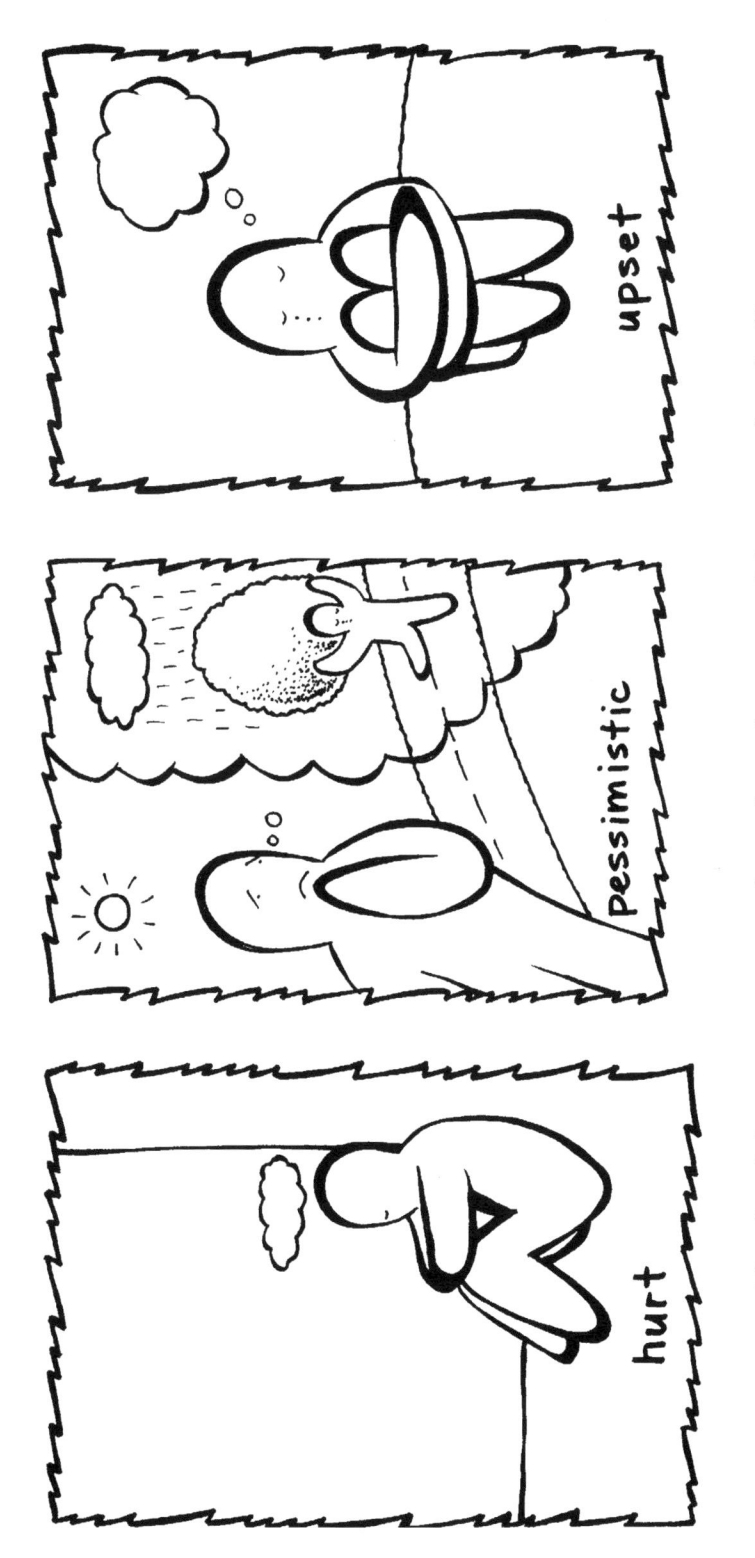

Charlie felt *pessimistic* about his chances of being a footballer.

The Blob Emotional Thesaurus

pleased

Individual feeling words

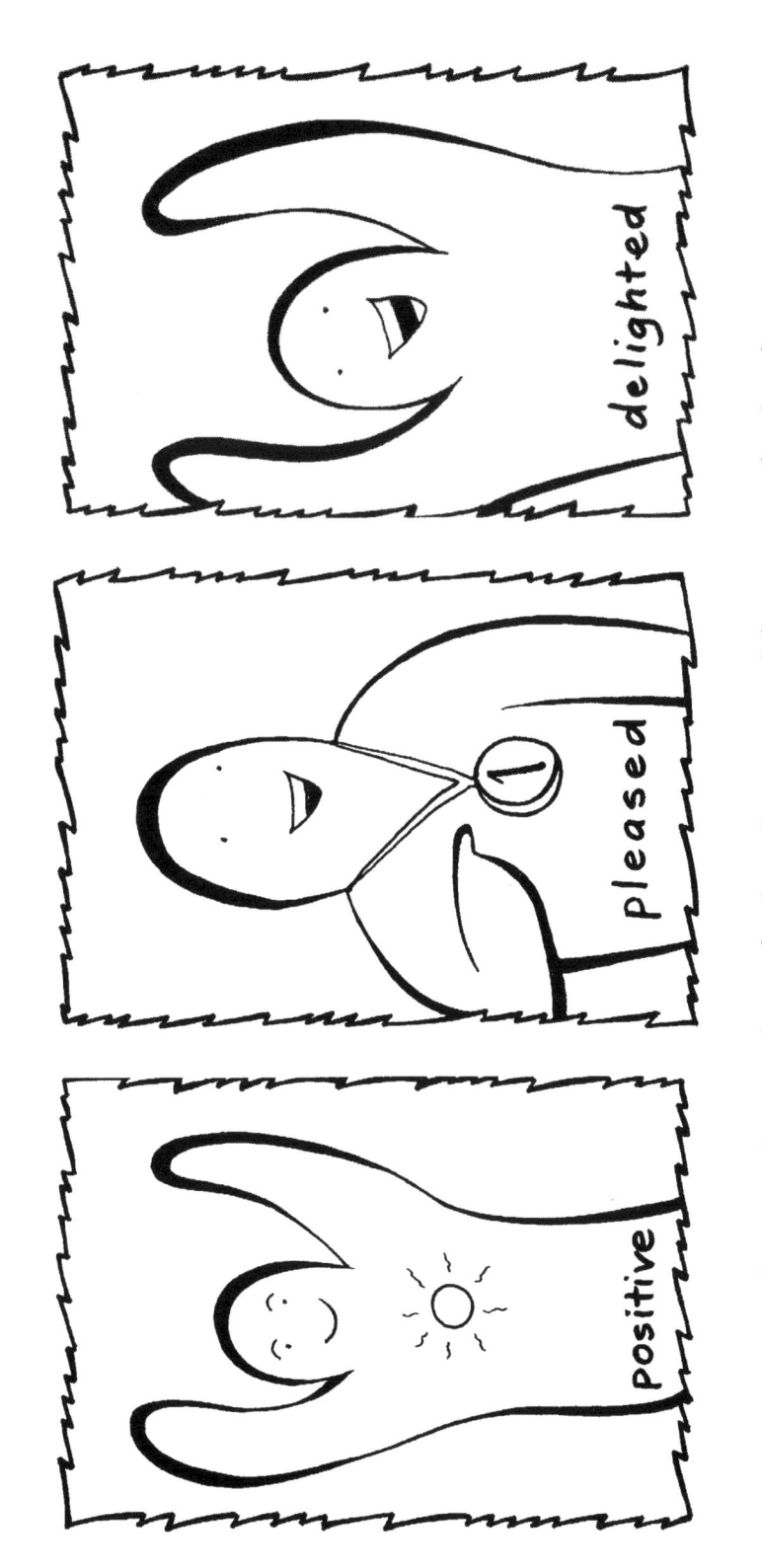

Mohammed was **pleased** when he received first prize for kindness and getting along with others.

delighted

pleased

positive

The Blob Emotional Thesaurus

positive

Individual feeling words

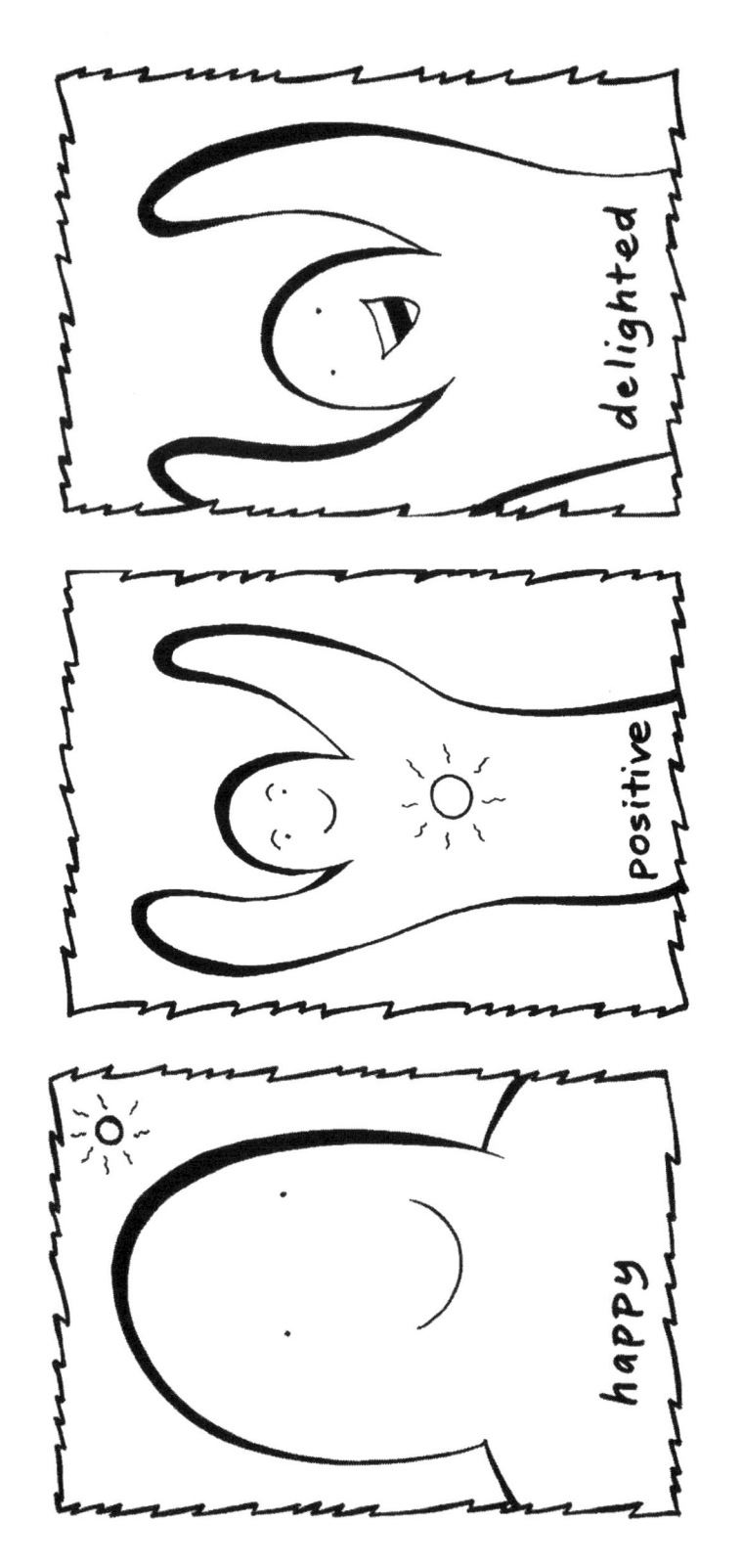

Heading off to church, Niall felt **positive** that something special was going to happen.

happy · positive · delighted

The Blob Emotional Thesaurus

possessive

Individual feeling words

Tilly felt very **possessive** about her collection of speciality spoons.

The Blob Emotional Thesaurus

pressured

Individual feeling words

burdened

pressured

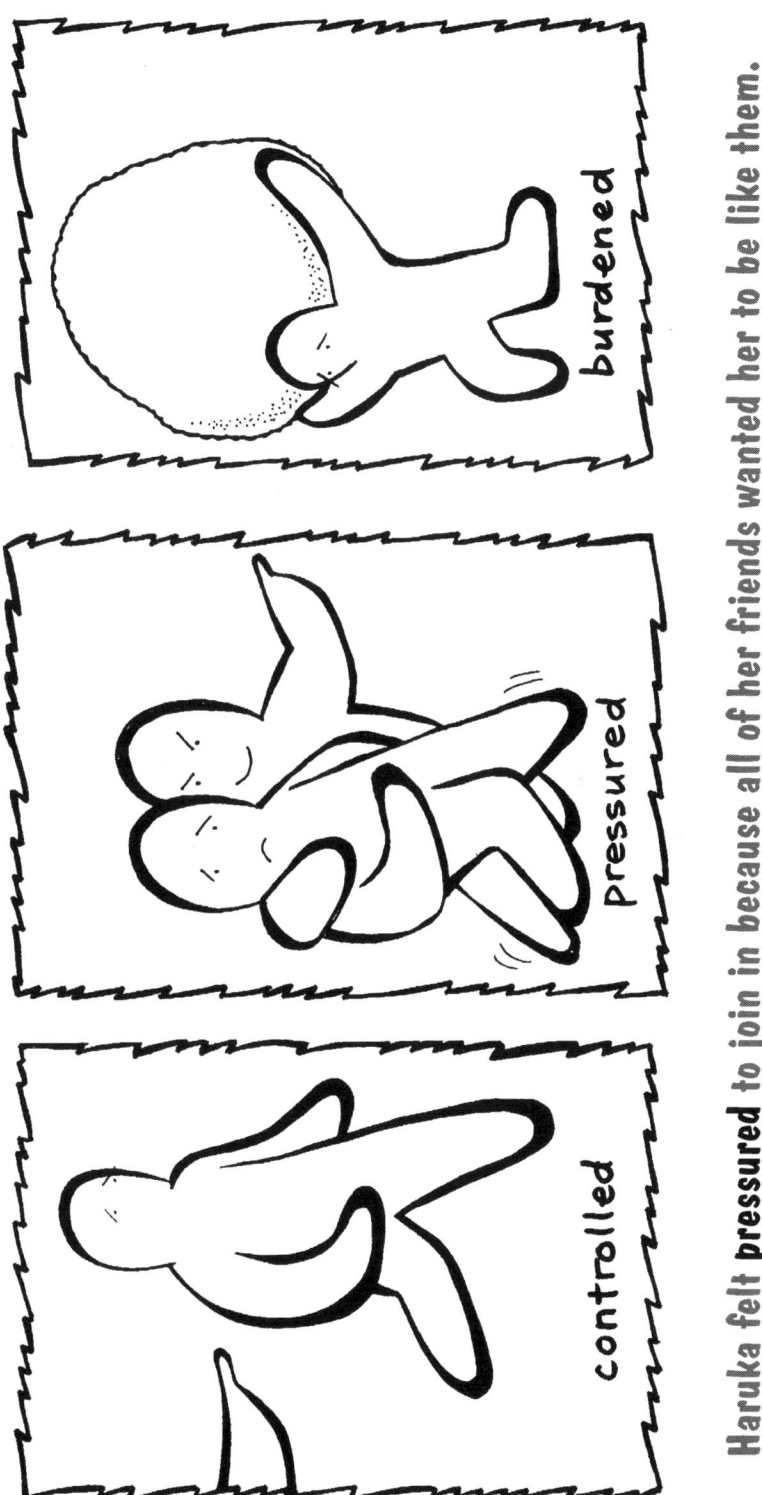

controlled

Haruka felt pressured to join in because all of her friends wanted her to be like them.

The Blob Emotional Thesaurus

proud

Individual feeling words

respected

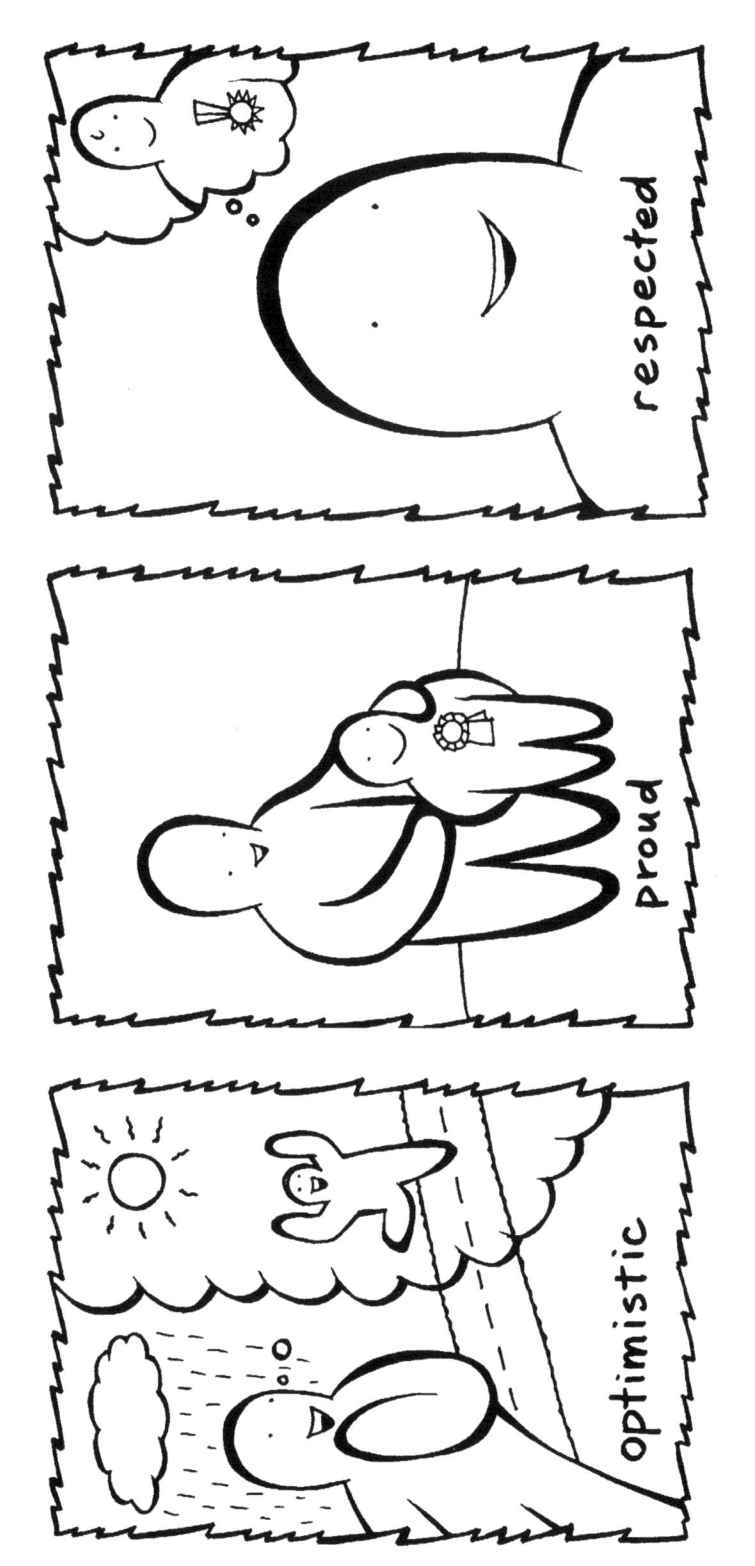

Proud

optimistic

Adrian was **proud** of Dylan's achievements, especially as he was only ten.

The Blob Emotional Thesaurus

purposeful

Individual feeling words

Liam felt **purposeful** as he headed off to the shops to buy his mother an Easter egg.

free

purposeful

organised

237

The Blob Emotional Thesaurus

puzzled

Individual feeling words

puzzled

bothered

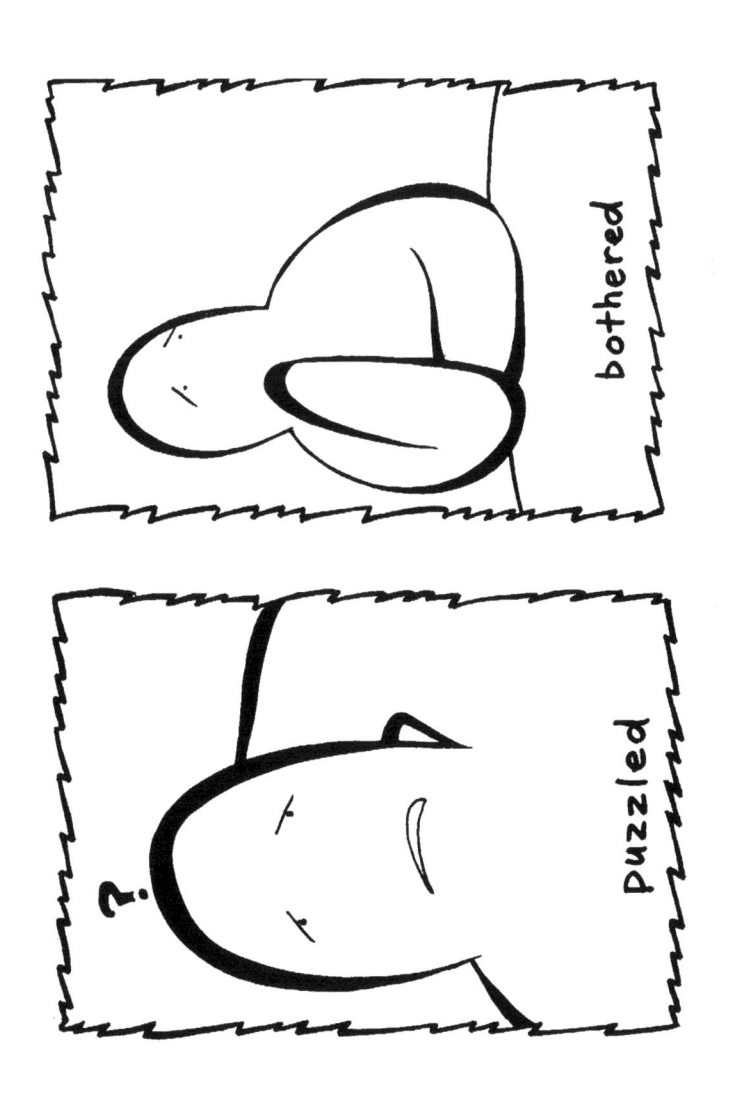

Tracy was *puzzled* by the strange smell she suddenly noticed in the hallway.

The Blob Emotional Thesaurus

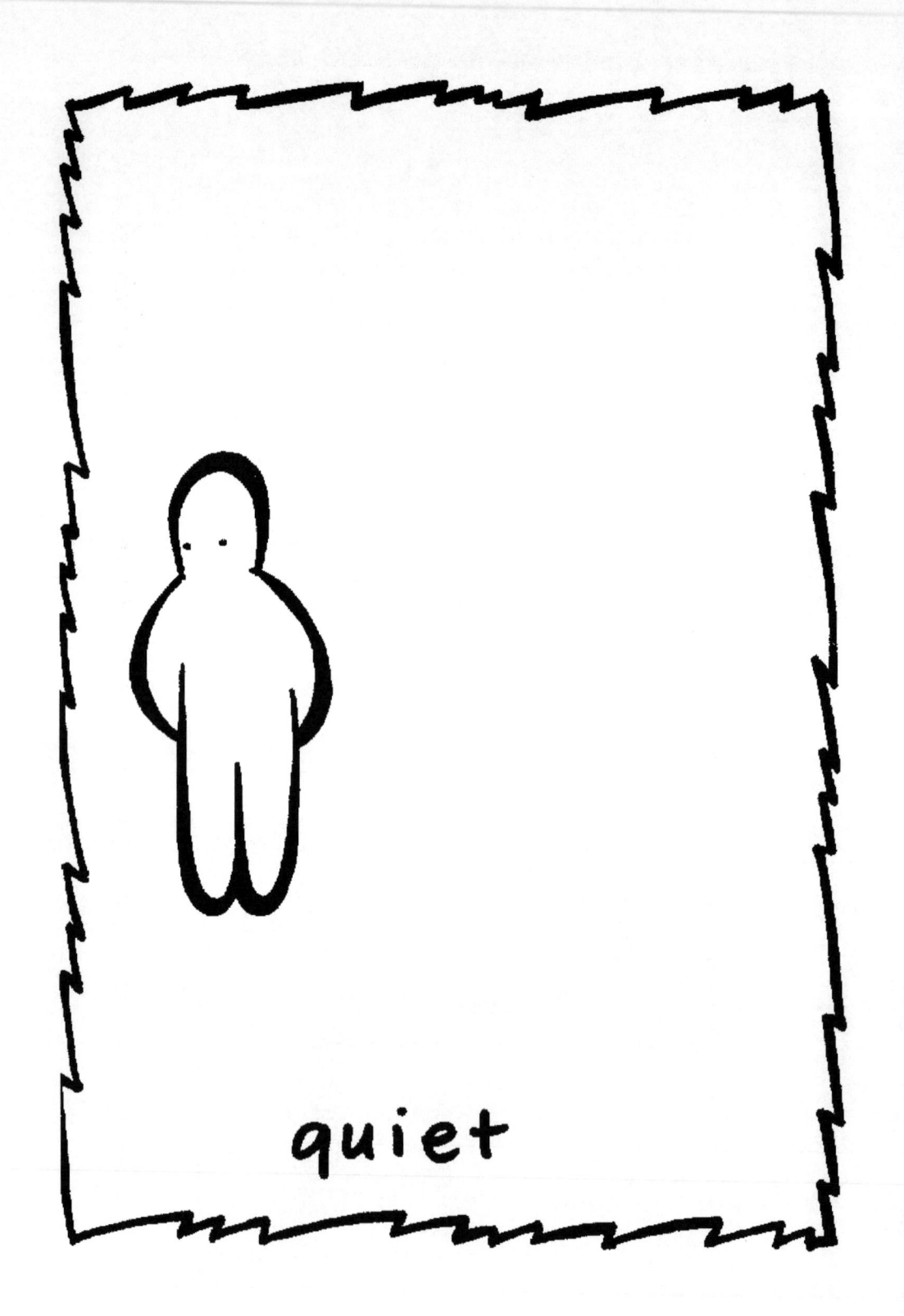

quiet

Individual feeling words

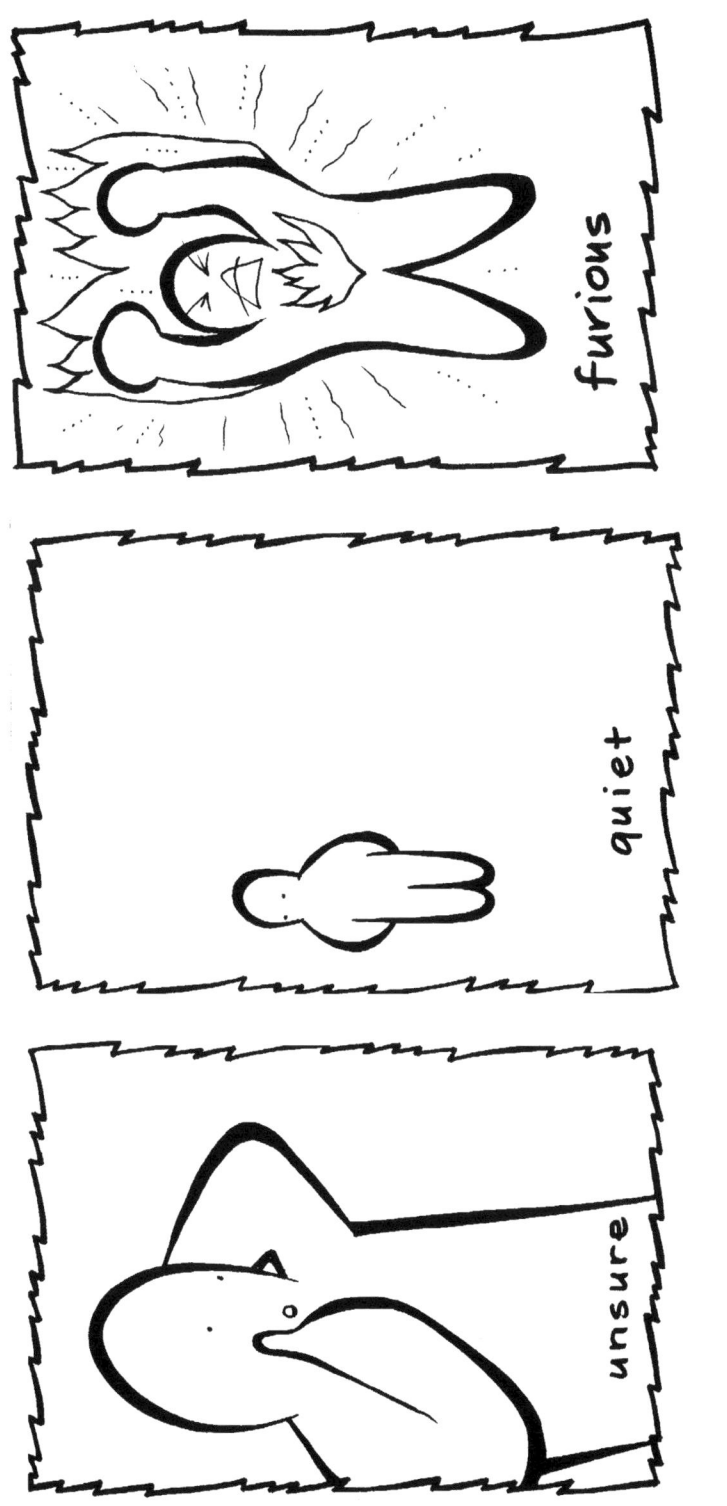

furious

quiet

unsure

Rachel was **quiet** as she pondered her response to his questioning.

The Blob Emotional Thesaurus

quivering

Individual feeling words

stressed

quivering

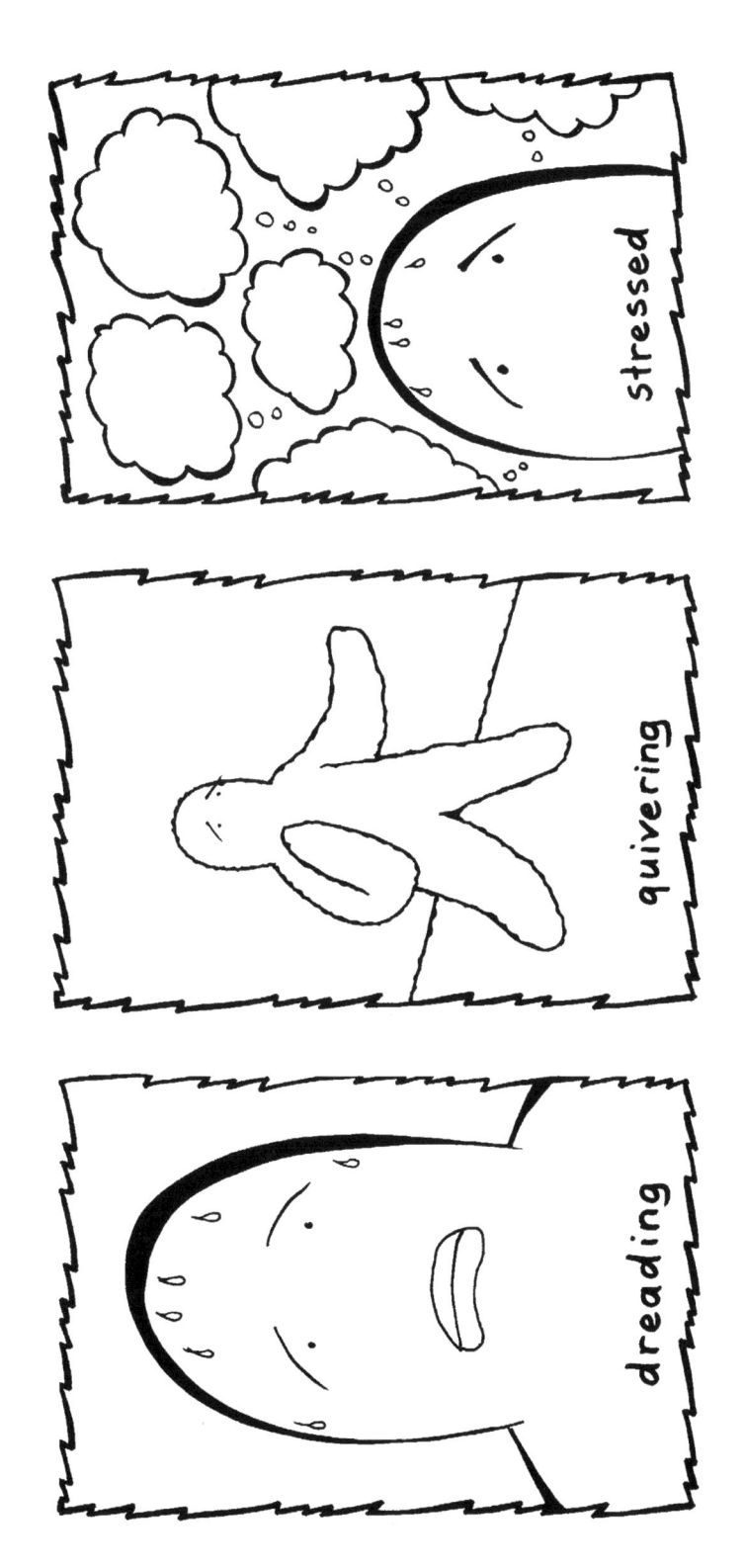

dreading

Steven was quivering as he walked into the haunted house for the first time.

243

The Blob Emotional Thesaurus

raging

Individual feeling words

volcanic

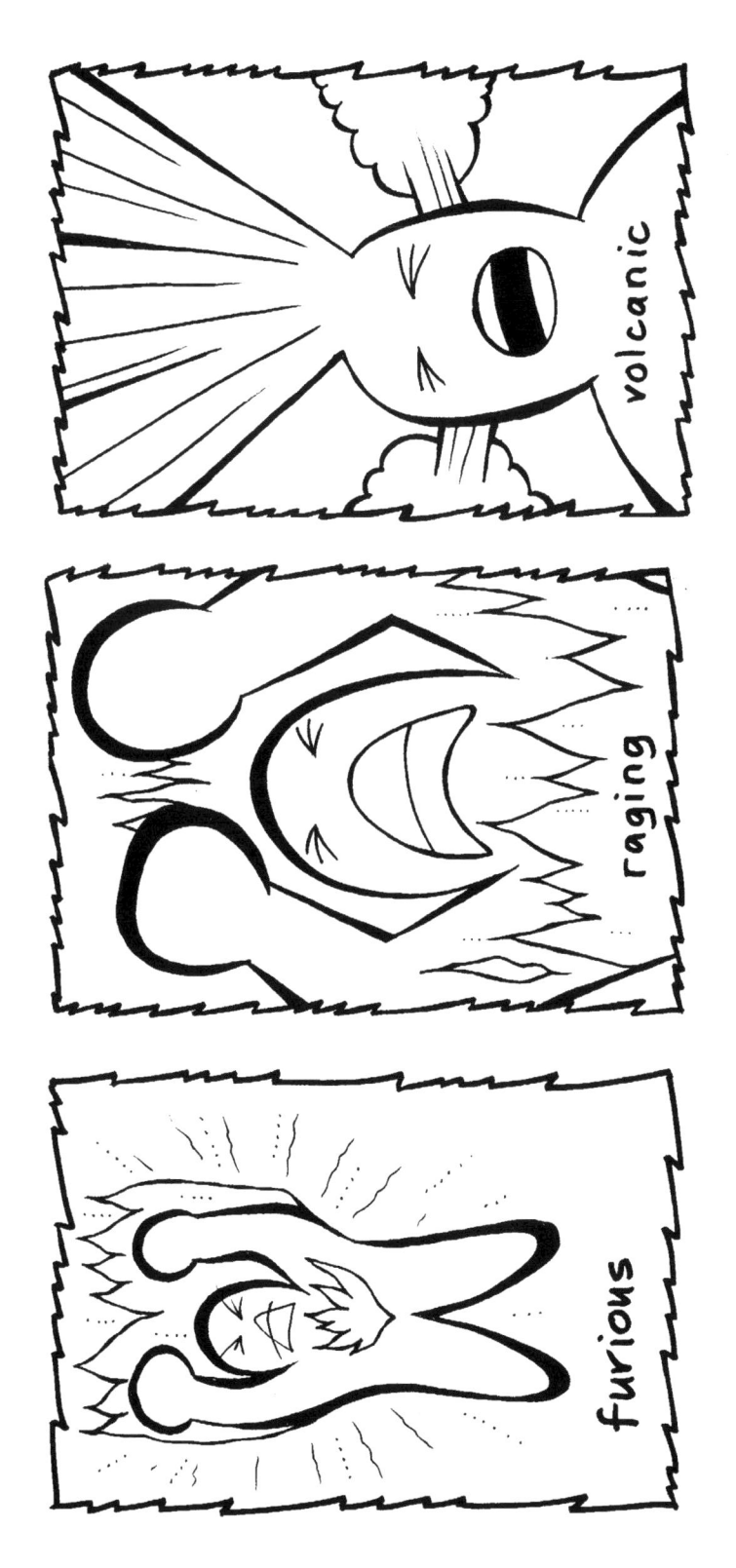

raging

furious

Minty was raging at the end of the racist film!

245

The Blob Emotional Thesaurus

rejected

Individual feeling words

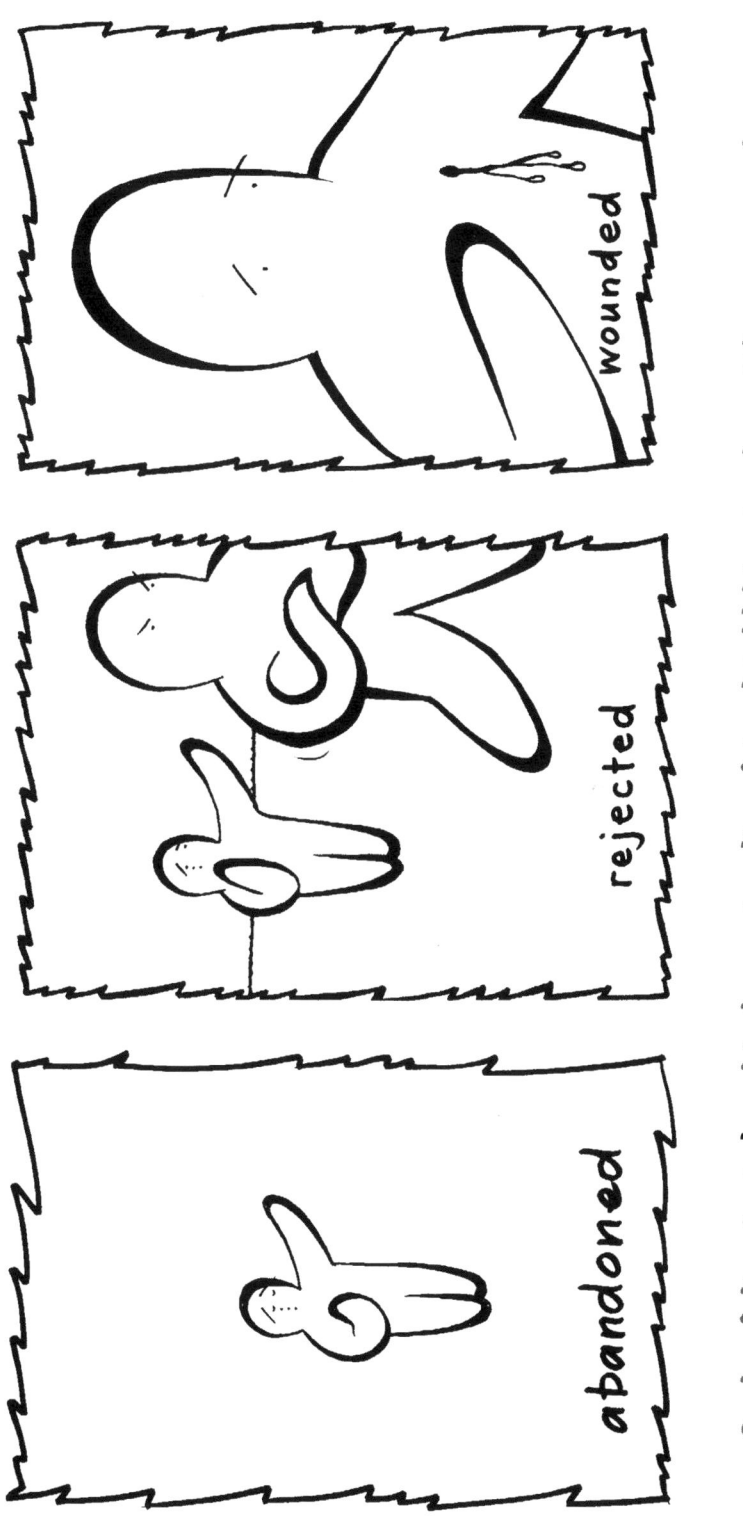

Carlos felt rejected as his long-standing friend told him to play with someone else.

wounded

rejected

abandoned

The Blob Emotional Thesaurus

released

Individual feeling words

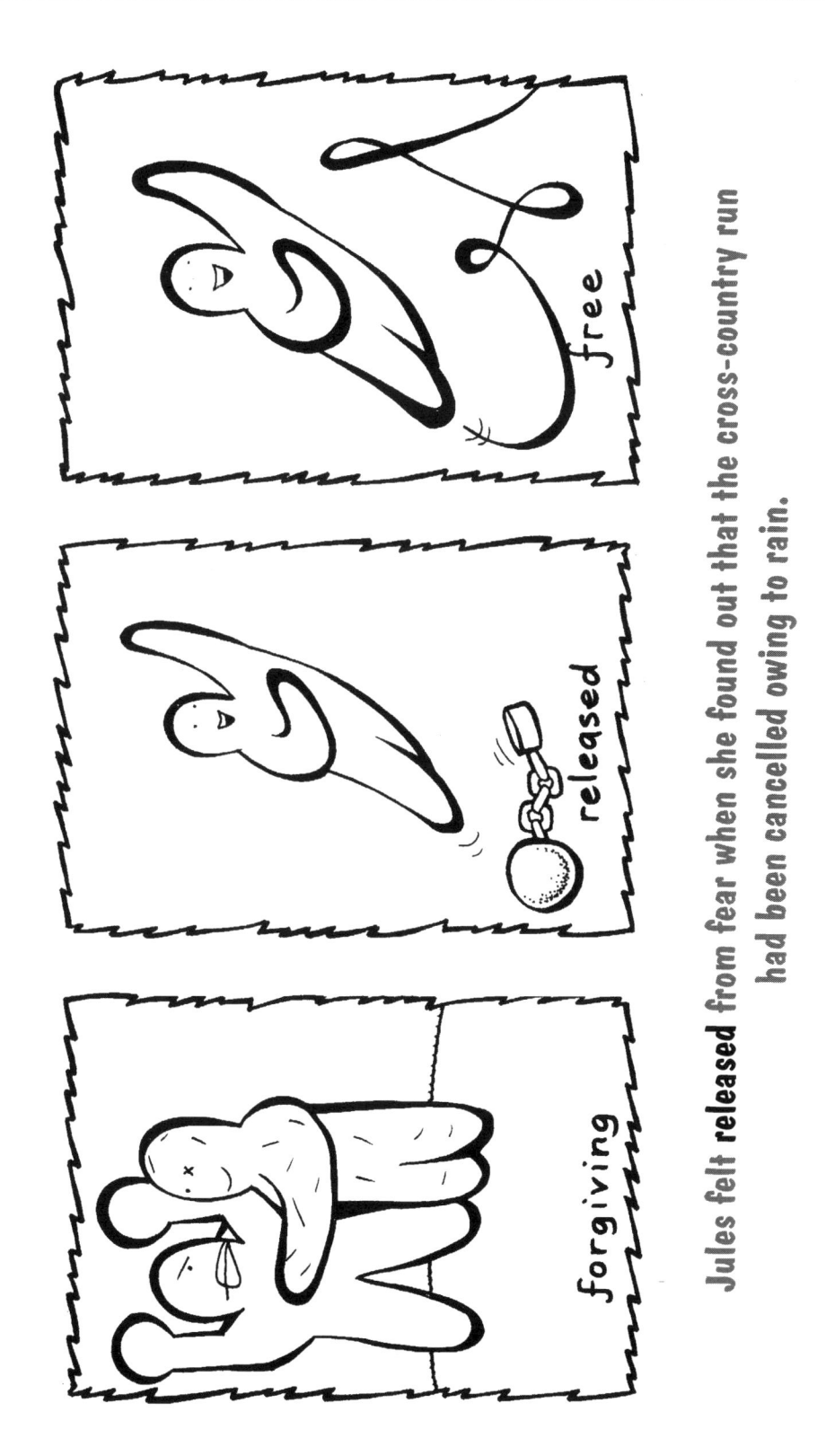

free

released

forgiving

Jules felt **released** from fear when she found out that the cross-country run had been cancelled owing to rain.

The Blob Emotional Thesaurus

relieved

Individual feeling words

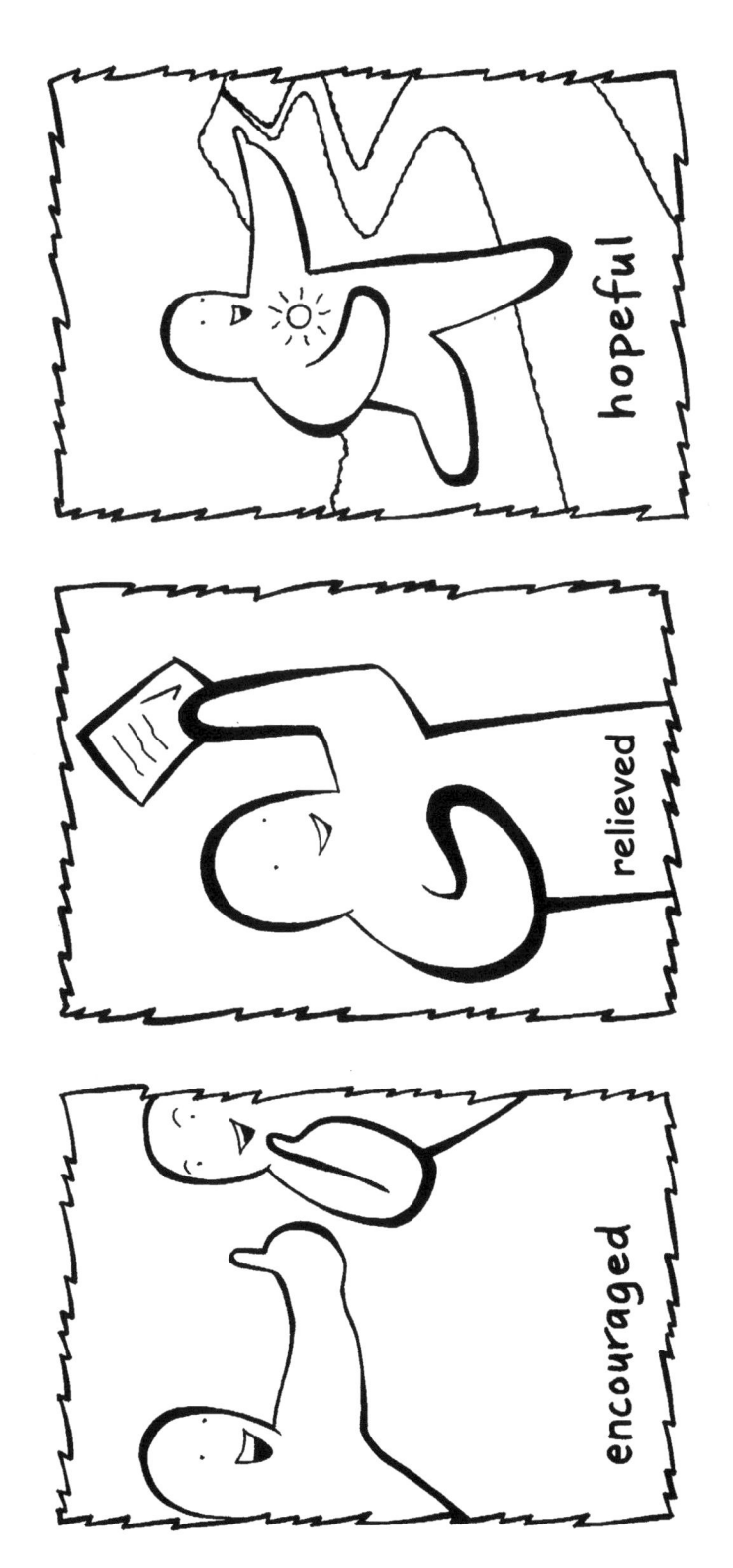

hopeful

relieved

encouraged

Bethan was very relieved when the exam results came back, and she had passed!

The Blob Emotional Thesaurus

respected

Individual feeling words

| wanted | respected | Proud |

Kate felt respected by her friends ever since she managed to make her first million from business.

The Blob Emotional Thesaurus

restrained

Individual feeling words

restrained

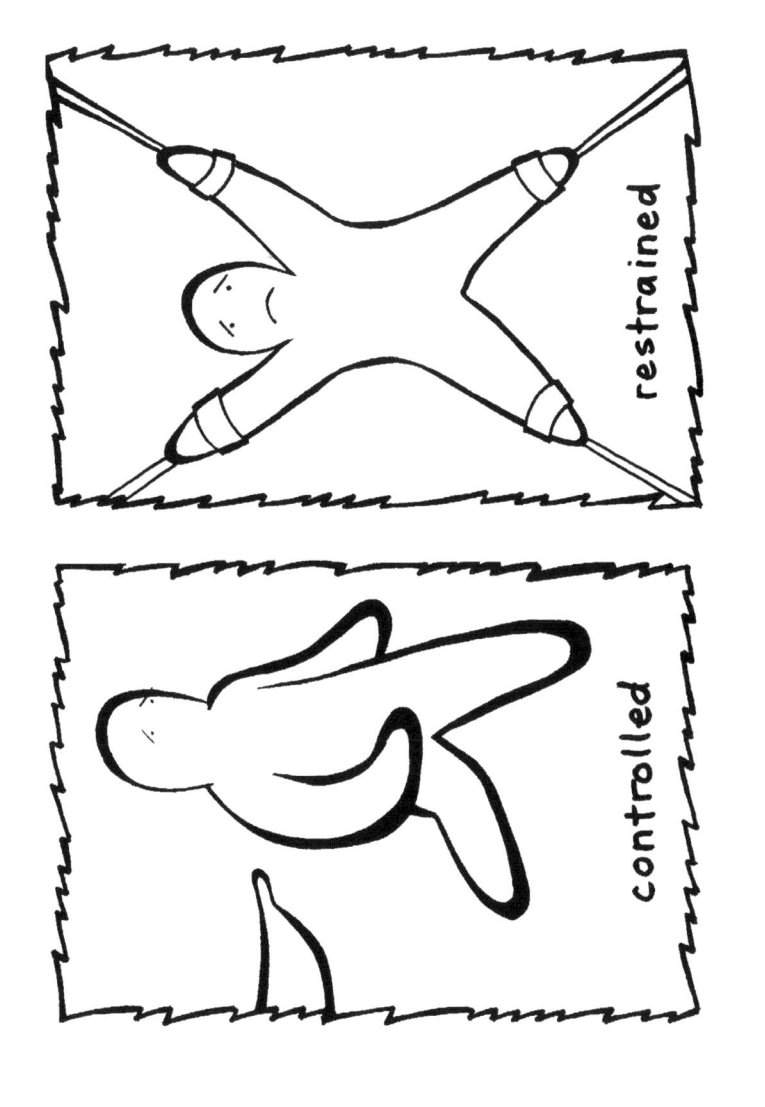

controlled

Juliet felt **restrained** by all the paperwork she had to carry out each day.

The Blob Emotional Thesaurus

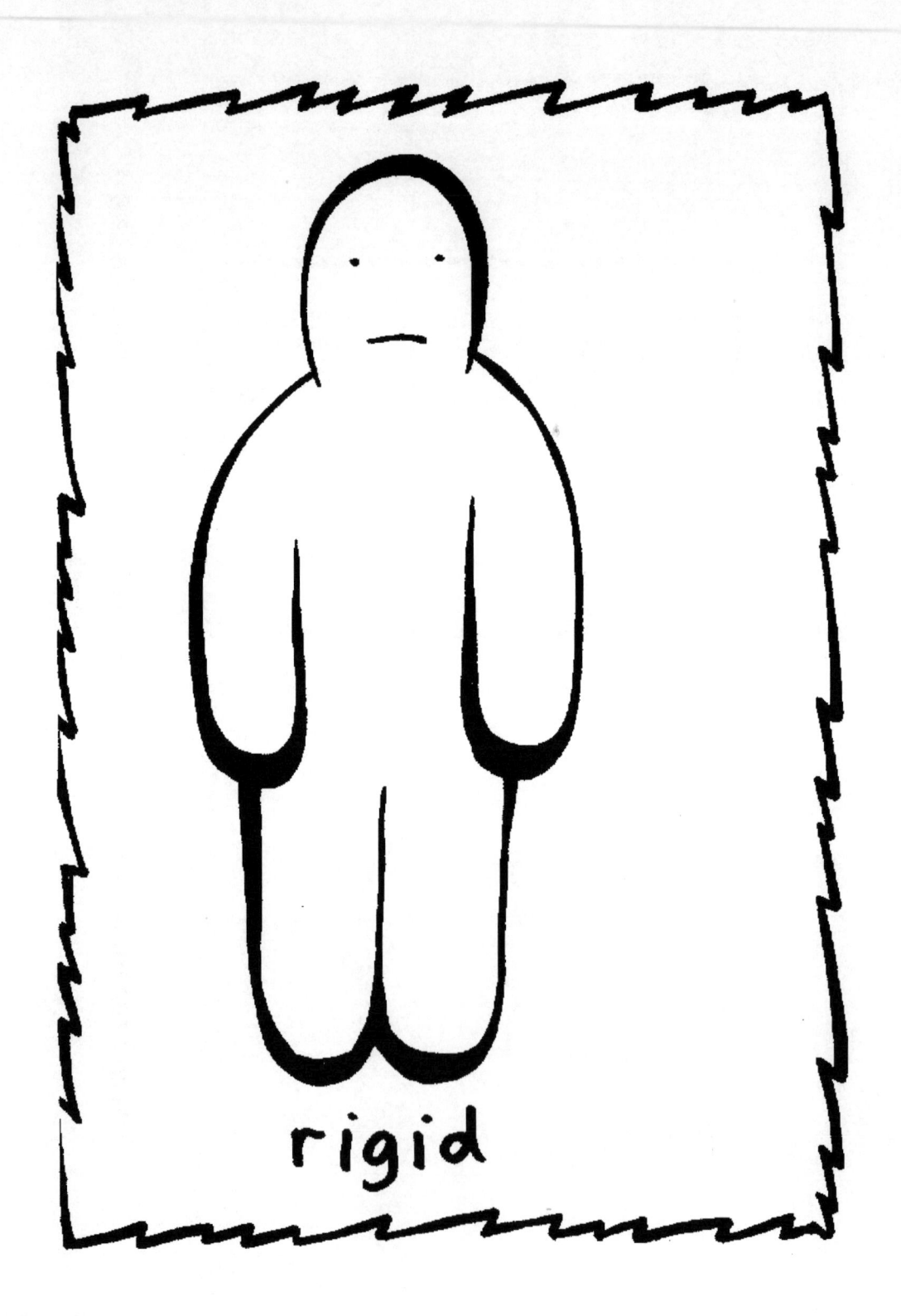

rigid

Individual feeling words

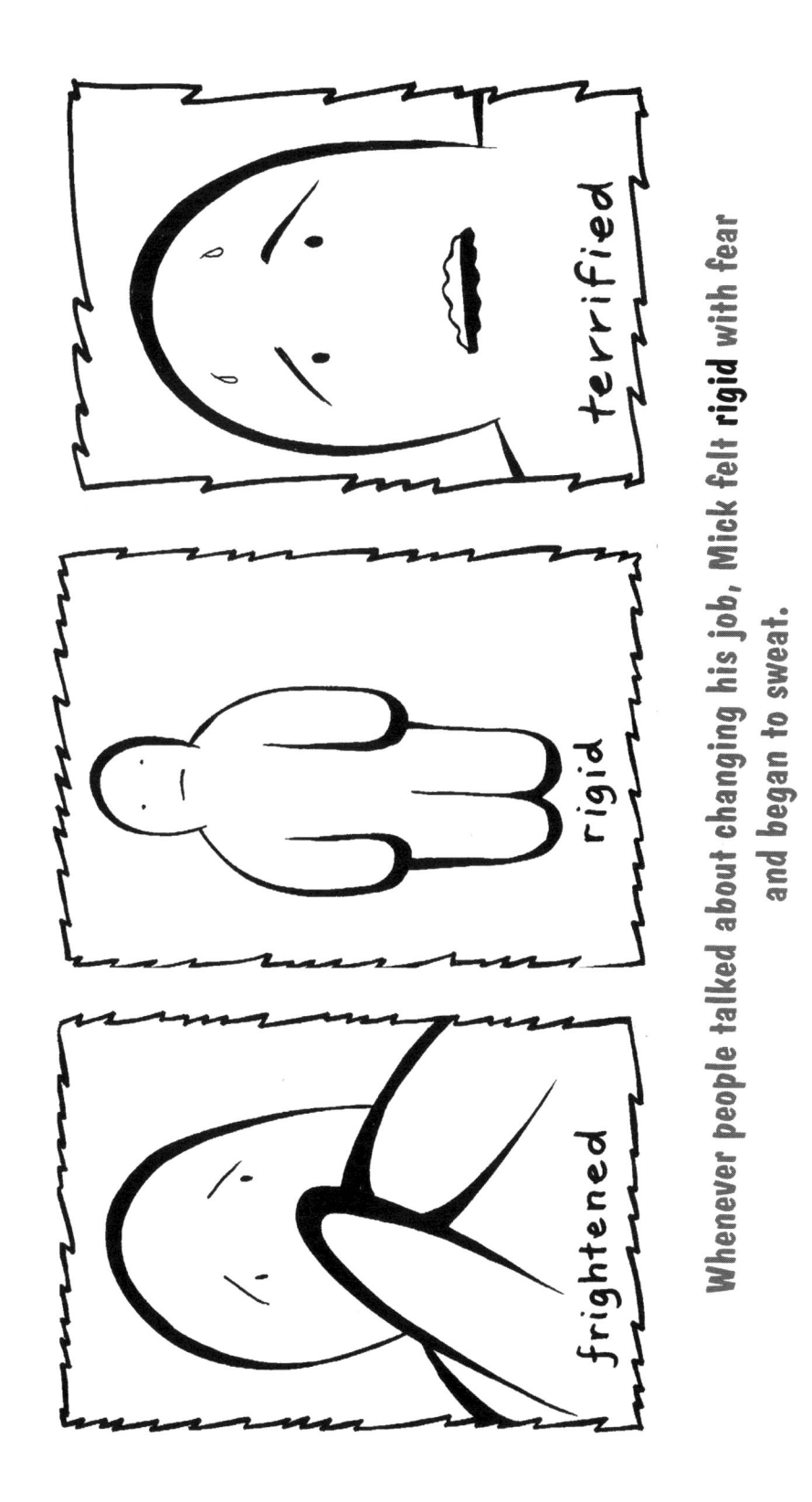

terrified

rigid

frightened

Whenever people talked about changing his job, Mick felt **rigid** with **fear** and began to sweat.

The Blob Emotional Thesaurus

romantic

Individual feeling words

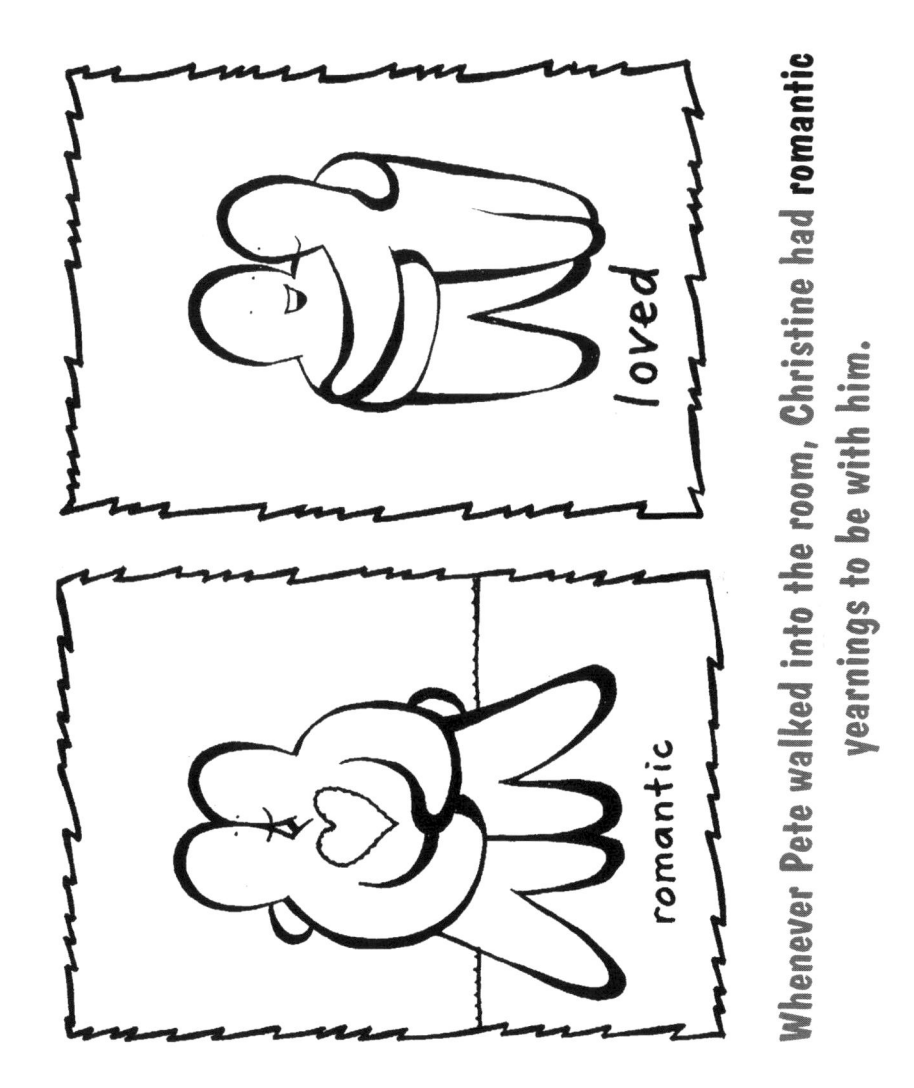

loved

romantic

Whenever Pete walked into the room, Christine had romantic yearnings to be with him.

The Blob Emotional Thesaurus

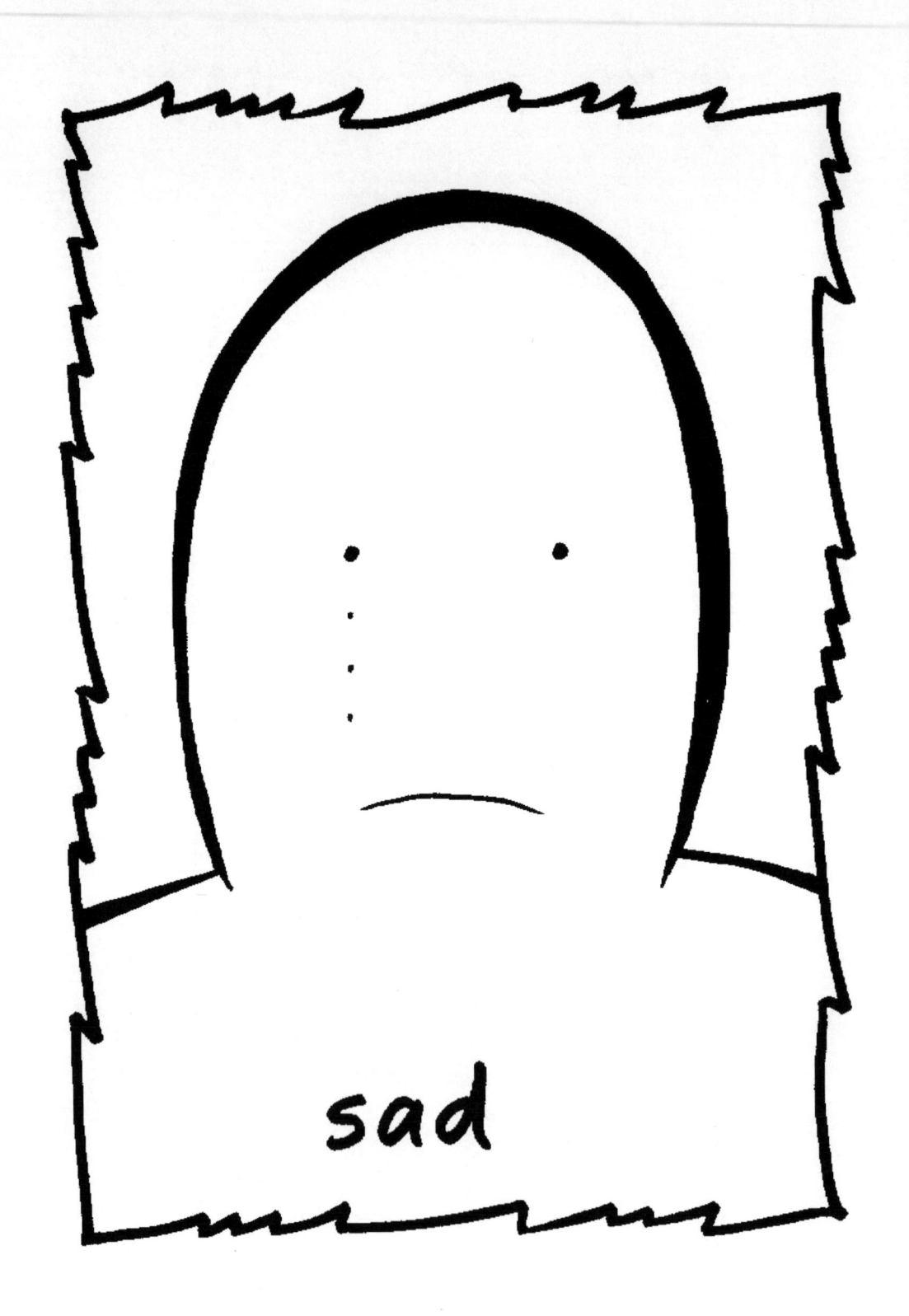

sad

Individual feeling words

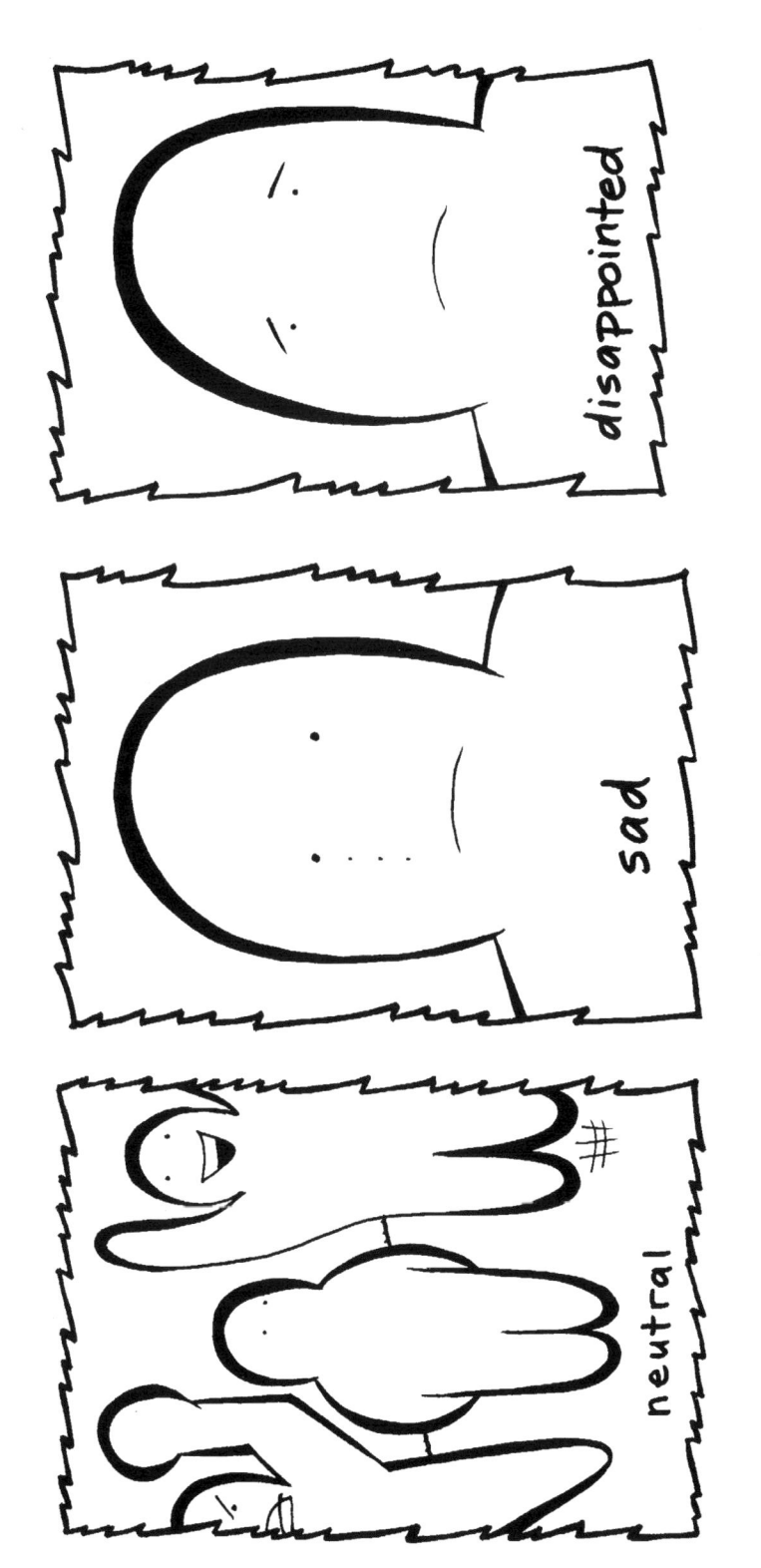

Pip was sad that his favourite team had lost for the first time.

disappointed

sad

neutral

The Blob Emotional Thesaurus

safe

Individual feeling words

confident

safe

satisfied

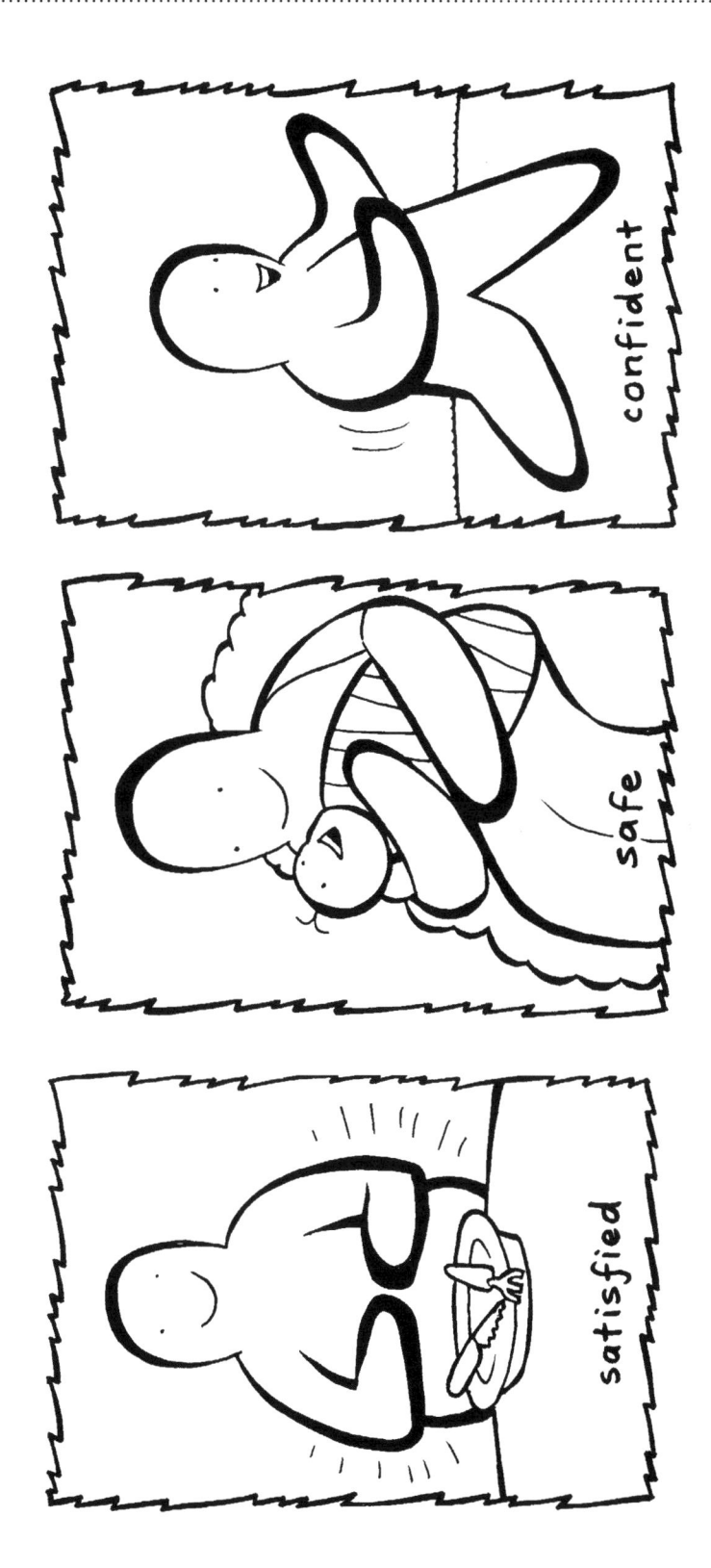

Now that Sky was home and dry, she finally felt safe and began to sigh!

The Blob Emotional Thesaurus

satisfied

Individual feeling words

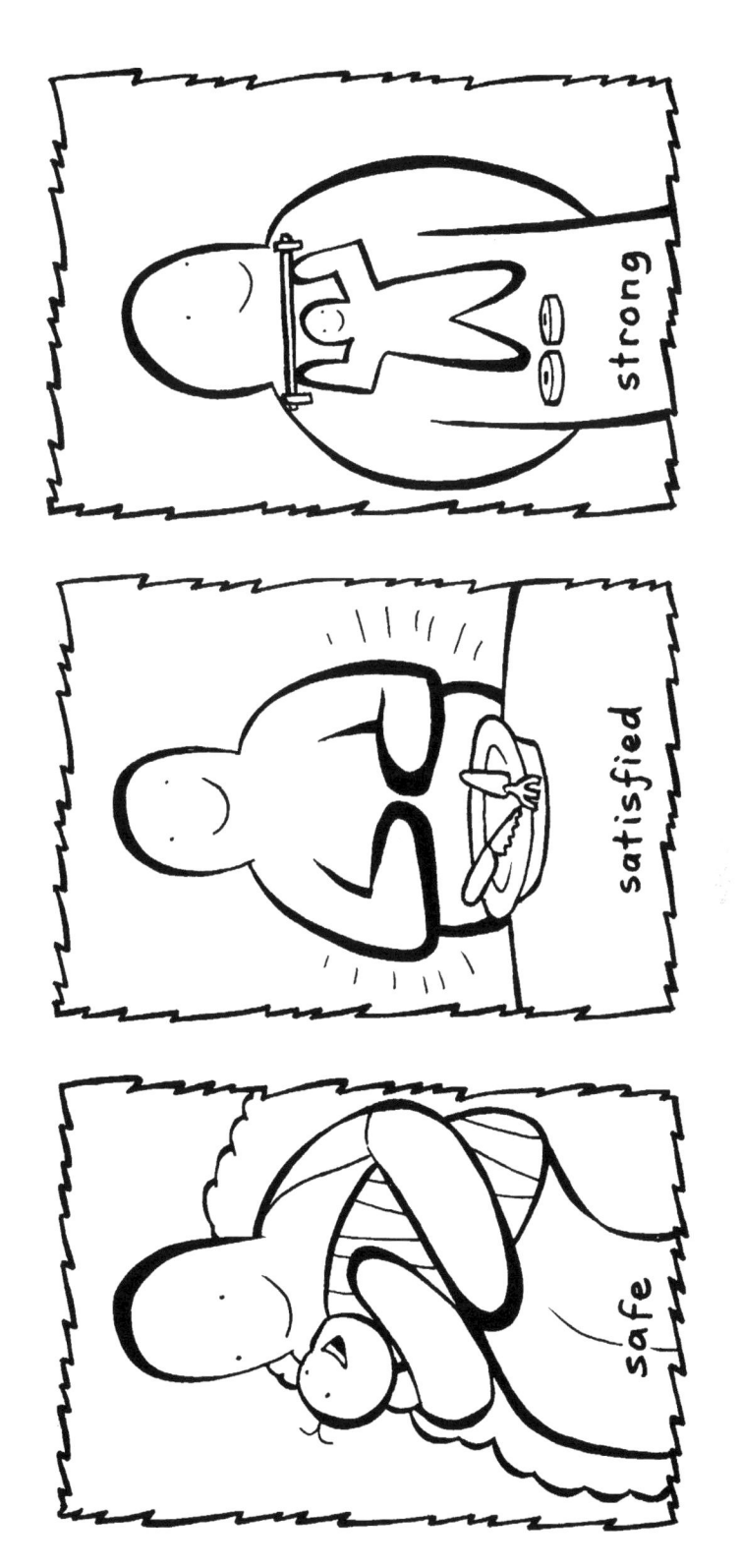

After lunch, Henry sat back in his seat, feeling very satisfied!

strong

satisfied

safe

The Blob Emotional Thesaurus

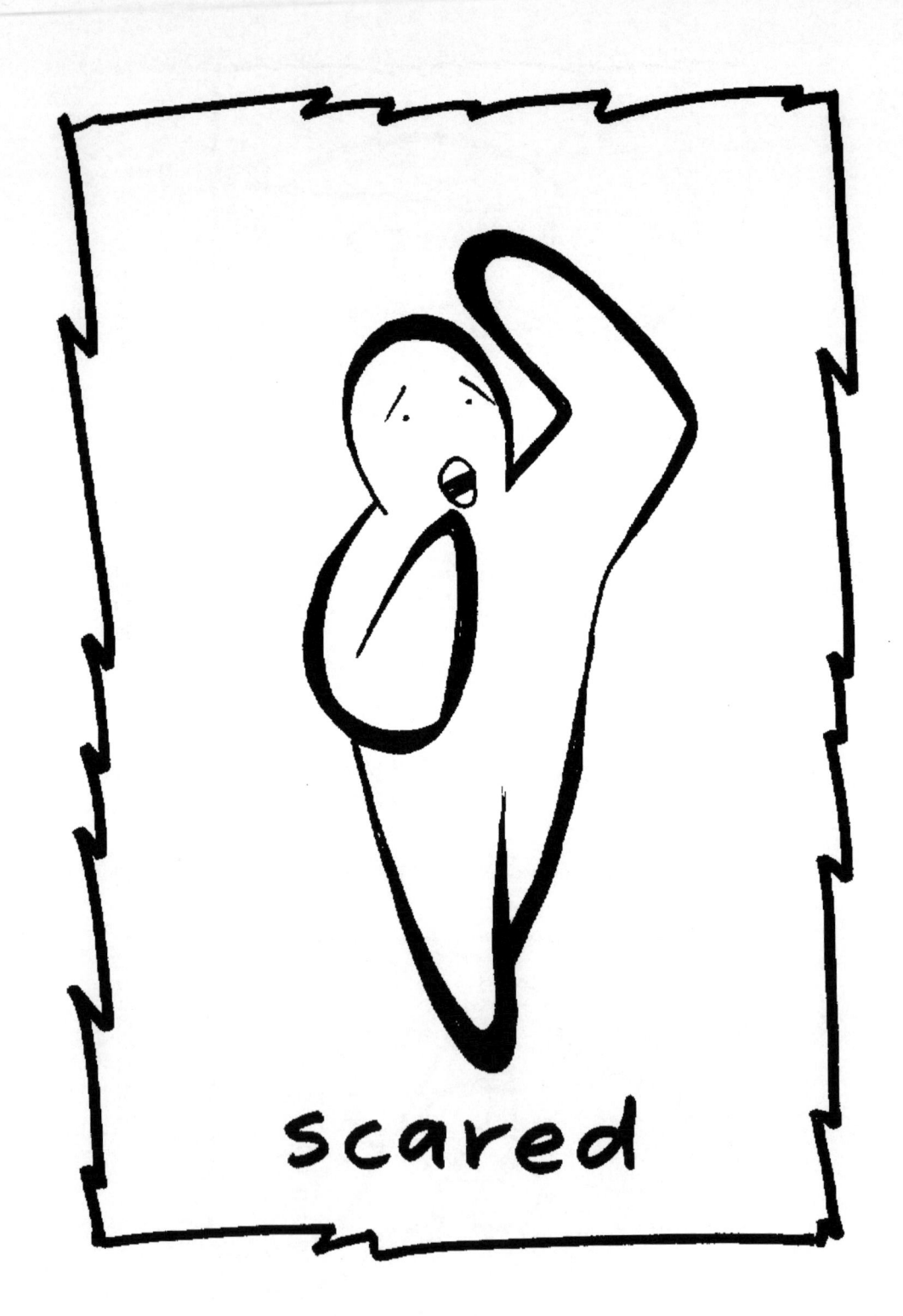

scared

Individual feeling words

dreading

scared

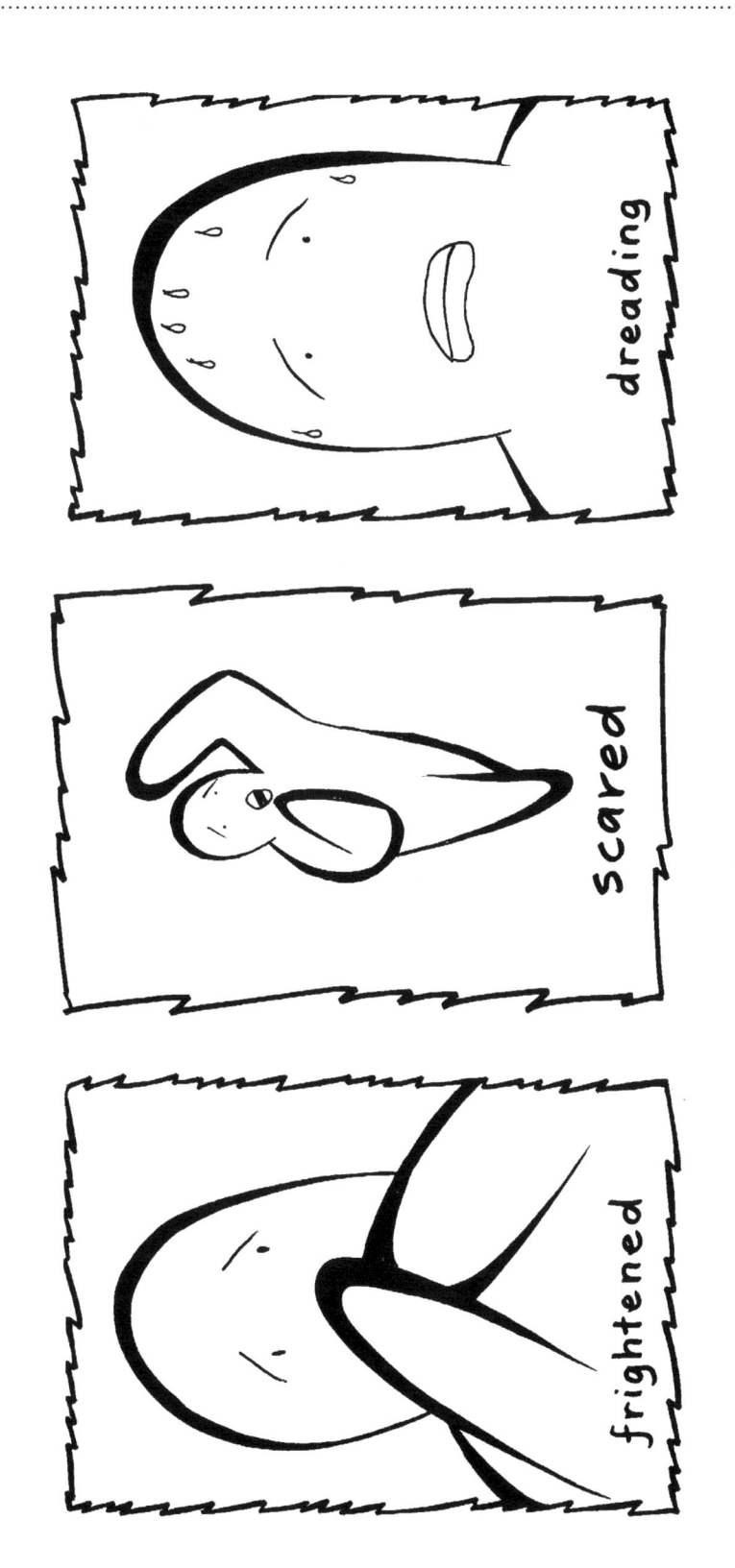

frightened

Melissa was **scared** by the sound of her bedroom door creaking open.

The Blob Emotional Thesaurus

seething

Individual feeling words

annoyed

seething

angry

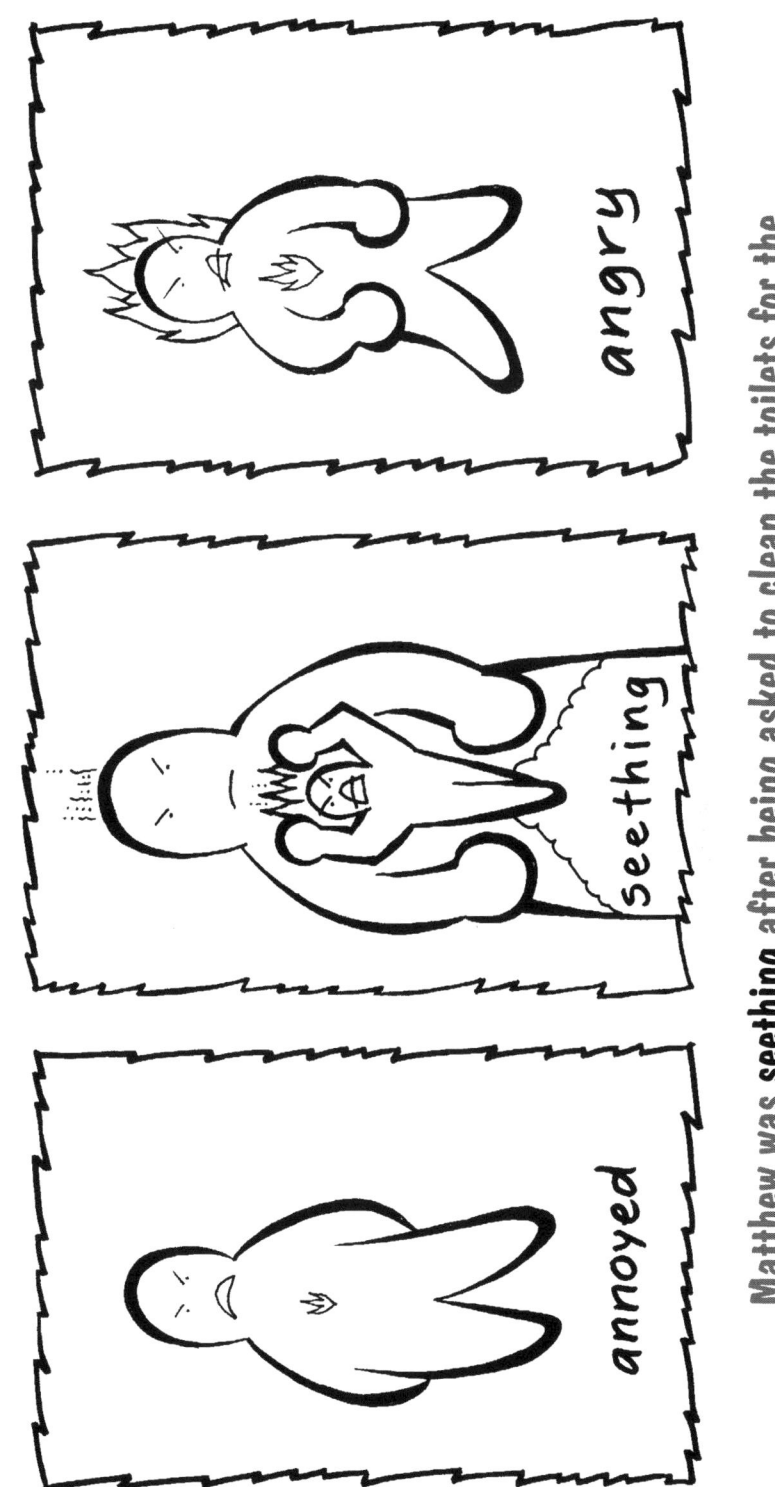

Matthew was **seething** after being asked to clean the toilets for the second time in the day.

sensitive

Individual feeling words

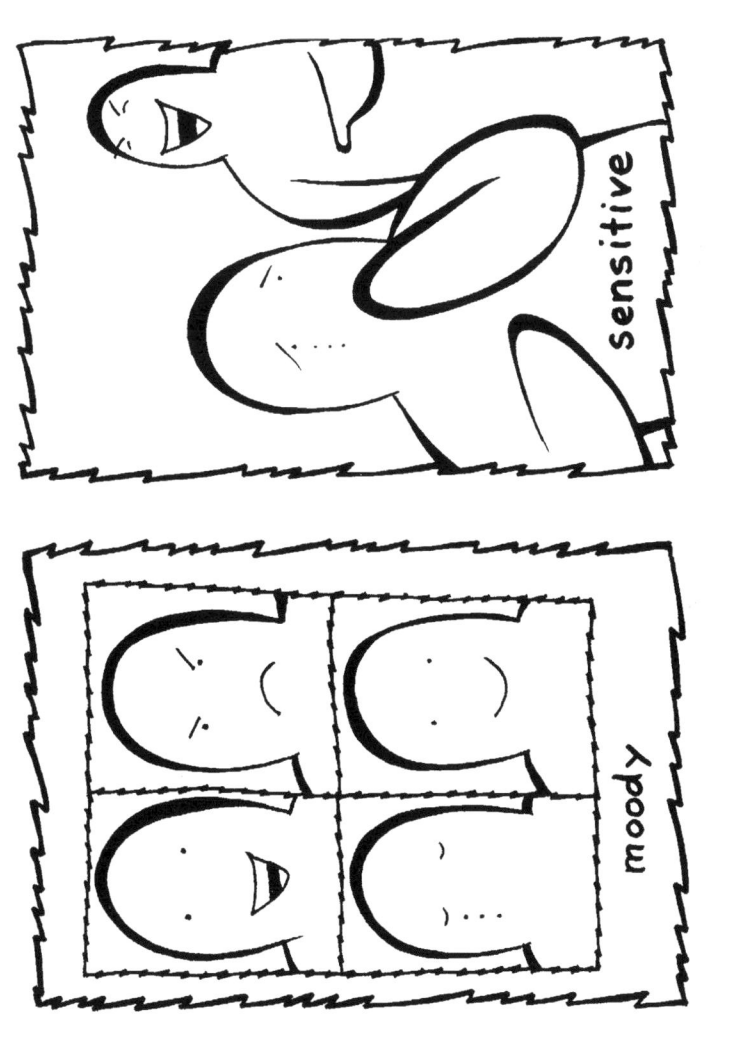

After a poor night's sleep, Douglas was **sensitive** to every comment his friends made about him.

The Blob Emotional Thesaurus

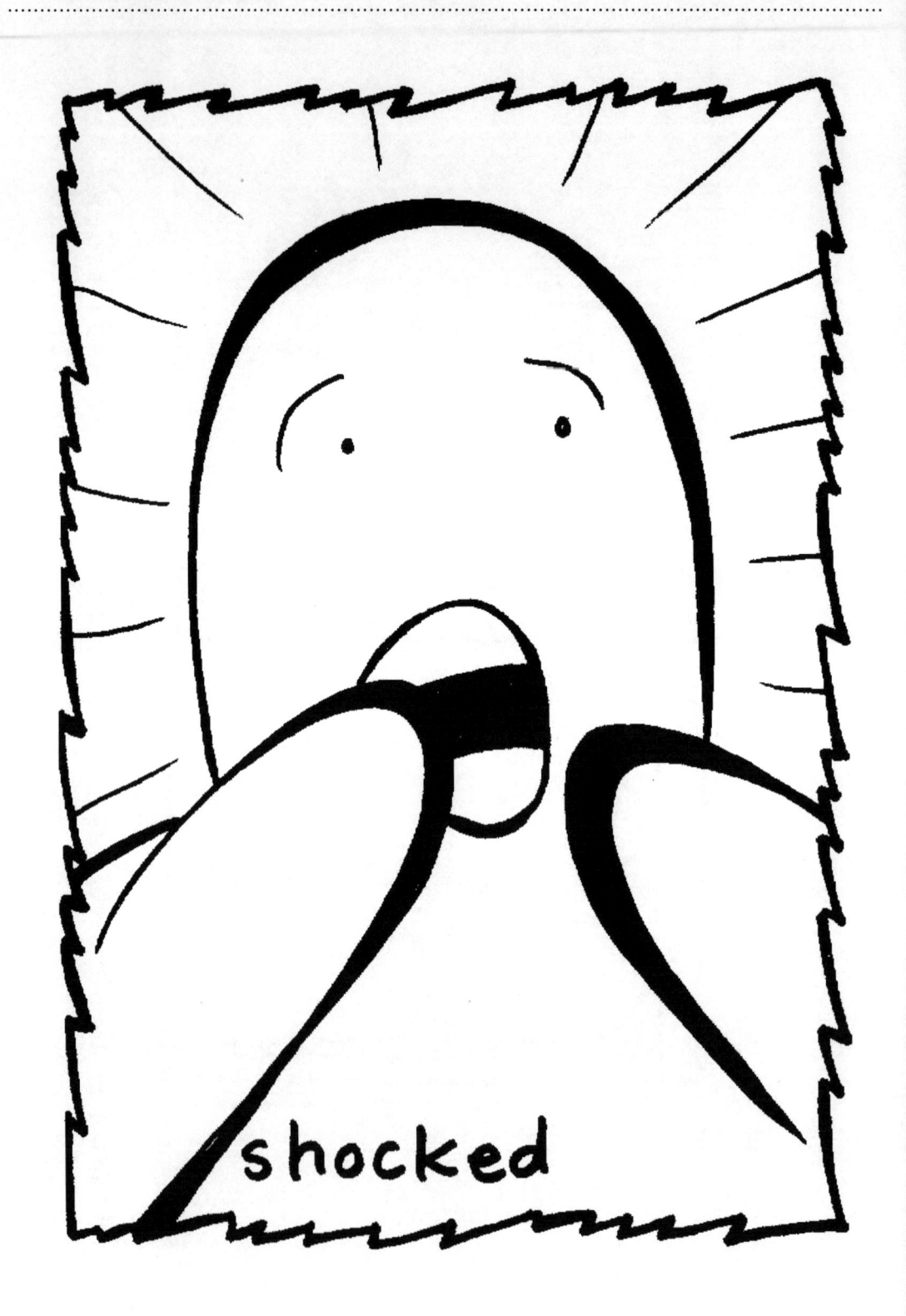

shocked

Individual feeling words

scared

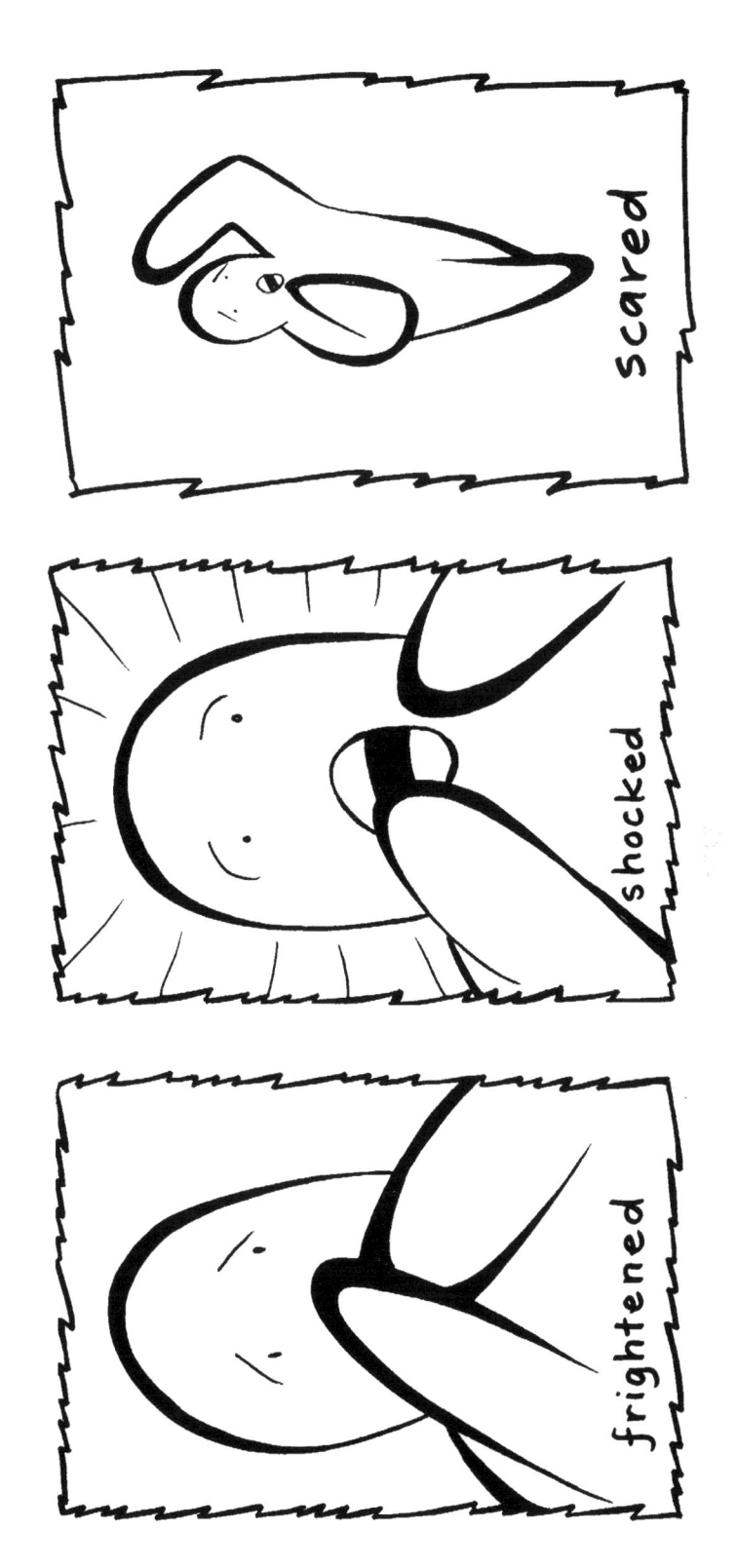

shocked

frightened

Kieran was *shocked* by the amount of homework he was expected to do each night!

The Blob Emotional Thesaurus

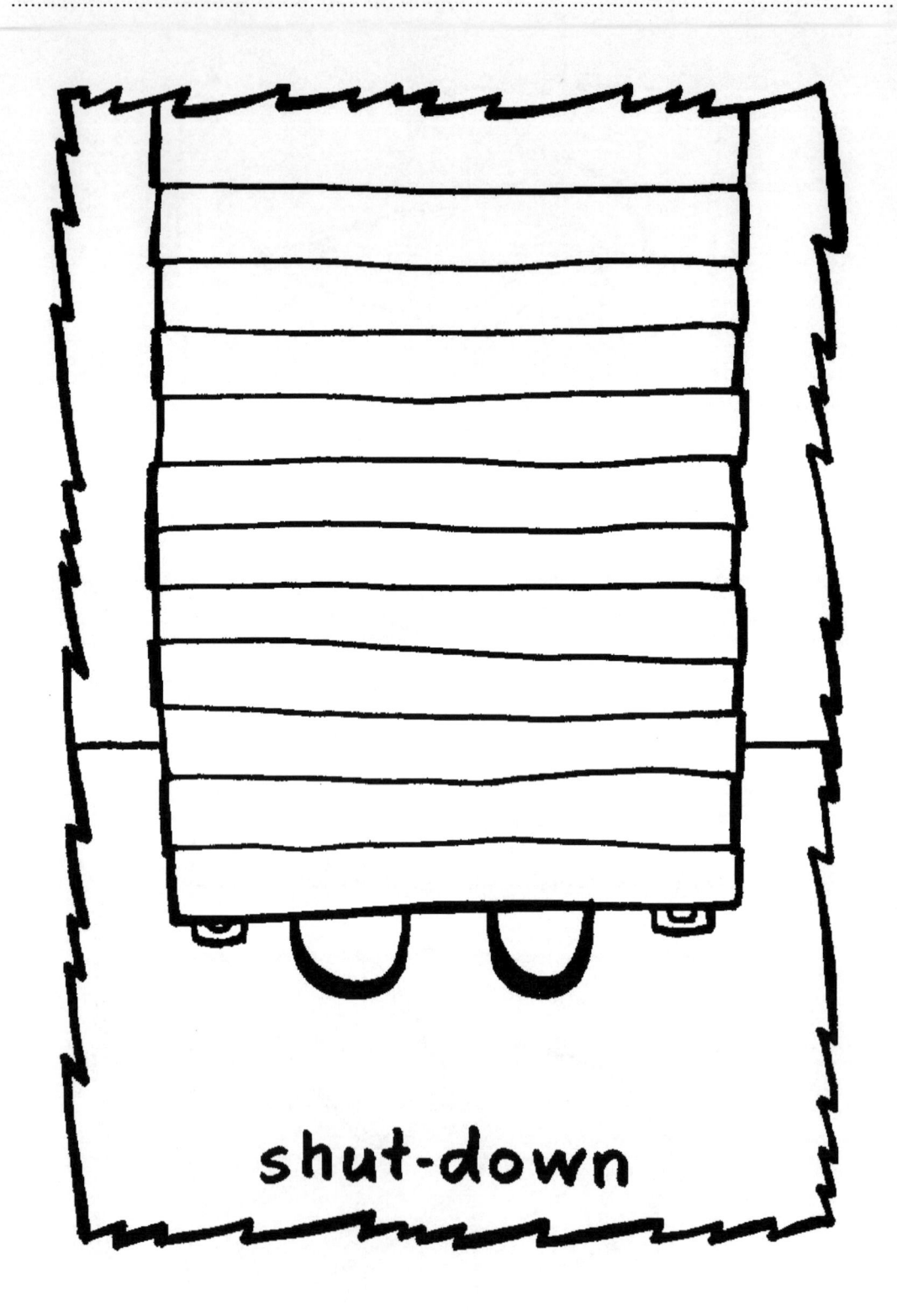

shut-down

Individual feeling words

depressed

shut-down

Emma's whole life had collapsed and she felt as if her heart had **shut-down completely**.

The Blob Emotional Thesaurus

stressed

Individual feeling words

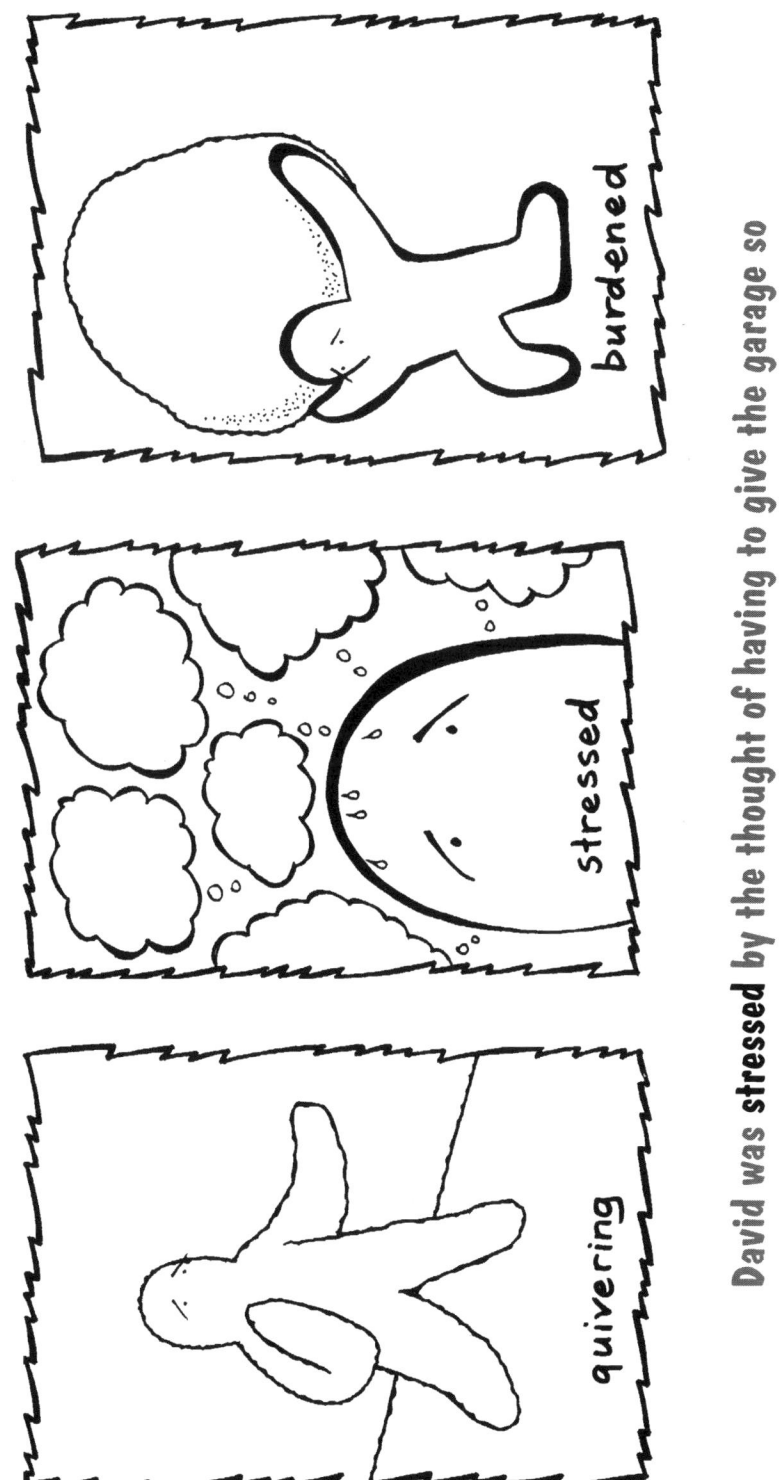

| burdened | stressed | quivering |

David was **stressed** by the thought of having to give the garage so much money to repair his truck.

The Blob Emotional Thesaurus

strong

Individual feeling words

courageous

strong

satisfied

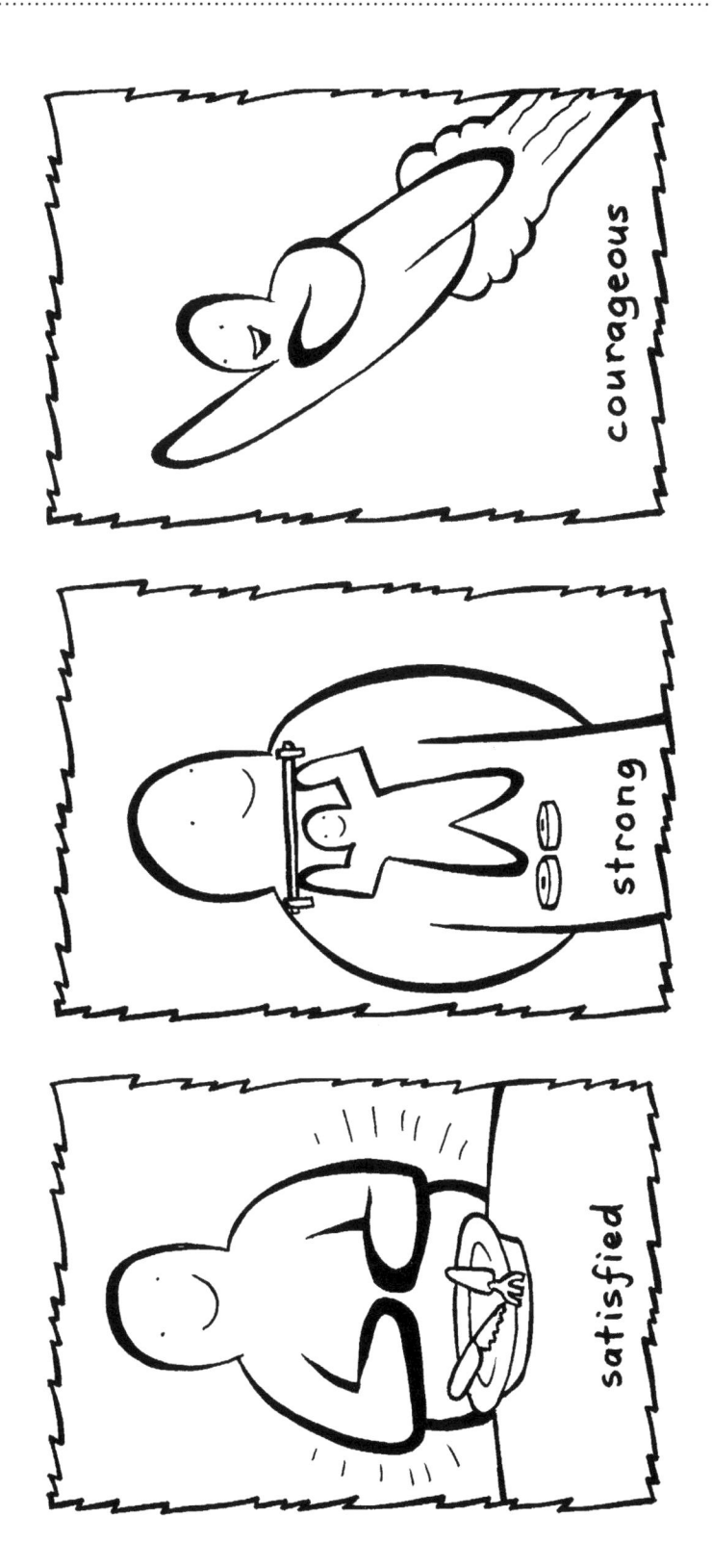

When others seemed to panic at problems, Jai felt strong and in control.

The Blob Emotional Thesaurus

stuck

Individual feeling words

trapped

stuck

isolated

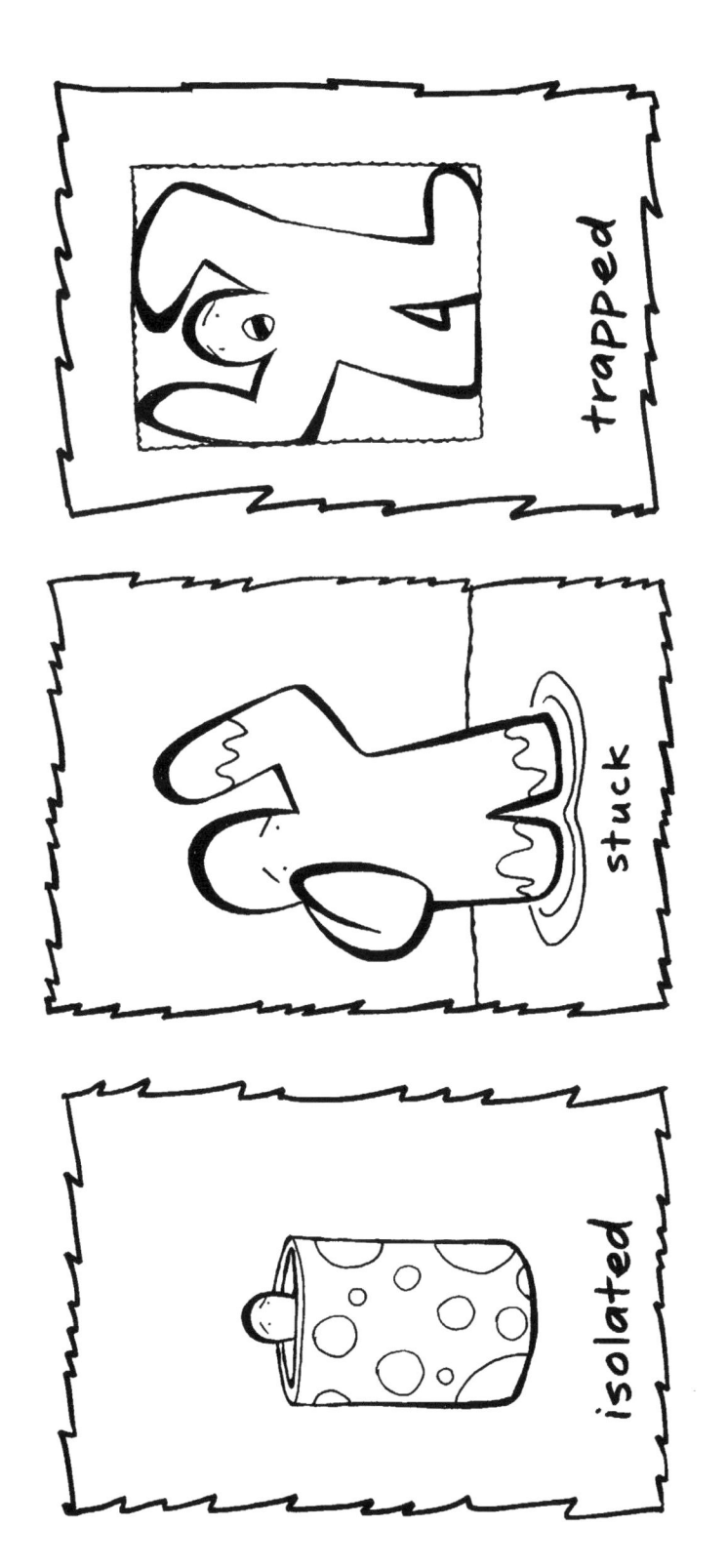

No matter what she thought as an answer, Cassie felt stuck — there was no way out!

The Blob Emotional Thesaurus

supported

Individual feeling words

Throughout his career, Phil had been **supported** by a wise and caring manager.

loved

supported

accepted

The Blob Emotional Thesaurus

tense

Individual feeling words

confident

tense

bothered

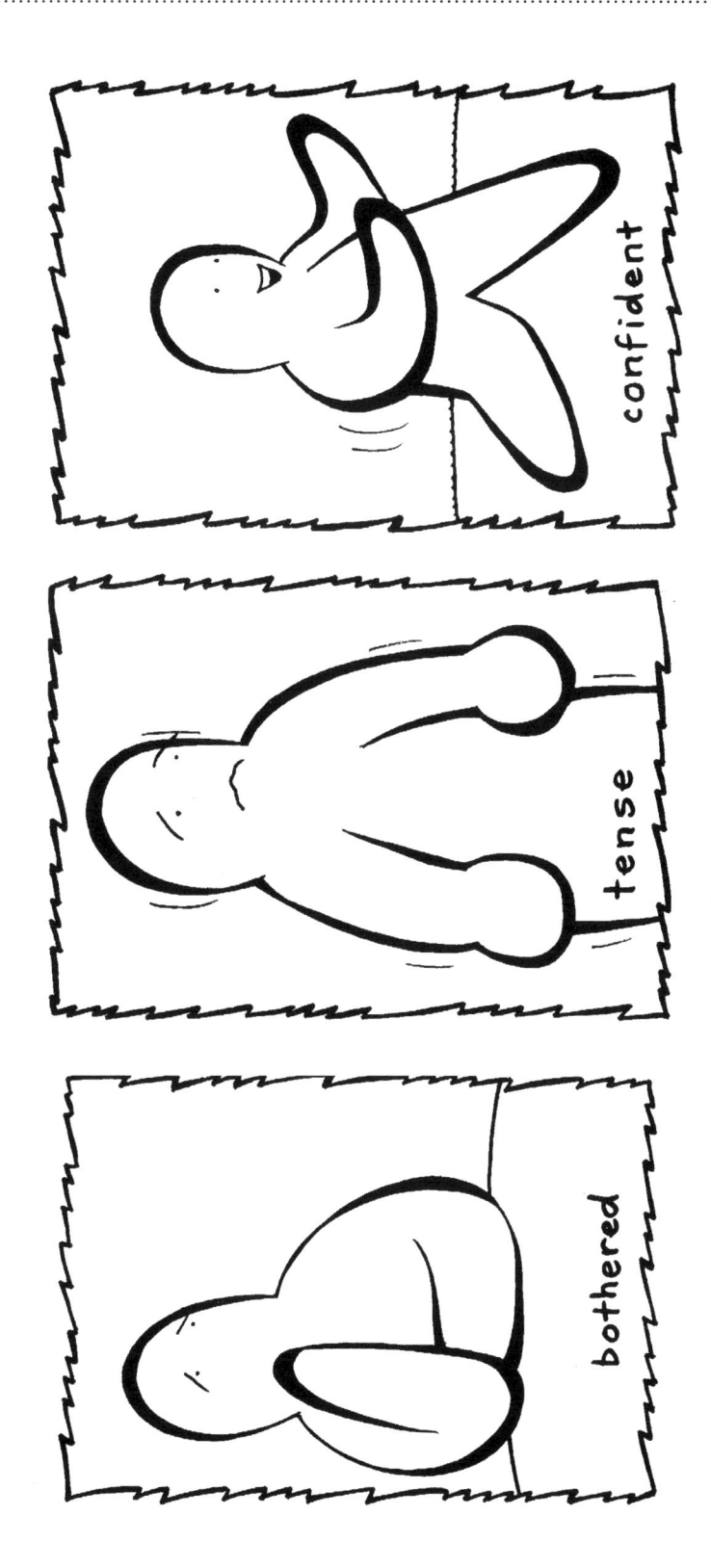

Julia felt **tense** as she walked into her first job interview.

The Blob Emotional Thesaurus

terrified

Individual feeling words

panic-stricken

terrified

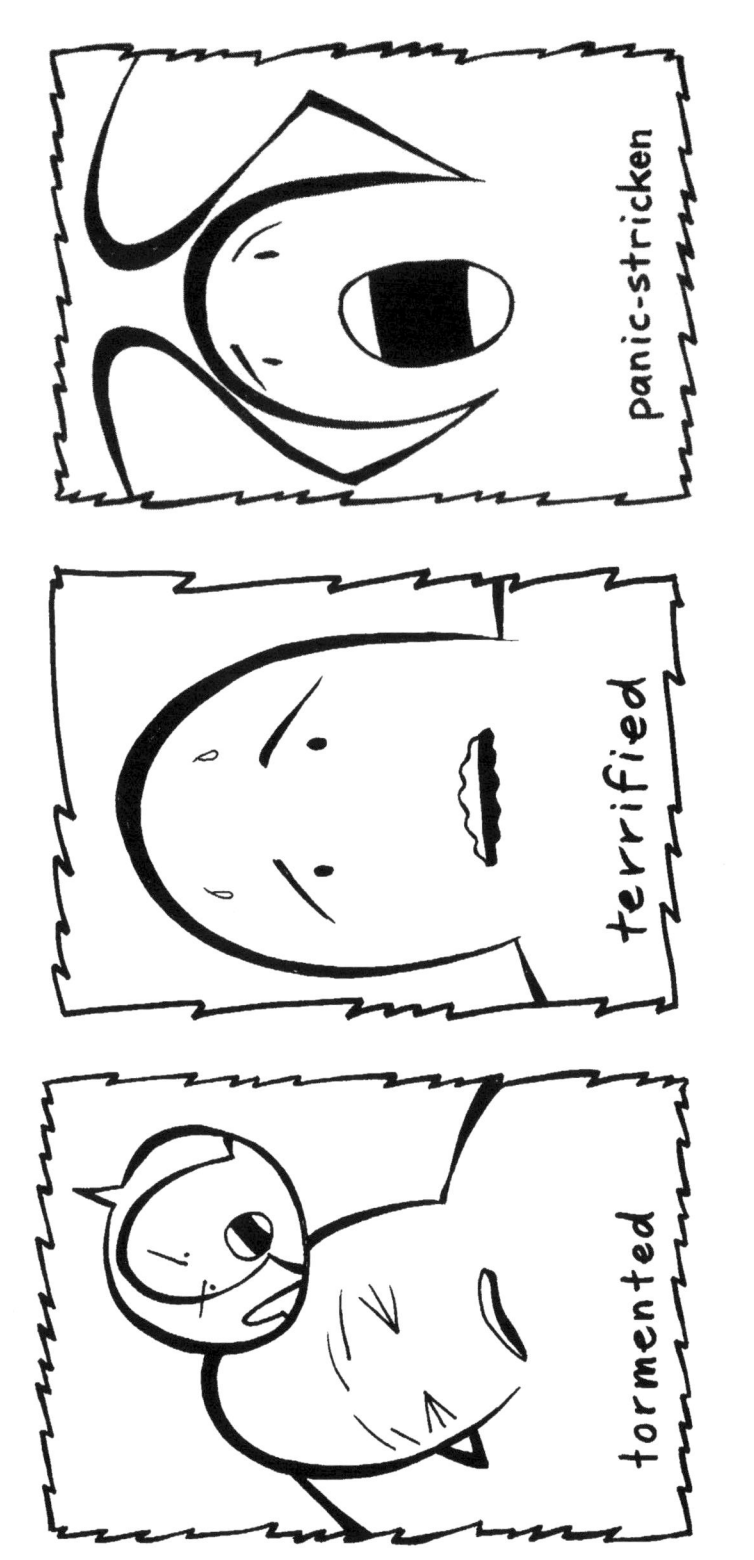

tormented

Jenni was terrified by the roar of the tiger walking slowly towards her.

The Blob Emotional Thesaurus

threatened

Individual feeling words

trapped

threatened

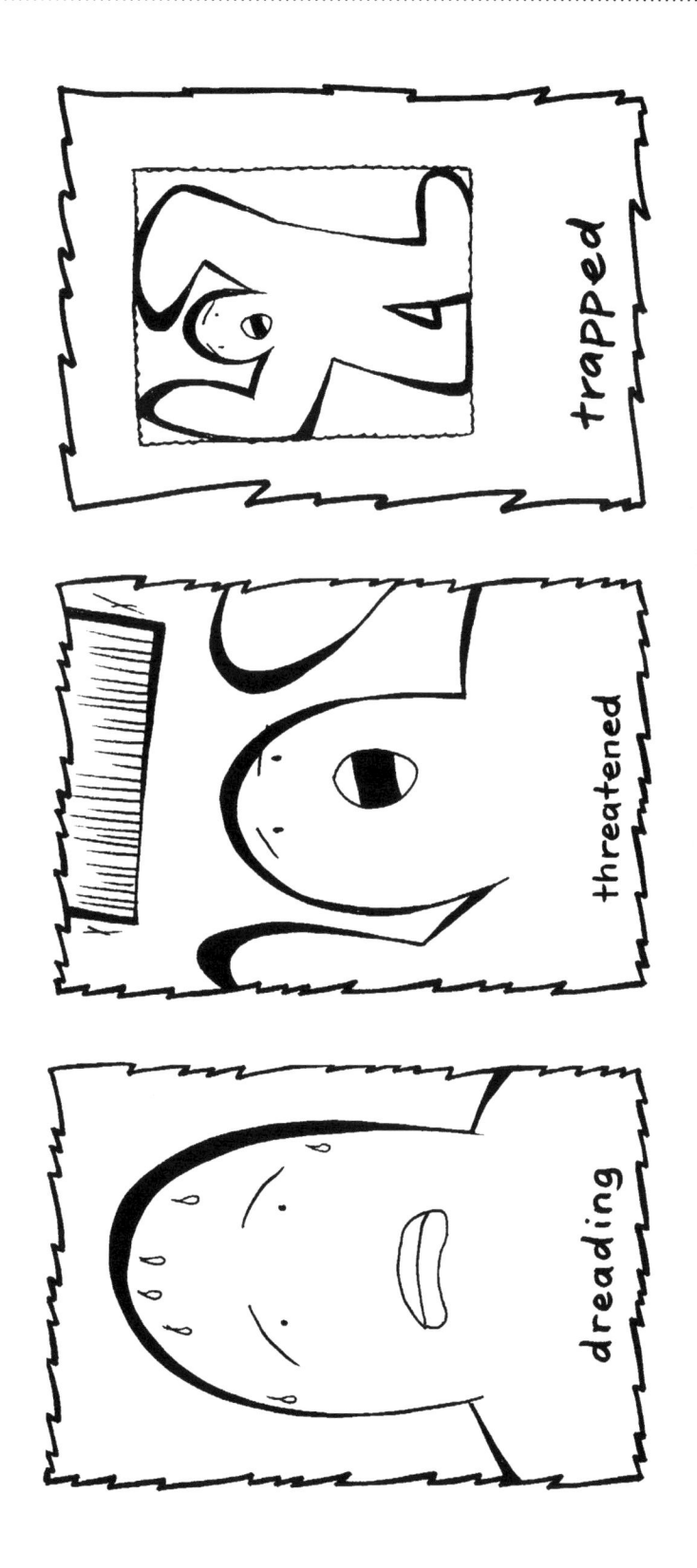

dreading

Gurmit felt threatened by the sound of footsteps behind her as she walked home in the dark.

thrilled

Individual feeling words

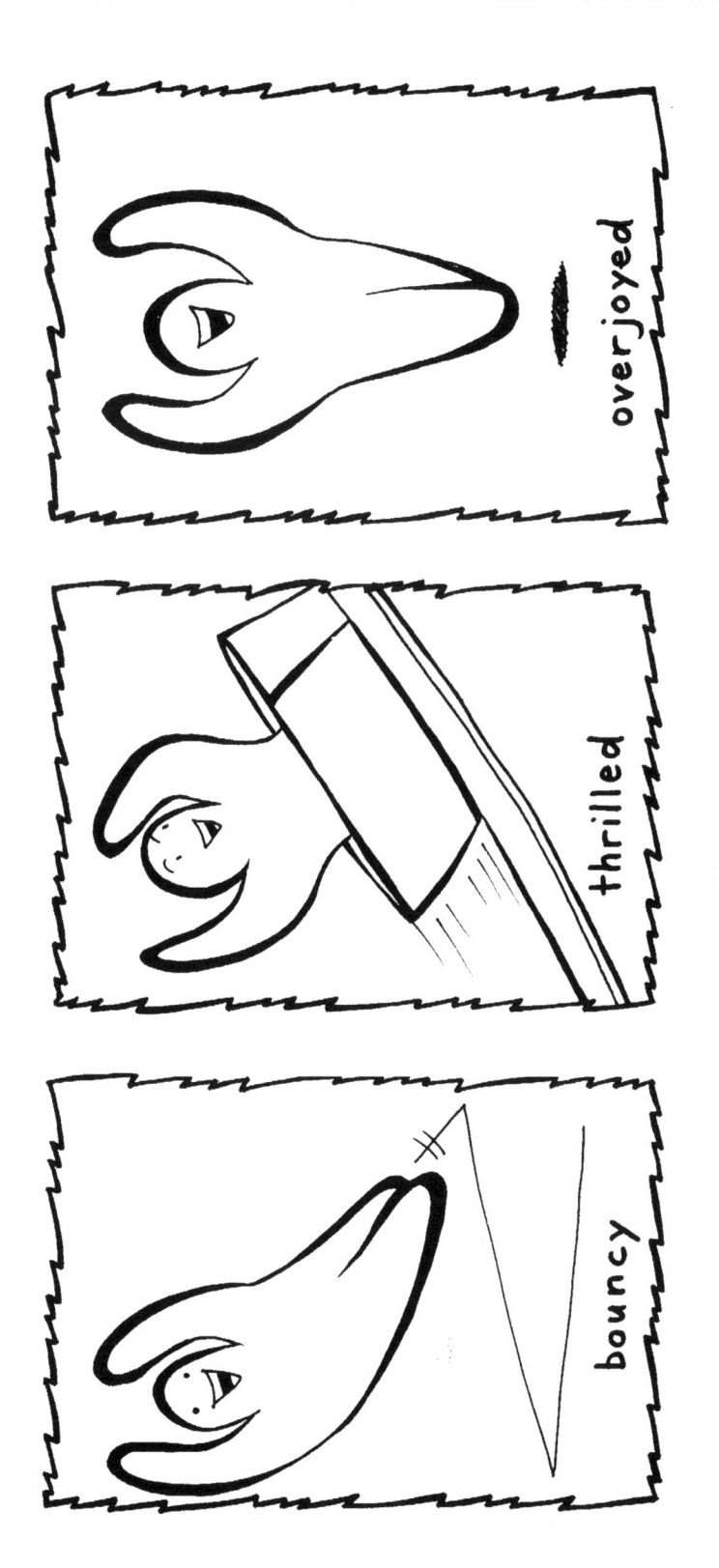

overjoyed

thrilled

bouncy

Will was thrilled by the adventure he and his family were on.

The Blob Emotional Thesaurus

tormented

Individual feeling words

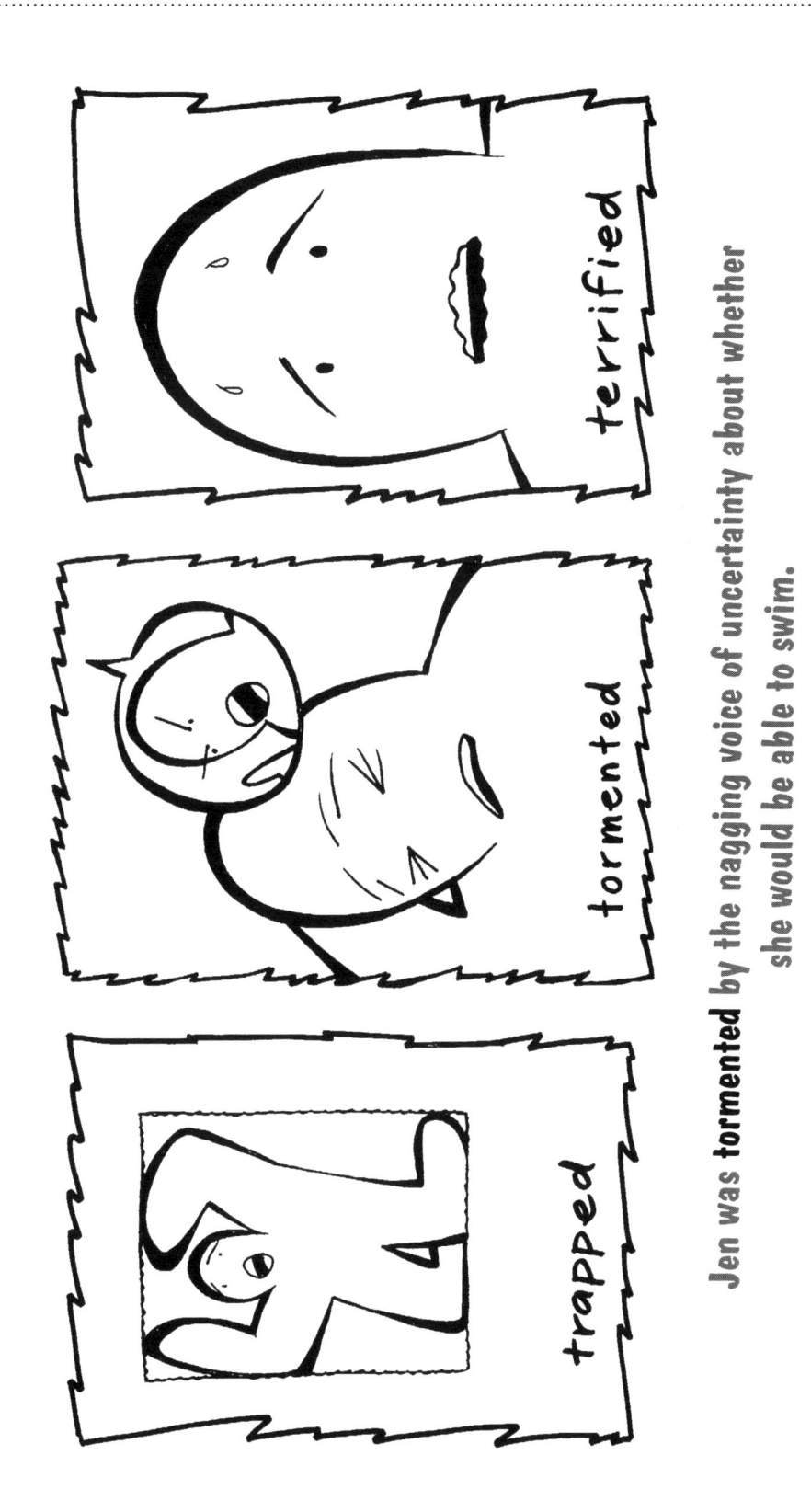

terrified

tormented

trapped

Jen was tormented by the nagging voice of uncertainty about whether she would be able to swim.

touched

Individual feeling words

close

touched

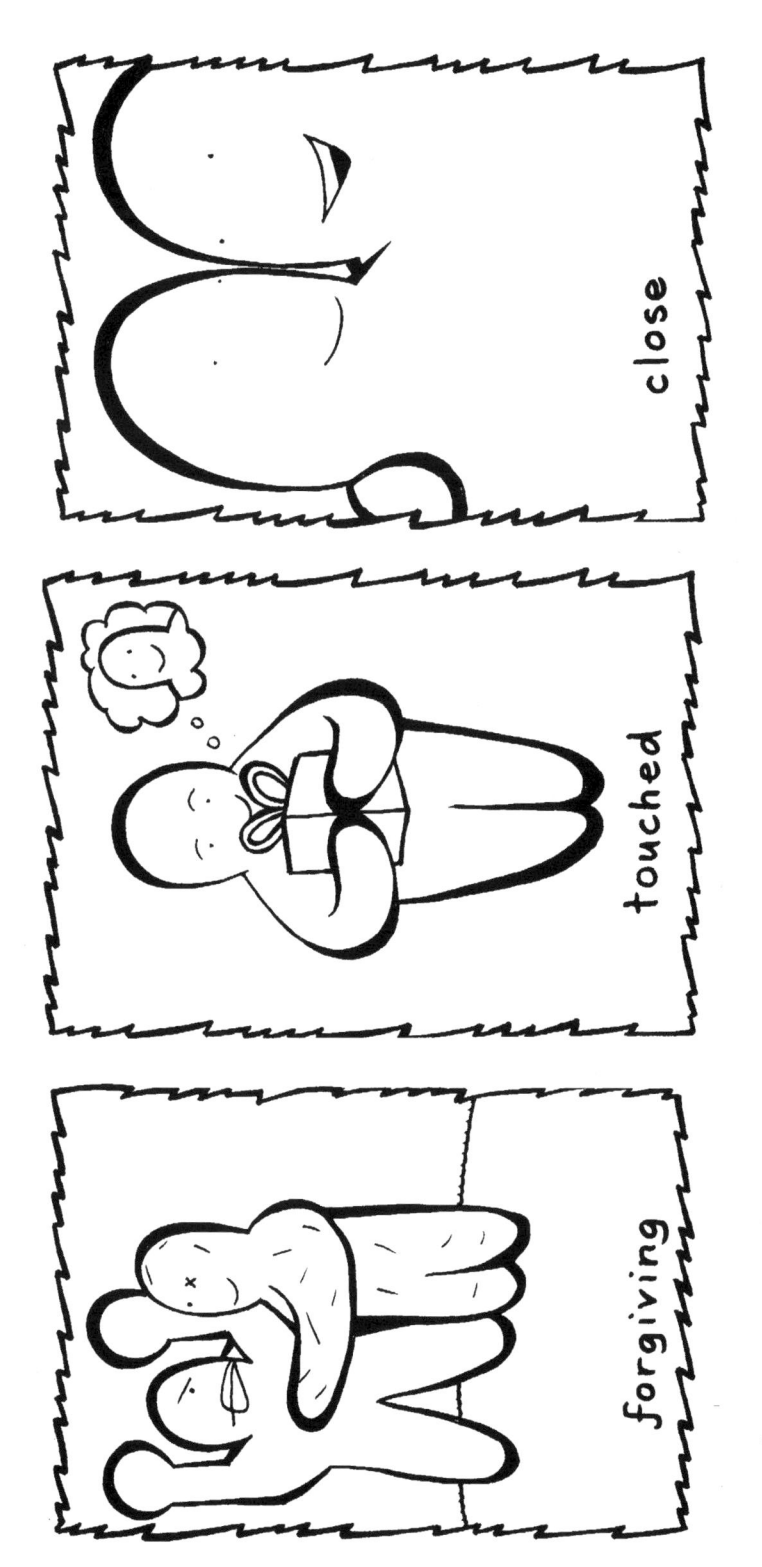

forgiving

Faith was *touched* by the gift on Valentine's Day, but didn't know whom it came from!

The Blob Emotional Thesaurus

trapped

Individual feeling words

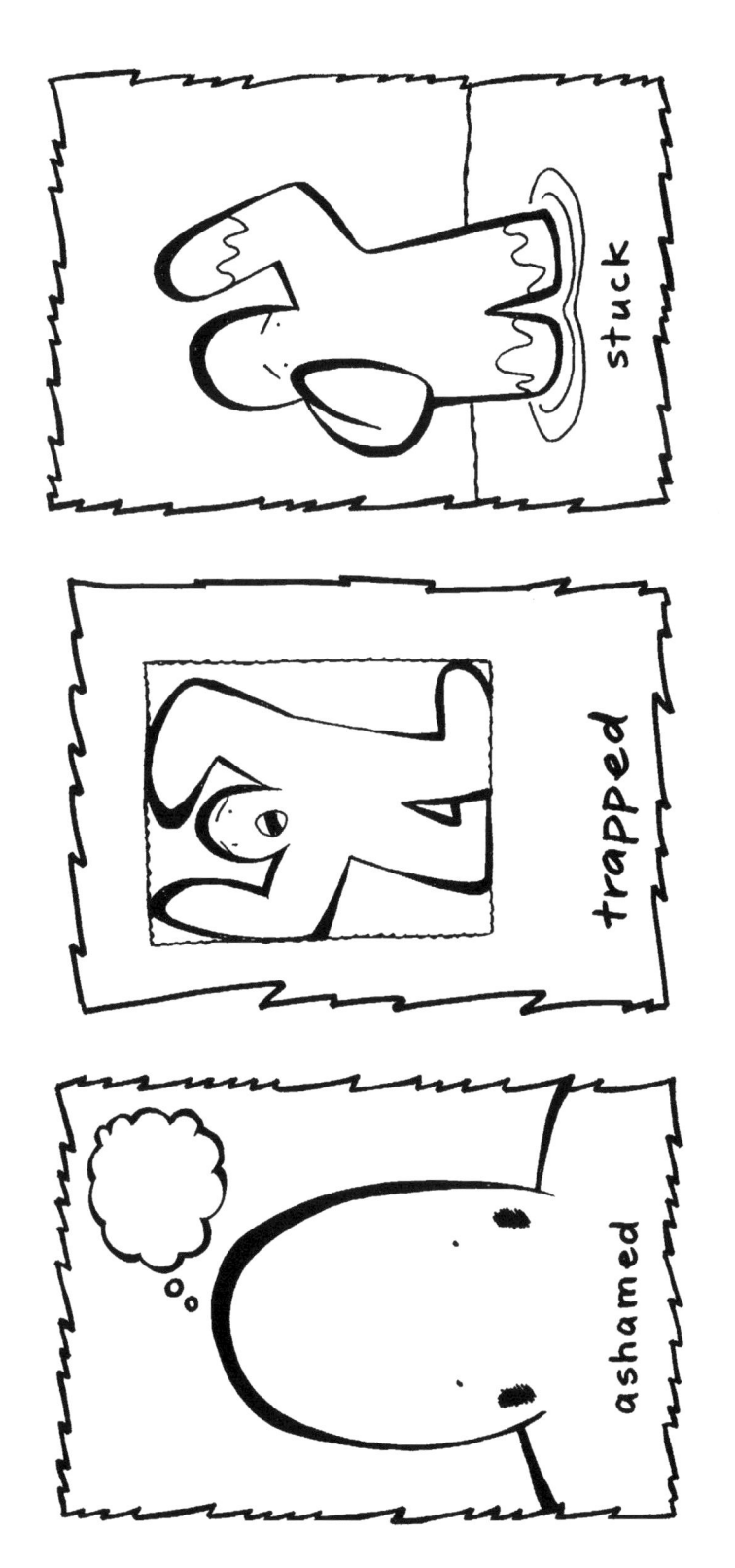

stuck

trapped

ashamed

Jeda felt **trapped** in the building, as the shouting of her friends filled the room!

The Blob Emotional Thesaurus

trusting

Individual feeling words

empowered

trusting

nurtured

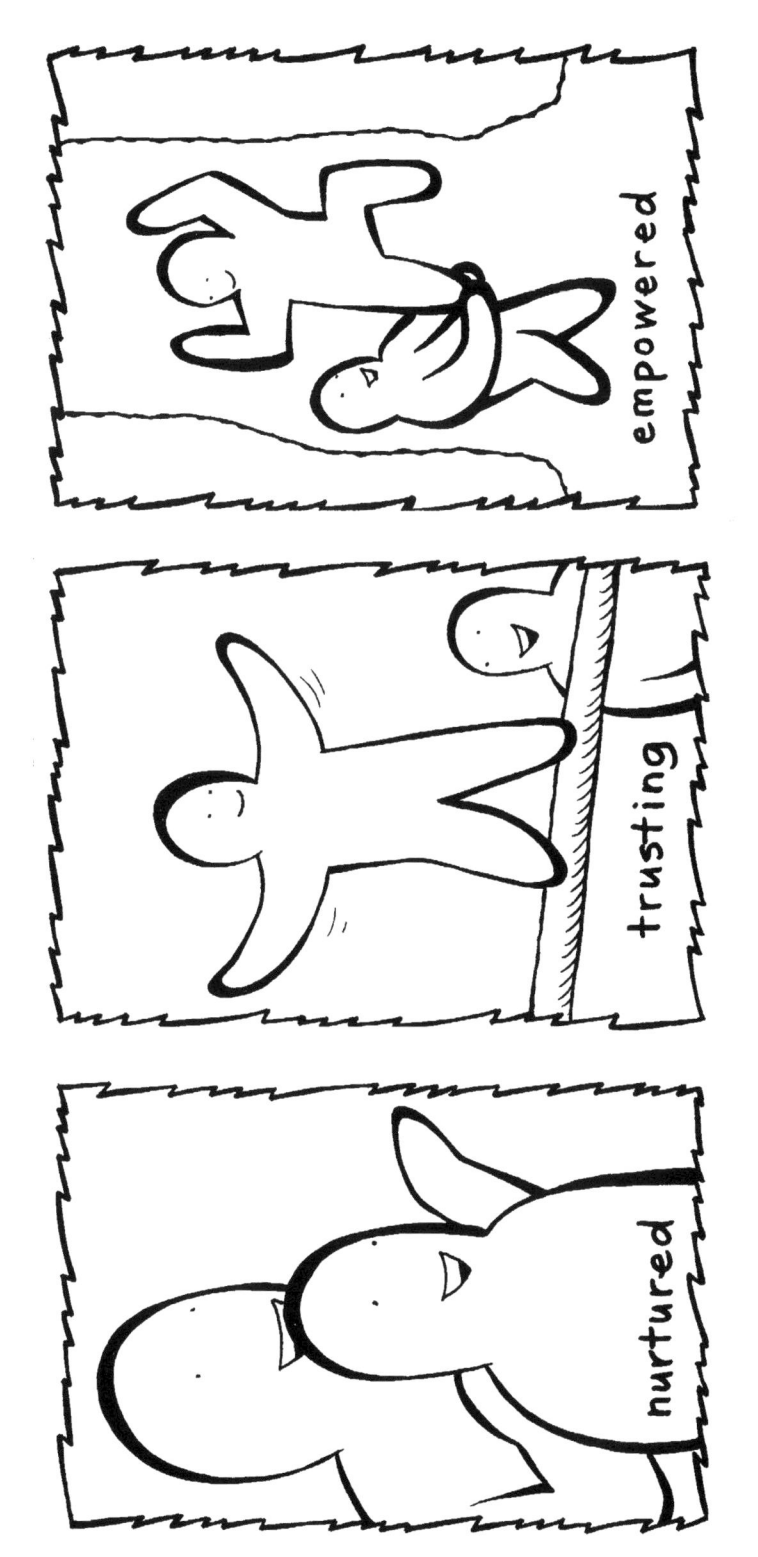

Because his boss showed real interest, Nick felt like trusting him with his career.

The Blob Emotional Thesaurus

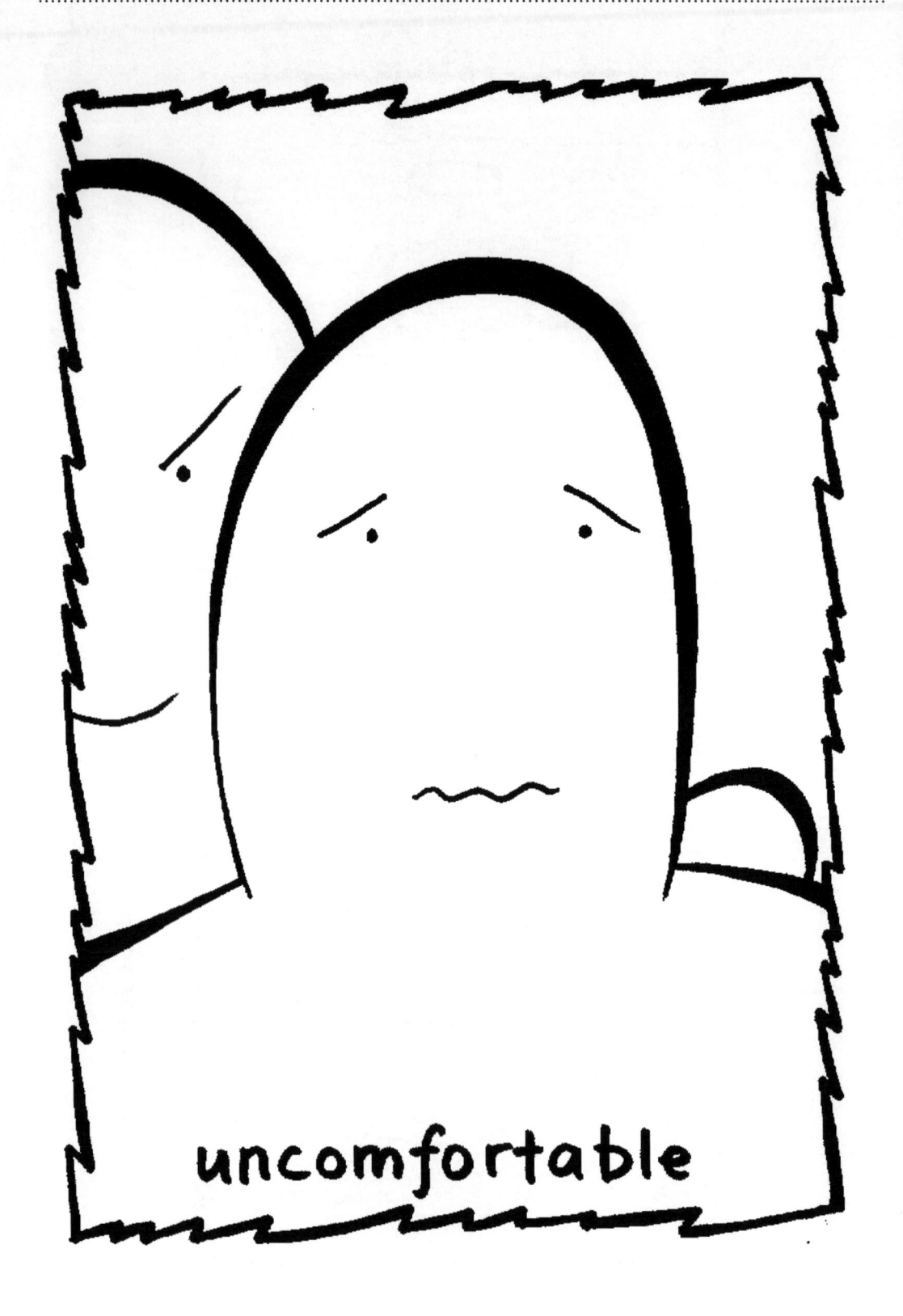

uncomfortable

Individual feeling words

tense

uncomfortable

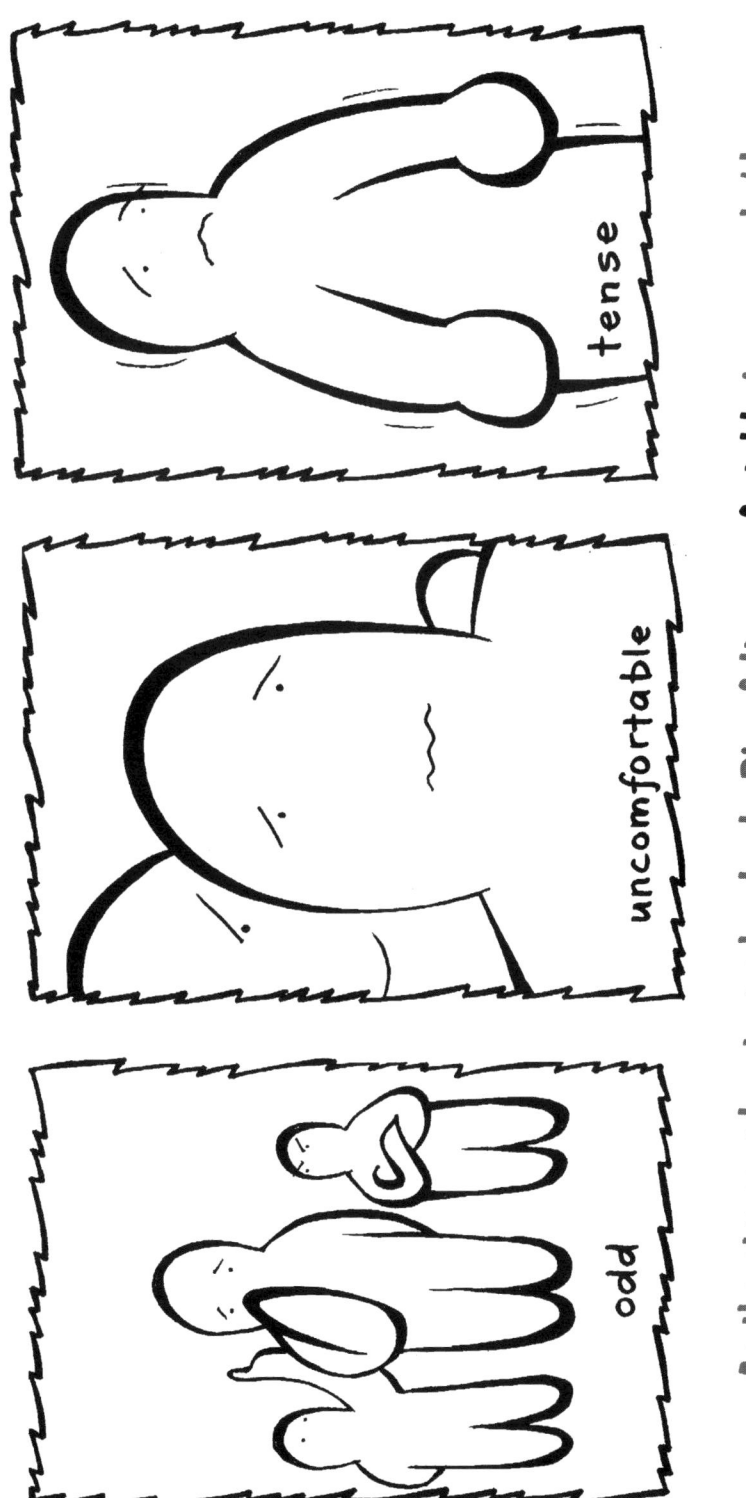

odd

As the stranger leant over her back, Bina felt uncomfortable in a way she'd never experienced before.

The Blob Emotional Thesaurus

united

Individual feeling words

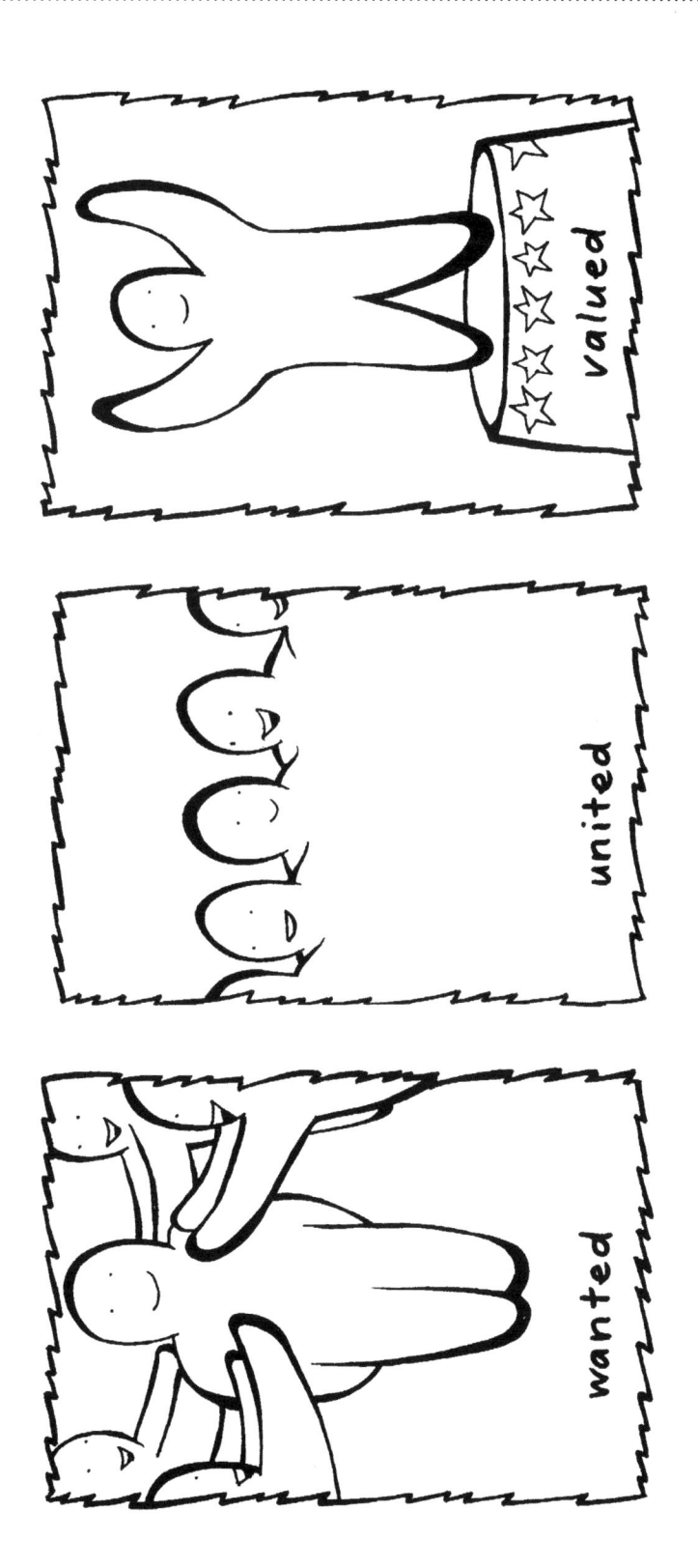

wanted

united

valued

Gita felt united with the others in her team after the first major incident was over.

The Blob Emotional Thesaurus

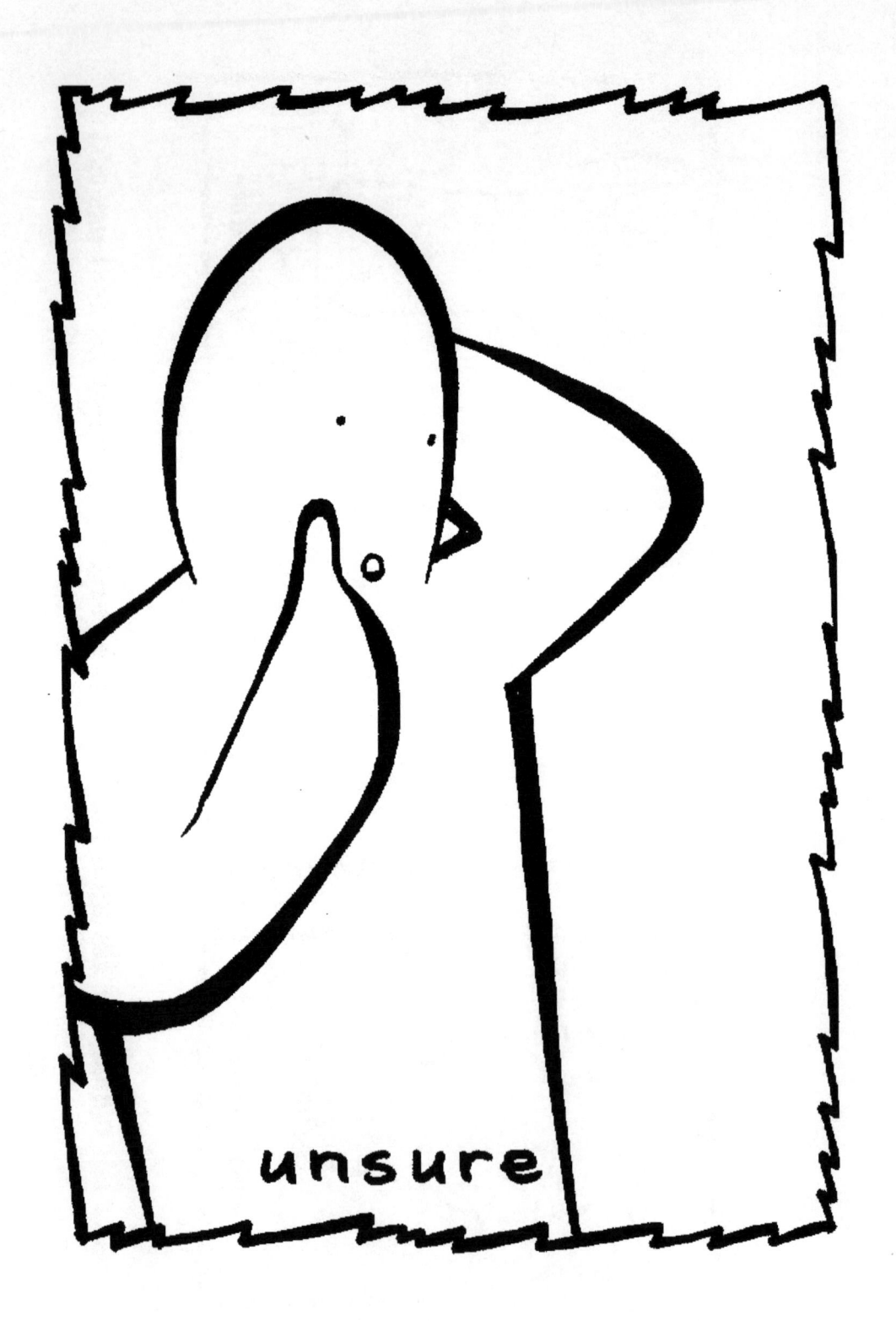

unsure

Individual feeling words

bothered

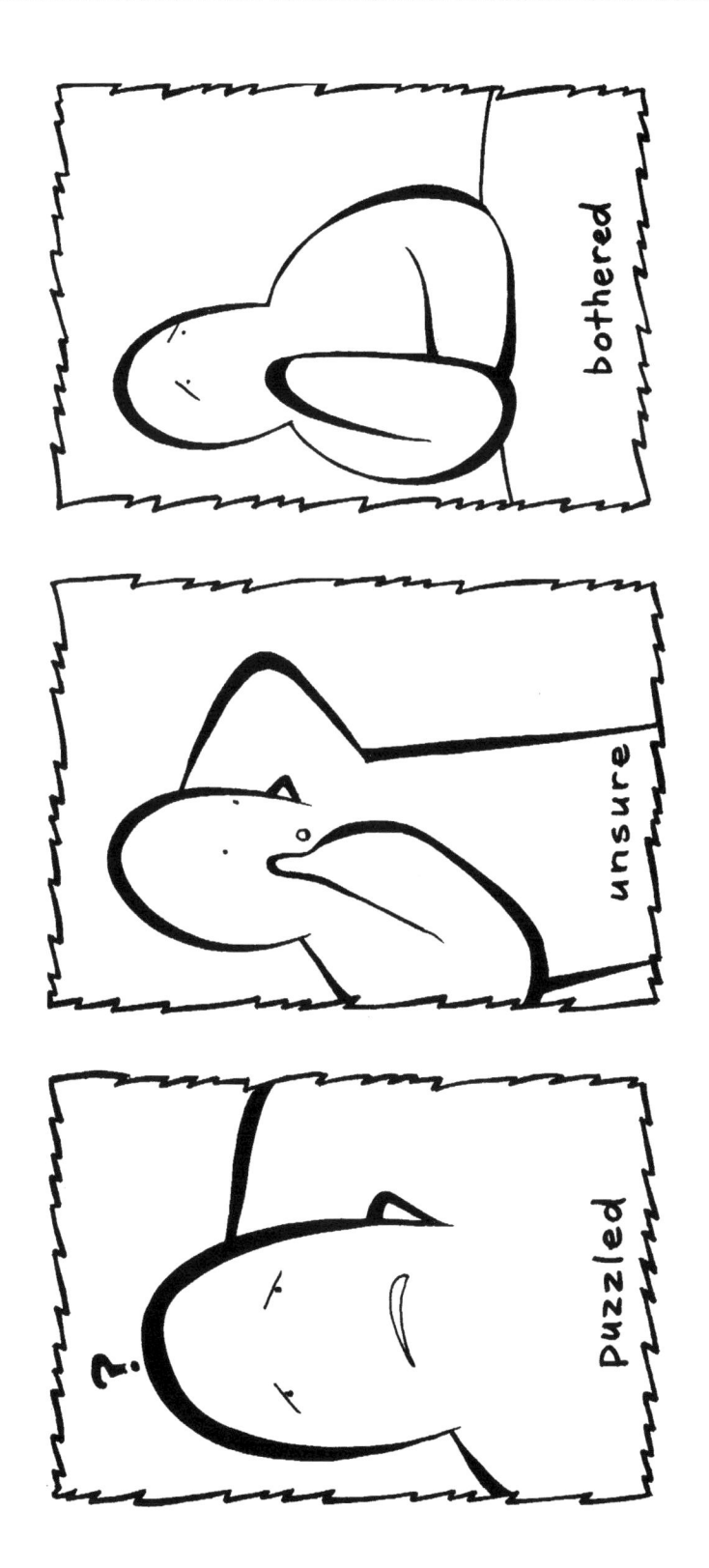

unsure

puzzled

Lee was unsure if his piano playing was the best way to entertain his friends.

The Blob Emotional Thesaurus

upset

Individual feeling words

hurt

upset

discouraged

Tricia was **upset** that she couldn't play with both her friends at the same time.

The Blob Emotional Thesaurus

valued

Individual feeling words

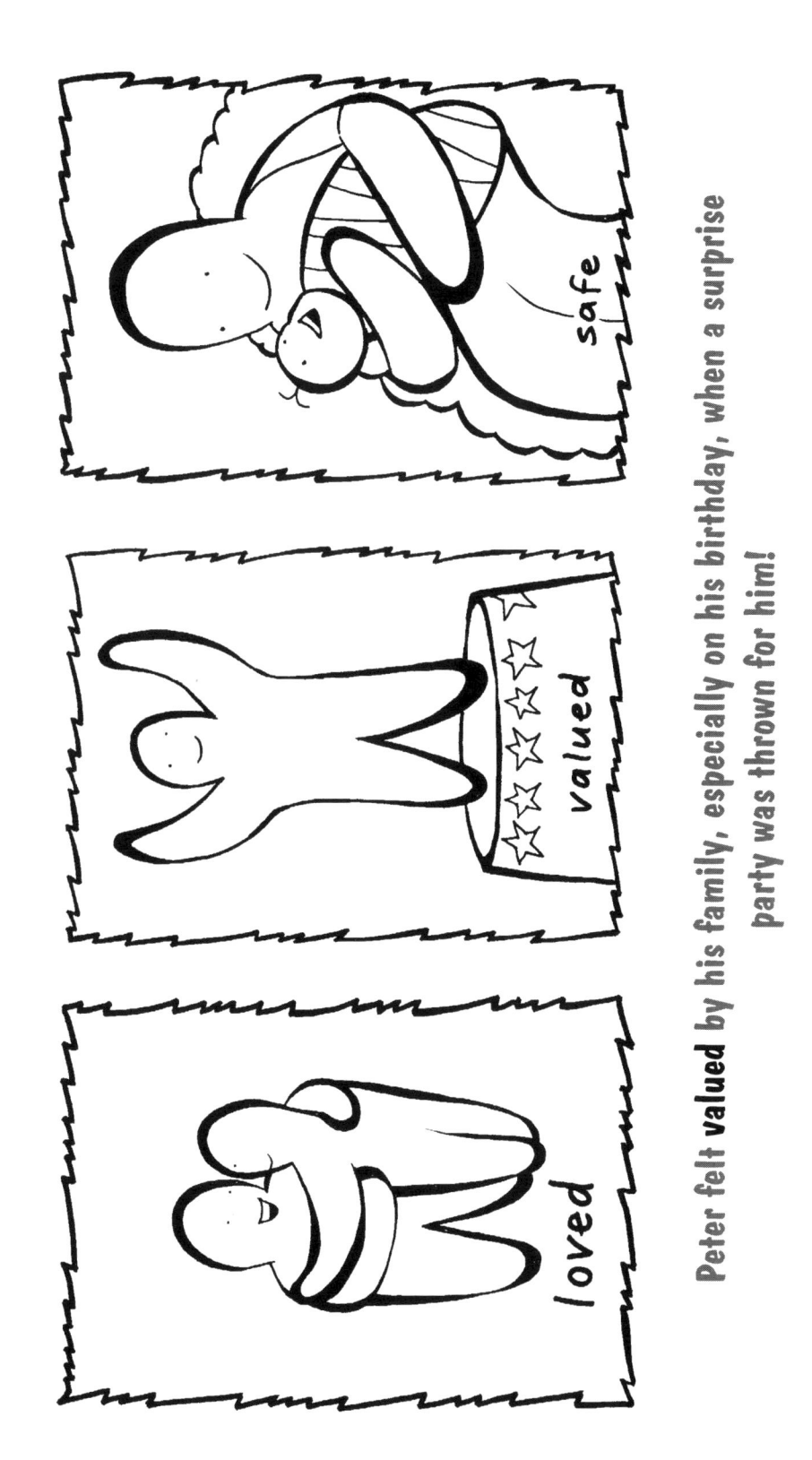

Peter felt **valued** by his family, especially on his birthday, when a surprise party was thrown for him!

The Blob Emotional Thesaurus

violent

Individual feeling words

evil

violent

volcanic

Billie thumped her friend because her feelings had finally turned **violent**.

The Blob Emotional Thesaurus

volcanic

Individual feeling words

violent

volcanic

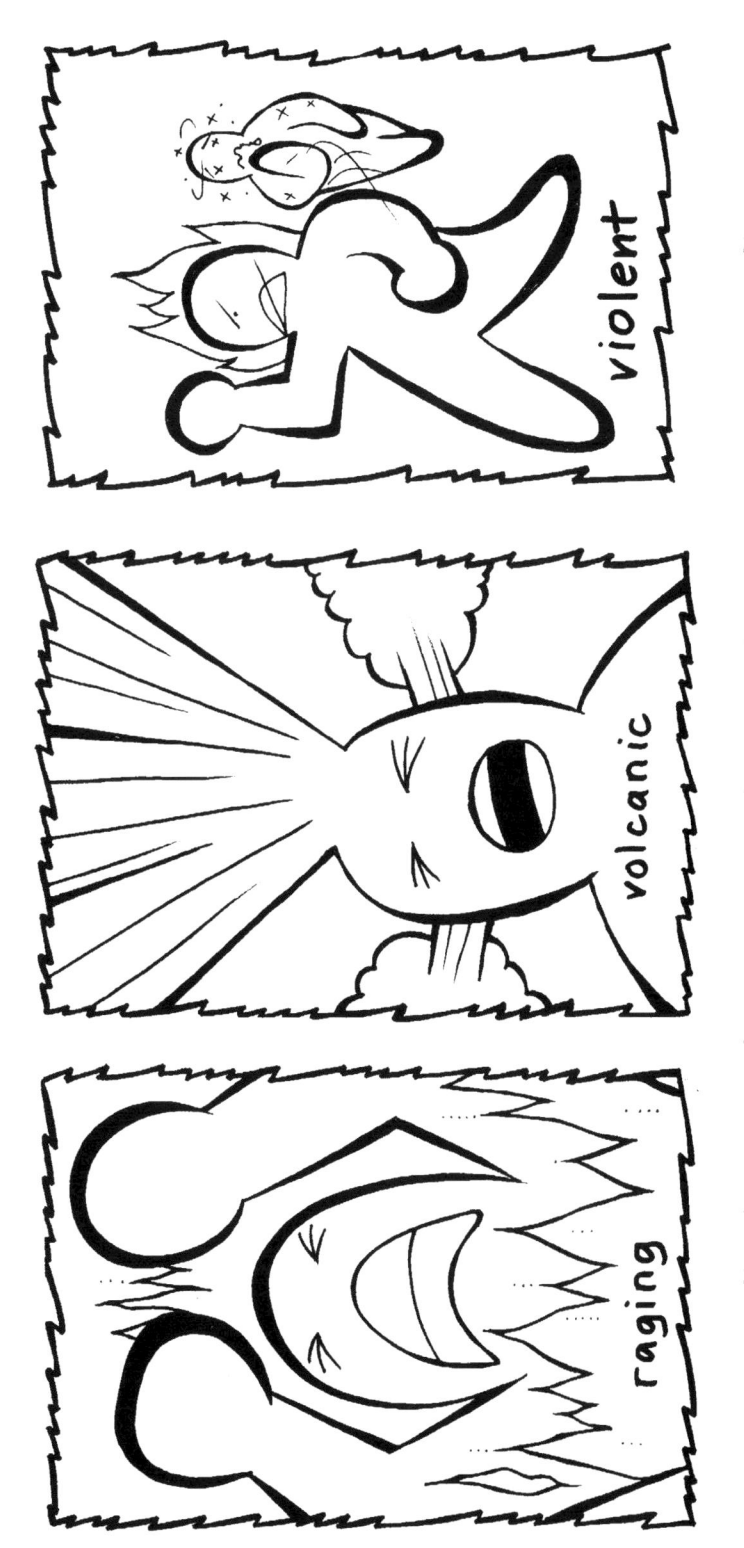

raging

Dudley became **volcanic** as something inside him suddenly snapped!

The Blob Emotional Thesaurus

wanted

Individual feeling words

nurtured

wanted

accepted

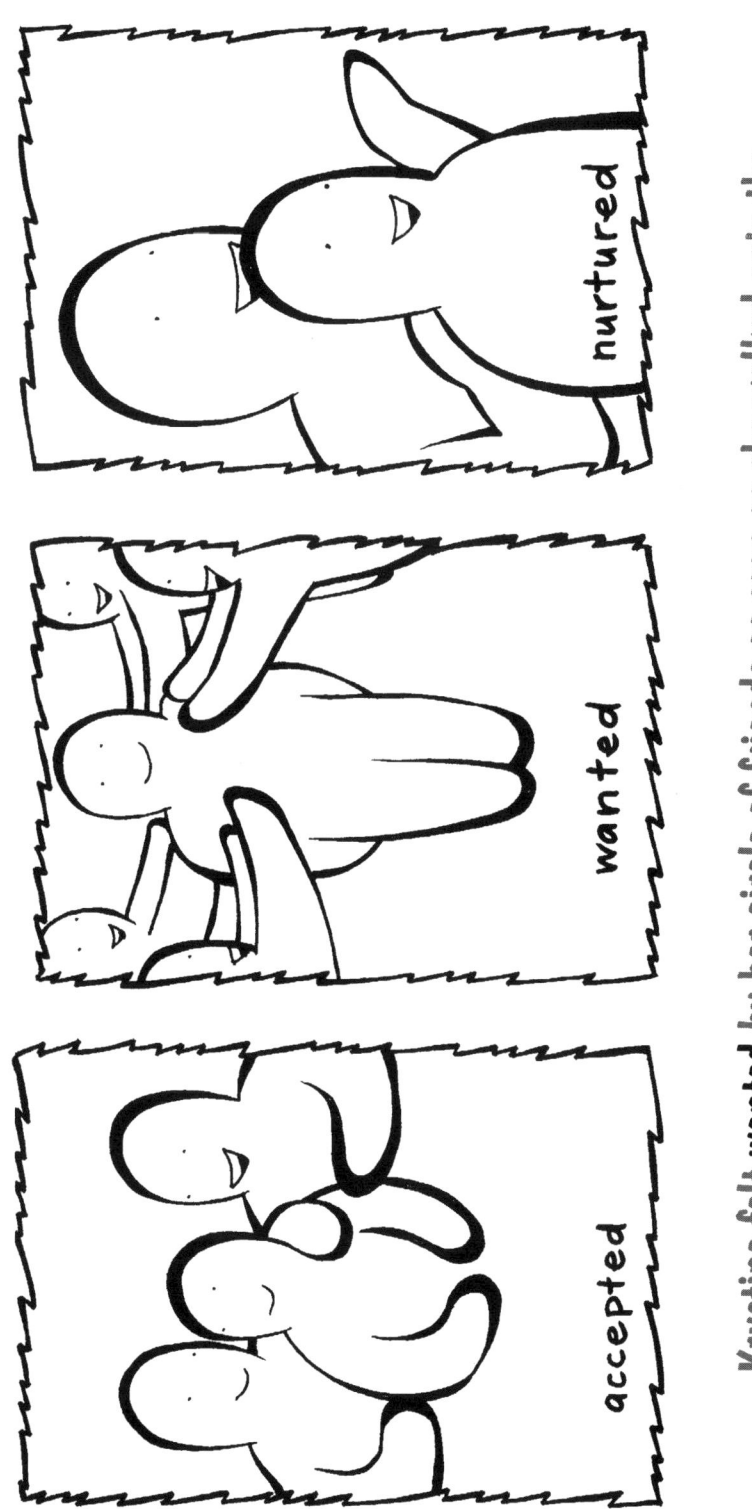

Krystine felt wanted by her circle of friends as soon as she walked onto the playground each morning.

The Blob Emotional Thesaurus

weak

Individual feeling words

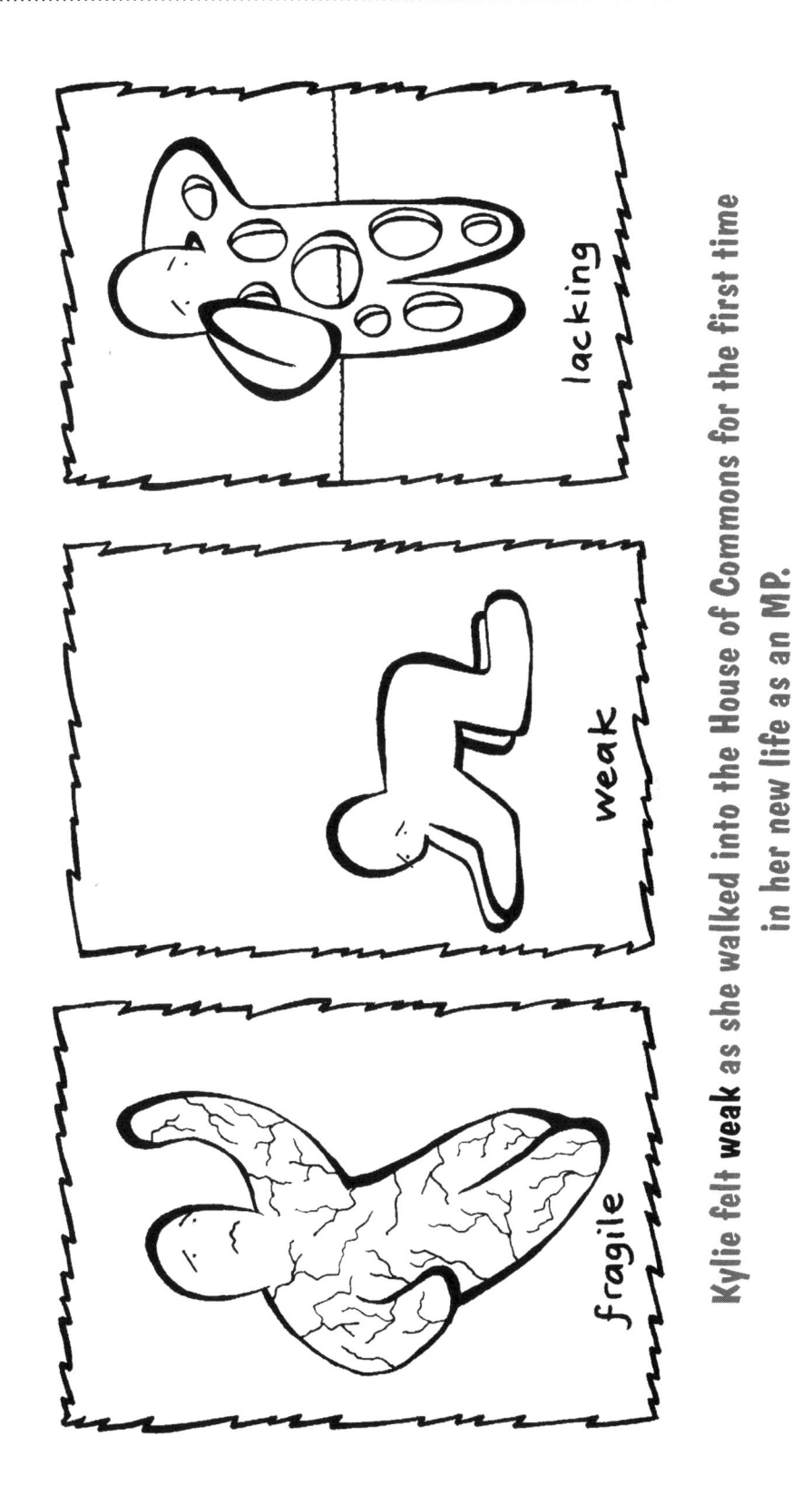

lacking

weak

fragile

Kylie felt **weak** as she walked into the House of Commons for the first time in her new life as an MP.

The Blob Emotional Thesaurus

worried

Individual feeling words

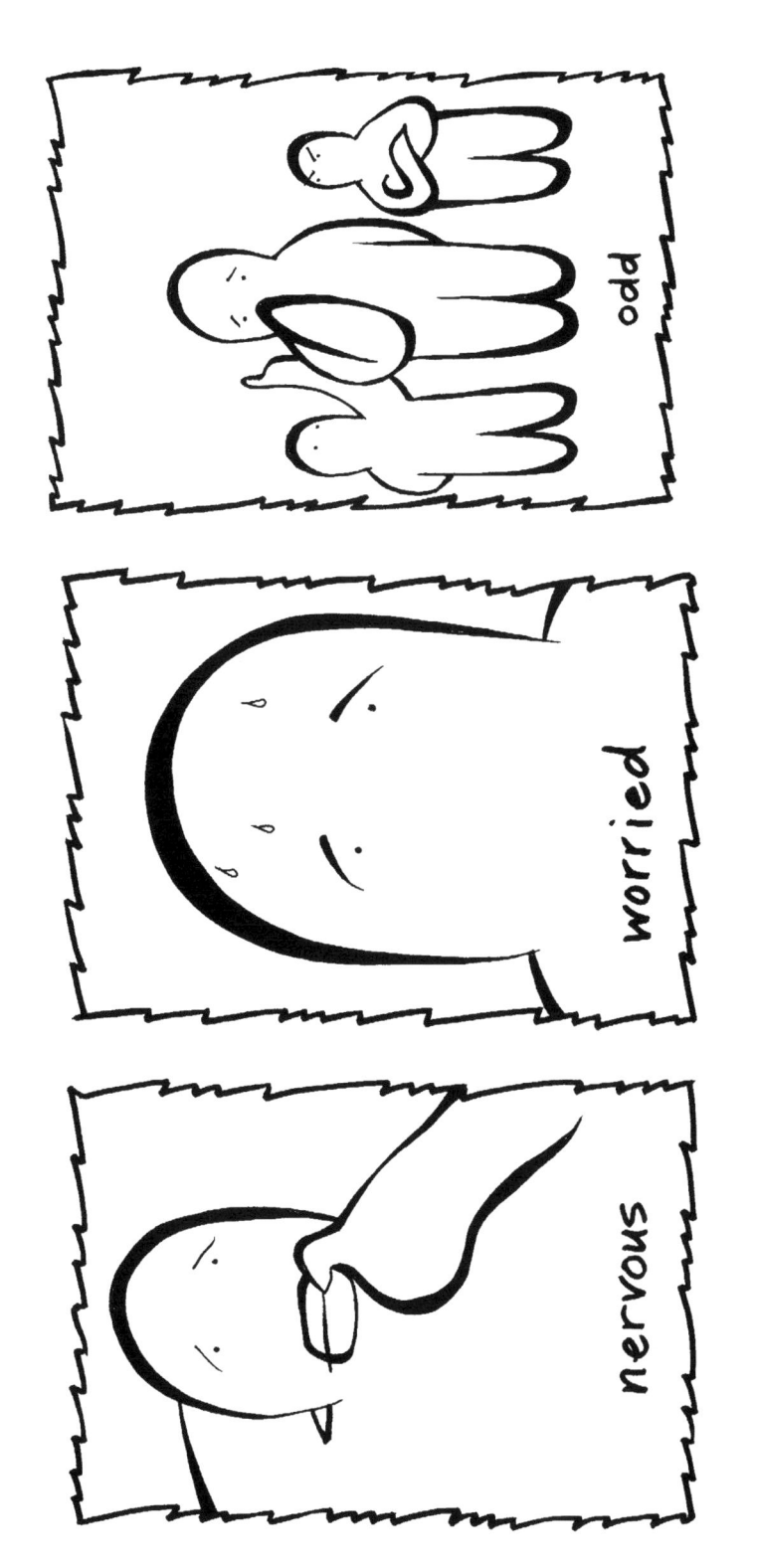

nervous

worried

odd

Alby was **worried** that his film may not be critically appreciated.

The Blob Emotional Thesaurus

worthless

Individual feeling words

numb

worthless

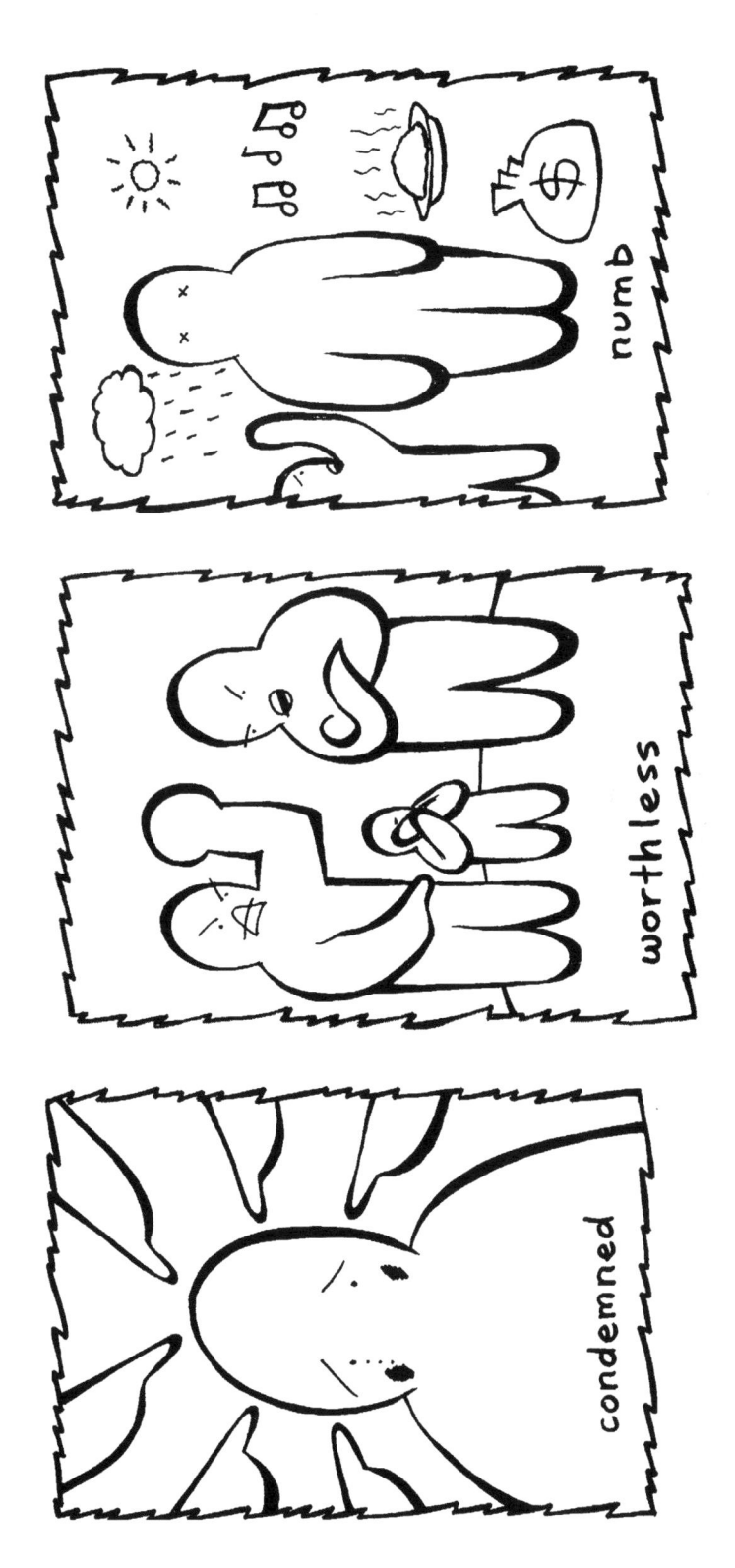

condemned

Glyn felt worthless after both his parents shouted at him for being forgetful.

Opposite pairs of feelings

Feelings are signals... can we read them?

© Ian Long + Pip Wilson 2013 www.blobtree.com

The Blob Emotional Thesaurus

calm

violent

abandoned

supported

accepted

rejected

Opposite pairs of feelings

amused

depressed

anxious

peaceful

bothered

satisfied

The Blob Emotional Thesaurus

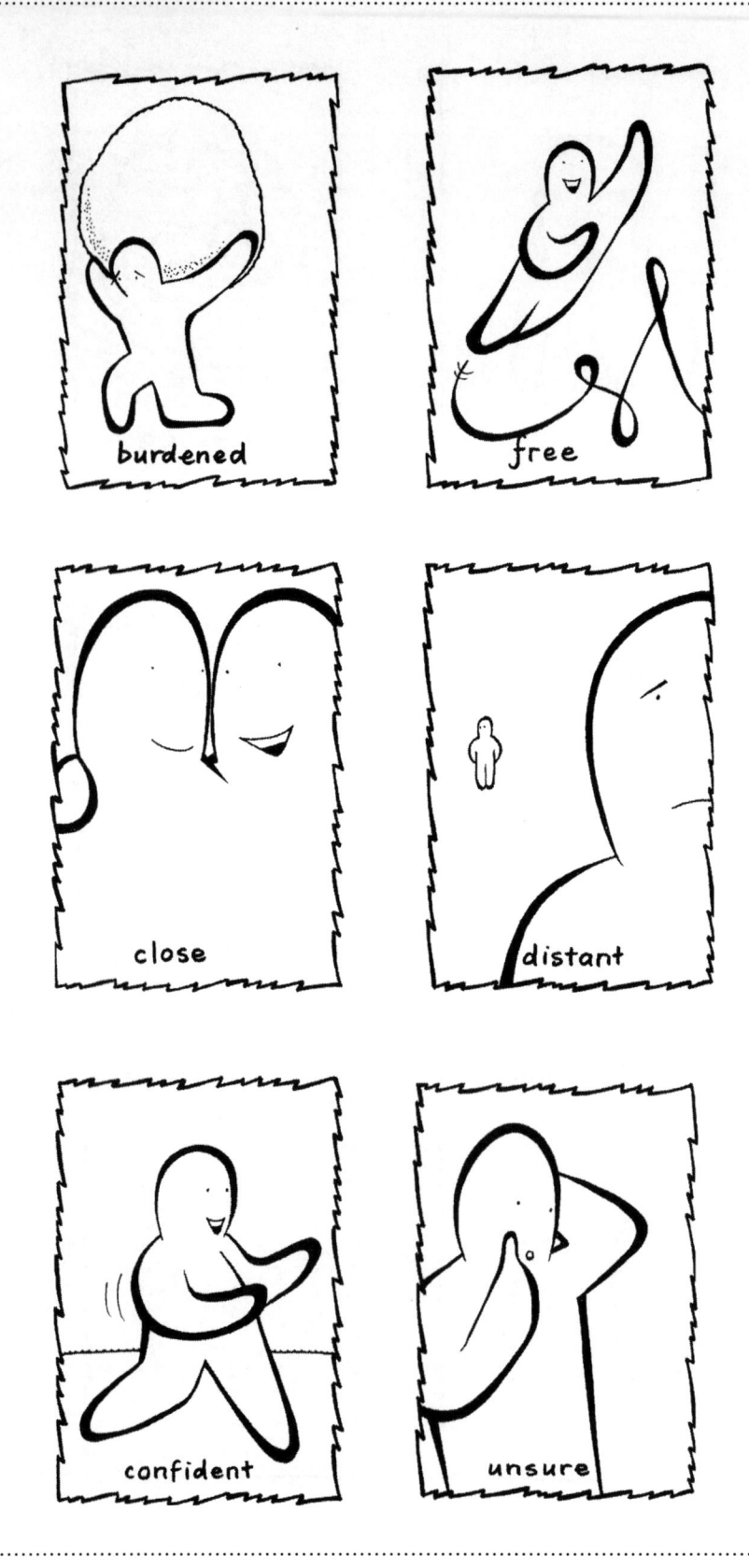

burdened

free

close

distant

confident

unsure

326

Opposite pairs of feelings

despondent

hopeful

disappointed

excited

discouraged

encouraged

The Blob Emotional Thesaurus

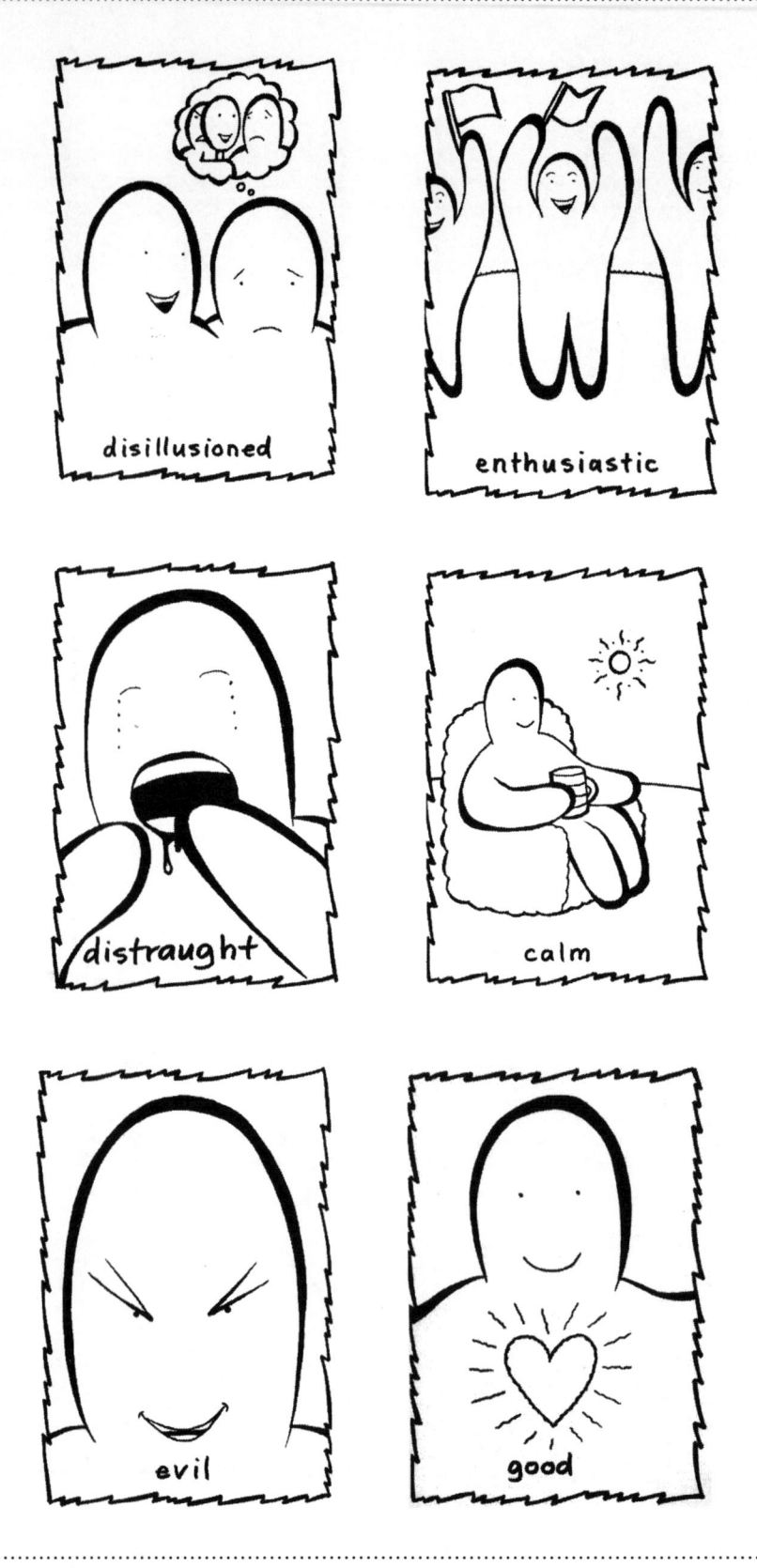

disillusioned	enthusiastic
distraught	calm
evil	good

Opposite pairs of feelings

forgiving

judgemental

fragile

strong

generous

possessive

The Blob Emotional Thesaurus

hated

loved

jealous

trusting

optimistic

pessimistic

Opposite pairs of

moody

overjoyed

proud

embarrassed

purposeful

lost

Emotional Thesaurus: feelings

safe	threatened
trapped	released
happy	sad

332

Opposite pairs of feelings

alone	united
enthusiastic	bored
positive	negative

The Blob Emotional Thesaurus

Everyone we meet is fighting a battle we know nothing about.
PIP WILSON